Developing Writing Skills

Prentice-Hall Canada Inc.
Scarborough, Ontario

Canadian Third Edition

Developing Writing Skills

William W. West
Stephen D. Bailey
Berenice L. Wood

Canadian Cataloguing in Publication Data

West, William W. (William Walter), 1925-
  Developing writing skills

Includes index.
ISBN 0-13-205328-4

1. English language — Composition and exercises.
2. English language — Rhetoric.   I. Bailey,
Stephen D., 1947-   II. Wood, Berenice L. (Berenice
Laura), 1947-   III. Title.

PE1408.W56 1981   808'.042   C81-094616-5

Supplementary Material: Teacher's Guide

Original Third Edition published by Prentice-Hall Inc.,
Englewood Cliffs, New Jersey, Copyright © 1980 by
Prentice-Hall, Inc.

©1981 by Prentice-Hall Canada Inc., Scarborough, Ontario
All rights reserved.
No part of this book may be reproduced in any form without
permission in writing from the publishers.

PRENTICE-HALL, INC., Englewood Cliffs, *New Jersey*
PRENTICE-HALL INTERNATIONAL, INC., *London*
PRENTICE-HALL OF AUSTRALIA, PTY., LTD., *Sydney*
PRENTICE-HALL OF INDIA PVT., LTD., *New Delhi*
PRENTICE-HALL OF JAPAN, INC., *Tokyo*
PRENTICE-HALL OF SOUTHEAST ASIA (PTE.) LTD., *Singapore*

ISBN 0-13-205328-4

Design: Joe Chin
Production Editor: Heather Scott McClune

    2   3   4   5   6   BP   86   85   84   83   82

Typesetting by Q Composition
Printed and bound in Canada by Bryant Press

Contents

Student Activities

Preface

Developing Writing Skills, Canadian Third Edition, is a writing program designed to refine the composition skills of senior secondary students. The text stresses writing as a process, leading students clearly and logically through the steps of prewriting, writing, and revising.

Chapters One and Two introduce students to the principles connected with writing as a process which underlie the text as a whole. Subsequent chapters open with examples of professional writing in the form being studied. By reading and discussing these models, students begin to understand the form and its possibilities and are given the opportunity to explore possible subjects for personal expression.

The Professional Models are followed by an explanation of the particular form of writing and the motivation for its use. Examples of student writing, with marginal notes to guide understanding, are included at this point to demonstrate how students have handled the writing assignments. Students then engage in a series of preparatory activities—writing, study, and discussion—focusing on skills and concepts. The Major Writing Assignment at the end of each chapter asks students to demonstrate proficiency in the skills they have learned.

Many of the Professional and Student Models were written by Canadians. We believe it is important for students to learn to write within the context of Canadian society and culture. Canada has a rich heritage in the written word. Students should appreciate the fact that they become part of that heritage when they write.

No one book can possibly teach everything there is to know about writing. We believe, however, that *Developing Writing Skills*, Canadian Third Edition, is a tool which can make better written expression a pleasant and rewarding goal for students.

Stephen D. Bailey
Berenice L. Wood

Acknowledgments

We would like to express sincere thanks to a number of people who have contributed to making this Canadian Edition of *Developing Writing Skills* a reality.

First of all, to Dr. William West whose helpful guidance and genuine enthusiasm have made our task not only easier, but emotionally rewarding as well. Dr. West is indeed a fine teacher and friend.

Henry Cunha and Dorothy Greenaway of Prentice-Hall Canada have given the kind of professional leadership to this project which would inspire any author. Dorothy has guided each phase of production carefully and patiently, offering helpful criticism and a host of valuable suggestions. Moreover, the editing and technical management of Heather Scott McClune are much appreciated.

We are also indebted to Mr. Fred Lepkin, Social Studies Department Head at Burnaby South Senior Secondary School, who helped in the preparation of Chapter 10, "The Library Resource Paper." A number of Burnaby South students whose writing appears in this book also deserve mention: Kal Gill, Nicola Marotz, Gregg Sewell and Janet Michel. Our appreciation is also extended to professors Herbert Rosengarten and Gernot Wieland of the University of British Columbia for information they provided on the development of the English alphabet.

We would also like to thank Mr. Bob Overgaard, Curriculum Consultant with the British Columbia Ministry of Education, and members of the English 12 Materials Selection Committee for their useful criticisms and comments.

Finally, to our friends and families who offered the kind of emotional support we needed when we needed it, we say thanks. Dianne Bailey has helped in many ways—proofreading, typing, and making suggestions, and Noeline Curtis did a first rate job of typing the manuscript. Even the younger set got in on the act. The Bailey Boys, Mark and Devin, while not fully grasping what all the fuss was about, offered a special kind of inspiration.

Stephen D. Bailey
Berenice L. Wood

Developing
Writing
Skills

1

Writing for Effective Communication

"...the activities we call reading and writing are in reality but two sides of the same coin;... the ability to put words on to paper effectively is closely related to the ability to take words off the printed page."

–Alan Dawe

Can you imagine how different your life would be if you did not know how to read and write?

Many of the things you take for granted during an ordinary day would no longer be possible if you could not read. You would miss the basic information you depend on for simple activities—everything from following instructions on a medicine bottle to obeying traffic signs. If you could not read letters, newspapers, and magazines, you would be out of touch with the world around you. Your understanding of that world would be limited even further without the insight provided by stories, poems, and novels.

If you could not write, you would be unable to record information and ideas for other people. In addition, you would lose the personal pleasure of keeping a journal to explore your private thoughts, creating an imaginary world in a story, or capturing your feelings in the words of a poem or song.

Try to imagine how different life in Canada would be if no one could read and write. The shape of our entire society would change. Obviously the printing and publishing industry would not exist. The absence of reading and writing would affect a surprising number of other organizations,

◀ In the Islamic world, writing was so important that it was used not only to communicate, but also to decorate buildings, household objects, even armour.

including the automotive industry, the business machines and computer industries, and electronic communication companies.

The reason, of course, is that the printing and publishing industry is a very important part of every one of these organizations. All facets of modern life—government, education, industry, commerce, health care, to name just a few—depend not just on communication but on *written* communication.

Even essentially visual enterprises, such as the movies and television, begin with writing. In the words of Robert Spencer Carr, a former Hollywood script writer, "Until the writer writes, the director has no job, the studios stand dark, the technicians are unemployed, and actors are 'at liberty'—meaning hungry."

Writing is involved not only in the finished product of many industries but also all along the way in the production process. It's easy to see the newspapers, books, magazines, periodicals, and advertisements all around you. In addition to these examples of printing and publishing that you see every day, there are many other kinds of writing: memos, letters, proposals, reports, inquiries, directions, cost estimates, contracts, agreements, and so on. All of these kinds of written communication make modern society possible.

Why Writing Matters

As a member of society, you are necessarily involved in written communication, at least as a reader. However, there are at least seven good reasons why just knowing how to read is not enough.

1. Writing helps you understand! Your teachers will tell you that the best way to learn something is to teach it. In some kinds of writing, you are explaining your ideas to a reader. This is one way of learning the material yourself.

2. Writing helps you participate! The number of new ideas in the modern world is growing at an amazing rate. Even within a single country the increase is vast. In 1977-78, the Canadian Patents Office granted 20 967 patents. This figure increased to 22 772 during 1978-79. These patents on "things" represent a fraction of the new ideas blossoming in every area of the world around you. Almost all ideas either originate in writing or are distributed in written form. How much better for you to participate in and influence this avalanche of new ideas, than to sit by and be buried by it.

3. Writing helps you think! As you prepare to write, you sort out and organize your ideas in order to express them clearly. That process of observing and organizing helps you perceive and understand. These

are the initial steps in the thinking process, and as you write, you gain control of many additional parts of the process. You make connections, you see differences and likenesses, you experiment with varying arrangements and patterns, you make inferences (logical guesses) about what things are and mean, you draw conclusions, and you make judgments. All these writing experiences give you new and clearer thinking habits for processing information and for conveying it orally and in writing.

4. Writing helps you enjoy! Everyone can experience the thrill of watching a goal scored during a Stanley Cup game, seeing the Royal Winnipeg Ballet, looking at a painting by Emily Carr, or reading a bestseller. What some students don't realize is that everyone can also enjoy the satisfaction of writing well. The fun of a hockey game is obvious, but the fun of writing comes from the satisfaction of expressing your own thoughts and feelings on paper. In fact, all the things mentioned above, from a Stanley Cup game to the Royal Winnipeg Ballet, can be enjoyed again and again through writing. Learning to write provides you with one more source of delight in your life.

5. Writing helps you lead! Whether in school, on the job, or in social situations, each of us comes in contact with people—equals or superiors in authority—whose ideas and principles may be in conflict with our own. In some cases such differences matter little and have little effect on the quality of our lives. In other situations it may be important to reveal and discuss such conflicts in order to resolve the differences, remedy injustices, or otherwise improve our lifestyles. The ability to write helps you to cooperate with people at a distance or to prepare ideas for future use. To influence others, to guide and help them, you need to be able to write.

6. Writing helps you create! Like other forms of artistic expression such as painting, music, or dancing, writing is an outlet for creative imagination. People have always felt the urge to create beauty, express emotions, or explore new experiences through language. Some of the earliest written records that have been passed down to us include imaginative stories about superhuman heroes and fabulous adventures. Whether you want to lead others into such worlds of fantasy and imagination or to give them insights into the significant events in daily life, writing allows you to entertain and enlighten others.

7. Writing helps you explore! Not all writing is intended for others to read. Sometimes you may wish to record your thoughts and feelings just for yourself. Writing poetry or keeping a journal as a private expression of emotions often lets you discover the significance of your experiences and helps you understand yourself better.

Although these are the main reasons for learning to write well, there are two additional reasons, which are related to the world you live in:

1. When you can write well you can communicate more fully to others the ideas, insights, emotions, and attitudes that you alone possess. People around you, your nation, and your culture need these from you. In the words of one writer, George Riemer, "Nobody remembers a nation for its readers."

2. When you can write well you can more easily realize your potential. You command the respect of those around you and thereby earn greater opportunity for self-realization.

(Activity 1A)

Considering the Role of Writing in Modern Life

Select one of the following tasks, complete it, and report to the class.

1. Select some major undertaking, such as constructing a ten-storey build-ing, building a bridge, starting a business, managing a political cam-paign, or manufacturing a mass-produced product. If possible, talk to someone actually involved in such an enterprise. Make a list of all the kinds of writing likely to be involved in this project. Include the prelim-inary and planning stages, such as raising money, getting contractors to submit bids on portions of the construction, attracting renters, draw-ing up leases, and so on.

2. Consider what the world would be like if learning to read and write in school were made voluntary and elective, as music and art are in many schools. Compare or contrast the roles, lifestyles, prestige, and self-respect of members of the literate and the nonliterate groups. Compare a day in the life of a member of each group.

3. Project yourselves into the future and imagine Phonovision (a system that enables you to see the person with whom you are speaking on the telephone); wristwatch-type television sets; computer access in every home to major world libraries; and other similar advances in commu-nication, either real or imaginary. List all the inventions you can think of, and then prepare a presentation describing communication in the future. (Be sure to include the roles reading and writing play in com-munication.)

4. Interview five to ten people in various kinds of jobs. Include people who work at relatively unskilled jobs as well as people in management positions. Ask them how important the ability to write well is in their work. List all the different kinds of job-related writing each person does.

5. Try to make a list of all the times you wrote something over the past week. Your list should include everything from short pieces of writing

like a telephone number or shopping list to longer items like a letter, a page in your journal, or a school essay. How many different kinds of writing did you do? How much of your writing was meant just for yourself, and how much was written for others to read? Sum up the reasons why writing is necessary and valuable in your life.

6. Choose a popular magazine or newspaper and review the contents carefully. How much of the writing in it is intended chiefly to communicate facts and information? Look at the number of items such as news reports and articles, advertisements, photographs, and interviews. How much of the writing is meant to entertain, to amuse, or to express emotions and opinions? Check the number of features such as cartoons, letters, humour, poetry, and personal experience stories. Would you say that the writing in this publication is intended chiefly to inform or to entertain the readers?

The Arrival Of Writing

No one knows exactly when or where writing was invented. Many cultures say that it was a gift of the gods. The Mayans of Central America, the ancient Egyptians, and the Japanese all have myths describing how writing came from divine sources.

The legend from the ancient Greeks about the origin of writing is especially interesting because it includes a warning about the limitations of writing and about problems that may arise.

THE MYTH OF CADMUS

Agenor, the king of Phoenicia, sent his son Cadmus to look for his sister Europa, telling him not to return until he found her. Zeus, the king of the gods, had carried her off. Cadmus consulted the oracle (a kind of prophet) of Apollo to ask for advice. The oracle told him to forget his mission and build a city of his own at the spot where he saw a young cow lying in the grass.

Cadmus set out as he was told, found the cow, and sent his companions off to a nearby grove for water. However, the grove was guarded by a dragon that devoured the men. When Cadmus came looking for his friends and discovered what had happened, he attacked and killed the dragon. Alone he could not have built his city, but the goddess Athena appeared and told Cadmus to sow the dragon's teeth in the ground. He obeyed her and, immediately, a small army of men sprang from the earth. Cadmus was frightened and quickly threw a stone into their midst to divert them. The men began to fight among themselves until only five men remained, and these five helped Cadmus build the city of Thebes.

Scholars interpret the story of Cadmus and the dragon's teeth symbolically. The stone represents the alphabet. As soon as it was cast among the people, they began to fight among themselves. In other words, when people have the tools to read and judge for themselves, dissension and death result. Is this a natural result of learning to read and write? To what degree is conflict the inevitable result of learning to read and write?

Historians think Cadmus of Thebes first brought the alphabet from Phoenicia to Greece about 1500 B.C. However, as you can see from the chart on page 7, other societies developed their own alphabets over a period of many centuries, using different kinds of drawn or written symbols to communicate meaning. These symbols are known as pictographic, ideographic, and phonetic alphabets.

Pictographic Writing.   The earliest kind of writing used little symbols called pictographs to express meaning. A pictograph is a simplified drawing of a definite object, like a tree or a fish, a person or the sun. An example of a pictograph system of writing is the Ancient Egyptian hieroglyphics shown on the chart. The early Chinese also used pictographs.

When these people wanted to communicate some information about an object like the sun or moon, they just drew simplified pictures of the objects involved. It is easy to see the main weakness in a pictograph system of writing. Pictographs can represent only definite objects, not abstract thought concepts or many spoken words. The information that can be expressed by *true* pictographic writing is very limited. For this reason, almost all pictographic writing gradually moves toward *ideographic* writing as communicators find themselves experimenting to find ways to communicate abstractions. For example, the Japanese verb "to come" (kuru, kimasu) is an abstraction created from three pictographs: *One man* ("hito") written 人 is shown beneath a *tree* ("ki") written 木 waiting for a *second man* ("nito") *to come*—so the whole abstract verb is expressed: 來

Ideographic Writing.   Next in the history of writing came ideographs, symbols for non-picturable things, actions and ideas. For instance, the early Chinese combined pictographs for "sun" and "tree" into an ideograph signifying "the east" and used pictographs for "sun" and "moon" to create an ideograph meaning "light." A system of writing using symbols to communicate ideas and thoughts in this way is called "picto-ideographic" or simply "ideographic." Such a system lets people express more complex or abstract ideas than they could using only pictographs to symbolize definite objects.

Phonetic Writing.   Phonetic systems of writing, like modern English, developed when some symbols came to refer to specific sounds in spoken language rather than just to specific objects. To the Egyptians, for instance, the symbol for "sun" was a picture of the sun. In spoken language, the Egyptian word for sun was "re." Eventually the sun pictograph was used in inscriptions to stand for the spoken syllable "re" as part of a longer word, not just to represent the sun.

ANCIENT EGYPTIAN		PHOENICIAN	ANCIENT GREEK	LATIN	MŒSO GOTHIC		OLD ENGLISH	MODERN ENGLISH
MONUMENTAL	CURSIVE				FORM	SOUND		
				A	λ	A	a	a
				B	ʙ	B	æ	b
				C	Γ	G	b	c
				D	ꝺ	D	c	d
				E	Ɇ	E	d	e
				F	F	F	e	f
				Z	G	G or J	f	g
				H	h	H	g	h
				—	ï or I	I	h	i
				I	K	K	i	j
				K	λ	L	k	k
				L	M	M	l	l
				M	N	N	m	m
				N	Ƨ	O	n	n
				—	Π	P	o	o
				O	⊙	HW	p	p
				P	Ʀ	R	p or r	q
				—	S	S	ϒ or ϒ	r
				Q	T	T		s
				R	Ψ	TH	t	t
				S	n	U	þ or ð	[th]
				T	ꭒ	CW	u	u
					ᴠ	W		v
					X	CH	ϸ/x	w
					Ƶ	Z	x	x
							y	y
							z	z

Written words are combinations of symbols that communicate meaning.

The Hebrews and Phoenicians took this process even farther. They developed phonetic writing, where the symbols they used represent *sounds* rather than objects. People who use phonetic systems of writing, like English, are able to form words for abstract ideas as well as specific objects. The Phoenician symbols illustrated on the chart on page 7 marked the beginning of a true phonetic alphabet.

When you examine the chart, you can trace the history of writing from simple pictographs to more advanced phonetic systems. Ancient Egyptian hieroglyphics were originally pictures which represented objects. Later, the Phoenician symbols represented sound in spoken language. Once the idea of using symbols to represent sound instead of ideas or objects was accepted, it spread quickly.

Notice how similar the Phoenician and Ancient Greek symbols look. The alphabet was brought to Greece from Phoenicia. Later, the Greek alphabet was borrowed by people called the Etruscans. In turn, the Etruscan alphabet was taken over by the Romans and was used as the basis for the Latin alphabet. Another version of the Greek alphabet was adopted by the Goths in the fourth century, but was discarded when the Goths became part of the Roman Empire. When you compare the Greek, Latin, and Gothic alphabets on the chart, you can see how similar they are to each other and to our English alphabet, which traces its origins back to them.

The Range of Writing

Jerome Martin, an educator, once described his own mind as similar to a "butterfly with hiccups." Can you see the image of the butterfly floating, settling down on an idea, and then suddenly, unexpectedly, hiccuping off in a different direction? Actually, the minds of many people function in this unpredictable, flitting manner. This kind of thinking does not lend itself to effective communication.

Readers and listeners need to have some idea of where you are coming from, what your purposes are, and where you are going. They need to be able to understand the background for what you say, to make connections between elements, and even to predict what you will say or do next. One writer is so cynical and doubtful about peoples' ability to communicate that he insists, "The only things you can communicate to other people are what they already know!" The statement, of course, is ridiculous because someone can tell you new ideas about atoms, astronomy, Russia, rice, and thousands of other things. Nonetheless, to comprehend these ideas you must understand the language, the vocabulary, the examples, the comparisons—even the patterns and structure of the words, phrases, and ideas. If the communicator's mind flits like a "butterfly with hiccups," you won't get much from the explanation.

For successful communication, you need order and arrangement, or structure. Fortunately, there is a wide range in the kind and amount of structure necessary for successful communication. For example, one of the greatest modern astronomers, Annie Jump Cannon, spent almost forty-five years at the Harvard Observatory scanning the heavens. During that time, she analyzed 286 000 stars, discovered 300 variable stars, 5 new stars, and a double star. Astronomers all over the world now look to her records, and astronomers hundreds of years in the future will read her descriptions. Annie Cannon could permit no inaccuracies in her work, for fear someone might confuse one of those 286 000 stars with some other one. Consequently, she "wrote" almost completely in mathematics and structured her work carefully. No room here for hiccuping butterflies!

Annie Cannon's work, as an example of structure, accuracy, and precision in scientific writing, can be placed at one end of a line of structure. At the other end of the line of structure might be the work of an experimental, creative writer such as Margaret Laurence. Of her work, she says, "Writing, for me, has to be set firmly in some soil, some place, some outer and inner territory...." Her work is also highly structured and organized. However, whereas Annie Cannon was describing the stars "out there," which can be located and checked for accuracy, Margaret Laurence is attempting to describe an "outer and inner territory" which is uniquely her own. Although her work is highly organized and patterned, it is her own pattern or map of experience, and at first some readers may find that they are unsure of the direction it is taking them. Writers at Margaret Laurence's end of the line of structure are "creative," not just because they are producing new and original works, but because they are interested in developing new and original patterns and structures.[1]

Now look at where various kinds of writing fall on the line of structure:

LINE OF STRUCTURE

Writing which must correspond precisely to objective reality	Structured, accurate writing in which the world's work is carried on	Free, unstructured writing for self-expression—no audience expected	Structured, creative writing of the traditional kind	Experimental writing using original structures and involving the writer's attitudes and vision of reality
Annie Jump Cannon's scientific writing	Business letters, laws, historical papers	Diaries, journals	Short stories, poetry, novels, essays	Margaret Laurence's writing

Activity 1B

Exploring the Degrees of Structure in Writing

Select one of the following tasks, explore it, and report to the class.

1. When you are ready, have someone give you one word. Without consciously thinking, write down the first word that comes into your mind as a result of the word you were given. Continue to list words, not pausing to think, as each new word suggests an additional word. Stop at the end of two minutes. Go back over your list, reconstructing how you got from one word to the next and trying to explain the connections among them. First, explain each connection; then write out explanations for the entire sequence. To what extent is your mind a "butterfly with hiccups?" How easily would a reader be able to follow a presentation that moved as your list moved, unless you reorganized and provided transitions and explanations?

2. An "ineffable" experience is an experience which cannot be expressed in words. Think of some time when you could not express in words the emotion you felt. It may have been anguish or joy or pride or elation or despair. Describe the setting, the event, and the situation which caused you to feel as you did. Then in a separate paragraph try to express the ineffable.

3. Find several examples of the kinds of writing in which the world's work is carried on. Analyze the structure or organization of each of the examples. Discuss the extent to which the structure or pattern limits the writer. Discuss the reader's need for structure.

4. One writer compared the organizing of ideas to the process of going shopping. She would walk hither and yon in a department store, going from one counter to another, retracing her steps and skipping whole areas as she pleased. That was the exploring, selecting part. Next she took her purchases, arranged them in what was, to her, the most interesting and exciting order. This was the organizing, arranging part. Then she shared her shopping trip with her invalid son at home, showing him one package at a time. She rarely told him about the items she put back or about the steps she retraced or about changing the order in which she bought things. (She always saved for last the toy she had bought him.)

   Choose a subject, such as discipline, homework, part-time jobs, or dating. With a group, bring up ideas on that subject. (Walk through the department store of ideas in your mind.) Jot down the ideas that you might put into a paper. It might help you in your selection of ideas to have in mind the main idea (the thesis statement). Arrange the ideas in logical order. Discuss to what extent the shopping trip and the composing process are similar.

5. Do you sometimes have trouble getting started writing a paper? Does your mind suddenly go blank? Try this technique. Look out the window or around the room. Think about how you felt when you got up this morning. What did you do yesterday? What are you looking forward to—or dreading—today? Write down whatever comes into your mind. Write freely for twenty minutes. Don't think about punctuation, grammar, spelling, or about the reaction of anyone else to what you are writing. At the end of twenty minutes, read what you have written.

   Discuss the results of this activity with a group or with the class as a whole. Share your paper with the others, or not, as you prefer. In your discussion, touch on these points:

   a. Did your mind behave like a "butterfly with hiccups"?
   b. Did you notice that, as the minutes passed, you began to write more quickly, more easily?
   c. Were your thoughts beginning to zero in on a central idea or theme?
   d. For what kinds of papers do you think this technique of free writing would be most helpful?
   e. Where, on the Line of Structure, would you place your paper?

Save your paper so you can compare it with another paper you will do when you reach Chapter 3.

Special Values of Writing

Near the end of World War II, the United States, England, and Russia issued the Potsdam Declaration calling for "unconditional surrender" by Japan. When Japanese Premier Suzuki was asked by the press on July 28, 1945, what his government planned to do, he declared that the cabinet was holding to a policy of *mokusatsu*. Since the Japanese word *moku* means "silence" and the word *satsu* means "kill," the literal meaning of *mokusatsu* is to "kill with silence." However, the word *mokusatsu* has come to mean two things: either "to withhold comment" or "to ignore." No one knows which meaning Suzuki had in mind. Did the cabinet intend "to withhold comment" until it received more information, or did it intend "to ignore" the declaration? The Domei News Agency chose the translation "to ignore." Nine days later, the United States dropped an atomic bomb on Hiroshima. Over 100 000 people died, possibly because of a misunderstanding.

   The problem with oral communication is that it is lightning fast—zip—and you've said something that cannot be retracted. If Premier Suzuki had written his reply, he would have had time to plan first and polish after-

A written record often lasts longer than the people who made it. This Assyrian tablet, telling of the Flood in Noah's time, is 2600 years old.

wards. He might have used a different Japanese word—perhaps *mokushi*, which means "to observe silence" and can be interpreted only one way.

This is one special value of writing: Because you can plan first and polish afterwards, you can be sure that you are expressing what you mean.

Another special value of writing is that you can record thoughts, impressions, and results and build on them over a long period of time. Speaking is like quicksilver: you say something, and the words vanish. Because the spoken word is so temporary, it's hard to have any complex, involved, and evolving structure in oral expression. Scientists, on the other hand, keep copious notes and use them to build their hypotheses and explanations and theories. Social scientists, literary scholars, and inventors all use written language to preserve their ideas. The writer Anais Nin kept a total of 150 manuscript volumes of her thoughts and impressions so that she built, over a period of many years, a wonderful storehouse of ideas.

Although it is not an intrinsic value of writing, a spirit of cooperation can be a byproduct of certain writing experiences. The most obvious example is a newspaper editorial, which is the official, institutional position of the newspaper regarding issues of concern to its readers. The editorial is the cooperative product of hours of discussion by the officials of the paper; of searching for examples and anecdotes to support the position; and of rewriting and editing one or more drafts. Even the magnificent translation of the Bible published in 1611, which we know as the King James version, was the result of years of cooperation by forty classical scholars. Although a single writer is often given credit for a book, most will freely acknowledge that, as the book grew over several years, a number of people contributed to its final form.

(*Activity 1C*)

Discussing the Special Values of Writing

Each of the following activities emphasizes one of the special values of writing.

1. Explain why the following are true:
   a. Why are most legal documents and real estate transactions recorded in writing and registered with the government?
   b. Why was the enactment by Hammurabi of a code of written laws considered a great step forward?
   c. Why do modern literary critics admire the "popular" poetry of some coffeehouse poets, who present their work orally, but reserve their highest praise for works which have been presented to the public in published form?

2. The next time you watch a television special, take five minutes immediately after the show to jot down some notes on the program's content. Put your notes away carefully. One week later, mentally review all you can remember about the show. Then look at your notes. How many details had faded from your memory? How much would you remember a year from now? Which of the values of writing does this experiment illustrate?

3. Cooperation on a piece of writing can mean assigning to different people the necessary tasks—originating the ideas, expressing them in written form, reorganizing and editing, proofreading. Discuss in what ways this method is helpful for a person learning to write.

On the first looking into Chapman's Homer

Much have I travelld in the Realms of Gold,
    And many goodly States, and Kingdoms seen;
    Round many Western islands have I been,
Which Bards in fealty to Apollo hold.
Of one wide expanse had I been told,
    Which deep brow'd Homer ruled as his Demesne;
        Yet could I never judge what Men could mean,
Till I heard Chapman speak out loud and bold. —
Then felt I like some Watcher of the Skies
    When a new Planet swims into his Ken,
Or like stout Cortez, when with wond'ring eyes
    He star'd at the Pacific, and all his Men
Look'd at each other with a wild surmise —
    Silent upon a Peak in Darien —

2

The Writing Process: An Overview

> *It is not generally understood that most writing takes place away from the typewriter. When you finally approach the machine, it is really the beginning of the end. Nine-tenths of your work has already been done; it remains to put on paper what you have already created. It is this creation process that takes most of the time.*
>
> — Pierre Berton

In 466 B.C. at Syracuse on the island of Sicily, south of Italy, there was a revolution that has had an influence on the way people have studied speaking and writing ever since! This book as well as many other textbooks you have used gets some of its ideas from this revolution.

Several tyrants had seized control of Syracuse, confiscated the property of many citizens, and exiled a large number of them. Finally, in 466, the people revolted, overthrew the tyrants, and invited the exiles to come home. Immediately, there were problems in the law courts. The exiles wanted their old lands and property back, but many records had been destroyed, the claims were often many years old, and the people had no deeds. The courts were flooded with claimants, and there simply were not enough lawyers to handle the business.

Into this confusion came Corax, a Sicilian Greek, and his pupil Tisias. They developed a little book called a *techne*, which was a kind of do-it-yourself manual on "How to Win Friends and Influence Juries." In short, Corax wrote the first book on how to make a speech and how to organize

◄ The manuscript of this poem by John Keats shows evidence of editorial changes and revisions.

FORTVNA LI FECE MAI ESSERE INSOLENTI

In 64 B.C., Cicero used rhetoric effectively to expose a plot by Catiline to overthrow the Senate of Rome.

a paper. For over 2000 years scholars have used the ideas of Corax, and you have learned some of them in various forms.

Later, in the first century B.C., the Roman orator Cicero built an outline of rhetoric, the art of using words effectively in speaking and writing. See if you think the elements of Cicero's outline cover what you have to learn in order to prepare papers.

1. Invention—the analysis of the communication situation and the audience, finding ideas to write and speak about, locating and selecting materials.

2. Disposition—the arrangement of ideas and arguments for maximum effect.

3. Style—the choice and arrangement of words to express ideas clearly, precisely, and vividly.

4. Memory—the ways of memorizing the material in order to present it exactly.

5. Delivery—the techniques needed for presenting the material orally.

Obviously, the last two points in the outline, Memory and Delivery, are useful in speaking but not in writing. Instead of these, let's substitute one that applies to writing:

> Mechanics—observing the conventions of manuscript form: spelling, capitalization, punctuation, paragraphing, and sentence structure.

Indeed, there is a good reason to focus on the four areas of Invention, Disposition, Style, and Mechanics as you learn to write. Several years ago, Educational Testing Service asked a number of successful people in various fields to rate three hundred first year university compositions. These business executives, scientists, attorneys, and writers were asked to rank the papers on a scale of one to nine with no fewer than four percent in any one category. They were to mark the papers and make extensive comments on them. ETS discovered much variation in the way the papers were judged. One reader might rank a paper "one" and another might rank the same paper "nine." No paper was in fewer than five of the nine categories and ninety-four percent were in seven, eight, or all nine. Then the written comments were analyzed by a computer to determine why the judges' evaluations differed so much. The computer revealed that each person was looking for different qualities:

1. Some were stressing content, ideas, and originality (Invention).
2. Some were stressing arrangement, patterning, and structure (Disposition).
3. Some were stressing word choice, sentence arrangement, and vivid imagery (Style).
4. Some were stressing capitalization, punctuation, spelling, handwriting, manuscript form, and paragraphing (Mechanics).

Educational Testing Service concluded from this research that, since no one knows what a particular reader will be looking for, a writer should develop skills in all four areas.

(*Activity 2A*)

Discussing the Divisions of the Writing Process

Consider each of the following questions.

1. Do the four elements, Invention, Disposition, Style, and Mechanics cover all aspects of learning to write? What others would you add?
2. From your personal experiences with writing and having your writing evaluated, which of the four elements do you think most people stress? Do you agree that this is the most important element? Defend your answer.

Steps in the Writing Process

You've just been reading and talking about how people judge writing. Now you're going to look at the steps in the actual writing process. The two are related to each other; and by using these steps, you can be sure that your writing will have the qualities people look for.

Every time you write a paper—whether you have a message to communicate, or an assignment to fulfill—it is necessary to go through six steps. Some of these steps may be unconscious, but you can probably do a better job if you are aware of the process.

Step One—Prewriting.   Before you begin to write, you think about what you want to communicate or about the assignment you've been given. You consider the situation, the readers, the time you have, the format you will use, what ideas you have and what research will be necessary, and how you will organize your paper. Obviously, before you even begin to write, you have a lot to do. Part of this step corresponds to Invention in Cicero's outline; that is, analyzing the audience and discovering ideas. Part of it corresponds to Disposition; that is, arranging ideas for the most effective presentation. Perhaps you haven't thought about how important this step is, how much time it takes, how interacting with others can help you, and how in-class time may be used effectively for prewriting preparation.

An important part of Prewriting is deciding why you want to write and who your reader will be. Whether you are writing to entertain or to inform, your purpose will determine such details as the form you write in and the language you use. Sometimes, for example, you may be stimulated to write in reaction to events which affect you or your community. When you write for such a purpose, you may choose the form of a letter to a newspaper editor or your Member of Parliament. At other times you may be required to write as part of a school assignment or a project related to your work. This kind of reason for writing may mean that a research essay or a formal report is the best choice of form. If your purpose for writing is personal satisfaction, your choices of form will be entirely different. Private self-expression may be best done in a journal or a poem, while imaginative writing intended to entertain others may take the form of a story or a play.

During Prewriting, you will be concerned with building a store of ideas and generating topics for your writing. Sometimes the Prewriting stage is simplified a bit if your teacher or your employer requests that you write about a specific topic. Most of your writing, however, will be the result of your desire to write about experiences, observations, or events which you wish to communicate to an audience. Often the hardest part of Prewriting is gathering information and recording experiences or observations. The following Prewriting activities may help to stimulate ideas for writing:

1. Regular entries in a journal or notebook.
2. Discussion with others.
3. Use of library reference material.
4. Study of literature selections.
5. Role-playing.
6. Sensory observation exercises.
7. Observation of films or pictures.
8. Listening to music.
9. Brainstorming ideas about a topic, individually or in a group.
10. "Clustering" groups of main ideas related to a general topic.
11. Building word caches for a variety of words to explore a topic.
12. Remembering vivid details about past experiences.

Step Two—Writing. The next step is actually writing the rough draft. If you have built an outline during the Prewriting process, you're off to a great start, but not everyone works well from an outline. Instead of using an outline, perhaps you will have made a list of ideas in approximately the order you expect to use them. In any case, you plunge right into your paper, using whatever organizational help you've prepared for yourself, and letting the paper grow and shape itself as you move along. You may think of new ideas that didn't come to you during the Prewriting step. You will reject some ideas that don't seem to fit and reorganize wherever appropriate. You won't worry too much about style and mechanics at this point because you don't want them to slow you down, but you may give them incidental attention as you write.

Most people perform this step alone because they don't want others to interrupt their train of thought. Thoughts flow better for many people when they compose by themselves, on a good Prewriting base.

This step involves you in Invention (finding ideas and checking them to see that they fit the audience and situation), Disposition (organizing), and Style (expressing ideas in appropriate arrangements of words). Therefore, this stage doesn't exactly correspond to any one of the sections of classical rhetoric.

You will find that your purpose, intended audience, and choice of supporting details all influence the form that your writing takes. Some experiences and emotions naturally lend themselves to narrative or creative forms while other topics can only be discussed in essay or report form. The chapters which follow deal with some of the forms you may wish to use at different times, ranging from essays expressing opinions or analyzing subjects, to letters, memos, and reports, to poetry, character sketches, and narration. Knowing about these various forms of writing will help you to choose the most appropriate form for your particular purpose each time you begin to write.

Step Three—Revising.   While writing the rough draft, the writer concentrates on getting as much as possible down on paper fluently, building on the ideas generated during Prewriting. Next comes Revising, the step which involves rewriting the rough draft to remove weaknesses in logic, organization, usage, and style. Revision involves four basic processes:

a. Adding material, such as examples, transitions, definitions, or summaries.
b. Deleting material, such as repetitions, clumsy expressions, or clichés.
c. Rearranging material, such as putting a main idea last for a more effective climax, or subordinating one idea to another.
d. Substituting material, such as finding the most descriptive words ("crept" instead of "walked"), or using more formal words ("informed" instead of "snitched").

It includes doing everything possible to reshape the rough draft into the most effective and artistic communication possible. For you to eliminate the revision process in preparing a school paper would show overconfidence, since even the greatest writers revise their manuscripts all the time.

Step Four—Editing.   Editing means going over the rough draft, reworking the words, phrases and sentences, correcting any unclear or illogical connections of ideas, and arranging the ideas in the best and most effective order. Effective editing calls for an objective, critical look at the piece of writing. Has it achieved the writer's purpose? Are the tone and style of language appropriate for the topic, the purpose, and the intended audience? Does the structure suit the information and ideas? Will the reader respond as the writer intends?

When editing your work you are concerned with using the correct conventions of English: capitalization, punctuation, subject-verb agreement, consistent verb tense, pronoun reference and agreement, and appropriate word choice. Check your English handbook for rules and examples concerned with the accepted language conventions.

Step Five—Writing and Proofreading Final Copy.   You are now ready to write your final copy. You will then proofread it to put the final polish on your work. You should look carefully at each sentence to be sure that no errors in the conventions of clear, correct expression slip past you.

Proofreading is often defined as a final check for accuracy before publication. This is a demanding task which publishers often leave to a whole battery of specialists. You don't have the services of a professional proofreader, as does the author of a book, and you have the handicap of working with your own material. It's much harder to find your own errors than those of another writer. Nonetheless, part of becoming an educated person is learning to be reasonably proficient at proofreading. The fact is that throughout life, both in school and out, you will not have someone to polish your writing for you. However, if it is possible and your teacher (in the case of assigned writing) agrees, you might work out some system of shared or cooperative proofreading in which you help someone else and he or she helps you. In any case, do not let the proofreading task interrupt your thought processes while you are composing. If possible, let a day or two elapse between editing your paper and proofreading.

Step Six—Sharing and Publishing. The purpose of most writing is communication. In a few cases, as the chart on page 9 indicates, you may write for self-expression without expectation or need of an audience. But in most cases, whether you are expressing ideas, opinions, judgments, inferences, attitudes, or emotions, you will be writing for an audience. One audience is your English teacher, who brings to your writing special background, skills, and experience. Another is a group of your peers; they can react to the content and form of your paper with openness and honesty. Reluctance to expose your paper to an audience may be a sign that you know you could have done a better job.

Your Special Revising and Editing Tasks

Two student essays have been included in this chapter to illustrate how the writing process of Prewriting, Writing, and Revising works. As you follow the student writers through the steps they took, you can see how they gathered and organized ideas and refined and polished their work to eliminate weaknesses in both logical organization and mechanical usage.

In the chapters that follow, you are going to be looking very closely at the kinds of Prewriting, Writing, and Sharing suitable for different kinds of papers. You will be looking carefully at models for each kind of writing to help you develop your own papers. Despite the fact that the kinds of writing will be different, the editing and proofreading processes will be much the same. Rather than repeat them in each chapter, we devote this chapter specifically to editing and proofreading suggestions. In this way, you will know the procedures when you are ready to work with the various kinds of writing. These procedures have been developed by writers, editors, and publishers over a long period of time, so take advantage of them to produce your best work.

SUGGESTIONS FOR REVISING AND EDITING

1. After you have written your rough draft, lay it aside for a day or two. Leave time to get some "distance" from your paper, so that you can be objective.

2. You may wish to read your whole paper aloud, as if someone else had written it. Check to see that it communicates what you had intended to say and that it sounds good to your ear. If it fails either test, try to locate and correct the problem.

3. Check the basic development of your paper: the opening, the thesis statement or main idea, the opening clues (if any) to your paper's organization, the logic in the order of your topics, the transitions, the ideas supporting your main points, and your conclusion. Use the four processes of revising—Addition, Deletion, Rearrangement, and Substitution—to increase your effectiveness.

4. When you're satisfied that your basic structure is good, reread your work and polish the phrases and sentences. Be sure that it reads smoothly, that the tone is appropriate, and that the whole paper produces the effect you desire.

5. After you have done your best to revise and edit your paper, share it with an interested friend. Together, repeat the foregoing process. Talk about any suggestions you have for each other, and seek additional help if you disagree.

After you have edited your paper, you are ready to proofread. If you can proofread your paper before making a final draft, you have saved yourself a step. However, if your rough draft has suffered from erasures, cross-outs, substitutions, writing between the lines, and other changes, you may need to recopy it before proofreading. As you proofread, you may need to make extensive additional corrections on this second draft. In most cases—for the purposes of your English class, for example—you will not need to prepare a third or fourth draft for the final copy. It is not unusual, however, in professional writing, to make a number of preliminary drafts. The standards set in your English class plus your own standards of excellence will help you determine when additional drafts are necessary.

SUGGESTIONS FOR PROOFREADING

1. Read slowly and carefully, sentence by sentence, being careful to let the meaning of each sentence register with you.

2. Pay special attention to natural phrasing of groups of words and the punctuation associated with them and with the ends of thoughts.

3. Use a dictionary to check spellings. Since some dictionaries will not have entries for all proper nouns, consider other sources of information. You may find that encyclopedias, biographical dictionaries, and updated yearbooks supply valuable information.

4. Use the style sheet on pages 383-393 to check major mechanical problems.

5. Consult other students and your teacher if you have specific problems.

6. After you have proofread your paper, share it with an interested friend. Repeat the foregoing process with each other's papers. Discuss any changes and be sure that you understand the reasons for them.

A WRITER'S CHECKLIST

Your teacher may suggest that you work with two or three other students in editing and proofreading teams to identify weaknesses in your own and others' writing. Whether you work alone or as part of an editing team, you may find a checklist helpful. The following checklist identifies how to revise a piece of writing.

I. **Selection of a Topic.** Does the writer:
   1. deal with a worthwhile central idea?
   2. have a definite purpose for writing?
   3. indicate a point of view on the topic?
   4. have a specific audience in mind?

II. **Organization.** Does the writer:
   1. choose the most appropriate form?
   2. include a clear introduction?
   3. place details in a logical order?
   4. group together details related to one idea?
   5. unify the writing by staying with only one main topic?
   6. use transitions to signal changes in direction of thought?
   7. include an effective conclusion?

III. **Development.** Does the writer:
   1. support the topic with facts, examples, and details?
   2. emphasize important points?
   3. show originality or insight?
   4. keep the reader's interest?
   5. select appropriate language and style?
   6. include colourful comparisons and images?

IV. **Mechanics and Usage.** Does the writer:
   1. punctuate correctly?
   2. use capital letters correctly?
   3. use accepted spelling?
   4. follow accepted grammatical usage?
   5. follow rules of pronoun reference?
   6. write in complete, correct sentences?

How Two Papers Developed

Roger Stryker received this assignment in English class: "Choose a controversial subject having to do with school. Present the arguments on both sides, and develop a position defending the side you believe is correct. Make your paper informative, persuasive, and interesting."

This is the way Roger developed his paper, following the first four "Steps in the Writing Process."

Step One—Prewriting.   Roger first considered all the possible topics. He took into account his purpose (as defined in the assignment), his probable audience (teacher and fellow students), his situation (his own available time, the length limitations, the available information, and so on). He did part of this thinking while doing other things—brushing his teeth, walking home from school, eating lunch. Part of it he did at his desk, remembering and putting down what he had thought of previously and thinking up new possibilities. He also casually discussed his assignment with his fellow football players, with his girlfriend, and at dinner with his parents. Then he brought this list of possible topics to the small group he was working with in class.

SOME IDEAS FOR MY POSITION PAPER

1. Require students to wear school uniform.
2. Maybe have soccer team during football season.
3. Eliminate student councils.
4. Decide that attendance in classes at secondary school shouldn't be compulsory.
5. There are more advantages than disadvantages to having a part-time job while attending secondary school.
6. Have a school work-day in which classes are cancelled so kids can do something for the community (planting bushes or picking up litter).
7. Work out recycling plans for paper, aluminum, etc., to earn money for clubs and conserve resources.
8. Improve library, especially back magazine collection for term papers and compositions.

Because this was a personal work sheet not intended for anyone else, Roger didn't hesitate to use fragments and abbreviations.

Each member of the prewriting group brought a similar list or a collection of ideas. Most preferred to bring a written list both to help them remember their ideas and to demonstrate to the group and to the teacher that they had made an effort to do their fair share. Only one student had a mental list.

The prewriting group pooled ideas, discarded some as uninteresting, too difficult, out-of-date, or inappropriate for the audience. Then each group member selected a single topic. Finally, the group consulted to help each person develop his or her topic.

Roger, with the group's help, decided to discuss the advantages and disadvantages of part-time jobs for secondary school students as his topic. The group helped him list these ideas to discuss in his paper:

Reasons to have part-time jobs:

1. Student earns own money, learns value.
2. Gets education from real life, not just books.
3. Learns to deal with adults as equals.
4. Gets experience with possible careers.
5. Has to learn to budget time and energy.
6. Makes decisions and accepts responsibility.
7. A chance to handle praise and criticism.
8. Puts skills learned in school into actual use.
9. Has money to save for a car, travel or university.
10. Gets experience dealing with the public.

Reasons not to have part-time jobs:

1. A job cuts out time for studying.
2. Hard to participate in school activities.
3. A job takes time away from friends and family.
4. Lots of time in life later for adult responsibility.
5. A job may be tiring and hard on the health.
6. Higher marks in school.
7. No time for hobbies and recreation.
8. Need good marks to get into post-secondary institutions.

Roger took this list, added a few more ideas, discarded some he didn't like, and made the following list of ideas to use in his essay. Although he knew how to make an outline, he preferred to work from a list.

Reasons to have a part-time job:

1. It helps to develop maturity in handling money.
2. Good for skills in dealing with the public.
3. Experience with possible future careers.
4. A chance to use the skills learned in school.
5. Learn to take responsibility and make decisions.
6. Budget time for job, school, and social life.

Reasons not to have a part-time job:

1. More time to study, higher achievement in school.
2. More time to spend with friends and family.
3. More chances for recreation and hobbies.
4. The teenager is not pushed into adult roles too soon.

This list is rough and perhaps illogical in some places, but Roger only used it as a guide. He didn't worry about order or arrangement. He is now ready for Step Two.

Step Two—Writing.   Following is the rough draft Roger wrote from his list of ideas. Some comments regarding suggested changes are shown on the left.

(*Activity 2B*)

Sharing Your Opinions

Read the draft without reading the editorial comments in the margin. As you read, jot down your own suggestions and comments. When you have finished, compare your comments with the marginal notes. Be prepared to discuss and defend your comments and the changes you suggested.

ROUGH DRAFT

Over the past ten years, one topic of discussion has taken up a lot of time over many dinner tables and in a lot of schools. This is the issue of part-time jobs for secondary school students, particularly those in Grades 11 and 12. In many secondary schools, about half the students hold a regular part-time job beside attending class full-time. While many parents and teachers see the value of part-time jobs for students, others are stupidly blind to it. Well, it's time for those people to wake up to the other side of the question and end their stupid objections.

Why object to part-time employment for students? Well, I suppose it's easy enough for a few rich mommas and poppas who can afford to give their kids money for clothes, a car, and recreation. Because their kids don't have to do anything but study and get good marks, they figure that the status of having such bright sons and daughters makes up for the drain on the parental pocketbook. They also figure that when these bright students graduate, they'll pick up more money in scholarships for university or post-secondary education. It would make more sense if scholarships were given to students who show a lot of all-around accomplishments. This might mean sports, community work, being

EDITING GROUP REACTIONS

Not a bad introduction. Probably could be more graphic and gripping. Could create more interest and excitement in the subject.

The word "stupid" is too harsh. Also, if any readers object to part-time work and you imply that they are stupid, they'll stop reading.

Good transition question. Oh, oh! The "well" is informal, and you're going to turn off many students with that comment about the mommas and poppas.

These comments about bright students and their parents will offend these readers.

You ought to leave out the whole section about scholarships and contributions to society. It's off the subject.

good in art or music—and, yes, even having one of those part-time jobs. It would be fairer for everyone concerned if scholarship money went to the students who showed that they needed it and tried to earn their own way. After all, these students are trying to contribute something to society so it can afford to provide scholarships.

They say that teenagers who don't work part-time have more time for activities that will contribute to all-around well-being. These are the guys who have more time to spend with their friends and families, so they can learn to form strong ties. These guys also get time to spend on their own hobbies and recreation. I don't think these are the only things that contribute to your well-being. If you're able to form ties to other people and develop your own hobbies for relaxation, you will, and that's all there is to it.

Well, why is part-time work valuable for secondary school students? I think that the main reason is that people learn to make decisions and take the responsibility for them. How would you feel if you finished secondary school knowing that you could already deal with adults and handle the public confidently? Besides, nobody asks you when you go to university or get a full-time job, did you graduate with all As or just a successful record? Nobody cares. As for handling money and learning to budget your time and energy, you can do that too. Handling a pretty full schedule. Now that's maturity.

Besides, it encourages you to get practical use out of the facts and skills you encounter in school, gives experience with possible future careers, and lets a person cope with how to budget time for a job, school, and social life.

Therefore, I think students benefit in a great many ways when they hold part-time jobs.

—Roger Stryker

"They" doesn't carry any weight. Can you name somebody? "Guy" is pretty informal.

Using what *you* think as proof is pretty weak. What proof can you offer?

"Well" is informal, but you do provide a good transition to your next main idea. It's not subtle, but it's clear. There's that "I think" again. What can you do to show that part-time work does this, whereas full-time school attendance alone does not? Since this is your main idea, maybe you could begin or end with it, instead of burying the idea in the middle.

You have a jumble of ideas right through here. Can you sort them, take them one at a time, and give some sort of "proof" or example in support of each one?

Do you think fragments are acceptable for this audience?

You shifted into the second person (using "you") in these paragraphs. It doesn't seem consistent with the earlier paragraphs.

Your ending is weak.

Step Three—Revising.   The comments placed beside the rough draft came from several students who met and shared comments on each other's papers. Roger reread his paper after putting it aside for a day or two. He then used the four revising processes: Adding, Deleting, Rearranging, and Substituting, to prepare an improved version of his paper.

Reviewing and Revising

Working individually or with a partner as your teacher suggests, prepare an improved version of Roger's paper. When revising the first version, make corrections and changes as suggested by the group's reactions. You may wish to go back to Roger's original notes for more material to strengthen the discussion, or you may add ideas of your own.

(*Activity 2D*)

Refining Your Opinions

Another student in Roger's class decided to write her position paper on "Our Inefficient Grading System." Like Roger, she began with the Prewriting step and then wrote this rough draft. As you read it, jot down your suggestions and comments just as you did with Roger's rough draft. Then compare your comments with the marginal notes.

ROUGH DRAFT

OUR INEFFICIENT GRADING SYSTEM

The present grading system used by most schools is an inaccurate, unproductive, and often unfair method of evaluating a student's knowledge and progress. However, many advocates of the system persist in maintaining that it is the only realistically feasible grading method available. This dogged train of thought is, in face of many new ideas and facts, so very untrue.

GROUP REACTIONS

Wouldn't it be a good idea to begin with a concrete example, story, or quotation to interest readers?

Your first sentence expresses what seems to be your thesis, but your paper goes beyond it to try to prove that some other system should be tried. Also, the three parts ("inaccurate," "unproductive," and "unfair") seem to be main divisions of your paper that you ought to prove. You do show that the system is inaccurate and unfair, but you ignore "unproductive." You ought to prove that, too.

The phrase "dogged train of thought" isn't accurate. In the first place, it's not a "train of thought," though the

The feasibility of the present grading system has only one point in its favour: simplicity. The calculation and transference of grades is quite simple for teachers and administrators, but so very unfair to the students. Grades are relative to so many things: classmates, quality of the teaching, difference in school grading scales, curves, and etc. How can educators continue to sacrifice the purpose of grades for simplicity? The purpose of grades is to evaluate a student's knowledge and to help pinpoint areas of difficulty so that they may be corrected. The present grading system does neither. How can educators continue to sacrifice these main objectives for the sake of simplicity?

Educators are incorrect when they maintain that the present grading system is the only method of student evaluation feasible. There are many new methods evolving today; many from teachers who are dissatisfied with the present system. For example, the Montessori Method, named after Maria Montessori, is based not upon relation to classmates, not upon tests, but upon achievement and progress. No distinction is made between school year (first grade, second grade, etc.), students' age, or grades (A, B, etc.). Instead, children are given tasks to accomplish and practise. Once the task is completed, the child is given something else to work at. The emphasis in this method is upon teaching children how to learn, instead of teaching them distinct subjects. The method takes advantage of a young child's tremendous ability to learn languages or mathematics at certain "sensitivity periods." Proof of these "sensitivity periods" is the ease with which young children can pick up language as opposed to the difficulty which older children have in doing the same thing. This is only one method of many. And it is working all across the country.

Another reason that the present grading is not the best available is the variance in which the final grades

advocates follow it "doggedly." "Untrue" is the wrong word. A belief may be untrue, but a train of thought would have to be "misguided" or something suggesting process.

Simplify the first sentence in the second paragraph. You're talking about "the system" not "feasibility." Keep the same subject in the second sentence as in the first. Why?

"So" in "so very unfair" sounds odd here. "Are relative to" could be simplified to "depend on."

"And etc." is redundant. Etc. alone means "and other things." Also, etc. should not be used in formal writing.

You really don't prove that the "purpose of grades is to evaluate." It could be a main idea for you to prove. If you use the three-part division in the first sentence, however, you have some overlapping.

The closing sentence of the second paragraph is a needless repetition.

Expletives (It is...There are...Here are...) waste words. Semicolons connect equal parts of sentences. This one doesn't.

You seem to be comparing apples and oranges, because the Montessori system is more than a grading system.

Clarify. Simplify. What you mean is that students are not placed in different classes according to grades, age, or scholastic achievement.

Discussion of a child's language ability seems way off the subject.

How do you "prove a sensitivity period?" What you prove is that "sensitivity periods" exist.

At the end of the third paragraph, what does "this" refer to? Is it the focus on tasks appropriate for sensitivity periods, or is it systems other than the Montessori Method?

The word "another," which begins the fourth paragraph, implies that the are calculated. Some teachers base the final grades on a curve based on the classmates' performance. Other teachers drop a low grade or allow for one grade to be dropped. In fact, the way in which grades are calculated vary with the teacher. The methods are limitless. They are also unfair. One student, under a certain teacher, covering a specified subject might get a high grade. But, if that same student were under another teacher, covering the same materials, he might very easily wind up with a low grade. The difference could be related to the ineptness of one teacher compared to another, or the poorness of one test to a better one. The point is, how can such diverse outcomes be overlooked so easily? There are better methods available and educators have the duty to investigate them.

Surely, such a grading system that misses its objectives by such a wide margin can not be maintained, especially when better methods are available. The educators of today have a serious obligation to society to investigate new methods and to implement improvements as soon as possible.

—Theresa Norton

idea in the previous paragraph and this new one are parallel. They don't seem to be. "Variance" is the wrong word. "Base" and "based" in the same sentence seem awkward.

The verb "vary" should agree with the subject "way."

Many people today object to letting the word "he" stand for people of both sexes. "Wind up" is too informal. Clarify what difference you are talking about. Also, the word "poorness" is not idiomatic.

"The point is" promises a "point," a statement, not a question. Also it seems a bit informal.

Your first task is to clarify your objective. Which do you want to do:
1) Prove the present grading system is bad?
2) Prove that other, better ones exist? or
3) Prove that the whole educational system is inferior to the Montessori approach?

You must limit your discussion of Montessori to its grading system only.

Step Three—Revising.   After Theresa reread her paper in the light of the group's comments and suggestions, she put it aside for a few days. Then she revised it. She added some things, deleted others, rearranged her material, and made some substitutions. Her second draft follows. As you read it, notice where she used each of these revising processes.

SECOND DRAFT WITH ADDITIONAL EDITING AND PROOFING NOTATIONS PRIOR TO TYPING IN FINAL FORM

OUR INEFFICIENT GRADING SYSTEM

Grace and Beth have been friends for a long time. In fact, all the way through Hawthorne Elementary School and East Junior Secondary School. They ~~have~~ were

CHANGES MADE AS A RESULT OF GROUP COMMENTS ON ROUGH DRAFT

Theresa has invented an opening story to attract the interest of readers.

always
always been in the same classes, and they have always earned the same grades. Suddenly, for the first time, at Washburn Senior Secondary they're in different classes—and, for the first time, they get wildly different grades. Difference in ability? Accident? No! They are victims of an inaccurate, unproductive, and unfair grading system which ought to be replaced.

The present grading system has only one point in its favour: it is simple. It enables teachers and administrators to calculate and transfer grades very easily. These grades, however, are so inaccurate, unfair and unproductive that educators should not continue to sacrifice major educational objectives for simplicity.

What are the purposes of grades? They should evaluate the knowledge and progress of students and show them where they need help. The present grading system, unfortunately, does neither. The experience of Grace and Beth is typical of thousands of experiences which point out its inadequacies.

The grading system, in many cases, is grossly inaccurate. Grades can depend on many different factors: the stimulation from classmates, the quality of teaching, the manner of evaluation, and other influences. It is perfectly possible for two students of equal ability, such as Grace and Beth, to receive such different grades that their marks bear no relationship whatsoever to their learning. If the two girls were to switch places, their grades for the next marking period might well be switched also. Such inaccurate marks couldn't possibly provide information about what students have achieved and where they need help.

Theresa has clarified her thinking. She will limit herself to discussing the grading system but she will prove both that it's bad and that it should be replaced.

To disarm the opposition, Theresa begins by giving credit to the present grading system for having at least one value. Notice the simplified first sentence. Then she will take up her three criticisms of the system one at a time and in order. Notice how the word "however" is sandwiched into the middle of the sentence so it doesn't use up a strong sentence-beginning slot.

This short paragraph puts grading into a context so that Theresa can more easily prove that the present system is inaccurate, unfair, and unproductive.

This reference to the opening story keeps the personal and concrete example alive and gives it additional effectiveness.

Here Theresa attempts to prove the first of the three charges she makes against the present grading system.

A grading system ~~which is~~ so inaccurate is necessarily unfair also. Because ~~each~~ *all* teacher~~s~~ calculate~~s~~ grades in the way ~~he or she~~ *they* prefer~~s~~, ~~there is great variation among procedures.~~ *procedures vary greatly.* Some teachers ~~base~~ grade~~s~~ on a curve based on student performance. Others have absolute standards. Some ~~teachers~~ figure in all grades. Others let students drop an occasional low grade or make allowance for incompletes. Any system ~~which is~~ so inaccurate and inconsistent ~~in evaluation~~ cannot possibly be fair.

Perhaps the worst thing about the present *grading* system ~~of grading~~ is that it is unproductive~~.~~ ~~That is,~~ it doesn't encourage either ~~the~~ student ~~who is earning high marks~~ *"A"* or ~~the~~ student ~~who is earning low marks~~ *"D"* to do ~~his or her~~ *their* best. The student ~~who is getting high marks~~ *"A"* thinks~~,~~ that ~~he is~~ *"I'm* doing fine~~.~~ ~~and doesn't~~ *I don't* have to work any harder. The student ~~who is getting low marks~~ *"D"* thinks that ~~he~~ *"I* can't do any better~~,~~ ~~so he doesn't~~ *I won't* try~~.~~*"* The present grading system doesn't encourage either type ~~of student~~ to reach their own potential. It is unproductive.

Some advocates of the present system maintain, however, that the present grading system is the only realistic~~ally feasible~~ system available. On the contrary, many new grading systems are evolving today~~,~~ ~~some of them even coming from teachers dissatisfied with the present system.~~ One interesting "grading system," which ~~is~~ a small part of ~~a completely different total educational package, is that~~ built into the Montessori Method. Maria Montessori based her grading, not on tests, but on actual observable achievement~~ and progress~~. She let students work at specific tasks, ignoring any age, ability, or grade-level differences. As students

Here Theresa handles the second charge she makes against the grading system—the charge that it is unfair. Note that she changed the order of her second and third points. Why?

Theresa takes up her third charge against the present grading system. Why does she save this one for last?

This transition prepares the reader psychologically for the "new" system or systems which might replace the present one.

Notice how Theresa now limits her discussion only to the grading portion of the Montessori system.

Notice how much of the earlier discussion of the Montessori system is now omitted, since it is not part of the grading system.

complete their tasks, they move on to more challenging and more rewarding tasks. There is no "grading" in the traditional sense. Students grade themselves by working at their own individual speeds and reaching their own levels. The Montessori "nongrading" or "selfgrading" system is only one of many ~~other~~ ways of handling the grading problem. Educators owe children and parents a better grading system, so they should seriously investigate some of the new methods available.

At the end of their first semester at Washburn Secondary, Grace and Beth discovered that the present grading system is inaccurate, unfair, and unproductive. In spite of the fact that they ~~and their work~~ were treated so differently, *Beth and Grace* ~~they~~ remained good friends and excellent students. Won't it be wonderful when the grading system actually encourages cooperation and friendship and productive scholarship, rather than being something good students must overcome?

—Theresa Norton

By referring to the opening story, Theresa uses the "envelope technique" to round out her paper.

Note how she repeats her main points in an unobtrusive summary.

After writing a second draft following initial revision Theresa has given her paper a second revision, completing editing tasks at the same time as the corrections on the preceding pages indicate. Theresa had asked another student to go over her paper with her. Since most professional writers have the benefit of this step, you, as a student learning to write, should have it also.

The one difference between you and a professional writer, however, is that you owe it to yourself to review any corrections to learn the reasons for the changes. To use an editor without learning from the process is both to deprive yourself of the opportunity of learning and to steal an undeserved grade by having someone else do your work.

After these processes of revising and editing, Theresa wrote her final copy and proofread it carefully. Her paper was now ready for the final stage of sharing and publishing.

Activity 2E

Locating and Correcting Errors

Copy the following paragraphs on a sheet of paper. Make all necessary proofreading corrections to remove errors. After you have corrected these paragraphs, your teacher may suggest that you work in a small group with two or three other students to check your corrections.

The availability of food plays a key role in detremining peoples eating habits. Certain foods grow well in 1 part of the world but poorly in another. Saltwater fish of seas and oceans differ from freshwater fish of lakes and. Why do you suppose the Chinese people eat rice and the Inuit eat blubber. People learn to survive on foods that are near at hand, and in doingso they acquire a tatse for the foods that they know. throughout human history our eating patters-what we eat and when and how we eat it have been influenced by culture, religion, and geography. In the modern World, a number of other things also affect our eating patterns.

Youll hear alot of talk about the benifits of travel, but I'am not so sure I agree with those poeple. Encouraging the rest of us to turn into proffesional tourists. They discribe travel as a great education in itself, pointing out the advantages of seeing other countries. Eating different kind's of food, visiting famous Museums and shopping in street markets. The 1st time I tryed to educate my self in this ways, the first forign meal I had, it made me so sick I spent most of my holiday in my hotel room. On my next trip, I fell while I was sightseeing and broke my ankle, when I tryed for the 3rd and last time to take another one of those educational tour's, the airline lost my luggage. I spent one uncomfortable week in Hawaii. But my suitcase enjoyed a glorious tour of England, france, denmark, and Spain before it finely got home two months later. The only thing, I've learned so far, is that travel is not for me.

There is only one trait that marks the writer. He is always watching. It's a trick of mind, and he is born with it.

—Morley Callaghan

3

Exposition

It was in Canada that the desire to write came upon me. It was in Canada that I first saw my name in print. I owe more to this Country and its people than I can put into words.

—Khushwant Singh

The second half of the twentieth century has seen an "Information Explosion." As Alvin Toffler has observed in *Future Shock*, a great leap forward in knowledge-acquisition occurred with the invention of movable type in the fifteenth century. Before 1500, about one thousand books a year were printed in Europe. About that many are now produced world-wide in a single day. Organizations based entirely on the "information sciences" have been formed specifically to keep business, industry, government, the military, and education up-to-date on the most recent world and national developments. A recent IBM advertisement expresses the current corporate view that "What you don't know *can* hurt you." Many executives and decision makers hesitate to make vital decisions without the latest, perhaps crucial, information.

Television and films have become popular modern sources of information, but for hundreds of years people have depended on exposition to extend and transmit knowledge. Exposition is the kind of writing that communicates information. Basically, it explains and exposes, or "puts forth," information. At one time, writers insisted that exposition should not be concerned with imagination or feelings or with convincing a reader to act in a certain way.

Things have changed, however, and modern writers know that presenting information alone is not enough. Good exposition appeals to the imagination and feelings of a reader. In many cases it will also lead the reader to act on the basis of the information given.

Your major writing assignment for this chapter will be an expository composition. You will prepare for that assignment by practising various techniques for beginning, developing, and ending expository material. If you master each component skill, putting them all together will not be so difficult.

Three Samples of Modern Exposition

As you read these samples of exposition, pay special attention to the four qualities people look for in writing: Invention, Disposition, Style, and Mechanics, which are described in Chapter 1. Look also for appeals to imagination, feelings, and decision making. Try to decide who the writer's intended audience is, and what details the writer has included to appeal to that audience. Look for techniques of effective exposition which you may want to use in your writing later.

I

THE NEW COMPUTER REVOLUTION

The new age of the computer has been called the second Industrial Revolution. Just as machinery amplified and extended the power of human muscles, so computers amplify and extend the power of the human brain. Although computers have definite limitations, there are virtually no areas of activity in the world today that have not been influenced by the computer to some extent. You cannot get through a day without being touched by this influence many times, whether or not you are aware of it.

Let's look at some of the areas in which computers are helping people to do their jobs better, or freeing them for more enjoyable activities.

In the areas of scientific research, engineering, and space science, computers have had the earliest, greatest, and most constant impact. In the world of business and finance, increasingly complex operations are possible only because of the computer's capacity to store and retrieve masses of information. In industry, many of the processes that transform raw material to finished product are controlled by computers.

Schools and universities have felt the impact of the computer age. Administrators use computers for record-keeping and scheduling and other routine tasks. Teachers use them as instructional tools. At the university level, major areas of study from architecture to forestry are making use of computers. Many universities that once made Latin a mandatory entrance requirement now require instead proficiency in at least one computer programming language!

There is still another area where the use of computers is growing rapidly. Since human beings play as well as work, it's not surprising that a major use of the computer is for fun. Chess champions have played exciting games with a computer as a partner. Swimmers touch electronic plates at the finish line. And for spectators, computerized ticket agencies can reserve seats, print tickets, and charge the cost to credit cards.

Perhaps the most important thing to keep in mind as we marvel at this computer revolution is this: Because computers can relieve us of doing routine mental tasks, we find ourselves with more freedom to develop our creativity. While computers carry on the more mundane work of society, we are free to organize, invent, create, and wonder—and put the computer to work producing the inventions and helping to discover the answers.[1]

II

Mention weight training to most women and they grimace at the thought of becoming muscle-bound. Yet thousands of Canadian women are entering the world of dumbbells and benches, bars and squat stands, both in comfortable clubs decorated with the feminine touch and in erstwhile "men only" gyms, where the smell of sweat still drifts out from under a cloud of Glade.

Robert Kennedy, a body culture author who publishes *Muscle Mag International* in Brampton, Ontario, estimates a 100% rise in women's participation in weight training in the last 12 months, and increases were reported by all the bodyshop owners I spoke to. Their female members aren't doing it to strike fear into families and friends; they've discovered that weight training is the quickest, most scientific way to reshape a body.

Robyn Goorevitch conducts the "Slender Salon" at the Moncton, New Brunswick YMCA, which has 300 women enrolled in its program, up from 200 last year. "Quite a number of women are enrolled in weight exercises," she says. "Most of them are into it for slimming. We give them flexibility exercises—we use weights a lot."

The Chaudière Health Centre in Lucerne, Québec says it has seen a 30% increase in women's enrolment in weight programs. And Janet Hudson of the European Spa Fitness Centre in North Vancouver says, "Women are into weight training much more heavily than they were. We now use weights in all our programs and the women are very enthusiastic."

A woman who works out with weights need not fear that she'll end up with arms and legs like Lou Ferrigno's. Ken Wheeler, who manages several Vic Tanny's clubs in Ontario, points out that women's bodies develop along different lines from men's. Women's muscles are less prominent and more esthetically pleasing. Even hard-working bodybuilding women will never look like Arnold Schwarzenegger because the male hormone testosterone plays an important part in the way muscles develop.[2]

—François-régis Klanfer

III

What's a *palimpsest* anyway? The word is not in everyday usage, but it is important to art historians. A palimpsest, by definition, is a canvas or parchment used over and over again: a painting on a painting on a painting. . . . Art thieves use palimpsests. How else could they get the *Mona Lisa* past French customs? Once safely through, the thieves would carefully rub off the top layer of an unremarkable work to reveal the smiling lady. You can find an everyday example of a palimpsest when you chip paint in an old apartment. The tastes of each of the previous tenants are preserved in chronological order with your color on top.

Land is also a palimpsest. A succession of human cultures, each with different priorities, has painted its record on the basic environmental canvas.

Today's shopping center was yesterday's orchard and before that a frontier farm and an Indian council ring. Probe back 40 000 years in North America and there is an environment totally unmodified by *Homo sapiens*.

It is good to celebrate places in the world where the crust of civilization is thin and broken. It is important that the palimpsest occasionally part to reveal the Old Master beneath man's paintings. It does not matter that the gaps vary in size. Some of them are relatively large: (we call these national parks and wilderness areas). Others may be as small and unexpected as a fringe of tall-grass prairie paralleling a railroad in the Midwest or a mossy boulder in New York City's Central Park. Beauty—and meaning—is in the eye of the beholder. What really matters is that the wild not vanish from the world that we have largely repainted. As curators we must be worthy of the delicate palimpsest we have inherited.[3]

—Roderick Nash

The Outside Structure

Every piece of exposition differs from every other piece, and by looking in textbooks, magazines, newspapers, and hobby kits, you can find many different types. Because exposition is the kind of writing that gets the world's work done, it is everywhere and of every type.

For our purposes, then, we'll leave out the instructive "how-to-do-it" type that makes no attempt to interest or to motivate. The kind of exposition you're going to produce is like the preceding models: short, focused, interesting, and purposeful.

This kind of exposition is easy to write because it has two structures: the *outside* structure and the *inside* structure. The outside structure consists of a kind of "wrapper" that goes around the main body of an expository paper. It consists of the introduction and the conclusion. Look at the beginning and end of each of the foregoing selections. (Sometimes the beginning will be just one sentence; sometimes it will be a paragraph or two. The endings vary similarly.)

A good introduction does two and sometimes three tasks as it prepares a reader psychologically for the main body of the paper. An introduction:

1. Arouses interest.
2. States the main idea or purpose of the paper.
3. Gives an overview of the main divisions of the paper (optional).

By the time readers have finished the introduction, they are ready to go on to the body of the paper.

Look at the preceding selections. Read the introductions carefully. Determine where and how each introduction arouses interest and reveals the main idea or purpose of the selection. None of the examples gives an overview of the main divisions of the paper. You will look at this task of an introduction later.

A good conclusion does one task and sometimes two as it wraps up the expository paper. A conclusion:

1. Summarizes the main points (optional).
2. Provides an interesting closure (ending) and a satisfying feeling of completion.

The introduction and the conclusion, which together "wrap up" the body of the paper, are the outside structure.

(Activity 3A)

Investigating Outside Structures

A newspaper or magazine must "earn" its audience. If it doesn't, people don't buy it, and the company fails. However, some publications are not required to "earn" their audiences. For example, certain technical reports, laws, directions, and so on, are required reading whether the writer has earned the attention of an audience or not. Students are required to read certain textbooks, interesting or not.

For this assignment, limit yourself to the kind of publications that are required to earn their audiences. Look at the beginnings and endings of selections from them and try to find out how they have used the outside structure of exposition. Be prepared to read in class, or to your group, the introduction and conclusion of one of your selections. Discuss the way the writer caught the interest of the reader, how the main idea was expressed, and how a feeling of closure was provided.

The Inside Structure

The inside structure of an expository composition consists of the material as it is organized in the body of the paper. Look at the different ways the three selections you have just read are organized:

1. The selection called "The New Computer Revolution" divides the material into paragraphs according to the various areas in which computers are being used.
2. The selection on women and weight training states that the once male-oriented sport of weight lifting is beginning to appeal to women, goes on to provide detail concerning the extent of this trend, and then concludes that weight lifting for women just might have a deeper significance than exercise.

3. The selection on the environment defines the word "palimpsest;" then it uses the comparison pattern to show how layers of civilization built on land are like a palimpsest.

Though each of these "inside structures" is different, each is closely tied to its "outside structure," and each develops the main idea or "thesis statement" set forth in the introduction. The thesis statement gives the main idea or purpose of the composition. Stating this idea is one of the tasks of a good introduction.

Following is a piece of writing that lacks an outside structure. The inside structure, or body, contains interesting historical information, factual information, and anecdotal details and examples. Yet, the lack of an outside structure to support the body results in problems. What do you think the main idea of this paper is?

I

The two-house parliamentary system established in Canada was modelled on that of Great Britain. The Americans, on the other hand, adopted a different philosophy of government and set up a system of "checks and balances" based on a clear division of power and authority among governmental institutions which oversee one another. This difference of philosophy is one of the most significant differences between the two types of government.

Canada, though, did not adopt the British system without alteration. Instead of a House of Lords, we, like the Americans, have a senate. Our senate, however, does not have the same function and powers of its American equivalent. As part of the legislative branch of government, the American Senate is an elected body. Canadian senators are created through government appointment. The Americans questioned the wisdom of an appointed legislative body. Perhaps they were wise to do so. Then again, perhaps the major issue we must face concerning our senate does not have to do with the matter of election or appointment. We cannot judge the effectiveness of governmental institutions on this one criterion alone.

Another important fact to consider is the nature of executive power. The role of the American president is, in many ways, autonomous. Unlike the Canadian prime minister, the president does not lead the government in its legislative debate. The Canadian prime minister, though, is a parliamentary fighter and has no austere power of veto. Perhaps Sir John A. Macdonald's government could have withstood the infamous Pacific Scandal if Macdonald had been able to remain aloof from the House of Commons and wield more executive power. But then, the Watergate scandal in the United States resulted in the fall of a president. So the presidency may not be as aloof and powerful as we might imagine. After all, unlike President Nixon, Macdonald came back into power and went on to finish his dream of a national railway. Again we see that we must think twice before seeking solutions to what we see as weaknesses in our governmental system south of the border.

Thesis Statement

A thesis statement is to a longer paper what a topic sentence is to a paragraph, and both thesis statements and topic sentences consist of two parts: a complete subject and a complete predicate. The complete subject identifies a topic and limits that topic to something the writer intends to discuss. The complete predicate presents an attitude toward or an idea about the topic that the writer will demonstrate or prove. A topic sentence, then, names the subject of a paragraph and states what the writer will prove or demonstrate about that subject. A thesis statement does the same for a longer paper. To write a thesis statement or a topic sentence, then, a writer must define the subject (if it needs defining) and present, in the predicate, an attitude towards or an idea about the subject. Here is a diagram of a thesis statement:

The Swiss	have chosen a neutral role in international affairs.

The subject   An idea about the subject

Here are the thesis statements of the first three selections.

Complete Subject	Complete Predicate
1. … the computer Revolution	is here
2. Thousands of Canadian women	are entering the world of dumbbells and benches, bars and squat stands …
3. Land	is also a palimpsest

As you look at the preceding thesis statements, which subjects seem to you to need defining? Has the writer done this? Do any of the predicates seem to need defining or explaining as well as proving? Has the writer done this?

It is not always necessary to express a thesis statement. Sometimes writers imply or suggest a thesis statement. A problem with implied thesis statements, however, is that sometimes readers do not really understand what the writer is trying to prove. Look for the thesis statement in the selection about government. Do you find it expressed anywhere? Is there an implied thesis statement? What is it? How could the selection be improved?

Activity 3B

Locating and Understanding Thesis Statements

Locate the thesis statement in each of the following passages. It may be stated or implied. Divide the thesis statement into its complete subject and complete predicate. Discuss with the class what tasks the writer must do because of the way the thesis statement is expressed.

The first one has been done for you.

1. Big. Tough. Monied. They're words that describe Alberta, and they have a nice masculine ring to them. Canadians tend to categorize Alberta as a man's country—a land of ranchers, roughnecks and red-necks, like Texas or Australia, with traditional values that leave little room for feminine influences.

   But in 75 years of provincehood the female fact has been pervasive and important. From the beginning, women suffered the isolation and loneliness of pioneer existence with an endurance more than the equal of their men's. Many of them, like Ukrainian women settlers at the turn of the century, cleared the land and harvested the crops while their husbands were away working on the railroad.[4]

   —Paul Grescoe

Thesis Statement:

Complete Subject	Complete Predicate
The female fact (in Alberta)	has been pervasive and important

The thesis statement indicates the writer's task—to demonstrate how women have made significant contributions to Alberta society during 75 years of provincehood.

2. You buy, collect, inherit, and hoard. And suddenly there comes a day when you have an irresistible desire to unload the excess baggage.

   Whatever it is that you have too much of, you want to eliminate it. This happens to all of us. The question then arises, how to dispose of the goods most advantageously? The answer depends on the types of items and why you want to pass them on.[5]

   —Harriet Webster

3. A few years ago, Noel Vietmeyer, a staff director of the National Academy of Sciences, was surprised to find in a collection of reports on tropical plants one with a curious title: "*Psophocarpus tetragonolobus:* Crop with a Future?" Neither Vietmeyer nor any other agriculture scientist would be suprised today. For the plant, better known as "the winged bean" because of the four winglike flanges on its pod, is now regarded as a great green hope among the experts who worry about new food sources for the overpopulated and under-developed world.[6]

4. What's in a no-name?
   Rich people think more about money than poor people do: that's usually how they got rich. So it shouldn't be any surprise that when no-name generic food products came to Canada, the people who hurried down to the stores to buy them were not the poor (who really *needed* cheap food) but the comparatively well-heeled, once again grabbing the bargains. The poor come later. As one food executive says, after surveying some elaborate marketing research: "The first to take the plunge were the more affluent. They are always more innovative and tend to be more cost conscious." After a lifetime spent in the bright ambience of highly touted brands, leaping into the darkness of generic products took a bit of daring.[7]

—*Saturday Night* Magazine

(*Activity 3C*)

Creating Thesis Statements

Working alone or in groups as your teacher designates, go through the following steps to prepare a list of at least ten possible thesis statements on which you might base an expository paper.

1. List subjects on which any teenager ought to be able to speak for three minutes without any preparation. What are subjects that most young adults know something about and have opinions about? (Begin with television, cars, health foods, and go on from there!) This is just a point of departure for building a storehouse of ideas on which you can write. Your life is filled with topics for exposition, and you can get many ideas from television, newspapers, magazines, films, libraries, conversations, experiments, and questionnaires.

2. Of all these topics, select ten that interest you. "Brainstorm" these topics so that you have some idea of your knowledge base. Consider your knowledge base and narrow each subject. For example, if the topic were cars, and your knowledge base were appropriate, limit yourself to "dune buggies." If the topic were television, you might select one particular program or "science fiction programs."

3. Now take five of the ten topics you chose and narrow them even further. Instead of "dune buggies," you might narrow your topic to "The plans I bought for a modified dune buggy."

4. When each topic has been narrowed sufficiently, it can serve as the complete subject of a thesis statement. If it's too broad for that, go through more narrowing steps. Now think of an idea you could communicate about each of the subjects you have chosen. This idea becomes the complete predicate of the thesis statement. Your idea should be something worth saying, something that isn't so obvious as not to need

proving or explaining, and something you can handle. Using the dune buggy example, you might decide to work from a thesis statement like: "The plans I bought for a modified dune buggy are too complicated for me to use."

5. Keep your original list of topics, your topic notes, your ten narrowed topics, and your thesis statements. Use all these as your storehouse of raw materials for future writing. Add to your storehouse from time to time, consciously expanding your supply of ideas.

Some Warnings About Topic Sentences and Thesis Statements

The suggestions you've just read for developing topic sentences and thesis statements are helpful. But, at times, you may have trouble developing a thesis statement on certain subjects. Some people just don't write effectively if they are forced to develop thesis statements before they write. Here are two warnings.

1. As you noted in Chapter 2, writing is, in itself, a process of discovery. Sometimes writers really don't know what they want to say before they begin to write, so they can't possibly begin by expressing a thesis statement. In such cases, they begin writing and the process of writing helps them clarify their thoughts and discover what they want to say. When they get to the point at which they know their thesis statement, they then go back over their work and make sure that everything pertains to the subject and supports that main idea.

2. Sometimes, for various reasons, writers do not express a thesis statement directly. For diplomatic reasons, they may not want to offend readers. For aesthetic and artistic reasons, they may prefer a more subtle approach. For psychological reasons, they may feel that the main idea will be more effective and longlasting if the reader has to discover it. These variations from the expository pattern are fine. Indeed, the most outstanding writers are probably the most subtle, seldom using anything as obvious as an overt, direct statement of purpose. However, for direct, simple communication, thesis statements are best for beginning writers.

Preparing Introductions

You've looked at the most important part of an introduction—the thesis statement—but the second part is almost as important. This is the part which arouses the readers' interest, gets them involved, and makes them want to continue reading.

Frank Luther Mott, a famous professor of journalism, developed a formula to explain why people choose to read certain selections rather than others. He calls his formula the "fraction of selection."

$$\text{Fraction of Selection} = \frac{\text{Expectation of Reward}}{\text{Effort Required}}$$

In other words, to get people to read what you write, you must show them that they'll get a high reward for little effort. If your reader is highly motivated because of previous interest in the subject or because the reading is required, motivation is less important. Nonetheless, it's a good idea to arouse interest by having a clear, interesting thesis statement and by writing clearly and sharply.

(*Activity 3D*)

Examining Interesting Openings

The following opening paragraphs show a few of the ways writers arouse interest at the beginning of an expository paper. Read each carefully to see what it contains. Discuss its advantages and disadvantages. Try to devise additional types of interest-arousers.

1. If you are going to a party and you know how to play the piano keep it a secret like a hole in your sock. Playing the piano at parties is the surest way to psychic scarification and social disaster.[8]

   —Mervyn J. Huston

2. The small, brown moths darkened the skies in New Brunswick in early July, cutting visibility at times to less than 275 m. Motorists who left the windows of parked cars open near Perth had to beat away the insects to get back behind the wheel. Since then, the moths have dropped eggs in massive quantities, and tiny .63 centimetres-long spruce budworms are now eating their way through 607 billion square metres of forests in Maine and southeastern New Brunswick. Evergreen spruce and fir trees stand brown and naked in the summer sun.

3. Choosing a lawyer is like buying a car: you should take both out for a test drive before making a final decision. Trying out a lawyer, however, is often an exercise conducted blindfold in a field glutted with contenders. Merely shopping for a lawyer can be as intimidating as the prospect of consulting one, but if you gird yourself with common sense and information, you the consumer can choose the expert to suit the case.[9]

   —Jane Widerman

4. No one can tell yet what mask to carve for Canada, which type to choose—a pulp savage or a bank teller, a civil servant or a broke hustler or a signalman helping to keep the peace in Cyprus or the Gaza Strip— whether the face should be serene and adventurous, or withdrawn and introspective. No one can tell for certain yet whether Canada is one nation

or two. The country reveals itself only slowly even to those who love it most, and much of its character still remains ambiguous.[10]

—Douglas Le Pan

5. "She's got an indiscreet voice," I remarked. "It's full of . . . I hesitated. "Her voice is full of money," he said suddenly."[11]

What Gatsby thought he heard in Daisy's voice is what any number of ambitious people sense they are sure to find in perfume, that it is "full of money."

6. What does Québec want?

It's simply not the right question. The way it's put, it calls for some kind of enumeration: some more of this, and a bit of that, and then a lot of this too. Etc. Ad nauseam. You answer it, you feel like you're talking about a recipe for political goulash. While the fact is that from now on Québec will always want more. Until it gets all. Because the question really is: What does Québec want *to be?* The answer: a homeland for a people; *'patrie'*; a nation in the fullest (English) sense of the word.[12]

—René Lévesque

7. Modern human beings must develop a universal social conscience. Walk through almost any village and you will discover on at least one edge of town the dirty, neglected, overcrowded tenements or hovels where the poor abide. In leaky-roofed shacks with torn, dingy shreds of wallpaper hanging from water-stained walls, the children huddle with pinched and hungry faces around the evening's scanty offerings. It is ironic that modern people have developed their technology to the point where they could relieve virtually all of such unnecessary suffering, but have not developed social conscience to the point that they are moved to do so.

(*Activity 3E*)

Writing Interesting Openings

Bring to class openings that you have written yourself or some you have found in current expository writing. Following are three activities to provide materials for a class discussion.

1. Look through several current magazines and make notes on the different kinds of openings you find. Bring examples of unusual openings to class. (Do not destroy library magazines.)

2. List on the blackboard various topics suitable for expository compositions. Select one of these and write an interesting opening for it. Discuss it with the class.

3. Choose two subjects from the list you prepared for Activity 3C (pages 45-46) and write openings for them. Exchange papers with each other in class for suggestions and corrections.

Thesis Statements and Inner Structure

There are many patterns of organization for the internal structure or body of a paper. These patterns are: development by details, arrangement according to space or time (chronology), comparison and contrast, analysis, synthesis, cause and effect, enumeration (listing), classification, definition, and example.

A good thesis statement in the introduction (outer structure) often suggests a way of organizing the body (inner structure). Planning and writing the inner structure will be easier if you are aware of the various patterns available to you.

Patterns of Organization.   A brief definition of each of the major patterns of organization follows. You will learn more about these patterns later in this chapter.

Development by details. The presentation of small portions of a whole or of items, often those which appeal to the senses, in order to support a generalization. What details, for example, would support the generalization, "It was a perfect day for snowmobiling?"

Arrangement according to space. This pattern is similar to development by details, but the details are carefully arranged to move logically from left to right, top to bottom, around in a circle, inside to outside, far to near, or in some other spatial pattern. This pattern is often used in describing a place in order to communicate the same feeling about it as was specified in the thesis statement or topic sentence: "His living room was a shambles."

Arrangement according to time (chronology). This involves arranging a series of events according to time sequence. Flash-backs and other distortions can be used for emphasis and effect, but the usual order is the natural order of time (chronological order).

> After that, everything happened too quickly, but I think the order of events was this—the dog started across the road right in front of the car, and Mr. Calloway yelled, at the dog or the car, I don't know which. Anyway the detective swerved—he said later, weakly, that he couldn't run over a dog—and down went Mr. Calloway, in a mess of broken glass and gold rims and silver hair, and blood.[13]
>
> —Graham Greene

Comparison and contrast. The juxtaposing (placing side by side) of two objects or ideas and showing, point by point, how they are similar or different. There are two basic patterns. Using the first pattern, you would describe the characteristics of one object fully before turning to the other. For example, in a comparison of a Ford and a Chevrolet, you would describe the engine, body, and transmission of a Ford and then the engine, body, and transmission of a Chevrolet. Using the second pattern, you would compare or contrast the engines of the Ford and Chevrolet, the bodies of each, then the transmissions of each.

Analysis. The examination of an object or idea by separating it into its component parts and elements. Since there are always a number of ways to do this, the purpose of the analysis must be determined. A different purpose will demand a different way of separating the elements of the object being examined. For example, a builder might analyze a house in terms of its materials—stone, wood, metal, plastic. But a person renting the house might analyze it in terms of its layout—kitchen, living room, bathroom, bedrooms. A good analysis should divide the item into parts so that no two overlap and nothing is left out. Both of these analyses would be faulty:

> The student body is divided into boys, girls, and redheads. (overlap)
> Canada is divided into Atlantic and Pacific Regions. (omission)

Synthesis. The opposite of analysis. In this pattern, the various parts or elements are examined and gradually the object or idea is perceived as a whole. Often this pattern is used to create a mood or atmosphere by putting together a number of sensory impressions. It is similar to development by details.

Cause and effect. Presenting the forces which are the causes of an event or reversing the order and presenting an event first and then specifying the causes.

> The explorer dropped a bar of soap into the steaming mouth of the hot spring. The soap lowered the surface tension of the water so that, immediately, a geyser spurted forth.

Enumeration. The listing of parts or elements of a whole. Enumeration is different from analysis in that the parts are simply listed rather than analyzed.

> Major Native groups of Canada's west coast include Salish, Bella Coola, Nootka, Kwakiutl, Tsimshian, Haida and Tlingit.

Classification. The grouping of items or individuals into groups on the basis of similarities. When you ask if something is animal, vegetable, or mineral, you are trying to classify it.

Definition. There are three definition patterns:

a. Nominal definitions—explaining the meaning of an unknown word by linking it with a known word ("Galluses are suspenders.")

b. Extensional definitions—pointing to an actual object to which the word refers ("That plastic disc those people are throwing back and forth is a frisbee.")

c. Formal definitions—naming the word to be defined, placing it in a class with which the reader is familiar, and describing the details that differentiate it from other members of that class.

Example. The description of a single outstanding and dramatic event, situation, or instance that demonstrates or proves the truth of your topic sentence or thesis statement.

(*Activity 3F*)

Determining Patterns of Organization Appropriate to Thesis Statements

Discuss which pattern of organization would be preferable in developing each of the following thesis statements. Skilled writers can sometimes adapt different patterns to the same thesis statement. Therefore, more than one response is possible for most of these items.

1. The government's attitude to threats of Québec separatism has evolved significantly during the past seventy-five years.

2. Contrary to popular opinion, the genitive form has five uses in addition to showing possession.

3. Tom Thomson's cabin, now located at Kleinburg, Ontario, remains pretty much as he left it.

4. A Moped is quite similar to a motor scooter, but there are definite differences.

5. From the foregoing information, you can readily see that Louis Riel was given to delusions about himself and his mission.

6. If the pioneer work ethic—the inner compulsion of our forefathers to work hard—has vanished, a number of forces have killed it.

7. The prevailing attitude towards authority in North America during the late 1960s was the product of complex problems during the period.

8. The *Marble Faun* was the most perfect statue I ever saw.

9. Chaucer's work had a profound influence on the English language.

10. The Italian sonnet is quite different from the Shakespearean sonnet.

11. A. Y. Jackson belonged to a group of Canadian artists who called themselves "The Group of Seven."

12. The various instruments in an orchestra belong to different families.

13. The Royals got worse during the game.

14. Every portion of the scene contributed to the growing feeling of terror.

15. From such varied arguments as those just stated, the Members of Parliament built the energy bill.

16. The fifty or more subjects taught at South Secondary are grouped into five departments.

17. The job of the mass media in Canadian society encompasses six major responsibilities.

18. The cafeteria is arranged for sanitation and efficiency.

19. Your attitude will depend in large part upon your understanding of the word "maturity."

20. The kinds of jobs open to secondary school students are quite limited.

Some Common Developments of Thesis Statements

Although the thesis statements you have just examined lend themselves to development of a certain kind, many thesis statements can be developed in any of several different ways. Read and discuss the following example.

Main Idea or Thesis Statement:

Teen-agers Today are Given Much Responsibility

Details. Teen-agers today are given much responsibility. Almost all teen-age boys and many teen-age girls have their driver's licences, and often their own cars. Frequently, they have either a sizable allowance or a part-time job which gives them considerable spending money. Even in school they are given many responsible assignments. Many office-practice classes handle a student-activity fund amounting to over ten thousand dollars, and often the student council plans every school activity, from pep rallies to graduation exercises. It is no wonder that both universities, and employers are pleased with the responsibility of today's young people.

Illustration or example. Teen-agers today are given much responsibility. Sharon Connors, for example, undertakes many important jobs at home, at school, and at work. At home, because her mother works, Sharon must prepare the evening meal and take care of Beth, her younger sister, between the time the sitter leaves and the time Mrs. Connors returns from the second shift at the factory. At school, because she is president of her class and secretary of the debating club, Sharon is always taking on new duties: making arrangements for the Graduation Dance, directing the sale of Graduation Yearbooks, or just maintaining the interest of her classmates in the activities she considers important. Her responsibilities at home and at school leave Sharon little time for work, but she manages to babysit on at least one weekend night. At these times, she is completely on her own as she cares for three-year-old Jeffrey and one-year-old Susan. If most teen-agers accept as much responsibility as Sharon does (and informal polls indicate that they do), they will certainly be ready for greater responsibilities at an earlier age than students in the past.

Cause or effect. For a number of different reasons, teen-agers today are given much responsibility. Pessimists say that they get their responsibilities by default. Adults, say the pessimists, are simply too busy (or irresponsible) themselves, so they let teen-agers take over. A few equally cynical people blame commercial interests for increasing the responsibilities given young people. Certainly it's true that North American business now recognizes teen-agers as an important market, and no doubt vested interests have encouraged teen-agers to open their own charge accounts and to assume important jobs for less money than adults could accept. But probably the most important reason that teen-agers have more responsibilities today is that as democracy has matured, North Americans have realized that accepting responsibility is an important aspect of their lives. Moreover, educators now realize that the best way to teach responsibility is to delegate responsibility. And finally, teen-agers have been given more and more responsibility because they have demonstrated their ability to handle it.

Comparison or contrast. Teen-agers today are given more responsibility than were teen-agers a generation ago. Today many students have joined neighbourhood action groups, and they are given the tasks of informing adults and even leading them in community programs. A generation ago, such teen-agers would not have been given such tasks and adults would not have followed their leadership. Many students rush from school to work and some of them have surprisingly large responsibilities on the job. The merchant who now trusts a teen-ager to deposit the day's receipts or to take charge of the store at night shows a confidence in his part-time worker that earlier employers would not have had.

Activity 3G

Developing Topic Sentences in Several Ways

Working as your teacher directs, plan the development of each of the following topic sentences into different kinds of paragraphs. These may be worked out individually or in groups. They may be shared orally, as brief topic outlines, or completely written out as those on teen-agers and responsibility.

1. The bedroom to which I was assigned was the most unusual I had ever seen.
2. Fewer students are going to university today than went ten years ago.
3. Macdonald enjoyed his train trip through the Rockies.
4. Becoming educated involves growing in many different ways.
5. Hillsborough Secondary offers all the girls' sports offered anywhere.
6. The electronic age began back in the 1900s.

7. Europeans usually want to see five major attractions when they come to Canada.
8. Discovering why an automobile won't start is quite easy.
9. The second she entered the ballroom, the mood of the moment seized her.
10. When the morning alarm rings, our household springs into action.

Aiding Your Reader with Definitions

Communication is possible only when people can identify experiences or information they all share. If you refer to a *proscenium arch* and your readers have no experience with the theatre, they may not know that you are referring to the arch that frames the opening in the wall through which the audience sees the stage. Whenever you are using a word or concept that your readers may not know, it is a good idea to provide either a definition or an example.

Definition Patterns. On page 51 you read briefly about three definition patterns. For a nominal definition, you simply identify the unknown word in terms of a word the reader is likely to know (Sockeye is a kind of fish.) For an extensional definition, you point to something in the real world. "Do you see Matthew's shirt? That's the colour I call cerise."

If you can explain one word adequately by simply giving another, or if you're in a situation in which you can point to an actual object, it may be unnecessary to give a more complicated definition. Your next choice might be descriptive definition—a kind of verbal pointing:

> When I talk about school spirit, I mean the kind of dedication that leads to service, as when the student council sold scrap and raised $2600 for the new p.a. system or when the yearbook staff sells candy at every single soccer and basketball game to support our yearbook.

Occasionally, however, you must use a formal definition. The formal definition follows this pattern:

Term to be defined ⟶	Name the word you are defining.	A python
Connector ⟶	Usually the word required is *is*.	is
Class ⟶	Use a class or category with which your reader is likely to be familiar.	a snake
Differentiating details ⟶	Describe the details that make this thing different from other members of the same class.	large, non-poisonous, crushes its prey to death.

Adding differentiating details.   In writing a formal definition, first place the referent (the word in question) in a class that the reader or listener already knows. Then give enough differentiating details to separate it from others in the same class: "A beagle is a dog . . . (present as many details as are necessary to distinguish a beagle from other dogs)."

Notice that the definition must be based on the principle of finding an idea or experience that the reader and the writer share. They must both have had experience with the class into which you place the word being defined and, of course, the word must fit that class. Make sure that you never define a word with other words that the reader is not likely to know (An opossum is an omnivorous marsupial.) Ordinarily, the search for shared experience as a basis for a definition means that the definition will be easier to understand than the original word.

The stage with proscenium arch, Massey Hall, Toronto.

(*Activity 3H*)

Working with Formal Definitions

Using a dictionary, prepare definitions for five of the following words. As you write out your definitions, remember to follow the formal definition pattern and to put the referent into a class that your reader is likely to know. Then add as many differentiating details as are necessary to distinguish the word from others in the same class. Be prepared to discuss your definitions in class. Note that the dictionary does not always follow the formal definition pattern and that you may have to select a single definition from among several given.

touchback	radar	moor	pilaster
plagiarism	vassal	phoenix	legume
blurb	sonnet	antivivisectionist	shaman
selvage	caduceus	ecology	haiku
laser	capacitor	vampire	Québec heater

Using Comparison and Contrast in Exposition

On page 49 you read a brief explanation of comparison and contrast. Sometimes you can clarify an item or idea you are explaining by comparing or contrasting it with another item or idea. If your readers are familiar with the second item or idea, they can readily make connections with the first.

Here is an excerpt containing both comparison, which emphasizes similarities, and contrast, which emphasizes differences:

> The words "education" and "training" are often used interchangeably, especially as the liberal arts courses are losing students and professors are tempted to shift their traditional role to preparing students for earning a living. A major difference between "education" and "training" is immediately apparent from looking at the etymologies of the two words. "Education" comes from the Latin words *ex*, meaning "out of" or "from" and *duco*, meaning "to lead." Education, then, attempts to lead out or draw out from within the individual what is already there. "Training" comes from the Latin word *trahere*, meaning "to draw" or "pull." Rather than leading out what is already inside, training seeks to pull the individual along a preconceived, external path.
>
> A second difference emerges from the first: Education benefits the individual, whereas training enables the individual to benefit others. For example, millions of dollars are spent on medical and dental training so that the individual doctors and dentists can use their training to benefit others.

A third difference is that education is general and theoretical, while training is specific and practical. In addition, education involves a kind of lifelong "learning to learn" commitment, whereas training is limited to a definite time period. Continued "in-service training" and updating may be necessary from time to time, but this cannot be compared to "learning how to learn" all kinds of things in all areas for a whole lifetime.

Finally, although liberal arts professors are currently having a hard time convincing potential students of this lifetime value, educators believe that education is its own reward, and they promise nothing more than the joys of competence, adaptability, and self-fulfillment. On the other hand, the rewards of training may include the satisfaction of being a skilled teacher, shoemaker, or physician, but along with that satisfaction come additional rewards—salaries, fees, recognition—from the outside world. Both education and training are necessary in human society, and most experts hope that students will choose to get a good education as a basis for their training, no matter what field they select.

According to the preceding passage, these are the ways in which education differs from training:

EDUCATION	TRAINING
Involves "leading out" what is already in the individual	Involves drawing the student along a preconceived path
Undertaken for the benefit of the individual	Undertaken for what the trainee learns to do or produce for others
General and theoretical	Specific and practical
Lifelong "learning to learn"	Limited period to acquire specific skills
Self-rewarding	Leads to external rewards

Each of the ideas listed above is called a point of comparison. In a formally written comparison, the two items being compared are examined carefully; and for each point of comparison for one item, there is a corresponding point of comparison for the other item.

The formally written comparison can be organized in either of two ways:

FIRST ORGANIZATION

1. All the points of comparison for Item One are treated.

2. All the points of comparison for Item Two are treated.

SECOND ORGANIZATION

1. First point of comparison
   a. The way the first point of comparison appears in Item One.
   b. The way the first point of comparison appears in Item Two.

2. Second point of comparison
   a. The way the second point of comparison appears in Item One.
   b. The way the second point of comparison appears in Item Two.
       Continue with all the other points of comparison.

   Although the formally written comparison and contrast paper should be organized around identical points of comparison and the treatment of these points should be in either of two particular orders, the fact is that many fine writers do not organize their work so precisely. Indeed, some feel that they would be inhibited by such precision.

(*Activity 3 I*)

Using Comparison and Contrast

1. Refer to Activity 3C, pages 45-46. From your list of topics, choose one for which the comparison and contrast pattern is appropriate. Write a paragraph or two in which you identify points of comparison and explain their similarities or differences. For practice, try each of the two organization patterns just described.

2. If the comparison and contrast pattern is not appropriate to your subject, think of some subject that lends itself to this pattern. Some suggestions follow. Choose one and write a paragraph or two using comparison and contrast.

maturity—immaturity	regional college—university
cheap—inexpensive	confident—brash
educated—uneducated	gifted—intellectual
radical—liberal	chivalrous—courteous
water skiing—snow skiing	chess—checkers
sports car—dragster	uninterested—unmotivated

Unity and Focus

Sentences and paragraphs rarely stand alone. Usually they are part of a longer unit of writing and must be tied in somehow with what has gone before and what follows. Sentences and paragraphs seem to belong together when:

1. They are on the same subject—giving unity to the material.
2. They are closely related to one another logically—having the quality of coherence.

3. They treat the subject from the same point of view—maintaining a single focus on the material.

The following paragraph consists of sentences on the same subject, but because the subject is treated from a different point of view in almost every sentence, the focus shifts and both unity and coherence are lost.

> My father is a member of our local volunteer fire department. When he is seen getting a call, I like to watch his instant response. The truck is always kept ready for these emergencies. The dust flies as he races towards the fire hall. By the time he arrives three minutes later others are also pulling in. Mom, in the meantime, listens in to the C.B. radio to find out the nature of the emergency. When everyone has gathered at the station—all within five minutes—the manned fire truck speeds off in the direction of the fire.

Focus and Variety.   Notice that the focus shifts in this paragraph because the subject changes from sentence to sentence. In the first sentence, the subject is *father*; in the second, it is *I*; in the third, *the truck*; fourth, *road dust*; fifth, *mom*; sixth, *the fire truck*.

Some students mistakenly shift focus because they believe that doing so gives variety to their paragraphs. Of course, variety is desirable, but not at the expense of unity, coherence, and focus. In general, avoid shifting unnecessarily from one subject to another. When you do shift, provide links to help the reader change subjects with you. Avoid inserting a passive-voice sentence (e.g., "When he is seen getting a call . . .") in the middle of a series of active-voice sentences. In the preceding paragraph, notice how the passive-voice sentence causes a shift of focus.

(*Activity 3J*)

Correcting Focus

Rewrite the sample paragraph so that *father* is the subject throughout. Achieve sentence variety by making some sentences long and some short and by combining some related ideas in a single sentence. Avoid using the passive voice.

Coherence

Sentences cohere when they have mechanical or logical connections. Some have both.

Mechanical connections.   A mechanical connection is one that results from the use of a connecting word or words ("therefore," "however," "besides," "on the other hand") or from the repetition of a word, phrase, or idea used earlier. Generally, a connecting word signals a logical connection as well; and sometimes the repetition comes when a substitute word, such as a pronoun or synonym, repeats an earlier idea.

Logical connections. A logical connection is a phrase that relates the ideas in two sentences, directing the reader to note cause and effect, sequence of events, idea and example, generalization and detail.

Example: Keremeos is very hot in the summertime. Therefore, the orchards must be watered continuously.

Activity 3K

Examining Sentences for Coherence

Discuss in class the mechanical and logical connections in each of the following pairs of sentences. Identify the words or phrases that make the connections and describe the relationships (e.g., cause and effect, contrast, sequence, etc.) they signal.

1. The way people stand, sit, or use their heads and arms often communicates a great deal about what they are thinking. As a matter of fact, linguists are making a serious study of "body language" so that people can understand one another better.

2. When the St. Lawrence Seaway was planned, officials were concerned about historical sites which would be flooded as a result of changes to the river. Now, thanks to the foresight of the Ontario-St. Lawrence Development Commission, Canadians can enjoy these heritage buildings which are now part of Upper Canada Village, a park complex near Morrisburg.

3. Some psychologists estimate that most human beings use only one-fifth of their brainpower. Imagine the great things people could accomplish if they could unleash this wasted resource.

4. As machines and inventions are perfected, such machines and inventions become more powerful and less wasteful. The first transatlantic cable, for example, required thousands of tons of pure copper cable to send one telephone message at a time; now, however, a satellite weighing only a few hundred kilograms can handle hundreds of such messages.

5. The explorer Thor Heyerdahl warned that we may kill off life in the oceans if we continue polluting the waters of the world. He described how in the middle of the Atlantic he sometimes disliked brushing his teeth in the stained and fouled ocean.

Transitions Between Paragraphs

Just as sentences must be tied together, so paragraphs must be tied together. Indeed, writers use many of the same connecting devices between paragraphs that they use between sentences. In addition, they are likely to use a "principle of transition" which can best be described as *look back and go forward*. In other words, they *look back* at what they have just said, and then *preview what they are going to say*. Some such "look back and go forward" transitions follow:

Look Back (Review)	Go Forward (Preview)
So much for the causes:	let's look at the effects.
But Shakespeare's genius does not stem solely from his mother's genteel influence	his education in the local Latin school surely contributed greatly to his preparation.
The preceding explanation is interesting, but inconclusive.	Another frequently-offered explanation is that . . . .
The apparent causes of the war were quite simple	but the real causes are another matter.

(Activity 3L)

Examining Transitions

From any expository material that you are currently reading (textbooks, magazine articles, editorials, how-to-do-it books), read six consecutive paragraphs. Pay particular attention to the beginning and ending sentences of each paragraph. Come to class prepared to discuss how the paragraphs are tied together.

Simplifying Your Writing

If you compare sentences written in English at different times over the last four hundred years, you will discover that, although words have grown longer, sentences have grown shorter. The reasons are twofold: First, many people won't read long sentences any more; and, second, good writers have learned to load more meaning into fewer words.

The second reason is important for you. To communicate successfully, you must discipline your mind to think clearly and choose words and structures appropriate to your meaning and subject. You are a little like a gardener who cuts away dead branches and pulls out weeds. If you learn the following techniques you will eliminate the "dead wood" in your writing and not burden your reader with unnecessary words. The grammatical structures are named in these examples, but if you do not know the terms, you can understand the processes by looking at the examples. You do not need to review your grammar to learn and use these techniques for simplifying your writing. You can study further examples in any comprehensive handbook of English.

Sentence combining exercises are also a good way to practise the manipulation of various sentence structures so that you can learn to achieve the effect you desire. Your teacher may make sentence combining material available to you.

A. Omit excess words from relative clauses. Change the clauses into either prepositional phrases or simple adjectives.

RELATIVE CLAUSE (R.C.)

He purchased a boat that was made of fiberglass.

R.C.

PREPOSITIONAL PHRASE (PREP.)

He purchased a boat of fiberglass.

Prep.

SIMPLE ADJECTIVE (ADJ.)

He purchased a fiberglass boat.

Adj.

B. Omit excess words from relative clauses and change the clauses into participial phrases.

RELATIVE CLAUSE (R.C.)

The boy who was tumbling on the mat looked tired.

R.C.

PARTICIPIAL PHRASE (P.P.)

The boy tumbling on the mat looked tired.

P.P.

C. Omit excess words from relative clauses and change the relative clauses into appositives.

RELATIVE CLAUSE (R.C.)

The test, which was our first examination of the year, disappointed me.

R.C.

APPOSITIVE (APP.)

The test, our first examination of the year, disappointed me.

App.

D. Omit excess words from subordinate clauses and change the clauses into infinitive phrases.

SUBORDINATE CLAUSE (S.C.)

The yearbook staff held bake sales at every game
in order that they could afford to pay for hard covers on the school yearbook.

S.C.

INFINITIVE PHRASE (I.P.)

The yearbook staff held bake sales at every game
to pay for hard covers on the school yearbook.

I.P.

(*Activity 3M*)

Simplifying Sentences

Follow the models in Sections A–D above.

1. Change the relative clauses in each of the following sentences first to prepositional phrases and then to simple adjectives.
   a. Richard likes paintings that are in the realistic style.
   b. The singer, who appeared in a red wig, was very funny.
   c. Karen and Bill frequently took a path that went beside the sea.

2. Change the relative clauses in each of the following sentences first to participial phrases, then to prepositional phrases, and then, when appropriate, to simple adjectives.
   a. Many students do not especially like books that are written for schools.
   b. Decisions that are made by students ought to be binding.

    c. The girl who is carrying the flowers is very pretty.

    d. The rug that is spread on the floor must be removed for dancing.

3. Change the relative clauses in each of the following sentences into appositives.

    a. Kate Federico, who was one of our Provincial Scholarship winners, was invited to speak at the Chamber of Commerce luncheon.

    b. Prime Minister Trudeau's decision, which was to invoke the War Measures Act, was very courageous.

    c. The "Summerhill" idea, which has students choosing their own activities and being responsible for their own learning, is becoming increasingly controversial.

    d. Fred's first trip away from home, which was a visit to Dartmouth, opened his eyes.

    e. The national concern for ecology, which is a fairly recent development, is opening up new careers.

4. Omit excess words from subordinate clauses in the following sentences and change the clauses into infinitive phrases.

    a. So that he might attract more attention for the forthcoming elections, Sam prepared a skit for the school public address system.

    b. The Penticton Herald ran an editorial saying that the Kettle Valley Railway should be preserved as a tourist attraction.

    c. In order that the class could get the value of writing more compositions, the students voted to ask for corrections on only every third paper.

    d. Mary wrote that she hoped that she could come.

5. Look through the compositions you have written so far this year. Locate any clauses that begin with *who*, *which*, or *that*. These usually signal relative clauses that can be reduced by using the techniques you have just worked with. Try reducing such clauses and see whether or not the sentences are improved. (Not all of them will be.) Share your experiences in your group.

Summary Endings

The final paragraph of a composition is the one that most readers will remember longest. Many writers sum up their main points and repeat their thesis statement in the final paragraph. Though such a summary is not always necessary, it is often effective.

Activity 3N

Examining Summary Endings

Be prepared to discuss in class how the following final paragraphs restate and emphasize the main ideas of the compositions they end. Working in a group, reconstruct the main paragraphs of the inner structure (the body) from the clues given here.

1. If tourists arrive at the border on a hot summer's day loaded down with furs and skis—and they have—it is because of what the movies told them about Canada. If Americans keep telling us "you're the same as we are"—and they do—it is because the movies have convinced them of that fact. If Europeans are baffled when they reach our shores to find that most of us live in cities—and they are—it is because the movies have misled them. And if Canadians continue to hold the belief that there is no such thing as a national identity—and who can deny that many hold it?—it is because the movies have frequently blurred, distorted, and hidden that identity under a celluloid mountain of misconceptions.[14]

   —Pierre Berton

2. There is little danger that salmon will become extinct. One of the great lessons of salmon conservation is that the fish have a tremendous capacity to increase in number, if given the chance. But unless we use more wisdom than in the past, and learn to control such adverse pressure as pollution, dams, and overfishing, there is no doubt that more and more streams will lose their runs of a handsome and delicious fish—one of mankind's major natural resources.[15]

3. So now you know what to expect if you play the piano at parties. You would be much wiser to take up the oboe. Nobody ever asks you to play an oboe at a party . . . not twice anyhow.[16]

   —Mervyn J. Huston

4. Both because of "progress" and in spite of it, the sailing ship may well displace many motorized tramp and trade ships, especially in the South Pacific. The higher costs of fuel, the simplified navigation techniques and improved weather prediction, the development of automation to replace crew members in setting sails, and the use of space-age materials in centuries-old sailing devices will all contribute to the return of sails. The square rigger is not dead!

5. Almost all women in the Soviet Union work outside the home, usually at menial jobs. They attend to household chores without help from servants, husbands, or modern appliances. They spend hours in line shopping for

hard-to-get items. They are passed over for the elevated, higher-paying, and easier executive positions. Despite emphasis on sexual equality in the Soviet Union, the life of the average woman remains very difficult.

Activity 3O

Writing a Summary Ending

Read the following incomplete composition carefully, then write a summary ending for it. Be sure to restate the main points in the order in which they appear in the body of the composition. If possible, try to restate them in different, more interesting words than appear in the original.

> When you see animated cartoons on television or at the movies, you often think of the huge studios of Walt Disney, Paul Terry, or Hanna and Barbera, but making animated cartoons is becoming increasingly popular in junior and senior high school, and even in some elementary schools. Most of these student-produced films don't have the slickness and professionalism of Terry-Tunes or Yogi Bear, but they're fun to watch and even more fun to make.
>
> The first thing to do in preparing to make an animated cartoon is to forget what you know about commercial cartoons and take a look at some of the simple cartoons. In "Boiled Egg," for example, a real egg is the main character, and as it was moved, photographed, moved, photographed, and so on, it shows very simply the egg's attempts to escape an unknown threatening force. In "Clay," a cartoon made by college students, a lump of clay is photographed, shaped one pinch at a time between photographs, into an animal and then, one pinch at a time, into another, and so on. In the finished cartoon, the lump of clay unexpectedly grows into one thing, swallows itself, and becomes another, and so on. In "Nébule" (N.F.B.) a black line becomes a magic cord to serve a small child's fancy. It becomes whatever the child wants it to be. The changes in the black line are presented against soft, pastel coloured backgrounds.

Activity 3P

Revising and Editing an Expository Composition

Before doing your major writing assignment for this chapter, sharpen your revision and editing skills by reworking the following expository composition. As you revise for style, clarity, and completeness, consider how you can improve the organization and content of the essay, and correct any grammatical or mechanical errors (sentence structure, spelling, punctuation) which are present.

ONLY THREE DAYS TO SEE

What would it be like to be sightless for your entire life? This is a question that people who have the gift of sight do not often cogitate upon. Helen Keller was a famous person who was blind from birth. She spent her life urging people to make better use of the precious gift of sight. Just what would you want to look at if you knew you had only three more days to see? What would you want to remember in the sightless days that would follow?

The first day would probably be taken up with looking at all the beauties of the natural world. You would want to be able to clearly remember the way the sky, the grass, the tree, the mountains, and the rivers look. As you smell the flowers, you would want to remember all their vivid colours.

The second day would be taken up considering again all the great achievements of man. Perhaps you would only have access to them through pictures in books. But you would want to remember the great buildings of man, the structures you would want to retain in your mind would represent some of man's greatest technological achievements.

The third day should be spent with friends and relatives. To say a farewell. To see them in the mind during future conversations would be a decided boon. Those special people will change as the years go by, but you will remember them just as they were on that last day of your sight.

If we all knew we only had three days to see, we would make better use of our gift of sight. We can't take something as vital as our sight for granted. Our personal worlds would be so limited without sight. But think of Helen Keller. She never even had three days to see. She never saw any of the beauties of the world.

> As you read, consider your intended audience. Decide whether continual use of the second person ("you") here is effective. Make this opening clearer and give it a precise focus. Is the transition between paragraphs effective here?

> Does this paragraph need to be developed with more specific detail? What about the other body paragraphs?

> As you revise this conclusion, go back to the introduction. Check the suitability of the entire outside structure of the essay and revise accordingly.

Major Writing Assignment

An Expository Composition

To write an expository composition, you must have an idea to communicate. Your first task, then, in writing a patterned expository composition is to choose a general subject you would like to write about. Next, you must gather all the ideas you can that are related to that subject. Can the topic

How many thesis statements could be developed for a composition about Newfoundland's offshore oil project?

be developed? Next, you must narrow that subject to a specific topic. The fourth logical step is to specify definitely and clearly the main idea you would like to communicate, and which details will be best to support or develop that main idea.

Unfortunately, human beings do not always operate logically. Many people must write out a complete rough draft before they can organize their thoughts sufficiently to specify their main idea. But having written a rough draft, having located and stated their main idea, they then rewrite their entire paper in terms of the main idea, or thesis statement. With a thesis statement to guide them, they can easily determine where they need to add more material, where they need to make certain points clearer, and where they should remove unnecessary details.

STEPS IN WRITING EXPOSITION

I. Determining your thesis statement
   A. Choose a general subject (for example, ecology).
   B. "Brainstorm" ideas and begin to determine possible methods of development.
   C. Narrow the subject to a specific topic (preserving marine life).

D. Write your thesis statement, a clear one-sentence statement of your main idea. (Dredge-and-fill operations must be halted to preserve the spawning grounds of marine species.)

(If you cannot develop a thesis statement at this point, proceed to II, and return to your thesis statement when it becomes clear to you.)

II. Developing your ideas
   A. Explore and research ideas for your paper (interviews, library research, conversation, experimentation, observation). Add to and subtract from ideas you have "brainstormed."
   B. List these ideas below your thesis statement in what seems to be a reasonable and effective order.

III. Writing your first draft
   A. Write a rough draft and leave it untouched for a day or two.
   B. Read your rough draft—preferably with an interested partner or listener—and check it against your thesis statement. Either revise your draft or rewrite your thesis statement, if necessary.

IV. Preparing your final paper
   A. Revise and edit your paper in the light of your critic's comments and your revision of your thesis statement.
   B. As part of the revision process, check the exposition pattern of your paper: do you have an interest-arousing beginning, and an effective ending? Check your transitions also. (In Chapter 5, you will learn how to provide an overview of the main divisions of your paper in your introduction.)
   C. Revise and recopy.
   D. Proofread this final draft.

Your teacher may ask you to submit the following materials together with your completed expository composition:

1. Your preliminary planning sheet, including
   a. General subject
   b. Brainstorming material
   c. Narrowed subject
   d. Initial thesis statement (if you had one at Step I D)
2. Rough draft of the paper, followed by your revised thesis statement.
3. Rough drafts of opening and closing paragraphs.
4. Complete second revision, (if you needed to prepare one).

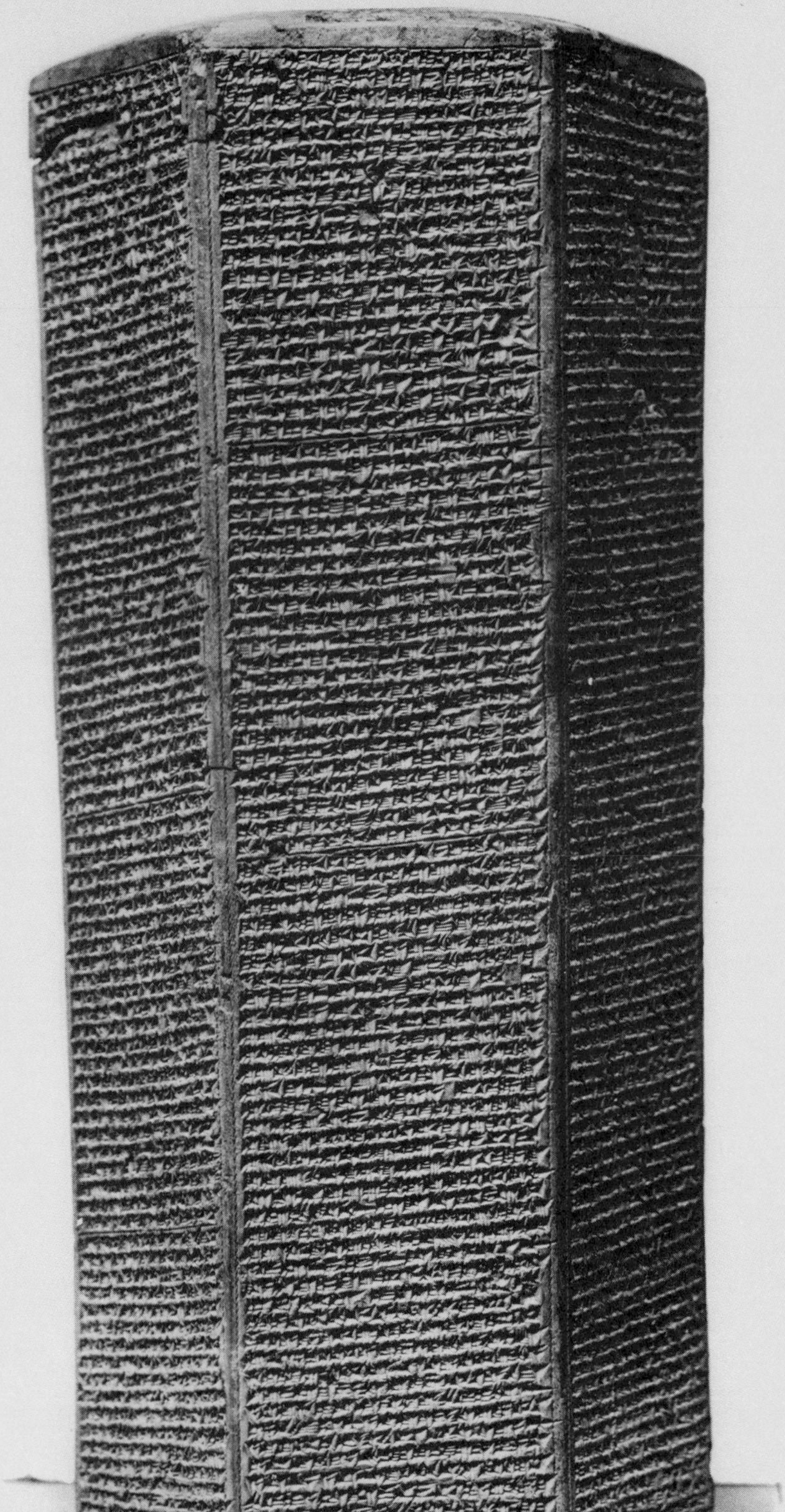

4

Paragraphing

In the previous chapter you practised organizing and writing the expository composition. In this chapter you will be given an opportunity to review and extend your knowledge of paragraphs, the "building blocks" for any kind of longer composition. Studying various aspects of paragraph writing will enable you to increase your skill in handling writing situations where several related paragraphs are required.

From the time you were in third or fourth grade, you have been given exercises in the writing of paragraphs, and you have been taught that an expository paragraph usually follows this order:

Topic sentence
Supporting details, examples, comparisons, analogies
Clincher sentence

We can elaborate by saying that an expository paragraph is usually a collection of sentences that makes a particular point, or attempts to convince the reader of something. These sentences are bound together by their common purpose: to clarify one point. In order to do this effectively the

◄ At one time, paragraphing as we know it today did not exist. This clay monument gives an account of King Sennacherib's siege of Jerusalem. Even if you knew cuneiform, do you think it would be easy to read?

writer needs to use at least three clarifying devices: (1) the topic sentence, (2) the key or operative term, and (3) the clincher sentence.

This definition adds one more element to your understanding of paragraphing: the *key* term. The operative or key term is a word or phrase in the topic sentence which states or implies the writer's attitude toward the subject of the paragraph. A good topic sentence communicates an *attitude* toward the idea it expresses. What is the key term, or attitude, in each of these sentences? (Sometimes a phrase or even several separated words will show the attitude.)

a. The completion of the C.P.R. in 1885 gave new life, verve, and optimism to the young country.

b. Mathematician Carl Gauss allowed his keen, restless mind to wander productively in fields far from his calling.

c. Fortunately, Ground Control in Houston was prepared to begin the delicate process of redirecting the satellite.

d. The inventors of the submarine and the airplane both resigned themselves to taking their inventions to other governments.

The inclusion of key terms, or attitudes, within your topic sentences enables you to write more easily and to communicate more effectively. Because you have stated your attitude towards your material, you can more easily select and control material to communicate that attitude. Because your readers quickly grasp the attitude you are trying to communicate, they can recognize the supporting ideas as they read.

Here are those same topic sentences without key terms. Obviously, it would be much more difficult to write effective and interesting paragraphs with such neutral topic sentences as these.

a. The C.P.R. was completed in 1885.

b. The mathematician Carl Gauss explored many different fields.

c. Ground Control in Houston began the process of re-directing the satellite.

d. The inventors of the submarine and the airplane both took their inventions to other governments.

(*Activity 4A*)

Adding Attitudes to Topic Sentences

Each of the following sentences could be used as the topic sentence of an expository paragraph. Yet each of them would be more effective and interesting if an attitude, or key term, were included. You can do this by adding an adverb, by adding an adjective, or by changing the verb or noun.

ADDING AN ADVERB (ADV):

The phonograph worked the first time Edison tried it.
Surprisingly, the phonograph worked the first time Edison tried it.
   (adv)

ADDING AN ADJECTIVE (ADJ):

Anthony voted with the majority.
Anthony voted with the *misguided* and *unthinking* majority.
       (adj)   (adj)

CHANGING THE VERB (V):

The detour went through Perth county.
The detour *meandered* through Perth County.
      (v)

CHANGING THE NOUN (N):

The Eiffel Tower was the centre of the Paris Exposition.
The Eiffel Tower was the *miracle* of the Paris Exposition.
      (n)

Rewrite each of these sentences to include an attitude:

1. Few of my fellow students know how they want to spend their lives.
2. Canadians have only recently learned that their resources are not limitless.
3. Recent developments in information science will change the way we get our news.
4. Napoleon Bonaparte was selfish.
5. The Pantheon is a famous building in Rome.
6. Some experts indicate that the weather will continue to become colder in the years ahead.
7. Some descendants of the Mayan Indians in Honduras still retain their traditions.
8. North American automobiles are becoming smaller.
9. Montreal's Expo '67 was a major world exhibition.
10. The Trans Canada Highway has added few additional routes in recent years.

Improving Paragraphs

Professor Edwin Peterson of the University of Pittsburgh added two more requirements for good paragraphs. He used the same pattern (Topic Sentence—Support—Clincher Sentence), but his requirements for topic sentences were more demanding. He used the formula SATP by which he meant:

Topic Sentence = **S**ubject plus **A**ttitude plus **T**ime plus **P**lace

The function of this formula is to limit the subject. Look again at the examples given in Activity 4A.

1. The phonograph worked the first time Edison tried it.
   This sentence would be more informative and more interesting if the writer had added a time and place.

   > Time (When) When he wrapped tin foil around a cylinder in 1877 . . .
   > Place (Where) . . . in his laboratory at Menlo Park . . .

2. Anthony voted with the majority.
   Anthony didn't always vote with the majority. The sentence only makes sense if the reader already knows the time and place being written about. It improves the sentence to add:

   > Time (When) During the zoning debates . . .
   > Place (Where) . . . in the City Council meetings . . .

3. The detour went through Perth County.
   Without a Time and Place specified, this sentence has very little value for the reader.

   > Time (When) The detour Ella took last summer . . .
   > Place (Where) . . . on her vacation in Ontario . . .

4. The Eiffel Tower was the center of the Paris Exposition. A place is already specified in this sentence, but the time has been omitted. The sentence is more meaningful when you give the reader the additional information.

   > Time (When) In 1889 . . .

(*Activity 4B*)

Adding a Time and Place to Topic Sentences

1. Look back over the ten topic sentences you expanded with attitudes in Activity 4A. See if you can make some of these topic sentences more meaningful by expanding them even further with a time and place. Follow the patterns above.
2. Look back in Chapter 3 at the ideas that you listed for possible compositions. Working as your teacher directs, develop five good topic sentences which include all of the SATP requirements: Subject—Attitude—Time—Place.

Discuss your topic sentences in class. After the class has discussed your sentences and improved on them, choose one of them to develop. Write a complete, unified paragraph of from four to ten sentences (up to 250 words). Use the standard expository paragraph pattern: topic sentence, supporting details, clincher sentence.

Different Kinds of Paragraphs

Even though you have learned the basic paragraph pattern, and even though this pattern has been taught for a long time, many people ignore it! Almost every day you can read an article like this:

Owner sure curse is on his farm

MIDLAND — (Special) — Peter Derks, owner of the Hog River farm near here is beginning to believe there is a curse hanging over its owners—past and present.

Mr. Derks, who came to Canada from The Netherlands 16 years ago, bought the farm in 1959.

Here's what has happened since:

In 1961 his house burned down.

In 1963, while working part-time at a grain elevator, he lost three fingers in a machine.

In 1967, his wife, Betty, was killed by a bull she was trying to put back in the barn.

In July this year a district slaughterhouse went bankrupt, owing Mr. Derks $1,487 —

more than half his annual profit.

In August, his barn loaded with $5,000 worth of hay and grain, burned down.

Two days later his car was stolen and burned.

Previous owners have had bad luck, too.

One had his barn burned down. Two years later he and his wife were injured in a car accident. Seven years later he died from the injuries.

Another owner lost a herd of prize horses which disappeared without a trace.

Another's baby fell out of a high chair and died.

Yet another owner dropped dead in the kitchen while still in his 30s.[1]

Why does the author break all the rules that you have been studying? The answer, of course, is that this newspaper writer is a professional and is doing so for a reason. Paragraphing is being used in a particular way, for a kind of emphasis in a particular kind of publication. Note how the paragraphing draws the reader to a number of facts which can be reviewed rapidly so that a certain emotional impact is created. Does the creation of this kind of "rhetorical effect" explain the writer's purpose here?

Actually, the way this writer uses paragraphs is probably an older way than the way you are studying. Many of us are inclined to think that the customs or symbols we know best have always been in existence, but that is not always true. For example, Sir Isaac Newton, who invented calculus, would not have known that π equals 3.1416! The symbol π, or Pi, was borrowed from Greek and introduced into mathematics by Sir William Jones after Newton was dead. And William Shakespeare could not have read the number 3.2 because the decimal point was introduced by John Napier in 1617. Shakespeare had died in 1616!

Similarly, the paragraph pattern you are studying would have been a mystery to Shakespeare or Susanna Moodie or even Edgar Allan Poe! All of these people, as well as the monks in the Middle Ages and the scribes in the Renaissance, would have understood the method of paragraphing used in the example above. They would not, however, have understood yours, for it was not introduced into the teaching of writing until 1866 when Alexander Bain first described it.

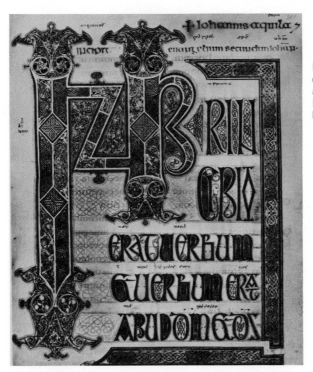

In medieval manuscripts, monks drew highly decorated letters to signal the beginning of a new section. The first three letters here are I N P from the Latin words In principio (In the beginning).

Until that time, writers indented and began a new paragraph whenever they wanted to, whenever they felt like it, whenever they wanted to signal something to the reader about a change or a break in thought. Monks first started this kind of paragraphing in the Middle Ages when they realized that readers needed warning signals to tell them to read the next section in a different way. The monks began placing the symbol ¶ to stand for *para graphein* (*para* means *"beside"*; *graphein* means *"the writing."*) They placed the paragraph symbol in the margin beside the writing to indicate to the reader that a new kind of material was coming. Thousands of years before the monks and scribes were copying manuscripts, the people of Meso-potamia were writing on clay tablets and other surfaces made of baked clay. Perhaps because of the difficulty of writing in this fashion and of the need to get as much as possible on a single tablet, little thought was given to paragraphs or margins.

Look at the illustration that opens this chapter. Baked in clay is the story of the siege of Jerusalem by Sennacherib, the king of Assyria. As you can see, the account was written without any thought of paragraphing to help the reader follow the story.

Alexander Bain's invention of a new kind of paragraph means that now there are two ways to paragraph. Perhaps you have been confused because you studied one kind of paragraph in school (Bain's very formal paragraph with a topic sentence, supporting details, and a clincher sentence), but you saw the other kinds of paragraphs in newspapers, magazines, and books.

The author of the following selection used the earlier kind of para-graphs.

II

The next bad thing I remember happening was the lie I told about the cat.

I am sitting at one of the long tables, I think in a reading class. Suddenly I have a fearful urge, a need, to assert myself, and I remark that at home I have a cat who can read and write.

"Oh, Nancy!" says the teacher. "No cat can read or write. Don't tell lies."

But it has become true. I *have* got, privately, at home, a remarkable cat who actually can read and write. In my mind's eye I can see her, the book propped up before her wise and whiskered face.

"I'm not telling a lie," I say. "She really can read and write."

The trouble that came to me after that! I was called, alone, into Miss Cavendish's study, where she sat, a thoroughly terrifying object by now, at her desk, in her robes.

"Nancy, you are telling a lie."

"No, I have a cat who can read and write." I clung to it as if everything—stability itself—depended on it.

My mother was got in touch with, paid a long call shut away with Miss Cavendish in her study, and emerged with red eyes.

"Nancy, you mean you can *imagine* a cat who could read and write," my mother said.

"No, I really have . . . " But here something broke. It was because I was looking at my mother. Watching her handsome, distressed face, I know that in the place where she and I live, there is no cat who can read and write. It is very much of a shock to realize this.

So then there are apologies exacted to Miss Cavendish, to the room teacher—"I'm sorry I told a lie." And after that there is a distinct difference, not only in the way I feel about school but in the way school feels about me, for I am branded as a liar, unreliable, at least for a time.[2]

—Nancy Hale

(*Activity 4C*)

Looking at Reasons for Paragraphs

Notice the paragraphing in the preceding passage and try to determine why the writer wrote as she did. Don't try to fit this kind of paragraphing into the formal pattern. Simply try to understand what it is that the writer is signaling to the reader. Discuss your findings in class.

Two Kinds of Paragraphs

Since 1866, when Alexander Bain introduced the new formal kind of paragraphing, there have been two types of paragraphing. To distinguish them, borrow a symbol from the mathematicians and call them Paragraph$_1$ and Paragraph$_2$.

Paragraph$_1$. The older, original kind of paragraphing. The writer indents during the course of writing a longer passage to signal that a change is coming. Paragraphs are set off for many purposes. They can be of any length. They rarely follow the pattern of Paragraph$_2$, and they are always a part of a longer piece of writing.

Paragraph$_2$. The paragraph invented by Alexander Bain. These paragraphs are actually "miniature compositions," or "minicomps." They have a beginning, a middle, and an end and are always limited to one subject; that is, they have *unity.* The sentences within such a paragraph all "stick together" or cohere. One rarely sets out to write one of these paragraphs the way one would write a letter or an essay or a short story. They occasionally occur in "real" out-of-school writing, but mainly by accident, rather than because someone planned to write one. One researcher found that this kind of paragraph comprised only about twenty-three percent of the paragraphs in contemporary expository writing. They occur much less frequently in such other kinds of writing as narrative, descriptive, and argumentative essays. They are, however, just the right length for a school assignment and, since they give excellent practice in miniature for learning to write full-length papers, the time you devote to writing these paragraphs is well spent.

How to Learn to Paragraph

As you study paragraphing, keep in mind the differences between the two types. Paragraph₁ is the kind of paragraph you will most often write outside of school, so learn how skilled writers indent to help their readers. Spend some time noting different uses for this kind of paragraphing. Writers use them to show the following:

1. Change of subject
2. Need for a break in masses of type (common in newspapers and magazines)
3. Change of time
4. Change of viewpoint
5. Change of tone
6. Change of place
7. Change of mood
8. Change of emphasis
9. Change of speaker
10. Emphasis
11. Change of style
12. Subdivision of thought

Outside of school, you will not be called upon very often to write the Paragraph₂ type. However, do your best to master this kind of paragraphing because as you select and express a main idea, limit it, support it, and drive it home, you are learning the skills you will use in writing long papers.

(*Activity 4D*)

Examining Reasons for Paragraph Breaks

Select six pages from any one of the following publications. Examine each paragraph break and try to determine why the writers began a new paragraph at each point.

Social studies textbook	*National Geographic*
Newspaper	*Saturday Night* or *Atlantic Monthly*
Science textbook	Editorial
Victorian novel	*Newsweek* or *Maclean's*
Modern novel	Modern short story from your literature text

Be prepared to report on the average number of words and sentences per paragraph, and the reasons the writer seems to have had for starting each new paragraph. Report also if you find one topic sentence developed in two or more paragraphs, or two or more seeming topic sentences developed in one paragraph.

Report also on any complete, formal Paragraph₂ types that you find.

More Kinds of Paragraphs

In Chapter 3, you looked at paragraphs from another point of view. They were classified as:

The Introductory Paragraph. As part of the outer structure of a paper, the introductory paragraph tries to interest the reader, name the subject of the paper, indicate what idea will be expressed about it, and perhaps show how it will be handled.

The Concluding Paragraph. Also part of the outer structure of a paper, the concluding paragraph provides closure and often summarizes the main idea or restates the thesis.

These are called "functional paragraphs" since they do specific jobs, or perform definite functions in a paper. Three additional types of functional paragraphs are:

The Transition Paragraph. Notice how the transition paragraph below creates a kind of bridge between the ideas which have preceded it and the new ideas which will follow. Like a bridge spanning a river, the transition paragraph carries you from one set of ideas across a gap to another set of ideas.

> But, although Descartes had come from an old, noble family and had the best classical and religious training available, he was hardly the reserved, ivory-tower philosopher. After a brief bawdy residence near Paris and a taste of soldiering in Holland, he enlisted under the Elector of Bavaria, who was then waging war against Bohemia.

What has the previous passage treated? What will the next passage treat?

The Parenthetic Paragraph of Explanation or Definition. Writers try to use words and ideas appropriate to their audience. Sometimes a writer may realize that readers need additional help. At such points, writers pause, put in a paragraph of explanation or definition, and then move forward with their main idea. The parenthetic paragraph of explanation is the second in the following example.

> Some of the best mathematicians today are working in an unusual, Alice-in-Wonderland world in which familiar objects are twisted, pulled, bent, and deformed—always with the provision that the surface not be torn, broken, or perforated. Topology, as it is called, is concerned with such unusual one-sided peculiarities as a *Mobius strip*.

Described by the German astronomer Augustus Mobius in an article published after his death in 1868, the Mobius strip is simply a long strip of paper with one end given a half-twist and then connected with the other end to make a loop. The unusual half-twist permits you to put a pencil in the centre of one side and begin making a line down the centre parallel to both edges and to continue until your mark extends down the centre of both sides of the strips and you are back where you started, having marked both sides of the strip, without having crossed an edge or having turned the strip over.

The preceding example doesn't quite follow the pattern of Paragraph$_2$, but good exposition is filled with this kind of parenthetical explanation. Because the reader needs the information, and the writer recognizes this need, a paragraph of explanation is used. It is a little side trip, rather than a sprint down the main street.

The Summary Paragraph. The summary paragraph often comes at the end of a paper as part of the concluding paragraph. Occasionally, a writer feels the need to remind readers what has been covered to a certain point. In this way the writer "keeps them together," makes sure of not losing anyone, and gets a fresh start for the next passage.

So far we have looked at the types of communications material the technical writer produces, at the audiences which read this material, and at the group processes used in developing the material. The foregoing analyses clearly indicate the nature of the skills the successful technical writer must have.

(*Activity 4E*)

Discussing Function Paragraphs

Each of the following brief paragraphs ought to be followed by a definition or explanation paragraph, a transition paragraph, or a summary paragraph. Working as your teacher directs, discuss the way you would write such a paragraph. Then prepare at least two of the five you have discussed. If you do not have the knowledge needed to develop the paragraph, go to the school or local library and research the topic.

1. Scientists can see individual atoms with an electron microscope. But most of what is known about atoms has come from studies with other instruments. For example, scientists may direct a beam of X rays at a small crystal of rock salt. Photographs of the X rays reflected from the crystal reveal the regular arrangement of its atoms. The distance between atoms in the crystal can be determined precisely.[3]

(A paragraph of explanation or definition is needed here.)

2. The mathematical theory of probability was formulated in the seventeenth century when a wealthy gambler, Chevalier de Mere, went to Pascal with a problem. "If one of two dice players must leave before a game is

finished, how should the stakes be divided between them?" Pascal, a mathematician, readily recognized that a fair division would be based upon the chances each has of winning the game at that point. In order to figure out the probabilities, Pascal made extensive use of the arithmetical triangle which now bears his name, Pascal's Triangle.

(A paragraph of explanation or definition should follow.)

3. The Reverend William Archibald Spooner is best known for the peculiar quirk of speech that has made his name a common noun. Without intending to, he would shift initial consonants between words, or interchange vowels in others so that his speech was filled with humourous surprises. Once when extolling the virtues of riding a bicycle, he exclaimed that he liked nothing better than to "pedal gently round on a well-boiled icicle." Another time he scolded one of his history students by saying, "You have hissed all of my mystery lessons, and completely tasted two whole worms." One unforgettable sermon on good intentions included the line, "All of us have in our hearts a half-warmed fish to lead a better life . . . ."

(The transition paragraph should be inserted here.)

Spooner served for twenty-one years as warden of New College until his retirement in 1924 and had an astonishing record of continuous residence at New College for sixty-two years. He was an extremely popular minister, serving a number of small parishes near Oxford. Also popular as a teacher, administrator, and counsellor, Spooner established an outstanding record as a professor. He wrote books and articles on subjects taken from literature, history, and geology, as well as religion.

4. Since Arabs believe that only Allah can foresee the future they consider anyone who tries to plan ahead as somewhat insane. Consequently, farmers refuse to estimate the crops their fields will yield, families are reluctant to plan to send children on for higher education, and insurance salesmen might as well stay home.

(The transition paragraph should be inserted here.)

We have whole "think tanks" full of futurists. The government pays planners and designers to develop various "scenarios" for the future. Every major business has a long-range merchandising and development plan. Families do their best to project their future needs for education, housing, and income. In a sense, the whole banking, investment, and insurance complex is based upon our conviction that we ought to look to the future.

5. The most ancient kind of writing system is the pictographic system, or picture writing, in which the subject under discussion is represented by pictures. Some traces of that system exist today, as when the Chinese or Japanese use symbols to convey the word "man" and to stand for "river" and to represent "rain." These symbols usually become so stylized that they no longer really look like what they "mean." At that point the language moves to a sound-based system, beginning with a *syllabic* system. Again, the Japanese can serve to illustrate this type of writing, for they use not one, but two syllabic systems when writing new words or foreign words for which they do not have a Japanese pictograph. Since every language has more combined sounds than it has unique sounds, the next logical development is the *phonemic* system in which each written symbol stands for a separate

sound, and combinations of symbols are used to represent syllables and words. English has a phonemic writing system. However, no natural language—that is, a language which has not been deliberately created by linguists and scholars—is completely phonemic.

(The summary paragraph should follow here.)

More New Kinds of Paragraphs

You've looked at Paragraph$_1$ types, in which the writer begins a new paragraph any time he or she wants to signal a change to the reader. You've reviewed Paragraph$_2$ types and looked at ways of improving their structure by improving the topic sentence. You've looked at a number of "Function Paragraphs," such as introductory, concluding, transition, definition-explanation, and summary paragraphs.

(What kind of paragraph is the preceding paragraph and why did the authors include it?)

But there are longer and more pleasing and more helpful Paragraph$_1$ types than those rather peculiar short ones on pages 75 and 77. In much good modern writing, these kinds of paragraphs are very effective, even if they don't quite follow the older patterns. Look, for example, at this sensitive paragraph. Notice that though it has unity and coherence and profound effect, it doesn't follow the traditional Paragraph$_2$ pattern.

I

At this crucial time my father died, and on the day I lost him, after a long illness that had made him grow remote from me, I found my brother Warren. We sat side by side on the piazza of our house on the strange April morning when we became fatherless. We watched the undertakers coming up the steps into the house, and going busily back and forth between the house and their terrible high black carriage. I felt cruelly little sorrow, considering how very deeply my father had cherished and loved me, perhaps because his cultivating love had helped to create the little girl whom I was now intent on destroying. Instead, his death gave me an exultant happiness because it strengthened and intensified my new awareness and adoration of cosmic things. It made me feel mature and experienced and proud because I could see it in the radiance of the new daybreak that was in my mind. Death was another of the great and ordered mysteries of life, and being so, it could never frighten me any more. In that revelation there was indescribable ecstasy and joy for the young mystic who was beginning to inhabit my mind and look out of my eyes.[4]

—Katherine Butler Hathaway

The opening sentence of this paragraph seems to promise to explain how the little girl found her brother. Actually, it does nothing of the sort.

It explains how she grew in sensitivity and awareness as a result of her father's death. Yet, everything in the paragraph fits together: it has unity and coherence; it makes sense; it moves the story forward.

Clearly, some other way of organizing paragraphs is operating.

These kinds of paragraphs have been around for a long time, but until recently no one ever described them or showed people how to develop them.

A New Way of Looking at Paragraphs

Professor Francis Christensen of the University of Southern California was very much frustrated by the paragraph pattern taught in schools. He looked at thousands of paragraphs written by outstanding modern writers. Finally, he developed his own description of the way twentieth-century writers prepare paragraphs.[5] These are some of the things he discovered.

1. Writers usually place their main idea in the first sentence of a paragraph.
2. Later sentences usually explain more concretely the idea of the first sentence.
3. Later sentences may give details about something in the first sentence, attributes or qualities (such as size, colour, or feeling), or comparisons with something in the first sentence.
4. The first sentence usually moves forward, but later sentences, as they explain the first sentence, often seem to move backward.
5. The first sentence is usually general and abstract, with later sentences providing a more concrete explanation.
6. The third and later sentences may explain more concretely any earlier sentences, as well as explaining the first sentence.
7. In order to be well-developed, concrete, and interesting, paragraphs must be fairly long.
8. Paragraphs have more interesting "texture" if they are fairly long and have several "layers of generality."
9. Ideas in a paragraph are either on the same level (parallel and equal—coordinate) or on a lower level (explaining, describing, exemplifying—subordinate).

These ideas will become clear to you as you look at the analyses of the following paragraphs.

The following paragraphs are set up to show how the sentences work together. A sentence which modifies, describes, or supports another sentence is indented to show that it belongs under that sentence. Arrows point from the supporting sentences to the topic sentence they describe to show how they relate to one another.

II

Although the bone structure of most of the North, the Canadian Shield, is perhaps five million years old, much of the land looks raw and new.

This is because a mere ten thousand years ago the entire region, except for the north-western corner, lay buried beneath a gigantic ice sheet.

The dome of the Keewatin ice sheet was two miles [3.2 km] thick.

Its own titanic weight made the ice sheet plastic and it flowed implacably in all directions outwards from several high-domed centres.

It scoured and gouged the ancient rocks, shearing off the surface soil layers and leaving behind an incredibly intricate pattern of waterfilled valleys, basins and deep coastal fiords.

When the ice eventually melted it left the land littered with debris that ranged from barn sized boulders to vast fields of shattered rock, and it enclosed the naked bones of the country with a complex design of morainic ridges, drumlins, and long sinuous eskers of sand and gravel.[6]

—Farley Mowat

This is the main idea of the paragraph.

This sentence explains the writer's reason *why* the land looks raw and new.

This sentence gives detail about the ice sheet and therefore follows directly from the one before it.

This sentence explains more about the ice sheet. All these sentences are at a lower level of generality and are more concrete than the first sentence.

This sentence describes more about the action of the ice sheet. A cause-effect pattern is emerging.

The first sentence moved "forward". All the others seem to move backward as they explain why the land looks new and raw in spite of its age. (Cause and effect.)

III

When I was a lad, I did not serve a term as office boy to an attorney's firm.

It was one of a number of omissions.

I did, however, work for a while as a file clerk in a credit agency.

Since I was sixteen years old at the time and had been graduated from high school, I knew a great deal and had opinions on a variety of subjects that I thought anyone else in the office would consider it a privilege to hear.

This sentence states the main idea of the paragraph.

This sentence, humourously, comments on the information in the first sentence.

This sentence adds more concrete information to the first sentence.

This sentence does not go back to explain the first. Instead, it moves backward to explain the one just before it.

I also thought that I discerned flaws in the way the office was run.

One fine day I was advised to keep a civil tongue in my head.

That meant "Be respectful to your elders," or less gently interpreted, "Shut up."

Although I did not know the word at the time (nobody did), I prioritized my interests, even as Jimmy Carter many years later suggested that the Democrats prioritize their platform.

Having a job was more highly-prioritized than not having a job.

Shut up I did.[7]

This sentence is parallel to the one before it, for both refer to and explain more concretely the idea in the third sentence.

This sentence, too, is parallel with the two before it in that it adds to the information in the third sentence.

This sentence refers to and explains more concretely the one just before it. It is at a lower level of generality, and it moves backward to explain that sentence.

This sentence, in explaining what the writer did, refers to the third sentence once more and explains more concretely and at a lower level of generality the idea "I did . . . work . . . as a file clerk . . . ."

This sentence explains more concretely the idea in the sentence just before it: "The writer prioritized his interests."

This sentence is parallel to the one before it in that both explain more concretely what the writer means by "prioritizing his interests."

These two paragraphs illustrate how concrete detail and "texture" can be created through having various levels of generality in a paragraph. Does the way in which each paragraph is organized reflect on the writer's purpose in each case?

IV

The house is alive.

It's a big creature and I live inside it.
Sometimes it likes my being inside and sometimes not.

It tries to talk to me and tell me stuff but I can't understand a word it says because we speak two different languages, the house and I.

Instead of words I hear gibberish and the gibberish eventually changes into drops of water that run down from the roof like rain, spilling across my window in wide sheets of water.

This is the main idea of the paragraph.

This sentence moves backward to explain more concretely the first sentence.
This sentence moves backward to explain more concretely the sentence before it.

This sentence moves backward to explain more concretely how the house shows the feelings attributed to it in the preceding sentence.

This sentence refers to the one before it, explaining more concretely the idea that the house and the writer speak different languages.

Whenever it rains I think I'm going to drown.

I can't see out, all I can see is the water sliding down the window, filling up the world.

This sentence, too, explains more concretely something in the one before it.

This sentence explains the one before it, giving reasons the writer thinks she will drown.

The house, being alive, can slam doors and open windows all by itself.

This sentence goes all the way back to the first sentence and explains in more detail and more concretely in what way "the house is alive."

Naturally, it could also trip me on the hall runners or catch my fingers in the kitchen door.

In explaining another way "the house is alive," this sentence is parallel to the one before it and refers to and supports the first sentence.

It could possibly lock me up in a closet, but it hasn't tried yet.

This is another parallel sentence referring to the house being alive.

Its works are down in the cellar: the guts, heart, gizzard, intestines, all the things you have inside you to make you function.

Not quite parallel in idea to the sentences before, this sentence is parallel to them in a logical sense because it refers to the first sentence and shows another way the house is alive.

I never go up into the attic because I don't want to come across any big fat gray housebrain up there.

This sentence is parallel both in content and logic to the one before it. It also refers to the first sentence and shows another way, in the writer's mind, the house is alive.

This paragraph demonstrates the nine principles listed on page 84. Go back to those principles and trace their operation in this paragraph. If there are some you do not understnd, ask your teacher for additional information.

Activity 4F

Analyzing Paragraphs

Look at the preceding paragraphs. Notice the placement of the broad and general topic sentence. Note that supporting sentences have been indented slightly under the sentences they support. Parallel sentences which refer to and support a preceding sentence are indented the same amount.

Now look at the following paragraphs. Read them carefully and analyze the way each sentence works in contributing to the paragraph. Then recopy the paragraph, indenting to show which sentence supports which idea. Compare your results with those of other students. Discuss those on which you differ and come to an agreement.

1. With profound relief he recognized his father coming around the bend on his horse. He was riding fast and his strong square face showed deep concern. His powerful shoulders were hunched forward against the cold, and strands of his long black hair had come loose from the *chonga* knot on his neck and from the red headband that had given him his name. Despite the cold, the horse was lathered.[8]

2. You just can't win with parents, Taf thought. You go out for a lot of sports, and they say you're neglecting your studies. You get good grades and don't go out for sports, and they say you're a bookworm. You join clubs, and they want to know what are you, a social butterfly or something? You don't join clubs, and they call you a loner or maladjusted. You hang around with a gang, and they say you're getting in with a bad crowd. There's no satisfying them, no matter what you do.[9]

3. Sonia outdid herself that morning. She was wearing a Spanish shawl that looked as if it had come off the top of a piano. It had a fringe and was embroidered in limes and pineapples in living color. She'd wound it around her smooth hair, draped it over one shoulder, and pinned it with a velvet rose. And under it she wore basic black, something like an evening gown, with beads following the seams on the skirt down to high-heeled suede boots. "She's really going too far," Alison said, though she only glanced at Sonia and kept a worried eye on me. Sonia swept past us on a cloud of *Evening in Paris* cologne.[10]

4. The Parkers lived in a modest, white stucco and wood frame house that looked, with minor variations, exactly like every other house in the neighborhood. It was a half-heartedly gabled box into which doors and windows had been cut, a squared-off, man-made mushroom surrounded by look-alikes in a vast anonymous sea of tastelessness. What had originally been intended as a lawn was a thick tangle of crabgrass. Along the outer walls of the house were sparse beds of emaciated petunias, columbines, and lilies of the valley.[11]

5. I rounded a curve, and the blacktop ended abruptly. White gravel began. At first, the new surface was a dull throb of sound from jittering wheels, but gradually the road became Dantesque. A curtain of dust particles moved sluggishly between me and the windshield. A car ahead of me threw up an explosion of dust into which I drove grimly, seeing its tail-lights, six red eyes, gleaming from time to time. Quadrilights glared suddenly as trucks roared past, ten feet high with gravel; metal clanged as stones struck the car.[12]

—Franklin Russell

Activity 4G

Following Christensen's Patterns in Paragraphing

The paragraph that follows has been built step-by-step according to the directions below. Note how each sentence is added as the directions suggest. After you have looked at the way this paragraph is built, write your own following the same directions. Then follow the directions for B and C.

You can get additional experience in building paragraphs in this way by coming back again and again to these sets of directions and building new paragraphs on different subjects.

A. 1. Choose the name of a place in which you like to be and tell how it makes you feel.

2. Name something in the place that contributes to that feeling and describe one detail of it.

3. Give additional information about the detail you described in the second sentence.

4. Now name something else on the same level as the second sentence and describe one detail of it.

5. Give additional information about the detail you described in the fourth sentence.

6. Give additional information parallel to sentence five for the detail you described in the fourth sentence.

7. Now go back and state in different words the feeling you described in the first sentence.

Example: (1) The shallow cave in the stone quarry makes me feel that I am back in prehistoric times. (2) Its narrow, jagged mouth shuts out the modern world. (3) The crude initials on the worn, brown limestone rocks look like the scratchings of cave dwellers. (4) The scorched, sooty fire pit at the back could be the home hearth of generations of these people. (5) It smells of wet wood ashes, pine pitch from half-burned logs, and scraps of bread and lunch meat from forgotten picnics. (6) Flat stones are crudely stacked, making a ring that encloses the fire pit. (7) Everything about that cave takes me back to the ancient people who could have lived there.

B. 1. Select one of your good friends and tell what you think of his or her personality.

2. Choose one aspect of that personality and describe it.

3. Choose another aspect of that personality; describe it.

4. Choose a third aspect of that personality; describe it.

5. Choose a detail about the aspect you described in sentence four and give additional information about it.

6. Restate the information from the first sentence in different words.

C. 1. Name one of your favourite possessions and tell why you prize it.

2. Choose one feature of that possession and describe it.

3. Describe in more detail the feature you named in the second sentence.

4. Write a sentence on the same level as the third sentence giving more detail about the feature you named in the second sentence.

5. Choose a second feature of your possession and describe it. This sentence should be on the same level as the second sentence.

6. Describe in more detail the feature you named in the fifth sentence.

7. Write a transition sentence which names the favourite possession you just described and connects it with another favourite possession which you might describe if you were writing a second paragraph.

(For additional practice, follow this same pattern in describing the possession you named in the seventh sentence.)

Major Writing Assignment

An Impromptu Composition

Paragraph₁ types are meaningless apart from the passage or selection in which they occur. Therefore, you cannot "practise" writing such paragraphs. However, you can and should practise writing Paragraph₂ types. There are occasions when you are expected to be able to write a clear, concise, well-organized paragraph. Some job and college applications and, indeed, some of your assignments in other subjects require a paragraph rather than a longer paper.

For your major writing assignment you will use your knowledge of paragraphing to write the kind of paper you may have to submit in your first college or university English class.

An impromptu composition is a composition written without advance preparation. To prepare yourself to write an impromptu composition on a specified topic, build a fund of general information on a variety of subjects. The best way to do this, of course, is to read widely. You will find that the information you have gathered can often be adapted to suit some aspect of the assigned topic.

For impromptu papers on a subject of your own choosing, the best preparation is to accumulate a list of topics that interest you and about which you have good solid information and definite opinions.

So much for content. The next step is to practise thinking quickly through the inside and outside structures of papers on several different subjects. Here your knowledge of the Paragraph₂ pattern will help you. The thesis statement of your paper corresponds to the topic sentence of the paragraph pattern. The body of your paper, the inside structure, corresponds to the supporting details of a paragraph. The conclusion of your composition corresponds to the clincher sentence of a paragraph.

For this assignment you will need at least two full class periods. On the first day, write your impromptu paper. Your teacher may either specify the subject or allow you to choose your own topic. Be sure to time yourself. You may have to shorten the body of your paper in order to allow enough time to write an effective conclusion. On the second day, work as your teacher directs on the finished composition.

5

Writing About Processes

Throughout your school life you study processes; after you leave school, you use directions constantly, both at work and in your leisure hours. How does something work? How do you make something? How do you organize something else? How can you get a job done? Sometimes you are a "receiver" of instructions, and sometimes you are a "sender" of explanations to other people. Knowing how to write compositions involving directions or instructions, those that describe or explain "how to," will help you with both activities. Perhaps the simplest kind of exposition, these kinds of compositions are generally organised in simple sequential order.

Although basically concerned with how something works or how to make something, compositions which give directions can vary greatly in subject matter and tone. Following are two examples of compositions written by secondary school students. One is informal and humourous; the other is serious. As you read them, note the comments in the margin. The suggestions and criticisms may be helpful when you write a similar kind of composition (See the *Major Writing Assignment* at the end of the chapter).

◄ Think of how the water you drink gets to your faucet—a complicated process. These ancient Roman water pipes were found intact after 1900 years. The one in the middle bears the name of Emperor Domitian.

Student Composition 5A

LEARNING TO WATER-SKI

Learning to water-ski can be quite difficult, but it is also very rewarding. If you have the determination and perseverance to master the fundamentals, you'll move into the great thrill of skipping back and forth across the frothy wake, lifting one ski in salute to the spectators, and perhaps even building a pyramid at thirty kilometres an hour.

But the first thing is learning to put the skis on correctly. Sometimes just getting into the rubber shoes fastened to the skis is pretty difficult. They wobble back and forth, jump out of the water (because of their buoyancy), and point the beginner in the wrong direction. It's a real problem, trying to hold the animals down, getting them stuck in the soft sand, and falling over backward during the process.

After you finally get your skis in place, you must be able to hold the skis upright until the boat can bring the ski rope to you. When the wooden handle drifts anywhere within grasp, you lurch desperately, lose your balance, and nine times out of ten must go back to Step One. Finally you get to the point where you have your skis pointed almost in the right direction, your feet almost in the shoes, and the tow rope marginally in your grasp. Now you're ready to make your first attempt at actually skiing.

Gritting your teeth, tensing your leg muscles, and waiting for the sudden shock, you yell to the driver, "Hit it!" As the boat accelerates, you relax your arms and let it pull you partially upright. Then, gently, you pull on the rope, and up you go to the beautiful, confident, soaring position—for the briefest moment before tumbling backward.

You repeat the foregoing steps with varying results and often ludicrous variations for perhaps a whole day. One variation is called the plough. For some reason or other, with the plough, the skier, unable to rise from the water, ploughs a spectacular third wake behind the boat. Another variation is the header, in which the sudden lurch forward of the boat throws the beginning skier head forward in a graceful, shimmering arc before the inevitable splashdown.

Finally, you master the skill, manage to stand upright, shift a little to either side. Then you stabilize, begin to relax, and even pull up on the rope and turn your skis to control your direction. Across the wake and back. And still standing. Now you're on the road to many hours of fun and excitement. You feel the satisfaction of having joined a small and select group. You can water-ski.

—Sherrie Aly

How interesting do you find this beginning? What technique does the writer use to make you feel her paper will be worth reading?

What is the natural order the writer follows?

How effective is the metaphor here? Is it "correct" as regards tone?

How effective are the phrases in series? Is there anything in the nature of a process composition that would make a writer use them frequently?

How much attention does the writer pay to concrete detail?

Do you approve of the use of the dash in this sentence? What is it supposed to do?

How realistic are these details? Should the writer avoid such interruptions in her main direction?

Are you prepared for the climax of the skier's desire to be a member of the "small and select group" of water-skiers, or has the emphasis been on something else as the reward?

Student Composition 5B

HOW THE HEART WORKS

Until the 1600s, when William Harvey discovered the circulation of the blood and the workings of the heart, no one really knew what the heart did or how it worked. It was believed that it had something to do with the blood, but people generally considered it to be the place in the body where love and courage are felt. Until Harvey's discovery, no one realized that the heart is one of the toughest muscles in the human body, and one of the most amazing pumps in the world. Though its size is like a clenched fist, it does enough work during a single day to lift a person weighing 58 kilograms almost 304 metres in the air. The heart is really two pumps side by side; one on the right and one on the left. The pump on the right pumps blood from the veins to the lungs. Then it pumps blood through the lungs to the pump on the left, which sends it through the body.

This is how it works. Each pump consists of two hollow chambers, like balloons in shape, and one above the other. The upper thin-walled chamber is called the auricle. The lower chamber, thick-walled and more powerful, is called the ventricle. The two chambers are separated by door-like valves that allow the blood to flow in only one direction. When blood enters the heart, it flows through the veins into the right auricle. The blood pours into the auricle and down through open valves into the ventricle. The auricle helps this flow slightly by a brief squeezing action just before the ventricle begins its constriction. As the ventricle contracts, the valves between the auricle and the ventricle shut to keep the blood from returning to the auricle. The blood can then go only one way—out the ventricle through other valves that open into the large artery leading to the lung.

On the left side of the heart, the pump has two chambers, exactly as on the right. The blood is pumped from the upper left chamber to the lower left chamber. The lower left chamber sends the blood to the main artery of the body, which is called the aorta. From the aorta, the blood runs on to the different branches of the arteries and is pumped throughout the body. The heartbeat continues involuntarily at a regulated pace and keeps the blood moving even at the farthest corners of the body; even though the right- and left-hand sides of the heart are two different pumps with no direct connection between them, they squeeze and relax in just about the same rhythm.

The most wonderful thing about this priceless heart is that it goes on beating throughout life, resting only a fraction of a second after each beat. It seems that

Are you interested by the reference to William Harvey and the date of his work? How might you eliminate the circular second use of the form of *work*?

Why does the writer use a simile in this passage? Why does he use an analogy?

Can you provide a more imaginative transition for this paragraph? What is gained in the simple, direct sentence?

Would a picture or diagram aid you in understanding this process?

Would you suggest any change in sentence structure here? What is your reason?

the heart must be a very complex muscle, yet the way it keeps alive the entire body is in reality a simple process.

—Bob Burke

What words weaken this final passage? How might you improve it?

Activity 5A

Discussing the Compositions

Although there is no single correct way of writing a composition which gives instructions or directions, discussing the techniques these students have used will help you understand some techniques you can use later. If you have read and discussed the comments and questions beside the models, you should be able to agree on answers to the following questions.

1. In Chapter 3 you learned about the organization of the "outside" structure of a composition and about the "inside" structure of a composition. To what extent has each writer followed the "outside" structure pattern? To what extent has each alerted the reader to the main idea? To what extent has each tried to interest the reader and to tie the composition together at the end?

2. The usual arrangement of a composition which explains a process is sequential. Is each of these models sequential? If not, why not? Do you believe that either might be improved if a different order were used? Why or why not?

3. In compositions involving explanation of a process, transitions are especially important. Call attention to any noteworthy transitions. Are any transitions weak?

4. Often in explaining processes, writers must clarify new vocabulary words or explain objects or relationships. Call attention to any such definitions or explanations. What words or concepts do you think should have been defined? How do you explain the writer's choosing not to define them?

Keep these discussion questions in mind as you read the following examples—how to do something, how something works, even how to avoid something.

I

WINTER AND THE OUTHARBOR JUVENILE

A crucial difference between then and now is the distribution of heat into a house. Whereas these days heat gets upstairs as well as in the kitchen, in those times it went to robust extremes depending on where you were.

You had the tropics and the arctic within the confines of one dwelling. There was the kitchen with the Waterloo or Maid of Avalon stoked to the dampers, red enough to read fine print by, with an iron kettle and so many iron boilers heaving up steam by the wholesale, and there you had the Amazon jungle. Not a degree under 90 [32°C].

Come into the kitchen from outdoors on the hand of being frozen. Like the sauna baths we read about in other countries the change greatly stirred the circulation, which is always good as regards hygiene.

On the other hand, if you rigged up for outdoors on a cold day you couldn't hang around the kitchen long once you had all your rigging on. You'd melt and run down into your boots.

The finest hour of the Waterloo stove was in the middle of a storm in the dead heart of the winter on the blackest night of the year with the wind a raging gale and the spray on the harbor sheet white and the frost bitter enough to crack the rocks and papers stuffed under the door to keep the draft out.

Then the only thing standing against the proceedings outside the window was the stove. The only thing, sir. It certainly got no help from the bit of clapboard and perhaps a bit of sawdust or goosegrass stuffed down between the chopped posts.

The bit of fire was all there was to stand against it. Give it a stir with the lifter, heave in a few more junks and see the flankers streaming away against the darkness.

But it was a different matter outside the kitchen. You might just as well bolt stark naked out the door into a ten-foot draft as go into the front room. Except that it was a little less windy.

No trouble to see your breath in the air in there, or your hand stick to the doorknob upstairs, or the frost on the bedroom windows devil-deep. A wonder the flame in the kerosene lamp didn't freeze.

Getting from the kitchen to the bed when the time came on a frosty night was a touchy business. First you had a drop of cocoa and a soda biscuit, then went out by the corner of the house, then came in and stood up by the stove to acquire as much heat as possible without scorching your garments. Then you made a bolt.

Off up the stairs with your beachrock in tow. It might sound sissy but it was a matter of survival. A beachrock—or a brick in homes that could afford one—heated in the oven and put into two wool socks.

Sling the rock under the bedding, discharge your prayers with blasphemous haste, then scravel off your clothes down to the knitted undergarments.

Even by that length of time you were shivering almost too much to blow out the lamp, but you didn't need to because you could hold your hand over the top of the globe and snuff it out and not get burned.

Then the straight dive under the bedclothes, if you could find the bottom of it. About eighteen layers of bedclothes and, no doubt, not one too many. Once under you might as well be caught in a mine cave in.

The beds dragged down in the middle like hammocks and with the heft of the clothes you were hard pressed to draw one breath after the other.

By this time the frost on the window was thick enough to shut out the light of a full moon and the ice in the pot under the bed solid enough to bear up a small foreign car. By the time the anti-freeze came along the modern conveniences were also available.

In the morning there was much the same drill except in reverse. You had your choice of taking a chance of putting on your clothes then and there or making a bolt for the kitchen with them under your arm.

All this, of course, is only a small part of winter as it affected the outharbor juvenile. Or the outharbor adult, for that matter. There were many other aspects to it, we know, both outside and in.

What effects it might have had in later years is a matter of opinion. But then, so is the effect on a juvenile of being reared in a house with the temperature in all parts at seventy degrees all year.

They're not likely to be so nimble on the stairs.[1]

—Ray Guy

II

HOT OFF THE PRESS AND INTO THE OVEN

This is the time of year when because of inclement weather and bad pitches by groggy newsboys, your Sunday newspaper may be arriving in a wet or soggy condition. Most people get angry at this state of affairs, maybe because they don't know how to dry and bake a good Sunday paper. Once you know how to do this, you may never fear getting a wet newspaper again.

My recipe for baking a newspaper was handed down in my family from one generation to the next, and even on the rainiest, snowiest, sleetiest days our family always has had the crispiest, tastiest Sunday newspaper on the block.

As a public service, it is my intention to pass on this family recipe to my loyal and devoted readers.

First, pre-heat oven to 300 degrees [150°C].

While you're doing that, drain off liquid from the paper and put aside.

Now get a sharp knife and start peeling off the sections of paper: the front section, then the society, sports, comics, etc. Wipe each section lightly with a damp cloth and roll to even out.

By this time your oven should be hot. If it isn't, you can study the wet football scores or the classified advertisements.

Once your oven is hot enough, arrange the sections of the newspaper on the racks of the oven, but make sure they do not touch each other or get in the way of the oven door.

Note: It is always best to put the comics on the lowest shelf so the color does not drip down on the black-and-white pages.

(If your paper is very, very large, you may have to bake it in two roastings. Therefore, select the sections you want to read first. Bake them, and then while you're reading them, stick the other sections in the oven.)

I know that the big question on your minds is how long to bake or roast a Sunday newspaper. This depends strictly on the paper. Give 15 minutes for each pound of wet newsprint. But every five minutes turn over the sections on the rack so that they don't get too brown. Some people prefer to cook their newspapers on a rotisserie which keeps going around in a circle, and this is probably a faster way to do it. But the danger is that if the paper touches the flame, it will go up in smoke and that won't leave you much to do on Sunday morning.

After you've allowed your newspaper first to simmer, then stew, and finally bake, you can test it to see if it's ready to be read. Take out the travel section, or the book review, and hold it in both hands. If the paper seems firm and stays up stiff of its own accord, it's ready. On the other hand, if it sags or falls apart while you're holding it, put the rest of it back in the oven for at least another 10 minutes.

Sometimes people make a mistake and overcook their paper. You'll know your Sunday paper is too well-done if it gets black around the edges and has a funny smell to it.

Your Sunday paper can either be served hot or cold to your family, and can also be sliced very thin or very thick, depending on how they like it.

If you want to read it cold, transfer to a cool, dry place and let stand 15 minutes.

The important thing to remember is that *anyone* can bake a Sunday newspaper. All you need for the ingredients are newsprint, rain, slush or snow, a hot oven and patience.

One more thing: There may be times when the news is so depressing that you're sorry you took the trouble to bake your paper. If this happens, just pour some cognac on it, light it and make it into a *flambé.*[2]

—Art Buchwald

III

HOW TO AVOID SHARK BITE

Never underestimate the power of the press. Since the release of *Jaws*, shark attack has vaulted from the number thirty-six position in popular fears (just behind ring around the collar) to number eleven. Even the sharks seem to have caught the spirit. Sightings near beaches have doubled in the past year, though many reports are inaccurate. The brave burghers of Miami Beach, for example, bludgeoned to death one ten-foot [3 m] invader, only to discover the victim was a baby whale.

Still, better safe than sorry. For those who wish to be prepared, here's the latest on how to preserve life and limb.

Elude 'em. Sharks don't have anything particular against humans; they are much too dumb to hold grudges. The going theory, these days, is that aggressive shark species eat everything that is accessible. The more you resemble easy prey, the more likely you are to get eaten. Hence the obvious precautions. Avoid swimming near concentrations of fish—natural bait for sharks. Avoid dead fish in the water—sharks have good noses. Avoid high-contrast clothing—sharks perceive contrast better than color. Don't splash around near sharks—it reminds them of wounded fish.

On the other hand, don't believe the myth that you're safe swimming in cold water. Few shark attacks have been recorded in water below 65 degrees [17°C] because few people swim in water below 65 degrees [17°C]. Shallow water offers little protection if it is close to a deep channel.

Repel 'em. Chemical shark repellents don't work very well. The U.S. Navy uses something called Shark Chaser, a mixture of copper acetate and black dye, developed during World War II. The copper acetate supposedly reduces shark appetitie, while the dye hides the potential victim. Unfortunately, the combination hasn't proved effective outside the laboratory.

What does work is a simple camouflage device called the Shark Screen. This is nothing more than a dull-colored plastic sack with a flotation collar, big enough for a person to fit inside. Sharks ignore it because it doesn't resemble an ordinary meal. And unlike Shark Chaser, the protection lasts indefinitely.

Kill 'em. The standard anti-shark weapon for divers is the bang stick. It's just a long pole with a shotgun shell and trigger device on the busines end. Unfortunately (as everybody who saw the movie knows), the bang stick will stop a big shark only if you nail the beast directly in the brain. Sharks have very small brains.

Other weapons may revolutionize the art. The Shark Dart, carried by Navy divers at Apollo splashdowns, punctures the skin with a hollow steel needle, then fills up the shark's gut with compressed gas. Very deadly. An electric dart, also being tested by the Navy paralyzes the monster with a thirty-volt shock. Disadvantage: when the battery wears out, so does the paralysis.

Probably the most appealing anti-shark weapon under development, though, is the porpoise. Porpoises defend their young by ramming predators at high velocity with their thick skulls. The Navy hopes to train them to do the same on behalf of divers. A big problem is getting porpoises angry enough to risk their own hides.

Eat 'em. Should you tangle with a shark and win, the following recipe will come in handy:

Shark à la Ross

2 lbs. [1/2 kg.] filet from young, medium-sized shark, preferably a Mako (no dark meat)
2 shallots, chopped
1/2 cup [125 ml.] parsley, chopped
1/4 cup **[65 ml.]** fresh basil, chopped
1/4 cup [65 ml.] dry white wine
1/4 cup [65 ml.] fish stock
4 tbs. [60 ml.] butter
1/2 lemon
salt and white pepper

Sprinkle the bottom of a buttered baking dish with the shallots, parsley, and basil. Pour in the wine and stock. Rub both sides of the filets with salt and pepper; place in the baking dish. Squeeze lemon juice over the fish and dot with butter.

Cook uncovered, in a preheated 350-degree [180°C] oven for 20 minutes, basting a few times with the pan liquid. Then brown under the broiler for a few minutes. Garnish with parsley sprigs and lemon wedges.
Serves 6.[3]

—Peter Passell

Activity 5B

Discussing the Professional Models

1. Refer to the discussion questions (page 96) based on the student compositions and apply them to the professional models you have just read.

2. In what respect do the student compositions differ from the professional models? Consider inside and outside structure, logical arrangement, transitions, vocabulary choices.

Suggested Topics for Your Process Composition

Here is a list of possible subjects for compositions describing processes. You may, of course, devise your own topic, dealing with something you are especially interested in. As you work through the activities that follow,

There are many steps involved in the process of building kitchen cupboards.

keep your chosen topic in mind. The techniques described and the examples given will help you write your own paper.

You will notice that the suggested topics have been divided into five categories. Into which category would you place each of the professional models? The student compositions?

1. How to do something: baby-sit; cook a meal; prepare an assignment; repair a toy or appliance; develop a personal quality; grow a crop; camp out; plan a trip, party, meal, game, visit, or campaign; get along with someone; pass time; learn a language, a trick, a sport, a stunt; run a publicity or public relations campaign; establish a business; improve race relations; keep or make a friend; track an animal; review a book; choose a wardrobe; earn spending money; collect coins; enjoy a vacation; hide embarrassment; study systematically; overhaul your car; tune up your car; show cattle; enjoy music; loaf; caddy; give artificial respiration; become popular.

2. How something works: camera, canal locks, helicopter, motion picture machine, radio, door bell, electric motor, gasoline engine, a political system, steam engine, vacuum bottle, precipitation cycle, fluorescent light, automation, binary computer, telephone, telegraph.

3. How to operate something: coin telephone, combine, mimeograph machine, automobile, automatic coin washer, pinball machine, tractor or end-loader, airplane, calculator, model airplane, outboard motor.

4. How to avoid something: making enemies, airplane crashes, accidents, being chosen for duties, being called on, blind dates, criticism, work.

5. How a process or system operates: passing a bill in Parliament; becoming a candidate for office; the Parliamentary System; International Monetary Fund; how a student council operates.

Making Your Inside Structure Clear

In Chapter 3 you looked at the relationship between the inside structure and the outside structure of a paper. You learned that the thesis statement or topic sentence specifies clearly what the paper is about and automatically provides direction and structure for many papers. Although the thesis statement or topic sentence is part of the outside structure, it definitely shapes the inside structure.

In addition to this major way of making the inside structure clear, writers have developed many other techniques you may want to borrow. Here are five of these techniques that are especially useful in organizing compositions dealing with processes although they are useful in other kinds of writing as well. An explanation and examples of each follow.

1. Specify in as few words as possible the major divisions or steps you will discuss.
2. Use topic headings to define and limit sections of your paper.
3. Use a combination of 1 and 2: Open with a list of main ideas and repeat them as topic headings.
4. Use a vivid image to help the reader *see* your subject.
5. Use a series of questions to control brief passages.

As you read the following examples, notice how each writer uses one of these techniques to make the inside structure clear.

> 1. Specify in as few words as possible the major divisions or steps you will discuss.

Here is a brief passage from a book by General Douglas MacArthur in which he specifies the major tasks he took upon himself as Supreme Commander of the Allied Powers in Occupied Japan after World War II. In the book, each of the short, crisp statements is developed in long, expanded sections explaining the process involved in each.

> From the moment of my appointment as supreme commander, I had formulated the policies I intended to follow, implementing them through the Emperor and the machinery of the imperial government. I was thoroughly familiar with Japanese administration, its weakness and its strengths, and felt the reforms I contemplated were those which would bring Japan abreast of modern progressive thought and action. First destroy the military power. Punish war criminals. Build the structure of representative government. Modernize the constitution. Hold free elections. Enfranchise the women. Release the political prisoners. Liberate the farmers. Establish a free labour movement. Encourage a free economy. Abolish police oppression. Develop a free

and responsible press. Liberalize education. Decentralize the political power. Separate church from state.

These tasks were to occupy me for the next five years and more. All were eventually accomplished, some easily, some with difficulty.[4]

—Douglas MacArthur

---

2. Use topic headings to define and limit sections of your paper.

Some writers have trouble trying to control the ideas in a long, continuous passage. The solution is to break up a long passage into short sections by using topic headings to limit and control the content of the passage. Editors of magazines and newspapers insert topic headings to help readers follow the main idea of a passage. You can use the same device to help you organize and control your ideas. If you've thought through the main divisions of your paper, you can use those divisions as topic headings on separate sheets of paper. Then you need only write the content for each topic and later provide transitions to link them. If you haven't thought your paper through, you can label each section after you've finished it. Then, as you continue, check to see whether what you have written deserves a new label or fits under the previous one. Some instructors feel that topic headings in a literary paper are too mechanical. If your teacher feels that way, simply pull out the headings and tighten your transitions when you make your final draft.

Here is the way one writer used topic headings to help control the content of a fairly long composition about how scientists are trying to save polluted lakes. The writer divided the body of the composition into five sections. Here are the topic headings for these sections:

1. Reducing the Source of Pollution
2. Increasing the Flow of Fresh Water
3. Using Chemicals to Neutralize the Pollutants
4. Aerating
5. Dredging

---

3. Use a combination of these techniques. Open with a list of main ideas and repeat them as topic headings.

The introductory paragraph of the following magazine article lists the major oil companies (the "seven sisters") and reveals the main divisions of the article.

THE SEVEN SISTERS STILL RULE

> There's no business like oil business.
> —C.C. Pocock, Chairman of Shell

A few years ago, such Ethel Mermanesque exuberance would have sounded strange coming from the chief of one of world oil's fabled Seven Sisters—Exxon, Shell, Mobil, Texaco, British Petroleum, Standard Oil of California, and Gulf. Though the sorocracy* had ruled the international oil trade since it began, the upheaval in the business that started with the Arab embargo of 1973 threatened to end this reign . . . .

Instead, five years after the energy crisis hit, the Sisters' power seems unshaken.[5]

*A coined word meaning "rule by a group of sisters."

Then the writer uses the names of each of the major oil companies as topic headings, making it easy to organize the content. This is the way a combination of the first two techniques works. Specify near the beginning of the paper the major divisions or steps you will discuss, and use topic headings to define and limit sections throughout the paper.

4. Use a vivid image to help the reader *see* your subject.

Like a line of washing billowing in the summer breezes, the provinces of Canada stretch from Pacific to Atlantic. Any talk of constitutional reform however, initiates interesting vibrations through that clothesline known as Confederation. The process of constitutional reform will have to work from strengthening the line itself towards replacing the pegs which hold the clothes to the line—while making sure that the often violent gusts which always accompany talk of constitutional reform don't blow everything away. The primary questions, then, are these, what must we accomplish, and how can we accomplish it as this crucial process unfolds before our eyes?

If you were writing this article on constitutional reform, what would you use as your four topic headings?

5. Use a series of questions to control brief passages.

By asking a question, you set for yourself the task of answering it. If your questions are carefully organized, you can take your reader—and yourself—right through a long paper and be sure that no one gets off the track. Here is the way one writer used questions to guide an explanation of the way a gasoline engine works.

How does the gasoline get from the tank to the engine?
What does the carburetor do?
What pulls the vapour into the cylinder?
What happens when the piston returns to the top of the cylinder?
What makes the vapour explode?
How is the cylinder cleared of burned gases to get ready for more vapour?

If you have trouble handling long passages, you can guide your writing by planning such a series of questions. Whether or not you use the questions as headings in the final paper doesn't matter.

(*Activity 5C*)

Planning Control of the Inner Structure of Your Paper

1. Choose one of the Suggested Topics listed on page 101, or another one that your teacher approves. List the main divisions that you will use in your paper. If possible, discuss the paper with one or more of your friends to clarify what you are trying to do. Make sure that they can follow your main divisions. Experiment with one or more of the preceding techniques for revealing the inner structure of your paper.
2. If you are unable to think through your main divisions before you begin to write (and many people cannot), write out a rough draft, trying to be as consistent and logical as possible. Then work with one or more of your friends to see whether or not your sequence of ideas can be improved. Experiment with one or more of the preceding ways of revealing the inner structure.

Combining Your Inner and Outer Structures

In Chapter 3 you looked at the outer structure of exposition and at the ways the inner and outer structures interact. In the activity you have just completed, you looked more closely at the inner structure. Now it is time to look at the way the inner and outer structures work together in compositions dealing with processes.

Although there are other patterns, this is the basic pattern of compositions concerned with processes:

(Outer Structure)	I. Introduction

      A. Arouse interest. (This may mean naming the subject you are writing about, showing that it's important, and putting it into a context.)

      B. State the main idea or purpose of the paper. (If this is clear from your title, this step is optional.)

      C. Give some clue as to the main divisions of the paper (optional).

(Inner Structure)	II. Body

Take up the major divisions of the paper in an appropriate and logical order. It will probably be sequential, but it could follow some other pattern. Make the movement from one division to another clear. Use topic headings, images, questions, or some other device.

(Outer Structure)	III. Conclusion

      A. Summarize the main divisions (optional).

      B. Provide interesting, satisfying *closure* (ending).

(*Activity 5D*)

Planning Your Whole Paper

1. Working as your teacher directs, try to build an outline for your paper following the preceding pattern. If you do not write comfortably from an outline, make a simple list of ideas, put them in an appropriate order, and go ahead to your rough draft. Then work out an outline from what you have written, rearranging the ideas in your rough draft if necessary.

2. Submit your outline to an editing group, a school friend, or an adult to learn whether or not your ideas are clear and you are ready to write (or rewrite).

Flavour in Writing: Avoiding Engfish

One of English professor Ken McCrorie's students jokingly misspelled "English" as *Engfish*. Now Professor McCrorie uses the word *Engfish* to refer to the kind of empty, impersonal, careless writing that may have no errors, but that also has no imagination or soul.

The first way to avoid writing *Engfish* is to find something you want to say and then write about it in such a way that a reader will understand and enjoy your message. The second way is to let your own personality colour your writing. Does the personality of the writer shine through in these passages?

I

The cinema is a ribbon of dreams.

—Orson Welles

II

...the true writer both of verse and of prose writes with his ear. ...

—John Macy

III

High up in the North in the land called Svithjod, there stands a rock. It is a hundred miles [160 km] high and a hundred miles [160 km] wide. Once every thousand years a little bird comes to this rock to sharpen its beak.

When the rock has thus been worn away, then a single day of eternity will have gone by.[6]

—Hendrik Van Loon

IV

It's always over so suddenly. We hit the end of summer like a traffic jam on Labour Day and are automatically lined up to go through the toll booth of another year.

Our biorhythms gave way to sociorhythms so long ago that we're now as geared up for the first day of school as any six-year-old. No matter what the calendar says, no matter what the thermostat says, ready or not, fall is here.

From now on, any warm day will be hoarded rather than savoured and our summer experience will be reduced to 2 x 3-inch [5 x 8 cm] Kodachrome slides and 8 x 11-inch [20 x 28 cm] essays of what we did on our vacations.

In a matter of days we will have completely covered up our tans with schedules and put on the layered look of obligations. We will all be carrying fall accessories like dentists' appointments and sign-up sheets for music lessons.

The speed with which we do our fall cleaning—sweeping summer out of our lives as if it were sand—has always amazed me. It looks as if we fear that one more minute or month of ease and we would all become permanently flaccid. Instead, September becomes our national tone-up month.[7]

—Ellen Goodman

(*Activity 5E*)

Considering Flavour in Writing

1. Most Canadian newspapers try to avoid a personal flavour in their news stories. Most business, government, scientific, and military reports aim at an impersonal sameness, as though no one had written them—as though they had somehow bloomed on their own with no human creator behind them. Most students in school are taught to write formally, editing out themselves and their own personalities.

   Working as your teacher tells you, consider the foregoing observations. Are they true or not? Why do you think much writing has become impersonal? What are the values of impersonal writing? What are the dangers? What do you want to aim for in your own writing? Why?

2. Very few textbooks show very much flavour or personality. Go to the nonfiction section of your library and check out a popular book from the applied arts (600s) or the social sciences (300s). Compare the flavour you find in that book with the flavour you find in your textbooks on a similar subject. Be prepared to point out what the differences are and the probable reasons for them.

3. Make a list of the elements which contribute to the flavour of a piece of writing. Try to work some of these elements into your compositions from now on.

Using Analogies to Clarify Explanations

In explaining processes—indeed, in all kinds of exposition—a communicator frequently must use a word or a concept which the reader or listener may not know. Since writers are unable to stop and show readers what they are talking about, often they do the next best thing: they compare the object or concept with something the reader knows. They use an *analogy*.

An analogy can be a comparison of the known and the unknown on the basis of a single similarity, or it can explain something by comparing it point by point with something else.

Many figures of speech involve a basic comparison:

METAPHOR:
Deerslayer *snaked* his way through the forest.

(The scout's movement is compared to the movement of a snake.)

SIMILE:
The announcement came *like* a thunderbolt.

(The effect of the announcement is compared to the effect of thunder and lightning.)

PERSONIFICATION:
Autumn *smiled* benevolently on the land.

(Autumn is compared to a smiling person.)

HYPERBOLE:
The chili sauce *tortured* his tonsils.

(The chili sauce is compared to an instrument of torture.)

Activity 5F

Examining Analogies

Keeping in mind that an analogy is a comparison of things in some way similar, notice how scientific writers in the following examples have used analogies to clarify their material.

1. Every civilization, born like an animal body, has just so much energy to expend. In its birth throes it chooses a path, the pathway perhaps of a great religion as in the time when Christianity arose. Or an empire of thought as built among the Greeks, or a great power extends its roads and governs as did the Romans. Or again, its wealth is poured out upon science, and science endows the culture with great energy, so that far goals seem attainable and yet grow illusory. Space and time widen to weariness. In the midst of triumph disenchantment sets in among the young. It is as though with the growth of cities an implosion took place, a final unseen structure, a spore-bearing structure towering upward toward its final release.[8]

—Loren Eiseley

2. Not long ago I chanced to fly over a forested section of country which, in my youth, was still an unfrequented wilderness. Across it now suburbia was spreading. Below, like the fungus upon a fruit, I could see the radiating lines of transport gouged through the naked earth. From far up in the wandering air one could see the lines stretching over the horizon. They led to cities clothed in an unmoving haze of smog. From my remote, abstract position in the clouds I could gaze upon all below and watch the incipient illness as it spread with all its slimy tendrils through the watershed.[9]

—Loren Eiseley

3. The normal healthy brain puts out "remarkable mileage." It consumes 1 teaspoon of sugar per hour. Using the terminology of industry, total operating costs are remarkably low. Energy output per hour is equal to that of a 20-watt light bulb. It is remarkable that while the combined brain energy of the group of men who worked on the atomic bomb did not equal the electrical energy consumed by the lights in an average office, nevertheless, they released atomic energy which is now being measured in megatons. Thus the brain is the control organ that directs the power flow of modern industry.[10]

—Robert K. Burns

4. A true perfume consists of a large number of odoriferous chemical compounds mixed in such proportions as to produce a single harmonious effect upon the sense of smell. In a fine brand of perfume may be compounded a dozen or twenty different ingredients and these, if they are natural essences, are complex mixtures of a dozen or so distinct substances. Perfumery is one of the fine arts. The perfumer, like the orchestra leader, must know how to combine and coordinate his instruments to produce the desired sensation. A Wagnerian opera requires 103 musicians. A Strauss opera requires 112. Now if the concert manager wants to economize he will insist upon cutting down on the most expensive musicians and dropping out some of the others, say, the supernumerary violinists and the man who blows a single blast or tinkles a triangle once in the course of the evening. Only the trained ear will detect the difference and the manager can make more money.

Suppose our mercenary impresario were unable to get into the concert hall of his famous rival. He would then listen outside the window and analyze the sound in this fashion: "Fifty per cent of the sound is made by the tuba, 20 per cent by the bass drum, 15 per cent by the 'cello and 10 per cent by the clarinet. There are some other instruments, but they are not loud and I guess if we can leave them out nobody will know the difference." So he makes up his orchestra out of these four alone and many people do not know the difference.

The cheap perfumer goes about it in the same way. He analyzes, for instance, the otto or oil of roses which cost during the war four hundred dollars a pound—if you could get it at any price—and he finds that the chief ingredient is geraniol, costing only five dollars, and next is citronelol, costing twenty dollars; then comes nerol and others. So he makes up a cheap brand of perfumery out of three or four such compounds. But the genuine oil of roses, like other natural essences, contains a dozen or more constituents and to leave many of them out is like reducing an orchestra to a few loud-sounding instruments or a painting to a three-color print.[11]

—Edwin E. Slosson

After you have read the preceding examples in class, be prepared to discuss these questions:

1. In each example, what is the unknown or obscure subject being discussed? What is the analogous object or situation and how does it help make the subject clearer and more interesting?

2. Although figures of speech are most often studied in connection with poetry, is their primary purpose (and likewise the purpose of analogy) only decorative? Do figures of speech and analogies actually help improve communication? How? What might be some dangers in overusing figures of speech and analogies?

3. These examples have all been taken from scientific writing. You have undoubtedly heard that this type of material is plain, straightforward, and unadorned. How do you justify the use of poetic devices in connection with scientific writing?

(Activity 5G)

Writing Analogy Paragraphs

Each of the following operations can be compared to one or more common objects or actions. For some, the analogy is so simple that the comparison can be communicated in a single figure of speech; for others, one or more paragraphs of development might be needed. After looking the list over and deciding on one or more appropriate comparisons for each item, discuss the list in class. If your teacher asks you to develop an analogy paragraph on one of the items, be sure to choose very carefully so that you will be able to get a complete paragraph. You may have to do some library work if you do not know these processes.

1. Growth of a stalactite and a stalagmite
2. Levelling action of a glacier
3. Growth of crime in a community
4. Chain reaction to a nuclear explosion
5. Precipitation cycle
6. Beginning, rise, and fall of a nation or civilization
7. How a computer works
8. How a three-stage rocket works
9. How a laser beam works
10. How a turbine works
11. Growth of prejudice
12. How a rumour spreads
13. How a stream is polluted
14. Development of a popular movement (ecology, feminism, others)
15. Drilling for oil
16. Social impact of school selection (how the school "assigns" people to varying roles in life)
17. The credibility gap
18. The Canadian Federal system
19. Government influence on news media
20. Vocational training
21. The expanding economy
22. The influence of advertising on consumption

Using Transition Words

Because the usual order in compositions involving processes is sequential, writers must be especially careful to let readers know how they are progressing in time and, if necessary, in space. Often they use such simple transitions as *first, second, third, fourth;* or *immediately, next, later, finally;* or some other combination of words, so that the relationship of each idea to other ideas is clear.

Transitions which serve as bridges between ideas, may be placed in five categories:

1. Time signals—*first, then, next, later*
2. Place signals—*on the left, nearby, in the centre, beside*
3. Minus signals for contrasting material—*however, but, unfortunately, on the contrary, on the other hand*
4. Plus signals for additional material—*and, in addition, moreover, besides*
5. Result signals for consequences—*consequently, therefore, hence, thus*

(Activity 5H)

Examining Transitions

1. Reread the professional selections and the student compositions in this chapter, or the analogy examples in Activity 5F. Be prepared to report on the types of transitions used. Try to classify the transitions in the categories mentioned in the preceding section.
2. After reporting on the transitions you located, investigate transitions in the equivalent of two book pages in one of the following:

Article in an encyclopedia	Cookbook
Popular Mechanics	Newspaper editorial
Home economics textbook	*Saturday Night* article
Social studies textbook	Athletic rulebook
Science textbook	How-to-do-it book

From the various types of writing you have investigated in questions 1 and 2, draw some conclusions about the kinds of transitions used in different kinds of writing.

Varying Tone in Describing a Process

Two speakers can address the same audience and say substantially the same thing, and the audience may jeer at one and cheer loudly for the other. Two writers can send substantially the same message to the same reader, but the reader may reject one and agree with the other.

The difference, often, is in the *tone* the writer uses. A student presiding over a school business meeting may be able, because of the formality of the situation, to rule a friend out of order and silence that person. If the same speaker, in any other situation, tried to order that same friend around, the response would probably be an angry refusal.

Similarly, in writing you assume an appropriate tone and a voice (an attitude, a point of view, a position with respect to the reader and your material). Because each situation is different, in half a dozen pieces of writing you will probably shift your tone half a dozen times. If you make the wrong decision in your choice of tone and voice—no matter how accurate your communication is otherwise—you probably won't get through to your reader.

(*Activity 5 I*)

Working on Tone in Process Writing

You can write out the solution to the following problem in about a paragraph. Read the problem in class and then write two separate process paragraphs answering the engineers' plea for help. In each paragraph, deliberately use a different tone and voice. Be prepared to read your paragraphs in class and discuss the different techniques by which you varied your tone.

> Two railroad engineers, each with a train 304 metres long, one eastbound and one west-bound, meet on the same track at a small town. In the town two small spurs of track, each of which will hold 152 metres of train, make an equilateral triangle with the main track. Neither engineer can figure out how the two trains can pass and continue each in its separate direction. Finally, they telegraph to the terminal for instructions.

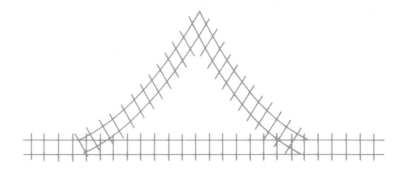

Perhaps in writing your explanations to the engineers you may want to assume one of these tones:

1. An apologetic office boy slightly embarrassed at having to straighten out a superior
2. A disgusted superintendent angry at being bothered
3. A dispassionate, unconcerned official, simply doing a job
4. A frightened yardmaster anxious to clear both trains so an express can use the track
5. An amused buddy of one of the engineers

(*Activity 5J*)

Writing Instructions

Writing instructions for someone else to follow is a special kind of "how to" task. Instructions must be properly sequenced, must break down the process being described into an appropriate number of steps, and must be presented concisely. They have as their purpose immediate action on the part of another person, so the test of their effectiveness is in the activity they generate.

1. You are walking along the street in front of your school and you have just been approached by a visitor to your community. Keeping in mind the criteria just outlined, compose a set of instructions, directing the stranger to a location familiar to you which your teacher will specify. Have someone in the class check your instructions for clarity and accuracy.
2. Working in small groups, appoint a member of your group to draw a picture on a piece of paper. The picture should not be *too* complicated. Now write a set of instructions which would guide someone in reproducing this picture.

When each group has completed its instructions, it should exchange them with those of another group. Follow your new set of instructions, drawing the picture on the chalkboard. Compare your chalkboard picture with the original on paper. If the instructions prepared for you are accurate and clear, the original and the chalkboard reproduction should be identical.

Improving Continuity by Improving Structure

As you explain your process, you must select grammatical structures that help clarify your ideas and improve your style. They must show the exact order and relationship of ideas, and they must make your writing easy to understand and pleasing to read.

The ability to make such choices of structure can be developed through much reading and writing. Be aware of examples of sound structure in your reading and practise them in your writing. Then you will become sensitive to the flow of sentences and the movement of ideas.

Major Writing Assignment

A Composition Dealing With a Process

You have gone through these steps in preparing to write compositions dealing with processes:

1. Examined and discussed student and professional models.
2. Considered a list of possible subjects.
3. Examined ways of making your inside structure clear.
4. Planned an outline combining your inside and outside structures.
5. Looked at ways of giving flavour to your writing and avoiding *Engfish*.
6. Examined analogies and worked out analogy paragraphs.
7. Examined and worked with process transitions.
8. Worked on tone in writing which describes a process.

Now you are ready to begin planning and writing your composition. Use the following as a checklist.

1. Prewriting—Have you thought (either alone or with a group) about a subject and ways of developing and structuring that subject?
2. Writing—Have you written out your rough draft?
3. Revising—Have you delayed your revision so that you can approach your writing with a fresh eye? Have you added, deleted, rearranged, and substituted portions of your rough draft?
4. Editing—Have you considered carefully the correct conventions of language?
5. Writing—Have you included all changes suggested during revision and editing when preparing your final draft?
6. Proofreading—Have you proofread both before and after preparing your final draft?
7. Sharing—Have you planned a way of completing the communication process so that you have an audience to react to your work?

y knilt auffi ⁊ Contre les pe/
ure nue bele Ou benne foient
fine peure tompteaulp de farme
uter les fruelles Ou peur tappe/
buele et foient Donez a manguer

Iterbentine est chaulde
et fuibe test la gome Dun
utbre nomt faum ⁊ Elle il betu
apume et fi Degaste bentofites elle
uetu la marriz et fi la confoite tar
en bfann uter brandes ou en tom
telles fane Delle auer fan me come
en fanfant fume en fuituffion
⁊ Pom efpramfon en fon fitt
fumee fur les charbons la quelle
fumee le partit feroint par bte
a bng buff ⁊ Pom la marriz
qui est chen fen fante teine on
fuppofitoue qui en fon onu ⁊ De

se meftie kronie la feme la fu
nue Delle come Ou est de efpran
fon mae pom la fuffocanon un
amontenu de la mariz la kronu
la feme par amont ⁊ Pom to
pre apoftine fon meffie ane farre
Dozet et fon milt fue ⁊ Ien la
nutt auffi en oronme credues po
feronidre et affemnder plante/
fuille que fen fant Delle diftille
est monlt epiellent a gome/ et a
puralifit et a tonte enflente ou
 filzanie de nufe et a donlem de
nufe quant fee maladie font
tanfee De freidiut et en Doit on
emdre le bten malade fur

6

Analysis

... one must always be impressed by the fact that our knowledge is only a collection of scraps and fragments that we put together into a pleasing design, and often the discovery of one new fragment would cause us to alter utterly the whole design.
—Morris Bishop

One of the most serious decisions you will ever make is only a few years away: How will you spend your life? What will you do for a living?

The following selection suggests that in order to answer these questions well you should *analyze* yourself and your personality.

The word "analysis" comes from two Greek words, *ana,* which means "throughout," and *lysis,* which means "a loosening." Analysis, then, means a loosening of the parts throughout, an examination of all of the separate elements making up a larger unit. Analysis is a very important skill and a very important pattern of modern communication.

As the world becomes more advanced and life for individuals in it becomes more complex, every major decision you make calls for you to weigh many different factors. Making the right decisions means examining complex situations in order to find the relationships among the details. The ability to see relationships and patterns is the ability to analyze. Analysis is important. It allows you to make the best possible decision in your own life. It also enables you to identify key elements or ideas and explain them clearly to others.

◀ The author of this fifteenth century book analyzed the different parts of plants to determine their medicinal value.

The following article suggests a way to analyze yourself to determine the type of work for which you are best suited.

I

GETTING TO KNOW YOU

What you do for a living should depend a lot on who you are and who you want to become. Sounds obvious, perhaps—but considerable numbers of people miss the boat on this important issue of choosing a career.

In our society, work tends to be a major piece of your identity. We label each other by our jobs and ask, "What do you do?" within minutes of meeting someone new. Work will probably influence your material comfort, your circle of friends and your feelings of self-worth and satisfaction with life. You can avoid joining the ranks of people who are dissatisfied with their work by making a conscious effort *now* to explore your own needs, talents and interests. Start by looking back on your personal history and applying this checklist:

1. Review all projects, awards, hobbies and other things that called upon your skills and abilities within the past three to five years. Which activities gave you the most personal satisfaction? Can you notice any pattern of areas in which you excel?

2. Now look at your past work experiences and extracurricular or academic activities. Which of these continue to interest you? Why?

3. Next list all of these favorite activities or involvements in order of preference. What specific skills did you use in each (such as managing money, working with people, organizing a system or taking responsibility)? Do you seem to prefer one type of environment over another?

4. Now start adding things up in terms of your past history and current feelings. Do you enjoy working with concrete, physical things, or abstract ideas such as time and space? Do you like to have assignments spelled out in detail or do you prefer to work independently? Are you an indoors or outdoors person? Do you work well under deadline pressure? Are you most comfortable spending time in a large group, with just a few people, or by yourself? Do you like to be in charge?

All of these personality traits help determine the type of work that fits you best. Try taking this checklist or a similar outline of your wants and needs to your career counseling office. With a rough sketch of the real you in hand, it's much easier to locate your specific options in the job market.[1]

Like many analyses, the one you have just read is informal and incomplete. It does not mention every one of the factors a person should examine before making a career decision. If you were analyzing a closed system, that is, one with a definite number of fixed parts, you would be able to make a definite, complete, and permanent analysis. Unfortunately (or perhaps, fortunately), human beings are much too complex for such a definite, complete, and permanent analysis. In analyzing yourself and many other aspects of the real world, you will have to be satisfied with a tentative and partial analysis.

Kinds of Analyses

As an essential skill, analyses of different types can be found all around us. Analyses can be descriptive, functional, or causal. In a later chapter you will be working with literary criticism, which is another form of analysis.

Your purpose for analyzing a situation or subject is the key to the type of analysis you do. The purpose determines what parts you consider and how you view the whole. For example, if you study a machine to see how and why it works and what its functions are, you are doing a functional analysis. If you examine the same machine and list or describe its various parts, you are doing a descriptive analysis. If you trace the factors which explain why this machine has become important to modern industry, you are doing a causal analysis.

Descriptive analysis. A descriptive analysis examines the parts of an object and shows how they appear. Usually the writer proceeds in some logical, spatial pattern, and usually in this type of simple analysis, the analysis is complete.

> The Atlantic was a huge, beautiful machine believed to be capable of crossing the Atlantic—hence its name. John Lamountane, one of the crew, had been in charge of its construction. It was fifty feet [15.5 m] in diameter and sixty [18.3 m] perpendicular, and was made of lacquered silk covered by a woven hemp net. At the bottom of the net was an iron load ring, below which was suspended a wicker basket. A special lifeboat, capable of carrying a thousand pounds [453 kg], was suspended fifteen feet [4.6 m] below the basket. The boat was encased in a heavy canvas jacket which acted as a sling and protective cover. A rope ladder enabled the crew to climb between boat and basket.[2]
>
> from *The Greatest Air Voyage Ever Made*
> —Jack R. Hunt

Functional analysis. A functional analysis describes how something works or functions. It is more complex than a descriptive analysis, for it must do two things: 1. describe the parts (though often less vividly than a descriptive analysis does), and 2. show how they work together. Again, the writer helps the reader by moving from one part to another in logical order. In the following selection, the writer uses chronological order (the order of time), rather than a spatial pattern. Sometimes, when describing parts which all work together at once, the writer arbitrarily specifies an order that the reader can understand—even though that order may not really exist! Functional analysis is very similar to the kind of writing you did in your composition about processes in Chapter 5.

> An electric bell must have a power source (either a battery or a transformer connected to house current), a wire to a push button, another wire from the push button to the electromagnet of the bell itself, an armature which the electromagnet can pull down with a spring that will return the

armature to its original position, a clapper attached so that it will move when the armature moves, a bell, or gong, for the clapper to strike, and another wire from the electromagnet back to the power source.

The power source feeds energy along the wire to the push button, but until the push button is pressed, it cannot get to the second wire and travel to the bell. As soon as the push button is pressed, however, electricity travels down the second wire and causes the electromagnet to pull the armature to itself. The movement of the armature to the electromagnet causes the clapper to strike the bell, but the same movement pulls the armature away from the current-carrying wire, stopping the flow of electricity. When the current stops, the electromagnet is deactivated so that it no longer attracts the armature, and the armature is pulled by a spring back to its normal position. In that position, it again makes contact so that current activates the electromagnet, and the process is repeated. As long as someone pushes the push button, the process continues, with the armature and clapper alternately being pulled to the electromagnet and the bell and then released.

Causal analysis.   A causal analysis presents, individually, the various forces which *cause* something. Often, there are many different forces that combine to make something happen. In such cases, causal analysis can be only tentative and incomplete. Can you imagine a writer determining all of the forces that caused World War II—or the decline of the Canadian dollar?

II

When we were kids, it was the cow that jumped over the moon. Now it's the cost of the cow that's sky high.

But blaming the cow isn't going to bring meat prices back to earth. No matter how much you beef about cost, you can't change a simple fact of life: the biology of the cow.

In large part, the price of beef has to do with the production cycle of cattle. It simply can't be any faster than it is. One cow can only give birth to one calf each year. And once that calf is born, it takes time to fatten it up for market. That may be as long as two years. Then there's another delay: If the farmers want to expand the herd, they have to keep the first offspring for further breeding. This postpones slaughtering another three years.

Five years have now passed from birth of the first heifers to slaughter. Next add to the supply cycle the fickle consumer. When supply is low, prices are high. Consumers buy less beef than usual. When supply is high, prices tumble, and consumers eat lots of meat.

But the farmers suffer. The low prices mean there's a large supply of cattle on the range. And cattle are expensive to produce. Low consumer prices don't give the farmers a sufficient return on their investment. So they sell off for slaughter a large number of stock. That makes things worse down on the farm. The large supply further depresses the market, prolonging the period of falling prices.

As the herd is cut back, consumer demand eventually exceeds supply. Prices start rising. The farmers experience good times, but not the consumers. In reaction to the high prices, shoppers switch to other protein sources. Demand drops off, discouraging the farmers from rebuilding their herds. Once demand picks up again, the entire cycle starts over. Generally it lasts 10 to 12 years.

Related to all this is inflation. Costs for transportation, feed, retailing and packing, and labor are increased.

Another factor is rising consumer incomes. When consumers have extra spending money, demand for beef is high. That, in turn, helps trigger even higher prices.

Today's high beef prices put us near the middle of the current cycle. Supply is low, so it's continuing high prices for the shopper.[3]

Each of the foregoing passages is one kind of simple analysis. Yet, each is different from the others. Sometimes an entire work follows the analysis pattern but at other times, as in the examples you have just read, just a part of a longer selection follows the analysis pattern.

In this chapter you will look at a formal procedure for using the analysis pattern. Later, as you gain confidence and security, you will move away from the formal pattern to a freer and more exciting style of your own. You will, however, use the same underlying thought process.

The Analysis Pattern

The analyses you have just read reveal a regular pattern. First, the writer begins by clearly stating the subject to be "taken apart." Next, the writer takes the parts one at a time and describes them. In the functional analysis (page 119), the writer goes to a third step and uses a kind of chronological order to show how each of the parts works. Go back to the examples now and locate in each of them the statement of the subject to be analyzed and determine the various parts to be examined.

There is one more element in the analysis pattern of thought. To analyze something effectively, you must do so in terms of some principle or purpose. This element differentiates the pattern of writing about a process from the analysis pattern. In your process composition (Chapter 5), you simply wrote an explanation of how something worked or of how to do something. In an analysis, you must first establish your point of view. For example, you could write an analysis of your family's car in at least a dozen different ways, depending on your purpose. Writing your analysis from the point of view of a safety specialist, you might consider the positive safety features (padded dashboard, collapsible steering column, seatbelts, safety glass) and the negative features (excessive engine power, single braking system, worn tires, faulty windshield wiper). Writing from the point of view of a mechanic, you might base your analysis on internal parts (engine, spark plugs, transmission, differential). Analyzing the car from the point of view of a used-car buyer you might write about the good points (late model, good paint job, good tires, low mileage) and the bad points (worn upholstery, dented fender, engine knock, no air conditioner).

Other people looking at your family car might analyze it according to other criteria; a junk dealer deciding which parts could be salvaged, an artist deciding whether or not it would be interesting as the subject of a painting, or even a thief deciding whether or not it would be worth stealing! (Think of what the thief might consider in addition to what the used-car buyer would list!)

Look around your classroom for a few minutes. Think of the various ways different people would analyze it in terms of their own purposes. Use your imagination to decide what each of the following persons would be looking for.

caretaker	teacher
good student	student wishing to avoid work
principal	lighting expert
librarian	interior decorator
psychologist	blind student
taxpayer	parent

Analysis, then, involves these steps:

1. Defining the subject to be examined.
2. Specifying the purpose, or principle, of the examination.
3. Examining the various parts.

The second step is particularly important, for by changing the principle of the analysis, you change the way you separate the subject into parts.

(Activity 6A)

Writing an Analysis

Write a short descriptive analysis of a classroom in your school. Analyze it from the point of view of one of the persons listed above. Follow the three steps recommended in planning your analysis.

Analysis of Simultaneous Procedures

In many very complex procedures, everything happens at once. Think, for example, of building an automobile. Various parts are built in various plants or factories. Workers in Windsor may be building the engine at the same time that workers in Oshawa are building the transmission. Brake linings are being manufactured somewhere else. Eventually, all the component parts are shipped to an assembly plant where they are put together to make a car. The analysis of this procedure could begin with any one of these parts, or at any factory, but to help the reader understand what is involved, some kind of order must be imposed.

The writer considers the various simultaneous operations, examines them carefully, and then determines the order in which to present each step or event. Presenting the steps or events in order helps the reader follow the operation even though the steps are really simultaneous rather than sequential. This kind of analysis is clearly related to the "functional" analysis in example two, but it is more complicated. In many "simultaneous procedure" analyses, the various parts may be abstractions, and the order they are placed in an arbitrary order based on the writer's guess as to what will be helpful for the reader.

Here is an outline for such a simultaneous procedure analysis.

I. Subject to be analyzed: The Industrial Revolution
II. Purpose of the examination: To understand what contemporary situations and events promoted the Industrial Revolution.
III. Parts to be examined:
    A. General agricultural and handicraft conditions in the eighteenth century
    B. Scientific progress
    C. Changing political institutions
    D. New agricultural methods
    E. Expansion of commerce
IV. Operation of the various parts in bringing about the Industrial Revolution (in order in which they will be handled):
    A. Social and political conditions at the beginning of the eighteenth century tended to keep economic conditions static.
    B. Scientific progress caused new examination of all customs, processes, and institutions.
    C. New political organizations came into prominence and the middle class began to have more power.
    D. Application of the scientific method caused the introduction of new methods in agriculture and production.
    E. Increased production caused expansion of commerce for new markets, removal of many peasants from the land to the cities, chronic unemployment, social unrest.

Clearly, in the foregoing example, all of the operations in Step IV took place simultaneously rather than one after the other. The writer chose to impose on them, however, an order that would be simple, efficient, and easy to follow.

Student Composition 6A

SIMPLE ANALYSIS

I. Subject to be analyzed:
   The changing Canadian environment.
II. Purpose of the examination: To determine the effect of various periods of development on the Canadian environment.
III. Parts to be examined:
   A. Pre-Columbian Period
   B. Settlement Period
   C. Colonial Period
   D. Early National Period
   E. Subsistence Period
   F. Modern Period

Time and the Changing Canadian Environment

Several hundred years ago, before European civilization was brought to the New World, the Atlantic region was wild and untouched by progress. The only inhabitants of this vast domain were Indians. The land was rich in natural resources. The forests were large and the ponds were clean and sparkling. Wildlife abounded all over the continent. The sea, the most obvious resource of all, was teeming with all the sealife agreeable to that environment. The balance of nature had been untouched by anything but nature herself. The sea, the wind, and all of the other elements worked together to build the strength of the land.

This natural beauty and bountifulness was not, however, to continue. The arrival of French colonists in 1604 and British colonists during the 1620s marked the beginning of a new era. Settling first in the area known as Acadia in the hope of finding a new way of life, they were soon to begin the long and ceaseless process of changing the land to suit their needs. At first the forests and wildlife were the haunts of the fur traders, who regarded these resources as unlimited sources of supply for the fur markets back in Europe. The forests also offered the wood needed to build and supply forts, homes, and villages. The land was cleared to permit farming, and the sea supplied much of their daily diet. These things in themselves did little to harm the land because in those days it was abundant in every way. However, these same things, if not controlled in the future, would tear down the environment. But the settlers knew very little about long-range conservation and

What is the subject of each of these sentences? How would you improve the coherence of the passage?

How effective in a description is a brief history of the location?

Would "bounty" fulfill the task of the longer word? Comment on which is preferable.

What makes this passage seem stilted? How can you make it more simple and direct?

Would you repeat "abundant in every way" here? Should the writer have used another expression here?

no one expects that they should have even understood the term. At that time, Acadia symbolized the new world, abundant in every way, beckoning to all to come and make a new life from its richness and chance for opportunity.

Later, as the New World was becoming settled, with Acadia becoming a British possession and part of what are now the provinces of Nova Scotia, New Brunswick, Prince Edward Island, and Newfoundland, a new breed of people came to inhabit the Atlantic area. These were the early breed, the tough, hardy ancestors of an era of well-respected people. These people were makers of the seafaring tradition. They were the fishers, the shipbuilders, the lobstermen, and that hardy bunch of whalers. There are many legends of these folks and their adventures at sea and ashore and all of these in some way or another show their pride in the land. Although the forests had now been considerably reduced, there was still no thought in the settlers' minds that the land was being abused. They used the land and the sea for their own personal existence and did not needlessly exploit its resources, so how could it be in danger?

On the other side of the continent, the western coastline was explored by the Spanish and British. In 1778, Captain James Cook entered Nootka Sound, Vancouver Island, and took possession of the country for the British. Following him were numerous traders such as Alexander Mackenzie, Simon Fraser, and David Thompson, who explored the western wilds, established trade routes, and built trading posts and forts. Colonists came west to settle in areas on Vancouver Island and the mainland. In 1858, the discovery of gold along the Fraser River brought an influx of miners and their suppliers. These groups also used the land and forests, the rivers and sea, for their own personal existence. Such activities as trapping, hunting, fishing, logging, and mining were seen as ways to use the natural resources of this great new continent to better human life, not as needless exploitation of nature. At that time, who thought that man might injure nature's delicate balance?

As the years progressed and those great mariners, explorers, traders, and gold miners became part of the colourful history of the past, the newer generations in Canada no longer followed in the professions of their ancestors because it was, quite simply, impossible to earn a living that way. Instead, the inhabitants of the Atlantic provinces turned to the trades of commercial fishing of all sorts, to the crafts of the individual artisans, and to the pursuits of those few who enjoyed the quiet life of the artist and writer. Across Canada, mass production and manufacturing began to develop in the

How would you improve the coherence of this transition?

How effective is the repetition of "nature" and "natural?" Can you rephrase these sentences to avoid the repetition?

areas which have become the industrialized centres. The rich expanses of the prairies were recognized as prime agricultural and wheat land, with the fantastic resources of the oil fields to be a catalyst for future growth and development. In British Columbia, the natural resources of the forests, which created lumber and pulp-and-paper industries, and the sea, which provided the basis for commercial fishing, became vital to the economic existence of the province.

We have come to recognize that some of these activities, if unchecked, are dangerous potential threats to our continent's ecology. Dumping industrial wastes, for example, could damage the balance of the Great Lakes, polluting vast expanses of land and the system of lakes and rivers. The damage such pollution could cause to animals, marine life, and human beings is beyond calculation. On the prairies, we have already seen what can happen if the land is over-used, as the 1930s revealed. Too little attention to the natural requirements of the vast prairie grasslands resulted in terrible erosion and dust storms, aggravated by prolonged drought. In the forested areas of both the east and west coasts, the temptation to log all usable timber for lumber and pulp-and-paper, could result in deserts of sawed-off stumps where once, beautiful green forests towered. Once again, the dangers of erosion and damage to the water systems are as real as the danger to the forest habitat.

In this paragraph, is the transition from one point to another done clearly enough to help the reader recognize when the writer moves from one major point to another?

A grim view of our future would be that the wild, free beauty that once marked the appeal of the Canadian landscape will vanish. The population may increase to the point of over-crowding the land available, and much of our wildlife will disappear. The loss of the forests and the lack of careful planning could cause the erosion of the coastlines in many places. Our fresh waters could be polluted by the carelessness of too many people. Our natural resources may be tapped to their utmost.

Though you may not be able to visualize the Canadian situation of today, what makes this paper a kind of description?

It is possible that the original spirit of the New World may still survive. The beauty is still there in the expanses of our land that are not yet touched. Behind it all are still the efforts of those who are concerned with the land. Measures are being taken to protect the environment and to conserve its resources, and hopefully the results of those efforts will be seen in the near future. Despite the factories, despite logged-off hillsides, despite our industrialized way of life, when a lone person stands on the shore of the Atlantic seacoast or walks through a tranquil forest, the beauty of the sea and the forest itself is still there, and the hope for the future is still there.

Is the word "hopefully" used correctly here?

How might a symbolic object be used at the end of this paper?

—Laura McDonald

Student Composition 6B

I have an extra-special feeling for those angelfish in the aquarium at the end of the hall. I doubt that it's the feeling that a lot of people would have. I think that most people are under the impression that angelfish are colourful little splashes of fins and scales, that they are beautiful, delicate creatures. These people are wrong. Angelfish are shiny, conniving little cannibals obsessed with the desire to eat.

The shiny beasts float lazily in circles, their beady eyes swivelling about, silently scanning the plastic seaweed for signs of food. Their fleshy pink lips are always puckering and unpuckering, their jaws chomping steadily as if the wanted food is there. The milk-coloured bodies look almost paper-thin, and I often wonder how so much food can fit into such a tiny animal.

Surprisingly enough, I haven't always had this hatred for those fish. It developed slowly, over a period of weeks. When I'd lift open the top of the aquarium at feeding time, the angels would always be there to greet me. I'd sprinkle the food on top of the water; the angels would float up and down underneath it like carousel horses, snapping at the frozen shrimp and making horrible popping noises that could be heard throughout the house.

I'll never forget the morning I forgot to feed them. When they realized that feeding time had passed, the ordinarily independent angels acted as one, singling out a smaller, weaker brother. Together they attacked and killed their victim, then divided the spoils, leaving only the cleaned skeleton sinking slowly to the Kolorbrite gravel below.

The irony, of course, is the name of the ugly beasts—angelfish. Devil fish would be much more appropriate.

—Cynthia D. Graham

This student composition is untitled. After reading it, suggest a title.

Do you think the subject of this paper is angelfish or an analysis of the writer's attitude toward angelfish? How do you know?

What technique does the writer use to make her description effective?

Why does she wait until now to define her "extra-special feeling" as "hatred?" Were you surprised? Find the words in the first paragraph that gave you a clue.

Notice how the writer uses imagery to make her descriptions vivid.

How would you rewrite this sentence to avoid the repetition of "forget" and "forgot?"

What device does the writer use for the conclusion?

I

BUYING A TYPEWRITER IS ALMOST LIKE BUYING A CAR: COMPLICATED AND COSTLY

Typewriters, like early Fords, used to be easy to buy. With only one color and one style available, the choice was simple: Take it or leave it.

Not so today. The marvels of modern technology have finally found their way to the once-lowly typewriter, making that instrument a complex piece of hardware. For business consumers especially, the range of available units now on the market is confusing, to say the least. More important, some of the latest models can perform functions never even dreamed of by the typewriter's principal inventor C. L. Sholes.

The truth is, typewriter purchases can represent significant capital expenditures for small companies. Whether the firm requires top-of-the-line units at the $1000 level or several less-sophisticated units at $500 each, the investment is one owner-managers will not want to make by the seat of the pants.

"Some typewriters are so poorly made that they cannot be relied on to perform for a month without trouble," says Ted Wirth, president of Buyers Lab, an independent testing company specializing in office equipment. "Others will last for ten years and be reliable throughout. Companies that fail to study the market before buying typewriters can wind up wasting thousands of dollars."

Few layman have kept up with the introduction of new typewriter technology in recent years. The types and categories of commercial typewriters now available include:

Portables: Experts warn against using portables for business use. Most are not durable, and they do not produce high-quality work.

"Trying to cheap out with a portable for business uses is bound to cost more money in the long run," adds Wirth, whose New Jersey-based company tests the typewriters of 38 manufacturers and publishes the findings in a booklet that sells for $55. "They are meant for term papers or letters to grandma, not business use. We recommend that business owners buy only those machines rated by manufacturers as office typewriters."

Intermediates: Lighter and less expensive than full-size office machines, intermediates are recommended for use in very small offices or remote locations. Priced from $350 to $475, they can perform well in such minor applications as occasional memo writing, shipping documents, and credit applications. Intermediates are not suitable for day-in, day-out use by a full-time typist.

Standard Type-Bar Machines: These are full-size office machines specially designed for use by professional typists. High quality standard type-bar units are durable and are capable of producing clear and attractive business documents. Prices range from $500 to $700.

Single-Element Models: The most advanced of the modern typewriters, single-element models have all of the type characters on a ball or cylinder rather than on individual keys. The beauty of the system is that changing from one type style to another is simply a matter of changing the ball, or element, and this is the major justification for purchasing single-element models. They are most expensive units, priced from approximately $650 to $1000, and are recommended only for those companies requiring the use of different type faces.

When purchasing typewriters, small firms should be aware that sometimes "less is more." Although most business machines are now electric, companies in remote locations and those that don't need sophisticated units may be better off with manual typewriters. The main reason for this is that service may be hard to get in remote areas, and manuals need fewer repairs.

The typewriter business is a highly competitive one, and there is a tremendous array of machines in each major category. Although a few manufacturers have come to dominate certain ends of the business—like IBM in the single-element field—independent consultants and distributors insist that other makes may be equally good and may cost less, to boot.

Prospective buyers are advised to compare several models, to test them out in the showroom and to make certain that repair and maintenance services are available. If full-time typists will be using the machines, it is also a good idea to involve them in the prepurchase testing. A typist's comfort with a unit has a major impact on efficiency. As a final precaution, Buyers Lab recommends checking with businesses that already use the machines to verify manufacturers' claims and statements.[4]

—Mark Stevens

II

WHAT'S ON THE LABEL TELLS A LOT ABOUT WHAT'S INSIDE

Oil can labels can tell you almost anything you need to know about today's motor oils.

There are two motor oil classification systems—SAE and API. The SAE grading system, developed by the Society of Automotive Engineers, rates oil by its viscosity (resistance to flow). The API system, developed by the American Petroleum Institute, in cooperation with SAE and the American Society for Testing and Materials, classifies oils on how well they perform and how they should be used.

Under the SAE system, oils are divided into eight grades (weights). Four of these are low temperature grades for winter use and include the letter "W", hence, SAE 5W, 10W, 15W, and 20W. The other four grades indicate high temperature viscosity: SAE 20, 30, 40, and 50. *The higher the grade number the heavier the oil.*

The development of additives called *viscosity index improvers* made multigrade oils possible. Two of the most widely used multigrade oils—SAE 10W-30 and SAE 10W-40—are thin enough for easy cranking at low winter temperatures and thick enough to lubricate an engine effectively at hotter summer temperatures.

API service classifications, which are identified by two letters, decribe the all-around performance of an oil in lubricating an engine and protecting it against sludge, tarnish, rust, and wear. The API system includes nine classes of service. Five of these—SA, SB, SC, SD, and SE—are for service station oils. The other four—CA, CB, CC, and CD—are for commercial oils.

Classifications beginning with the letter "S" for "Service" describe passenger car oils used generally in automobiles and light trucks. Those beginning with the letter "C" for "Commercial" designate oils for truck fleets, heavy equipment, farm vehicles, and the like.

What in this opening appeals to a reader? Why would anyone want to read on?
What does this paragraph do for a reader?

Why should this paragraph be separated from the previous one?

The original article used two topic headings to help the reader keep the main divisions of the article clear. Where would you put such headings? What would they be?
How does this paragraph prepare you for the discussion that follows?

You can see that this paper has been very carefully analyzed into main divisions and subdivisions. Because it is so carefully thought out and organized, it is very easy to outline. What would you place at each point on this outline?

I. Introduction
    A. Why subject is important
    B. Division of content
II. Body
    A. 1.
       2.

SA, a straight mineral oil with no additives, and SB, which contains only a small amount of anti-oxidant and anti-wear additives, but which is non-detergent, are now largely obsolete. They have been superseded by oils of more recent API classifications.

SC, a detergent oil which provides some control of high and low-temperature deposits, wear, rust, and corrosion, met car manufacturers' warranty requirements for 1964-1967 models.

SD, with higher detergency and anti-wear characteristics, provides greater engine protection than SC oil. It can be used when SC is recommended. SD oils met warranty requirements for 1968-1971 models.

SE oils provide the highest current quality and are recommended for all cars, vans, and light trucks, including older models, which formerly used SC or SD oils.

Certain SC oils are recommended for older cars which burn large amounts of oil because of poor mechanical condition.

Lawnmowers and other 4-stroke cycle engines now use detergent oils of SC, SD and SE quality, whereas manufacturers used to specify straight mineral oils.

B. (Digression)
C. 1.
    2. (Named—but a discussion is omitted.)

In the outline there would be several subpoints under A.1, A.2, C.1, and C.2. What would they be?

Why did the writer omit a discussion of C.2 in the body? Why does a reader not feel cheated?

One of the claims of the advertising industry is that good ads keep the public informed of new products and of ways of deciding which purchases are in their best interests. How would you rate this advertisement on its value to the consumer?

Why do you think the article omits the traditional conclusion?

If you wanted to end this article effectively and drive home its message what kind of a conclusion might you provide? How do you rate this article as to outside structure? Inside structure?

III

Canada was never Hollywood's favourite word. In fact the moviemakers went out of their way *not* to use it. In scores of cases, the only way you knew a movie was about Canada was when a Mountie or a French-Canadian trapper hove into view.

Take a look at the titles: the words Canada and Canadian scarcely ever appeared. Instead, every possible euphemism was used to get around those dreadful words. But everybody knew, when a picture came out using code words like Northwest or Big Snows or Great Woods, that the setting was north of the border. More than 170 movies bore that kind of code in their titles; only eight dared to use Canada or Canadian.

Code Word	Number of Titles
North, Northwest, Northern, Northwoods	79
Wild, Wilderness or Trail	50
Mounties or Mounted	37
Klondike or Yukon	18
Snow	11

Even best-selling Canadian classics were carefully de-Canadianized by the moviemakers. It's been largely forgotten that there was a period in Canadian literary history when certain Canadian novels were in furious demand by an international audience and therefore by the movies. Of the five best-selling Canadian authors of all time, four have had their classic novels transferred to the screen by Hollywood. They are: Ralph Connor, Mazo de la Roche, L. M. Montgomery, and Robert W. Service. Only the work of Stephen Leacock, perhaps the biggest seller of them all, has never been given feature film treatment.

These best sellers were all unmistakably Canadian—a fact that in no sense conspired against their popularity. The first American printing of Ralph Connor's novel *The Sky Pilot*, for instance, was 250 000 copies. The novel's eventual sales exceeded one million copies.* Hollywood bought it, of course, but then proceeded to de-Canadianize it. The only Canadian reference in the entire picture is to the fact that the Sky Pilot comes from Montreal. Presumably the setting is the Canadian Rockies; but the movie was shot on location at Truckee, California, and the saloons, gun-fights, and even the costumes are those of the American wild west. The major trade reviews didn't even mention the story's Canadian origin but praised the picture as "an exceedingly good western"[1] with a "collection of thrilling punches."[2]

The other big best sellers were given a similar laundering. Service's novel, *The Trail of '98*, is all about the Klondike gold rush but the only evidence of any Canadian location in the movie is a fleeting shot of a British flag at the summit of the Chilkoot Pass.

The picture made from Mazo de la Roche's prize-winning novel, *Jalna,* had only three direct references to Canada and a few indirect ones. The characters were shown speaking with English accents, living in a panelled English manor, dressed in English tweeds, indulging in English upper-class slang (meself, old gel) and being waited on by jovial Cockney servants, all of whom knew their place.

The movie version of L. M. Montgomery's classic novel, *Anne of Green Gables,* did have a few references to Prince Edward Island and an opening scene or two showing the gentle island landscape, but its sequel, *Anne of Windy Poplars,* was not identifiably Canadian. Except for a single reference to Charlottetown it could just as easily have been made in the American midwest, and there were undoubtedly thousands of movie-goers who thought it was.

The situation has not changed. When Margaret Laurence's important Canadian novel, *A Jest of God,* was made into the film *Rachel, Rachel,* the location was changed, for no very good reason, from Manitoba to Maine.

It's a curious kind of attitude, when you think about it: make use of the Canadian classic novels; make use of the Canadian background; make use of the mounted police; but try not to mention Canada. As far as I can tell, ours is the only country that Hollywood treated in this fashion. But then it wasn't as easy to take a novel set in the African jungle or the China seas or the English countryside or a Graustarkian palace and camouflage it to the point where it might have taken place somewhere in America.[5]

—Pierre Berton

---

* A later Connor novel, *The Man from Glengarry,* sold five million copies.

Discussing the Analysis Papers

1. To what extent have the writers of these papers written "off the tops of their heads" and to what extent have they done library work, personal research, and interviewing in preparing the articles? What is the danger in using reference material? What are the relative merits of basing your writing upon library research and basing it upon general personal background?
2. What comments can you make on the organization of each paper? Do you think each writer was conscious of an outline such as that on page 123?
3. How concrete are the papers? Do you find any particularly good comparisons, figures of speech, appeals to the senses, examples, or supporting details?
4. In what ways do the papers differ from each other? Can they all legitimately be considered analysis papers?
5. Could the student compositions in Chapter 3 have been classified as analysis compositions? What are the distinguishing marks of an analysis composition?

(Activity 6B)

Outlining an Analysis Paper

Refer to the outline that precedes Student Composition 6A on page 123. Choose one of the professional writing samples and build a similar outline for it.

Faulty Analysis

If someone promised you an apple pie but gave you one with a big slice removed, you'd probably be quite disappointed. And if someone promised you a new motor but gave you a box of miscellaneous parts, some from a Ford and some from a Chevrolet, again you'd be disappointed.

The reader of faulty analysis may feel a similar let down. The introduction to an analytical composition promises the reader, in effect, to take a given subject apart and to examine all the necessary parts.

Sometimes a writer does not produce the neat complete analysis the reader expects. Usually such a flawed analysis errs in one of three ways:

1. It leaves out some of the parts.
2. It includes some parts that don't belong.
3. It treats some of the same parts twice, often using different names for the same things or looking at them in a different way.

Acknowledging incomplete analysis.   If you are analyzing a mechanism or a closed system, you can list all of the parts and treat them separately. However, there are many things that do not lend themselves to a neat, tidy, complete analysis. As you examine natural processes, complicated ideas, and many aspects of social studies and literature, you can't be sure that you have located all pertinent parts. In these cases, make your reader aware that there are other aspects of the subject you are analyzing which you will not be dealing with. There are a number of ways to do this. You may use a phrase like "Among the contributing causes are ... ," "A partial examination reveals ... ," or "There are many facets of this complex subject; however, I shall discuss just four." Avoid the use of etc., an abbreviation for the Latin words et cetera (and others). Most people feel that this suggests incomplete thought or a hasty analysis.

(*Activity 6C*)

Examining Faulty Analyses

Examine the following outlines for analysis papers. Be prepared to discuss each one and explain how you would improve it.

OUR SCHOOL
I. Administration
   A. Faculty
   B. Maintenance
II. Students
   A. Clerical
      assistants
   B. Cheerleaders

BENEFITS OF ATHLETICS
I. Conditioning
II. Friendship
III. Sportsmanship
IV. Status
V. Team spirit
VI. Impossibility of part-time
   work

LEISURE TIME ACTIVITIES
I. Quiet things
   A. Read
   B. Watch TV
   C. Dream
II. Active things
   A. Swim
   B. Ski
   C. Bowl
   D. Play tennis
III. Community things
   A. Help at recycling
      station
   B. Volunteer at
      hospital
   C. Join youth
      organization

Activity 6D

Revising and Editing an Analysis Composition

The outline for the subject "Benefits of Athletics" has been used to build the following paragraph. Read the paragraph carefully, and apply your revising and editing skills to correct errors in mechanics and logical thought. Your teacher may suggest whether you should work alone or with a group.

"Benifits of Athletics"

There is many benifits to participating in atheletics, whether they be part of an extra-curricula programme at school or a community sports team. We all recognize the importance of keeping your body in shape, and so the physical conditioning involved in such sports programmes are valuable to you. Also considering the value of friendship. Team-mates and even competitors oftentimes go on to become good friends after the games' are over. After the games are over, the basic good rules of sportsmanship learned on the team is helpful in conducting yourself well in life. Everybody appreciate's the status they would earn as part of a championship team, everybody enjoys the same feeling of status wearing their team jacket and representing there school or community even when you don't win. Also taking into account the real spirit of togetherness known as "team spirit," a positive advantage. And last but not least, participating regularly in atheletics effects a students' life because they soon discover the impossibility of part-time work when giving up there sparetime for sports.

Major Writing Assignment

An Analysis Composition

Reread the articles and compositions at the beginning of this chapter and note that most of them require some research. Choose one of the subjects listed here or another one approved by your teacher, and write an analysis composition.

Whether or not you do your best work writing from an outline, think through your analysis before you begin to write. Identify the audience you intend to address. Use the procedure explained near the beginning of this chapter:

1. Subject to be analyzed.
2. Purpose, or principle, of the examination.
3. Parts to be examined.

If you work well from an outline, or if you and your teacher think that you need experience in outlining, develop an outline that follows this form:

I. Introduction
   A. Arouse the reader's interest.
   B. Introduce the subject. Define or explain it, if necessary.
   C. Suggest the purpose or principle you are going to use and indicate why this analysis is important, interesting, or worth doing.
   D. List, in the order you have decided on, the main parts you will examine. Be sure that, in the body of the composition, you treat these parts in the same order as you list them here. (This step is optional.)

II. Body

(For Descriptive and Causal Analysis)
Take up and describe or explain each part (in the order you listed them if you had Part D in your Introduction).

(For Functional Analysis)
   A. Take up and describe or explain each part (in the order you listed them if you had Part D in your Introduction).
   B. Show how each part works or functions. Use either chronological or spatial order or work out an arbitrary order the reader can easily understand.

III. Conclusion
   A. Review for the reader what you have analyzed and why you did so. Vary your wording so that this reminder is not too obvious.
   B. End your composition with an application of what you have presented, an indication of something in the future connected with your subject, a mention of a related subject. You might want to refer to the limitations of your analysis and suggest the possibility of further study.

Be sure to use what you learned in this chapter. The following are some possible analysis subjects from which to select your topic:

Causes of a historical event

An organization (team, class, government, unit, scout troop, club)

Aspects of an institution (church, school, university, department)

A work of art (painting, mural, statue)

Factors causing a social change (pollution control, inflation)

Manufacture of an item

A job or profession

Issue in a current election

Operation of a community organization

Values of a particular activity (group, philosophy, tradition, idea)

A concept or idea (mercantilism, ethics, scientific method, morality, or other idea to be handled analytically)

A scientific experiment or process

A hobby

7

Opinion

We all have opinions, but some of us happen to be right.

—Louis Dudek

All people have personal opinions about and reactions to events in the world around them. An opinion is based not on absolute certainty but on what seems to be true or probable. Pressure is often very strong to make individuals give up their personal opinions and reactions and accept those of a group. Consider this story.

A sailor on a submarine became very ill. The captain surfaced near a tiny South Pacific island and radioed for a helicopter to come and take the sailor to a hospital.

Two islanders, who had never seen modern machines, watched the transfer of the sailor to the helicopter. Then they rushed back to their village to report the wonder they had seen: A great fish had burst from the water, and two men had climbed out of an opening on its back. Then an enormous bird came from the sky and hovered near the fish. The two men lifted a third man from the great fish and stuffed him into the belly of the bird. Finally, the bird flew away, the men climbed back into the fish, and the fish sank into the sea.

The village elders scoffed at the story. Fish have no openings on their backs, and no bird is big enough to swallow a man. After much discussion, the two islanders agreed with the elders. They admitted that they could not possibly have seen what they had seen. They agreed that the event had never happened.[1]

◀ Demonstrations with placards are often used as public forums for the expression of opinion.

137

It is hard to believe that the islanders could have been persuaded to reject the evidence of their own eyes. You probably cannot imagine anyone persuading you to deny something that you have actually seen. It might be much easier, however, to persuade you to deny a belief or an opinion which, of course you can neither see nor touch. Maintaining an opinion, a belief, or an idea in the face of opposition is difficult because each is an abstraction that you cannot verify with your senses.

Individual opinions are important in helping people discover truths and adapt themselves and their institutions to changes in the world. In some countries, people are denied the right to express their opinions. Even in an open, free society it often takes courage to express an opinion that is unpopular, and the right to express oneself freely must be carefully guarded. As the French philosopher Voltaire said, "I disapprove of what you say, but I will defend to the death your right to say it." In the seventeenth century, the English poet John Milton put it this way: "...he who destroys a good book kills reason itself." The same thought was expressed by Benjamin Franklin: "...when Men differ in Opinion, both Sides ought equally to have the Advantage of being heard by the Publick; and ... when Truth and Error have fair Play, the former is always an overmatch for the latter...."

An instance of people exchanging ideas and defending their opinions has been taking place in Canada's north among members of the Dene Nation. These people have been very concerned about the effect of the construction of an oil pipeline through their homeland in the Mackenzie Valley. In fact, the issues at hand are broader in scope than the adverse effects of a pipeline. The Dene see their struggle as one dealing with their right to be a self-determining people living on their own land as they have always done. To express their point of view, the Dene have issued a "Statement of Rights" which asserts their claim to their ancestral lands. The Government and the oil companies in turn have been pressing for their rights and interests. The result has been such government commissions as the Mackenzie Valley Pipeline Inquiry which has sought, through discussion and debate, to resolve the many complex issues involved.[2]

The important point to be made here is that debate can take place and that the people of the Dene Nation have taken advantage of their right to make their position known to those with decision-making power. For this reason, it is important for *you* to learn to express your opinions intelligently and effectively.

Opinion papers are similar to both the expository papers you worked with in Chapter 3 and the persuasion papers you will read in Chapter 8. All three are organized in much the same way, opening, as a rule, with a thesis statement (implied or clearly stated) followed by supporting information and arguments. The differences are these:

1. An expository paper attempts to communicate information.
2. An opinion paper attempts to convince readers of the validity of an opinion.
3. A persuasion paper attempts to motivate readers to act in some manner.

Here are some examples of opinion papers.

I

COME BACK, KRAZY KAT

You may not have noticed; but the comic strip is dead. Newspapers still carry something referred to as comic strips, but these are just a pallid remnant of the former art. When was the last time you lay on the floor with the funnies spread out in front of you like a gaudy carpet?

In 1896, W. R. Hearst trumpeted the New York *Journal's* first comic section as "eight pages of iridescent, polychromatic effulgence that makes the rainbow look like a piece of lead pipe." The comic strip was conceived, and thrived, as a creature of newspaper circulation wars. But times change, and for the last 40 years every cost rise and economic hiccup has been inspiration for newspaper editors to reduce the size and number of their strips. Television, they say, has destroyed comics as a readership draw.

Until 1940, the typical Sunday comic covered a full-size newspaper page—approximately 15 by 20 inches [38 × 51 cm], which makes 300 square inches [1936 sq cm]. Today, the average Sunday comic is printed at about four by nine inches [10 × 23 cm], which is 36 square inches [232 sq cm] or 12% of the area of an old Sunday page.

Besides being visually unexciting, miniaturized comics do not have much scope. A modern Sunday page, such as *Shoe* or *Garfield*, contains four to six tiny panels, with a maximum of 15 words per panel. In one of Frederick Opper's turn-of-the-century *Happy Hooligan* strips, each of the 12 panels could contain three or four balloons, with up to 50 words each. Happy Hooligan was a well meaning simpleton, with a tin-can hat and a knack for finding trouble; his page was a complete skit, a comedy of manners that is impossible in today's strips.

In its golden age, the comic strip was a vehicle for more than burlesque. Milton Caniff, in his 1930s drama *Terry and the Pirates,* portrayed the crackle of attraction between the sexes, the love between friends and the grief of death; his seedy oriental settings evoked the mood and tension of a Graham Greene novel. George Herriman's *Krazy Kat* started as the misadventures of a cat, a mouse and a dog; but the poetically twisted language made the most touching, ethereal comic strip of all time.

This is not to say that contemporary cartoonists are doing bad work. On the contrary, the level of craftsmanship has never been higher for it takes an artistic acrobat to do anything in so confining a format. But it is a very different art.

The resonant mix for character and conflict has been replaced by the rapid 1-2-3 knockout of the punch line. This is a hellishly difficult form of humour to write and can be rapier sharp, as in *Doonesbury*. But it can also be formulaic, as in such strips as *B.C.* and *Animal Crackers*, where the laugh line is yet another clever insult or wry reflection by a perpetual loser.

I have observed that people no longer know how to read the old strips. I can tell by the rapid sweeps of their eyes that they are making the relentless push toward the boffo payoff; when there is none, they snort and change the subject. It seems we have lost the taste for entertainment that requires involvement and effort. In the age of T.V. laugh tracks and fast food, comics are also predigested for the consumer.

There is no use in decrying the trend or damning modern sensibilities. The nature of popular art is to reflect the lives of the people to whom it is sold. This nonetheless leaves us dinosaurs, who loved the funnies as they were, with little else to do but weep and gnash our teeth.

Some book publishers, spurred by European examples, have recently begun to issue hardcover comic strip books and adult comic magazines. If comics have a future, it seems likely to be in these formats. Meanwhile, the old strips—and some new ones—are beginning to appear, framed, in art galleries. But this is the veneration imparted to a popular art form after its vitality has gone.[3]

—Arn Saba

II

AFTER I, THE DELUGE

When I was a lad, I did not serve a term as office boy to an attorney's firm. It was one of a number of omissions. I did, however, work for a while as a file clerk in a credit agency. Since I was sixteen years old at the time and had been graduated from high school, I knew a great deal and had opinions on a variety of subjects that I thought anyone else in the office would consider it a privilege to hear. I also thought that I discerned flaws in the way the office was run. One fine day I was advised to keep a civil tongue in my head. That meant "Be respectful to your elders," or less gently interpreted, "Shut up." Although I did not know the word at the time (nobody did), I prioritized my interests, even as Jimmy Carter many years later suggested that the Democrats prioritize their platform. Having a job was more highly prioritized than not having a job. Shut up I did.

I now take a civil tongue to mean much more than that. Mere politeness is part of it, though the temptation to place *mere* before politeness ought to be resisted. The alternative to a code of conduct is, if not chaos, certainly confusion and embarrassment, and language is conduct. Not that I am arguing for freezing the language. I would hate to take American English out of a cryogenic compartment in a hundred years and find, after the ice is chipped away and the language has thawed, that it sounds as it does now. I think I would put it back in.

How *does* it sound now? It does not sound civil.

■ A scholar writes, "Our children currently have no viable role models to emulate." Heroes they would have been called not long ago. And heroines. But that is too straightforward:

"Father, I cannot tell a lie. With my little hatchet, I chopped down the cherry tree."

"I'm proud of you, George. I was saying to your mother only last week that one day our son will be a role model for generations of Americans yet unborn."

■ A New York specialty shop advertises items "for all the giftees on your June list." I hope it spreads to Scotland:

"Wha hae ye there, lass?"

"'Tis a wee giftie for the giftee."

"Aye, would some power the giftee gie us ..."

■ "Scientists, investigating spontaneous glucagon secretion in the immediate postnatal period, study groups of infants cross-sectionally and longitudinally." Cross-sectionally should not alarm anyone: it means at the same age. Longitudinally means as they grow older.

■ A man is put in jail in Dubuque, Iowa. It isn't called the jail any longer; it's the law enforcement center. Time is served there longitudinally.

■ When the soil-collecting scoop on Viking I on Mars fails to function, an anomaly team goes to work to set it right. No hits, no runs, no anomalies.

■ Washington churns out its usual nonsense. The chief of the United States Capitol Police posts a notice: "Vehicles will be parked chronologically as they enter the lot" (1975 models in this corner and 1973 models over there). The Undersecretary of the Treasury, Edwin H. Yeo III, is asked about additional loans to New York City: "If we find the reasonable probability of repayment is slipping away from us, then we'll have to respond in terms of extension of future credit." If they don't pay what they owe, we won't lend them any more.

■ A weather broadcaster in Marlboro, Massachusetts, calls small storms stormettes. Massachusetts come from a large Massachus.

■ In Kansas City, Missouri, television viewers are told about "the heavy storm system that performed over our area last night." Music by Rossini.

■ An airline stewardess urges her passengers to "have a nice day in Cincinnati or wherever your final destination may be taking you," and an investment company writes: "We have exceptional game plan capabilities together with strict concerns for programming successful situations." My final destination is taking me far away from game plans, capabilities, programming, and situations, there to have a nice day.

■ A professor, Sam Schoenbaum of Northwestern, explains on ABC television why William Shakespeare was so eminent a playwright: "He had a tremendous commitment to his own medium, the stage." All the world's a medium, but the professor appears to believe that Shakespeare could have left the theater for television or Hollywood.

That is how the language sounds now. A civil tongue, on the other hand, means to me a language that is not bogged down in jargon, not puffed up with false dignity, not studded with trick phrases that have lost their meaning. It is not falsely exciting, is not patronizing, does not conceal the smallness and triteness of ideas by clothing them in language ever more grandiose, does not seek out increasingy complicated constructions, does not weigh us down with the gelatinous verbiage of Washington and the social sciences. It treats errors in spelling and usage with a decent tolerance but does not take them lightly. It does not consider "We're there because that's where it's at" the height of cleverness. It is not merely a stream of sound that disk jockeys produce, in which what is said does not matter so long as it is said without pause. It is direct, specific, concrete, vigorous, colorful, subtle, and imaginative when it should be, and as lucid and eloquent as we are able to make it. It is something to revel in and enjoy.[4]

—Edwin Newman

Student Composition 7A

TOMORROW WILL BE BETTER

"...If the last 50 000 years of man's existence were divided into lifetimes of approximately 62 years each, there have been 800 such lifetimes. Of these 800, fully 650 were spent in caves.

Only during the last seventy lifetimes has it been possible to communicate effectively from one lifetime to another—as writing made it possible to do. Only during the last 6 lifetimes did masses of men see the printed word. Only during the last four has it been possible to measure time with any precision. Only in the last 2 has anyone anywhere used an electric motor. And the overwhelming majority of all the material goods we use in daily life today have been developed within the present, the 800th lifetime."*

By beginning with this quotation from Alvin Toffler's *Future Shock*, I want to emphasize how far human beings have come in such a short time and to show that the whole trend of human life has been upward. During their long history, people have constantly progressed, and I believe that Canadians are no different from others. People will continue to progress, and life in the future is going to get better, especially in Canada.

The first way that life will be better is in material things. Scientists have already developed thousands of new products that are waiting in the wings for us to call them. Already computers can provide hundreds of services to every household and do chores ranging from paying bills to helping the children with their homework. Optical fibers offer new, cheaper, and more durable ways of communicating. New building materials promise longlasting, carefree luxury at less cost. New engines and transportation systems should make our old, heavy, dirty, and inefficient cars, trains, and buses obsolete in short order. I don't think anyone questions the ability of scientists and inventors to make our lives better if we can afford what they offer.

Some people are worried about whether or not the Canadian political and economic system can provide the kind of structure that will make it possible for us to use the new inventions. They say that science is at least twenty years ahead of social science, and it's in the realm of social science that Canada will fall down. I don't agree with that either. Canadians have always been imaginative, creative, and flexible and above all adaptable. But in addition to that, they are beginning to look to experts and planners in social science just as they have looked for years to scientific experts.

How do you feel as you read this long introductory quote without knowing why the writer used it and what it is supposed to prove? What might be better?

The writer has been inconsistent in the spelling out of numbers. What would you suggest as policy for a passage with lots of numbers in it?

Now you know what the quotation is supposed to prove. What better organization might the writer have used?

How effective is the thesis statement? Are you clear on what the writer will try to solve?

How do you feel about such clichés as "waiting in the wings"? What other image might be more appropriate here? Why is this one not appropriate?

The writer did not give clues to the structure of the paper, or an overview. What are the main divisions?

Why does the writer not offer proof, authority, or other justification for this idea?

How effective is the change at this point to the second section of the paper? How would you label this section?

Point out some informal phrases and constructions here and elsewhere. How do you feel about them in this kind of paper?

A model for this aspect of North American society is Herman Kahn, the director of the Hudson Institute, who works in a "Think Tank" with dozens of scientists and social scientists on problems ranging from disarmament to foreign aid to new sources of energy. "Centre of Excellence" is the term used for the Canadian equivalent by the Science Council of Canada. An example is the Sheridan Park Research Centre in Mississauga, Ontario, organized to improve industrial capabilities and to direct industrial research in such problems as the disposal of dangerous chemicals and the nonpolluting disposal of sludge. Supported by the Ontario government with some funding by private industry, Sheridan Park is an example of Canadian efforts to combine social awareness with industrial development. I don't believe any problem is too great when we go after it this way.

Some people are worried that Canada will go downhill because of the energy crisis and its dependence on foreign energy. I don't think this is a major problem. In fact, I think the only reason it's a problem even now is that we are too humane to use the substitute power we could easily get in a few years. Think what would happen to all the oil-producing countries if we suddenly stopped buying oil! And if we went all out on solar energy, kinetic energy from windmills, tidal energy from ocean installations, gasahol, woodburning conversions, and atomic power plants, and coal conversions, not to mention oil shale and even methane from manure, we could leave OPEC in the lurch right now, or at least within ten years.

Of course, the new demands of the developing nations are a problem, especially when they control raw materials we need and when our money has gone down in value. Canada is working though, through the International Monetary Fund and other agencies, to give those countries both political and economic stability and to help them build industries of their own, so they won't demand that we continue giving them handouts.**

The Canadian Industrial Development Agency funds high technology programs in other countries. Its objectives are to fund and encourage projects in Third World countries which in turn purchase high technology components from Canada. Thus both Canada and some of these developing countries benefit and work together cooperatively on their development.

One other thing people worry about is that Canadians won't face the challenge of the future. They are concerned about the fact that our materialistic way of life provides for everybody, creating a society of individuals who are uninterested in important things

What kind of image does "works in a Think Tank" evoke? How would you rewrite this sentence?

If the writer has not acquired this kind of information from general reading, where might he or she find it?

What justification, or proof, does the writer offer for this belief?

Should the writer define any of these terms?

and lack commitment to their country's future. Marshall McLuhan commented: "Canada is the only country in the world that knows how to live without an identity."

If there's one thing I'm sure of, it's the fact that Canadians will rise to any challenge put to them. When the going gets tough, the tough get going, and Canadians do just that. They can tighten their belts if they have to, use less energy if they must, and get along without some of the luxuries they took for granted. I think, however, that science will keep providing more ideas and products, the political and economic system will change and adjust, the energy crisis will go away, the developing nations will—with our help—begin to build for themselves rather than trying to steal from us.

All of these forces will make life in Canada better in the future, even if there's a lag for a few years. I don't think any of these forces will fail in the long run, but if they do, I'll fall back on the Canadian citizen to meet the challenge. If necessary, we can start all over, and that might give us a better life, too.

—Vernon Marks

*Alvin Toffler, Future Shock (New York: Random House, 1970),p.15.
**Ron Chernow, "The IMF, Roughest Bank in Town," *Saturday Review,* February 3, 1979, p. 17.

†Marshall McLuhan quoted in Laurence J. Peter, *Peter's Quotations* (Toronto: Bantam Books, 1979), p.67.

Another Kind of Opinion Paper—Satire

The preceding three examples are varied in tone and development. The tones range from humourous to serious, and the methods of development include support by statistics, factual examples, specific details, and personal observations. However, these three pieces of writing have one main point in common. Each writer states specifically the thesis or opinion which is the basis for the piece of writing.

Also based on opinion, but very different in tone and development, is the barbed humour known as satire. Satire exposes common follies or weaknesses to public view, with the intention of making people aware of how ridiculous some ideas or actions really are. A satiric writer often appears on the surface to be making one point, but uses devices like irony and ridicule so that the reader comes to realize that the writer actually supports the opposite point of view.

Read the two satiric pieces which follow, and decide what opinion each writer really wants to convey.

III

LOTOLAND

Little Debbie Gimbeau has never tasted avocado and shrimp. She does not own an Arabian pony and has never been to Martinique. Unlike her schoolmates, she has never known a home with a sauna, has never been chauffeured to fencing class, has never studied Fine Art in Siena. Life, for Debbie Gimbeau, is fraught with hardship, and she is not alone. There are thousands of Debbie Gimbeaus—children who wake each day to bowls of Shreddies and paper routes, children who wear orlon sweaters and who have no scuba tanks. They are the unlucky ones. They are children whose parents have never won a lottery.

Once they were referred to as the underprivileged. Now, in the wake of the economic revolution that has swept the country, unfortunates such as Debbie's parents are known as the New Losers, the people left behind by the laws of chance. Their existence might be traced to 1969 when an amendment to the Criminal Code exempted the government from antigambling laws. More accurately, their origins can be found in the landmark federal budget that a few years ago ushered in a new economic age, transforming Canada from a land of long shots into what Jimmy the Greek calls "just a society of lucky stiffs."

It was in the spring of 1981 that the federal government abolished the economy and launched the most elaborate lottery scheme the world has ever seen. Although a bold move, it was a decision that came as no surprise to anyone; for years it had been apparent that the only thing the government could do with any degree of efficiency was run lotteries. Singularly helpless at fighting inflation and unemployment, strangely unmoved by the disappearance of the dollar and Québec, Ottawa nonetheless managed to persuade overtaxed citizens to spend $10 on lottery tickets that had a one in 800 000 chance of winning—people were twice as likely to be hit by a falling satellite—but which paid off at odds one-tenth of that. Clearly, with the chutzpah to con an entire population, the government was wasting its time on pedestrian concerns like inflation.

As economic revolutions go, this one was surprisingly simple. Federal taxes were raised a mere 10 percent, thereby giving Ottawa control of all the money in the country. This capital was then invested in high-risk, high-return commodities. With these monies the government inaugurated a massive series of million-dollar lotteries. Held every 15 seconds, the draws corresponded precisely to the number of Canadians in the most recent census. In theory, everyone could become a millionaire.

Has the gamble paid off? Preliminary indicators are that it has. Department stores report that sales of ascots, blazers and white yachting caps have sky-rocketed, while a French businessman, speaking from a Paris kennel, estimates that poodle exports to Canada have tripled. And a recent survey has shown that 80 percent of all Canadian households now subscribe to *Country Life* and *Gourmet* magazines.

The new economic system is not without its flaws, and inflation is certainly one of them.

But there is a bigger problem. While certain lucky lotophiles have won grand prizes three or four times, the sad fact remains that there are people, like the Gimbeaus, who do not win things, however favourable the odds. "Maybe I'm jinxed," says Clement Baddleboine, a Vancouver accountant and father of four, "but I've never won anything in my life—not a door prize, not a raffle, not even a coin toss. And now my children are paying for it."

The plight of the losing class is indeed a tragic one. While neighbours and friends give charity balls, take courses in Japanese flower-arranging and attend tennis camps, the habitual holders of unlucky numbers are forced to wear imitation Wallabies and count their change in restaurants. "Sometimes I don't think I can bear it," says Rhona Geffler, a petite blonde who wears seven rabbits' feet and who, after two years of empty hopes, is physically incapable of uncrossing her fingers. "When I think of the chintzy Laura Ashley prints, the crummy Nina Ricci perfume, the tacky Gucci handbags, all the junk that the nouveau lucky squanders its millions on, it makes me sick. And I bet not one of them could answer a lousy skill-testing question."

Sad but true. As lotomania and its countless variants take the country by storm, reason, it seems, has given way to "the breaks." Whether passing fad or new reality, luck is now the cornerstone of Canadian society.

Students were the first to feel the effect of loto-consciousness. As high school literacy levels dip lower and lower, it had become increasingly difficult for universities to screen applicants—most students cannot read, much less write, an entrance exam. Selection of candidates by lottery has proven to be a happy solution. "It's a good system," says a Moncton high school principal, Hiram Needles. "It teaches these kids what life is all about."

Hospitals were the next to follow suit. In an effort to relieve overcrowded and understaffed emergency wards, accident victims are asked upon arrival to pick up a number from an orderly's hat. Lucky winners are wheeled immediately to surgery. The less fortunate are thanked for expressing an interest in modern medicine and asked if they would care to donate their bodies to science.

In a precedent-setting case a Supreme Court judge asked defence and prosecuting attorneys to draw lots rather than waste time presenting their arguments. The decision has met with criticism, but its supporters are vocal. "Don't knock it," says Sammy Scarpelli, recently found not guilty on 37 counts of murder. "You ain't gonna win if God don't love ya."

Odds are, the demands of the losing class will continue to fall on deaf ears. The insufferably lucky have, thus far, proven unsympathetic to the sad predicament of the Debbie Gimbeaus. It is hardly surprising; it is a common belief among winners that in order to win, somebody has to lose. For the luckless, there remains little hope. In a stormy confrontation with New Loser protesters, the new prime minister—his name was picked from a barrel last week—outlined his policy in a terse statement. "That's the way the cookie crumbles," he said. For Debbie Gimbeau and the other strangers to fortune, the future indeed looks bleak.[5]

—David MacFarlane

IV

HOW TO DRESS LIKE A LOSER

Listen: Elizabeth Storms didn't make the rules, so don't blame her when she tells you that what you're wearing right now isn't doing your career any good. I mean, if you think your powder-blue leisure suit and your white penny-loafers express the Inner You, that's O.K. with Ms. Storms. All she's saying—

and she's paid to say it by companies such as London Life and sober-sided law factories such as Thomson Rogers, in Toronto—is that people who dress like John Turner tend to get treated like former or potential finance ministers, and people who dress like aluminum-siding salesmen tend to get doors slammed in their faces.

Ms. Storms is only 23, a University of Toronto psychology dropout who spent two years studying marketing and design in Boston. Also, she's got an entrepreneurial streak. And so, instead of competing with arts graduates for some underpaid job as a proofreader in a publishing house, she formed a company last year called Storms, and hung out her shingle as an "image consultant." Yes, we know it sounds silly. But silly or not, she's now pulling down a good income advising employees of various large companies how to dress.

Her first client was a large and stately Toronto law firm, which asked Ms. Storms to talk to the clerical staff. Too many of the women were turning up in jeans and low-cut dresses—dreadfully bad for the appropriate image. "I think they hired me because it's so much easier for an outsider to talk to employees about the way they dress," she says. "From the boss, they'd resent it. Coming from me, they listen."

Analyzing the accoutrements of everyone from CBC television hosts to legal stenographers has given Ms. Storms a wealth of insight into how and what your clothes communicate to other people. Bow ties communicate dishonesty, for instance; blue pinstripe suits and thin gold watches communicate power.

Ms. Storms is thus not only an expert on how to Dress for Success; she's also eloquent on the subject of how *not* to dress. In the interests of accentuating the negative, then, we present on these pages Ms. Storm's choices of the worst things a business person can wear. Read and heed, or prepare yourself for a demotion to the mail room.[6]

—Alexander Ross

(*Activity 7A*)

Discussing the Opinion Papers

The entire process of supporting opinions is so complex that Daniel Webster once said when complimented on a speech of opinion, "I have been preparing for that speech all of my life." Your opinions and your thinking processes have indeed grown throughout your life, but a look at how to support an opinion may help you think and write more clearly.

1. The purpose or thesis statement of an opinion paper must clearly state the opinion that is to be supported. What is the thesis statement, or opinion, of each of these papers?

2. Although opinion papers are based on opinions, they must include concrete and specific examples and facts. Have the professional writing

samples and the student samples all used concrete, specific examples and facts?

3. The introduction to this chapter suggests that many opinions are controversial and that sometimes a person with a strong opinion encounters opposition. How controversial are the subjects in the model papers? Under what circumstances might any of the foregoing papers encounter opposition?

4. Working with a partner or small group, take one of the thesis statements of the two student samples and make a list of the kinds of concrete specifics and facts you might use to support such an idea. Jot down the outline you might develop if you were writing the paper.

5. Satire is one of the most interesting and readable ways writers communicate their opinions. Discuss some opinions you have about life in Canada and think of how you might present one of these opinions satirically. Use some of the techniques the writer used in the last model.

Selecting Valid Opinions to Support

Perhaps you've heard someone end an argument by saying, "Well, everyone is entitled to an opinion." Yes, in *some* cases a person is entitled to an opinion. In matters of taste, for which there are no "right" or "wrong" answers, everyone is entitled to decide such questions as "who has the best personality" or "what is the most enjoyable sport." But an argument on a matter of taste is silly; people should discuss such an issue to reveal why they think as they do, rather than to convince anyone that theirs is the "correct" opinion.

Matters of fact. On matters of fact, such as whether Québec or British Columbia reach farther north, no one can have an opinion. To support, discuss, or argue a matter of fact is a waste of time. Look up the information and set the record straight. Québec reaches farther north than British Columbia and that's all there is to it.

Matters of judgment. One can legitimately argue and write about matters of judgment. Although people may not agree on a matter of judgment, as they must on matters of fact, a person can prove that an opinion is reasonable or believable. But even in this area, some people are not entitled to an opinion. Those who have little background on a subject or who have not taken the trouble to become informed are not entitled to discuss it. To support an opinion one must investigate the facts and then make a judgment.

Three kinds of opinion. As you prepare to select a subject for your opinion paper, consider the major areas in which you have had experience. Then think in terms of three kinds of judgments:

1. *Generalization*—What conclusion or generalization can you draw from a series of facts or events? For example, few students come to see the school play, *Macbeth*; no one tries out for the essay contest; the debate team is defeated in the first round of eliminations.

What do these facts mean? Perhaps "Our students are no longer interested in cultural activities," or "Interest in speech is declining," or "Homework no longer leaves time for extracurricular activities," or "Our school spirit isn't very good." Whatever your opinion, you must prove that you have made a valid generalization from the facts. The more supporting facts you can provide, the more believable your generalization.

2. *Evaluation*—What is it worth? Football requires a player to practise at least fifteen hours a week for three months each year. Are its values worth the time? What is football worth? Or, for another example, you've just read *Lord of the Flies*. How much time did you invest? Was it worth it?

3. *Interpretation*—What does it mean? The residents in your town have just voted down a proposal for a new library. What does this vote mean in terms of inflation, the prevailing goals and values, voter turn-out, the future development of the town, and the other needs of the town? Or, the valedictorian, a top tennis player with an outstanding personality, was just turned down by McGill University. What does it mean in terms of university admissions generally, McGill, your school, and the student?

(*Activity 7B*)

Recognizing Different Kinds of Opinions

1. Read the editorials in your daily newspaper for three days. Copy the title and the thesis statement of each. Come to class prepared to discuss the kind of opinion (generalization, evaluation, or interpretation) that each represents. See whether the newspaper has based any editorials on matters of taste or matters of fact.

2. Bring to class three carefully worded opinions you would like to base a paper on. Be sure they do not concern matters of taste or matters of fact. With your teacher's help, determine the best one to use as a basis for the Major Writing Assignment for this chapter.

Patterns of Reasoning

The two basic kinds of reasoning are *induction* and *deduction*. Writing an opinion paper is, in a sense, an exercise in reasoning. You may decide to present specific evidence to support your opinion and lead the reader to draw certain conclusions. This process is called inductive reasoning. Or, you may begin by stating your opinion and, by a pattern of deductive reasoning, examine specific instances in the light of that statement.

Inductive reasoning.   Induction can be visualized as a triangle sitting on its base with the vertex, or point, up.

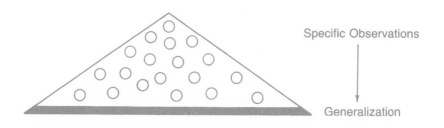

The movement of thought is from the top down. In using induction, you begin with individual observations (the point of the triangle) from which you draw a conclusion or generalization (the base line). The following sample demonstrates one of the pitfalls of inductive reasoning:

> There was once upon a time a census officer who had to record the names of all householders in a certain Welsh village. The first that he questioned was called William Williams; so were the second, third, fourth. ... At last he said to himself: 'This is tedious; evidently they are all called William Williams. I shall put them down so and take a holiday." But he was wrong; there was just one whose name was John Jones.[1]
>
> —Bertrand Russell

The census officer begins with separate observations (the four people whose names he checked personally) and then makes an "inductive leap" to what is called a "hasty generalization"—"They are all called William Williams." You recognize at once the weakness of that generalization, but do you recognize the nature of your inductive leap when you say, "Those North-siders are really poor sports. We played them last year and they hissed when we won"? This is called stereotyping, and it is another example of an error in inductive reasoning.

Deductive reasoning.   Deduction can be visualized as a triangle with its base up and the vertex down.

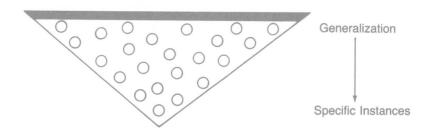

The movement of thought, again, is from the top down. In using deduction, you begin with a broad generalization (the top side) and apply it to a specific instance (the vertex). The following sample demonstrates some of the pitfalls of deductive reasoning:

At their first meeting, Sherlock Holmes said to Dr. Watson, "You have been in Afghanistan, I perceive." Later he explained how he knew:

> "From long habit the train of thoughts ran so swiftly through my mind that I arrived at the conclusion without being conscious of intermediate steps. There were such steps, however. The train of reasoning ran, 'Here is a gentleman of a medical type, but with the air of a military man. Clearly an army doctor, then. He has just come from the tropics, for his face is dark, and that is not the natural tint of his skin, for his wrists are fair. He has undergone hardship and sickness, as his haggard face says clearly. His left arm has been injured. He holds it in a stiff and unnatural manner. Where in the tropics could an English army doctor have seen such hardship and got his arm wounded? Clearly in Afghanistan."[8]
>
> —Arthur Conan Doyle

Holmes' reasoning *seems* to be very good and it's great fun to read, but would you be willing to accept his generalizations and his logic?

Anyone with the air of a military man is or has been a soldier.
Watson has the air of a military man.
Therefore, Watson was a soldier.

Anyone with a suntan has been in the tropics.
Watson has a suntan.
Therefore, Watson has been in the tropics.

Anyone who holds his arm in a stiff and unnatural manner has been wounded.
Watson holds his arm in a stiff and unnatural manner.
Therefore, Watson has been wounded.

And finally:

Any English army doctor with a tanned and haggard face and a wounded arm must have been wounded in Afghanistan.
Watson is an English army doctor, has such a face and such an arm.
Therefore, Watson was wounded in Afghanistan.

(*Activity 7C*)

Locating the Reasoning Patterns

Read the following items carefully, locate the main idea in each, and determine whether the conclusion is justified. Write any sentences necessary to complete the thought pattern, as in the examples in the preceding section. Be prepared to discuss in class whether or not the reasoning is logical and acceptable.

1. Fish have no openings on their backs, and no bird is big enough to swallow a man. Therefore, you could not have seen what you have reported you saw.

2. When truth and error have fair play, truth always wins. In order to have fair play for truth, you must play fair with error. Therefore, when people who promote false ideas are permitted to present their opinions, truth will win out in the end.

3. One of the concerns of the Canadian Government is to create jobs in the North and open that part of the country to economic development. An oil pipeline through the Mackenzie Valley would provide jobs. Therefore, the Dene Nation should give its support to the construction of a pipeline.

4. Because of the delicate ecological balance of Canada's north, oil companies should not be allowed to build pipelines which will interfere with the plant, animal and human populations which have inhabited this land for countless generations.

5. Freedom of speech and freedom of the press are very important in democratic life. In order to be sure you do not suppress good ideas, you must accept the expression of all ideas. Therefore, people must be allowed to speak even when their ideas are unpopular.

6. Many provinces need new sources of money. Half of the provinces find various lotteries a profitable source of income. Therefore, the rest of the provinces should institute lotteries.

7. The idea of wealth without work is non-productive and harmful. Government-approved lotteries promote the idea that wealth without work is possible. Therefore, the provinces should not approve lotteries.

8. Our society depends heavily on technology. Technology provides us with many conveniences. Because these convenience free us from work and effort in daily life, we are becoming morally and spiritually bankrupt.

9. The alternative to a code of conduct is, if not chaos, certainly confusion and embarrassment. Language is conduct. Therefore, it is important to have a pretty strict standard for acceptable language.

10. If you add -*ettes* to the word "storm," to mean "small storms" then probably any word that ends in -*etts* or -*ettes* has been made from another word in the same way. Therefore, Massachusetts means "small Massachus."

11. Because of our complex twentieth century society, it costs more to have our cars fixed.

12. Because everybody is taken care of, Canadians are uninterested in important things and lack incentive.

Fallacies of inductive thinking.   From examining the examples in Activity 7C, you must have become aware of how often and how subtly you use "logical" reasoning and how difficult it is to keep from becoming illogical. Errors in reasoning are called fallacies. The following sections describe briefly several of the basic fallacies of inductive thinking.

"Inductive leap" leading to a false generalization.   The basic pattern of induction is to observe a large number of specific cases and then "leap" to a general conclusion. Thus a scientist may have burned several hundred pieces of copper and then generalized, "Copper burns with a green flame." But because he has not tested every piece of copper in the universe, he cannot be absolutely certain that all copper everywhere burns with a green flame. He has made an inductive leap because he is *reasonably* sure. The Welsh census taker in the story on page 150, made an error because he based his generalization on too few observations. How many times do people generalize from too few cases: "Vans are no good. Ours got no mileage at all."

Stereotyping. This is a common fallacy of inductive reasoning. It is similar to hasty generalization. It is the mistake you make when you assign a certain quality to all members of a group, ignoring their individual differences. "I wouldn't bother with anyone who lives up on the hill. They're all snobs" is an example of stereotyping. Try to be aware of this fallacy in your everyday life—in conversations with friends, in judgments you make yourself, in the newspapers and books you read. Prejudice results from the error of thinking in stereotypes. Every time you say, or hear someone else say, "Oh, what can you expect. They're all alike!" one of you is making a statement about an entire group without considering individual differences among the members of that group.

Post hoc, ergo propter hoc.   Translated into English, this phrase means "After this, therefore because of this." Another name for this fallacy is "mistaken causal relationship." It designates the fallacy of assuming that, because event B followed event A, B must have been caused by A. "A black cat ran in front of my car. A little later I had an accident. All on account of that cat!" "I wore my T-shirt wrong side out for the Upton game, and we won. From now on, I'm going to wear my T-shirt wrong side out for a game."

Ignoring the question.   There are many different ways to ignore a question. One way is to change the subject: "I don't care whether good grades help on university and college admissions or not; a fellow gets an awful lot out of athletics." Another way is to shift from the issue to the character or personality of an opponent: "Here I am discussing the values of athletics with Smiley, and he's never even made first team. How would he know anything about it?" Or, you can use an emotional appeal that may have nothing to do with the argument: "The value of athletics? It's the very lifeblood of the free enterprise system. Competition. That's it!"

Fallacies of deductive reasoning. As was explained on page 151, in deductive reasoning you begin with a generalization and apply it to a specific instance. This kind of reasoning takes the form of a syllogism in which two statements (the major premise and the minor premise) are made and a conclusion is drawn from them. See page 151 for examples of the syllogisms Sherlock Holmes may have used to arrive at his conclusions. The following sections describe some common fallacies in deductive thinking.

> Everything in the paper is true.
> I read the story in the paper.
> Therefore, the story is true.

And what happens if the conclusion is not stated so that something inside the smaller circle also falls within the larger circle?

> Gold is very heavy.
> This rock is very heavy.
> Therefore, this rock is gold.

The conclusion, of course, is false because the minor premise is weak: something other than gold may be very heavy; consequently the rock may fall outside of the "gold" circle.

False Syllogism. To understand the basic pattern of the syllogism, think of the major premise as setting up a large circle. (All human beings are mortal.) Then think of the minor premise as setting up a smaller circle inside the larger circle. (Socrates is a human being.) Finally, think of the conclusion as indicating that the statement in the larger circle must apply to whatever is in the smaller circle. (Therefore, Socrates is mortal.) But what happens if the major premise is false?

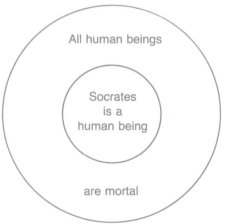

Either-or. Probably the most famous example of the either-or fallacy is Patrick Henry's "Give me liberty or give me death." The famous patriot was suggesting that only these two alternatives existed. This assumption, that in a given situation only two alternatives exist, is called the "either-or" fallacy.

Words with changing meanings. Words often change meanings depending upon the context in which they are used; if you are not alert, you may be caught in a semantic trap. "Anna is very *smooth*. We need a *smoothly* operating student council. We should elect Anna president." In its first use, *smooth* means "diplomatic, gracious—perhaps sophisticated or tricky." In the second use, it means "efficient." The reasoning is illogical.

Begging the question. In this fallacy, the arguer assumes as true something that must be proven. "Our unwieldy Bill of Rights should be changed." (Is it really unwieldy? Prove it!) "The least valuable course in our high-school curriculum, health, should be cut to one day a week." (Is it really least valuable? Prove it!) "Shakespeare's sonnets are great literature because Shakespeare was a great writer and he wrote them." (The arguer assumes that a great writer must always write great literature. That the sonnets themselves are great must be proven.)

Non sequitur. A sequel is a book or an event that follows another. A *non sequitur* is simply a statement that doesn't follow from what has gone before. "Sally Cinema is gorgeous, and she recommends Cruncho cereal so it must be great." (Cruncho cereal may have little to do with her looks.) "Charley McKinney is a great quarterback. I'm going to vote for him for Student Council president."(The last sentence implies that greatness on the football field signifies greatness as a student representative. It doesn't necessarily follow.)

A knowledge of these basic fallacies of reasoning will be very helpful to you now and when you are working with Chapter 8, Argumentation and Persuasion. As you read the articles and the student compositions, watch for patterns of reasoning and be alert for any fallacies in the arguments presented.

(Activity 7D)

Finding Obvious Fallacies

Locate and list the fallacies in the following statement. Bring your list to class and be prepared to discuss it.

"You want to know what I think about cheerleading clubs in high school? Well, I think they're wonderful. Yes, I think they're very beneficial. I've been in one for two years, and I've had a wonderful time. Certainly, that proves they're very beneficial.

"Let me give you an example: I went out for cheerleading and only three weeks later I was elected prom queen. I certainly think cheerleading clubs are very important.

"I see you're quoting Sandy Barron in your article too. Why, she doesn't know anything about cheerleading. She's just a little grind who studies all the time. Well, I look at it this way: either you're a grind and study all the time or else you're a normal, well-balanced person interested in cheerleading. You're either one way or the other—and who wants to be like Sandy?

"Why, I've even heard that she's so interested in study that she's going to go to summer school when she doesn't have to. That proves she's crazy, doesn't it?

"This is the way I look at it: school is supposed to produce a well-rounded individual. In order to be well-rounded, you've got to be in extracurricular things, so I like all kinds of extracurricular things, especially cheerleading. Besides, who likes to study anyway? Ask anybody. Go ahead: ask all of my friends. (But don't ask Sandy, she wouldn't know.)"

Qualifying Your Statements

A broad, general statement can be a sign of fuzzy thinking or of an intent to deceive. However, careful use of the English language enables you to say exactly what you mean. You can make a statement more precise, even more truthful, by qualifying it in some way. You do this by adding to the statement a word, phrase, or clause. In this way, you change the statement enough to make it convey a more exact meaning.

GENERAL STATEMENT

St. Stephen's Secondary School is the best school in this province.

QUALIFIED BY ADDING

A *word:* St. Stephen's Secondary School is the best private school in this province.
A *phrase:* According to the principal, St. Stephen's is the best school in this province.
A *clause:* St. Stephen's is the best school in this province if you happen to be a straight A student.

The next time you are tempted to make a broad, general statement ask yourself, "What is it that I really want to say?" Then qualify your statement so that you cannot be easily misunderstood.

Activity 7E

Qualifying Opinions for Exactness

Take each of the following "opinions" and qualify it in such a way as to make it more precise. Without naming the grammatical structures you used, just record the qualifying words and notice the difference they make.

1. The government hurts poor people by destroying their homes and building roads for people who can afford automobiles.
2. Life is harder in Canadian cities today than it was fifty years ago.
3. Police officers are treated unfairly.
4. Canadian conservation policies are failures.
5. Every day in every way we're getting better and better.
6. The government is not responsive to the changing needs of people.
7. Adults don't like the music of young people.
8. Science will solve all our problems.
9. Cable television is the hope of the future.
10. Political figures are highly honoured today.
11. Insurance laws are unfair to teenage drivers.

Good English in an Opinion Paper

One definition of "good" English is that it is the language which, in a given situation, communicates best. A message may be grammatically perfect and rhetorically eloquent, but if it is not understood by readers or listeners, then it hasn't done the job the writer or speaker intended, and it's not "good" English. The opposite is also true. A message may be phrased in broken, almost illiterate language, but if it does the job the writer or speaker intended, in that sense it's good. Of course, from other points of view— for example, from the standpoint of permanent literary value—it might be poor. Some people, such as the writer of the sample you read on pages 140-141, insist that language cannot be effective if it is "bogged down" in jargon, or "puffed up" with inflated words.

Some linguists say that if the thought is clear, the language will be clear and, because of its clarity, effective. Therefore, the most significant step in writing an opinion paper is getting your thinking clear. You may be able to think through your idea before you begin to write or you may want to explore the idea by writing about it.

A second element in presenting an opinion effectively is that of selecting the language which is acceptable to your audience for your specific situation and purpose. For example, your friends accept one kind of language when you are chatting informally. They expect another kind of language when you write to them. There's also a difference between what they expect in an informal, friendly note in which you make plans for a party and a more formal plan for several sessions of your church youth group. And, of course, if your minister is going to read the plans, you will use language that is even more formal.

(*Activity 7F*)

Exploring the Nature of Acceptable Language

There are a number of language items or expressions that at one time were not considered acceptable as standard English. Some of these have gradually come to be accepted; others are still considered nonstandard.[9]

Discuss the following sentences from the point of view of a speaker of standard English. Are there any language items in these sentences that you would not accept? Are some of them appropriate under certain circumstances? Are there some that may be considered standard usage in the future?

a. We're back so far I can't hardly see the stage.
b. It seems like we've been here for hours.
c. Jason insists that he didn't break the window but I seen him.
d. I would of gone if I'da known the Blue Bombers were playing.
e. Liz won't buy a chance on the raffle. She says she never has no luck.
f. Carol, my little sister, wants to go to the movies with you and I.
g. I asked him why he was so late and he goes, "Well, I ran out of gas."
h. Would you bring them books to the library, please?
i. My dog he deserves a medal for saving that baby.
j. You can loan Jerry the money if you want to, but you may not get it back.

Major Writing Assignment

An Opinion Paper

By now, you have chosen one of the three carefully worded opinions you brought to class for Activity 7B. You will now use it as the thesis statement of your opinion paper.

To formulate your thesis statement, complete this sentence:

I believe strongly that _____ .

Then cross out the first four words. What remains will be your thesis statement. Remember that to make your opinion acceptable, you must support it with facts, opinions of authorities, logical reasoning, and, above all, specific examples.

Outlines for opinion papers differ. If you choose to write a satire like that of David MacFarlane, for example, you must develop your own order. If you wish to follow a fairly standard pattern, however, you might look closely at this outline of Arn Saba's article on comic strips.

TITLE: COME BACK, KRAZY KAT

> *Thesis statement:* It seems we have lost the taste for entertainment that requires involvement and effort. In the age of T.V. laugh tracks and fast foods, comics are also predigested for the consumer. (Thesis statement is held until third paragraph from the end.)

I. Introduction
   A. Arouse interest: Start with a direct address to the reader, "You may not have noticed..."
   B. Indicate subject and suggest its importance: Describe comics as they used to be and as they are now: refer to them as "art."
   C. Suggest thesis: Indicate that present day comics are a "pallid remnant" of former years.

II. Body
   A. Give historical description of what comics used to be.
      1. 1896, in the pages of New York *Journal*.
      2. 1940s, the typical family reaction to papers.

   B. Analyze some reasons why comics now are not as good.
      1. Visually unexciting, comparing examples from turn-of-the-century and today.
      2. Older strips covered wide range of emotional situations.
      3. Older strips had more complex characters and conflicts.
      4. Older strips required more attentive reading than today.

III. Conclusion
   A. Acknowledge that modern comics represent modern lives and ideas.
   B. End with repetition of opening idea that older comic strips are now recognized as art and are displayed in galleries as such.

Although the thesis of this article is a negative view of the subject rather than positive, the overall pattern of organization is clear, and it is one that you may be able to use as you work.

8

Argumentation and Persuasion

A newspaper is only a thought-throwing machine, a reflex of the popular mind. If it is not, it cannot live. We are not disposed to send our proof-sheets to anyone to correct.

—Amor de Cosmos, editorial in the
B.C. Colonist, Victoria, 1859

Today, at least in democratic societies, people have respect for each other's ideas and they often try to work together to make intelligent choices. This approach has changed the meaning of the words "argumentation" and "persuasion." Argumentation has come to mean presenting the one course of action or judgment that, in a given situation, is preferable to all others. Persuasion goes one step further. It refers to the fair, logical, and reasoned ways one motivates others to act on or believe in what has been set forth as the best or the most intelligent choice.

Argumentation and persuasion, then, no longer mean a contest in which one side loses and the other wins by any means possible but rather, a cooperative search for truth based on logic and the most complete set of facts possible. Your responsibility to other people and to truth is to search for all the facts that you can find on an issue, work with others to determine the intelligent choice, and then support this position by evidence and reason. You may, of course, organize your material to make your position attractive to certain audiences, but as an ethical persuader in search of truth

◀ The Speaker's Corner in Hyde Park, London, is known as a place where people can express their views, argue, and debate in public.

161

for the good of all, you should be willing to change your position as new information emerges, and you should never think of others as "things" which you can manipulate for your own purposes.

You use argumentation and persuasion every day. Think back over last week and try to remember how many times you've argued over such unstated propositions as "Resolved, Mom and Dad should let me have the car on Saturday night," or "Resolved, I should get a little extra allowance to go to the concert next week."

Argumentation and persuasion are all around you, and it is not at all surprising that different people and different groups come to different conclusions. Here are two examples of attempts at persuasion in which different courses of action are suggested.

I

HEAT SAVES

Worried about heating costs this winter? How would you like to have a house that can be heated for $43 a year in Montréal or Toronto, $66 in Winnipeg, $50 in Saskatoon or Calgary and only $38 a year in Vancouver? We're not talking about an expensive experimental house, either. It's a production model available in a number of styles and sizes at prices as low as $41 000 (plus land)—and only $2000 more than it would cost to build the same house to conventional standards, says its designer and builder, Keith Funk of Concept Construction Ltd. in Saskatoon.

There are three reasons why this house uses one-seventh as much heat as a standard house. One is upgraded construction, more of what is already being required in new homes—additional insulation, tighter construction, more efficient design. The ceiling is insulated to R50 instead of R18, the walls to R30 instead of R14, and the basement to R28 instead of R12.

The second energy-saving measure is the use of solar heat—but not the kind that requires large collector panels on the roof, storage tanks in the basement and a forest of pipes and pumps to circulate the heat. That type is called 'active' solar heating, and is still considered too expensive to be economical in Canada.

'Passive' solar heat, on the other hand, is the kind we've been using in our homes for years—it warms our walls and streams through our windows on sunny winter days. The Saskatoon house is simply designed to collect more of this heat and use it more efficiently.

A 25 foot [7.3 m] window wall facing south catches 200 square feet [55 square m] of sunlight, but only one-third of it enters the house directly. Behind the rest of the window is a black concrete block wall that soaks up heat like a sponge during the day and radiates it to the house at night. An aluminized, multilayer insulating blind inside the window, controlled by a sun sensor, makes the most efficient use of heat radiation, summer and winter.

The third way this house reduces heating costs is by controlling the ventilation. Leakage replaces all the air in the average house about once every hour during the winter months—as often as every 30 minutes in some loosely built older houses. Even the tightest house built to present construction standards probably loses all its heated air 10 to 12 times a day. In a well insulated house, that can represent as much as 35% of the total heating bill.[1]

—Harris Mitchell

II

The nuclear power industry is gearing up to build about 40 reactors across Canada by 1990. Close to $50 billion will be spent on the reactors, mining equipment, refineries, heavy water plants, a reprocessing plant and waste disposal facilities—the machinery for tapping nuclear power. This represents a huge growth in the nuclear power program: at present there are only seven commercial reactors operating, all of them in Ontario.

This program is gambling with the health, social well-being, and prosperity of Canadians. The pay-off—if there are no miscalculations, no accidents—will be more electricity than we really need. The risks may not be worth taking.

Danger: Radiation

The main cause for concern in this huge program is the radioactivity associated with uranium and its products. The effects of radiation range from quick death at the extreme, to cancer, and mutilated (deformed) offspring, depending on the amount and kind received.

Normally very little radiation (about one percent of the allowed maximum) escapes from the reactors themselves into the environment. The management of radiation from mining operations and from waste disposal has a less reassuring record. Already we have problems. Maximum levels have been decided upon by the federal and provincial governments, but they have often been exceeded.

The Serpent River, flowing into Lake Huron, has three times the Ontario maximum radioactivity, because of mine tailings (waste) from Elliot Lake uranium mines. The radiation from drinking water is not expected to endanger the health in the short term—but people who have lived there all their lives are understandably concerned about the longer term. Elliot Lake miners also appear to have suffered from radiation: they are three times as likely to get lung cancer as the general population.

In the town of Port Hope, where unacceptable levels of radiation were found a few years ago, a clean-up still hasn't been completed. In reality, anything contaminated with radiation cannot be cleaned. In the case of Port Hope, 'cleaning up' means moving the soil from the town to other dump sites. Many years will pass before society knows for sure the impact of these radiation burdens. Meanwhile more nuclear activity is sown, like dragon's teeth, across the country.

High level (highly radioactive) wastes from the reactors pose a more serious threat: they remain toxic (harmful) for a quarter of a million years! Canadian scientists are considering putting these wastes in glass blocks and burying them. The U.S.S.R. and France have already looked at and rejected the idea of burying wastes in granite. In fact, no safe disposal method has been found, yet if expansion continues, 143 000 tons of waste fuel will be around by the year 2000. We will never know if we have harmed future generations through our ignorance in handling these wastes.

Choosing the Path

Despite these risks, nuclear power is promoted as our salvation in a world of dwindling oil and gas supplies. The feeling is that we are trapped; we must go 'electric'. However, we do have options. One is increasing efficiency.

It has been estimated that the efficiency of energy use in North America could be doubled. Presently, energy escapes through windows and roofs; it flows down drains into our rivers; it lights high-rise office buildings at night when no one is around. Examples of the possibilities for improvement are everywhere: superior gas mileage in new cars; new office buildings designed to use one-third the energy of older buildings; efficient appliance designs.

Since nuclear electricity is not a particularly efficient source of energy, leaning more and more on it may in fact tend to move us further from efficient use of energy. Approximately 70 percent of the energy obtained in the form of heat from nuclear plants is rejected into nearby rivers or lakes. Further losses occur in transmission lines. There is plenty of room for improvement, then, and nuclear electricity may not fit well into an efficient future.

Other Sources

There is also room for improvement in matching energy sources to the tasks at hand. Basically, there are 'low-grade' or disperse energy sources, and "high-grade" or high temperature energy sources. The sun provides a low-grade source, while electricity is high-grade.

Some tasks, such as lighting and telecommunications, require electricity, but for other tasks using electricity is like cutting butter with a chainsaw. It's overkill. Low-grade sources such as solar heat, can do the job. Since one-third of our energy is used to heat homes, apartments and commercial buildings to a comfortable room temperature, low-grade sources could play an important role in our energy picture. We're not trapped yet.

Soon we may be. This program does not just mean nuclear plants. It means an economy in which our energy supply will take a far greater bite out of available capital than ever before. In the next 15 years we will spend half our energy budget to supply electricity, which will only amount to one-third of our energy supply. These are estimates: actual costs may be much higher, because costs of nuclear plants are rising faster than the rate of inflation. Point Lepreau Nuclear Station, originally estimated at $466 million, could easily end up costing over $726 million.

The nuclear power program also means that much of our economy will be oriented around electricity: more appliances, more industries, and more transportation systems will use electricity. Our normal lives will depend more and more on this huge system, going back will be harder.

Sir Brian Flowers, Chairman of Britain's Royal Commission on Environmental Pollution, cautions against rushing down the nuclear path: "Please ask yourself if that's the path down which you want to go. Stop and think before you take the next major step. Stop and think."[2]

—Jan Marmorek and Barry Spinner

You can readily see that the subject of these messages dealing with the energy crisis is a very tangled and complex problem. You can see also that these messages do not permit a detailed examination of all the facts. Such methods of persuasion require you to dig deeper into the issue if you are to make your own intelligent choice. Look back over the discussion of reasoning in Chapter 7 (pages 149-156). Then reread the two pieces on the energy crisis. Examine the reasoning closely. Look for fallacies. Whenever you read anything that attempts to persuade you to think or act in a certain way, subject it to this kind of critical, careful reading.

(Activity 8A)

Discussing the Examples

Consider the following questions:

1. What motivates each of the messages? What does each writer expect to achieve by getting this message to the public?

2. What is the "voice" each of the writers uses? Who seems to be speaking to you in each of the selections? How does that voice influence your attitude towards and your acceptance of the messages? Is writing in a "voice" other than your own dishonest?

3. What techniques do the writers use to draw you into their arguments, to make you *feel* something about the energy crisis? Can you find examples of techniques such as: use of statistics, loaded language, vivid examples, figurative language?

4. Which of the messages seem to offer the most information and the most logically supported argument? What difference might the "medium" in which the material appears make? How does each of the arguments attempt to provide for the different "levels of audience," which range from the superficial "skimmer" to the more intelligent and concerned student of the problem?

5. From your studies of these messages, formulate some statements about strategies of argumentation. What factors are basic to an effective argument?

6. Consider the use of such devices as: sentence fragments, one-word "sentences," one-sentence paragraphs, lists, repetition of phrases, quotations, reference to well-known people and organizations. How does each of these devices as used by professional writers reflect principles related to presenting an effective argument? To what extent should you use these devices in your writing?

Following are three examples of relatively good arguments—papers in which truth is sought through the use of logic and facts. Read them carefully in class and note the comments to the right of the student composition. When you write your next major composition, you will be preparing this kind of paper.

Student Composition 8A

WE ARE NOT ALONE

We have been taking our first feeble steps toward venturing out into the solar system and eventually beyond. Yet we are not alone in the universe. Mass evidence, supporting the belief that Unidentified Flying Objects (UFOs) do exist and have appeared on earth, includes UFO sighting reports by credible observers, physical evidence, and the censorship of UFO information by governments.

First of all, the UFO sightings serve as their own supportive evidence. In the United States, a Gallup Poll reported that five million people in that nation were willing to admit that they had seen strange objects which they felt were UFOs. In fact since the first UFOs first appeared in number, in 1946, they have been reported by every nation on earth, including Canada. Obviously, a high percentage of the reports are false. Yet this still leaves a substantial number of cases where competent witnesses (including astronomers, airline pilots and local police, and military and civilian radar operators) report objects which cannot be identified as either manufactured or conventional in terms of natural space bodies. One such incident took place at Fort Knox, Kentucky, U.S.A., on January 7, 1948. This is the classic case of Captain Thomas Mantell, a veteran fighter pilot, who lost his life while in pursuit of a huge spherical object which was crossing the state of Kentucky.

Secondly, there is physical evidence that UFOs have been present in a given location. This evidence includes markings on the ground and fragments of debris discharged from the UFOs. In many cases the debris is confiscated by government personnel. However, some UFO evidence has slipped out of the government's hands, and reports that leading scientists have often been unable to identify the substances have followed. Other physical evidence includes thousands of photographs of UFOs. In Taormina, Sicily, in 1954, a United Press photographer filmed several UFOs. A crowd of thousands watched these UFOs until an Italian jet arrived and chased them all away. Still other UFO effects include: unexplained stoppage of motor cars, interference with radio and TV, and electrical power failure. Many claim that the great New York—New England blackout on November 9, 1965, was directly connected with the UFO that was observed earlier that day.

Thirdly, support of UFO's existence is based on the fact that government agencies are deceiving the people by hiding known factual information on UFOs. Attempting to protect the public from panic (as the ob-

Can you suggest a more gripping and dramatic beginning for this paper?

Do these structural clues indicate interesting and substantial proofs for the writer's thesis? What is her thesis? How forceful is this argument? Do you object to the mechanical transition?

How would you rewrite the sentence beginning "Yet this still leaves..." to make it clearer?

What other transition than the mechanical "Secondly" would you suggest here?

Will you accept this undocumented report from "leading scientists?"

Would you insert a qualifying adjective between the words "several" and "UFOs?"

Is this a case of "begging the question?" What proof must you demand before you will accept the generalization presented here?

vious reason for the Armed Forces' traditional policy of identifying flying objects as weather balloons etc.) is something that cannot be indefinitely sustained, particularly when the source of presumed potential panic is a mass of peculiar things that persist in flying around where large numbers of people can see them. An excellent example of government censorship of UFO reports is the still undisclosed information of the numerous sightings by American astronauts. The motives of the American government must be questioned. Why would both the voice messages and the television broadcasts from the Apollo be censored to be released, when and as the government sees fit, if there were nothing that was being concealed?

UFOs exist as something unknown to our present understanding and are visiting earth. For one must realize that only people with immature minds quickly reject as impossible or alarming all that which lies outside their own physical experience or beyond the understanding of their limited imagination.

—Ellen Francis

How can one argue against this kind of reasoning?

What should the writer do to make the statement on government censorship believable?

How would you rewrite this topic sentence?

What error in reasoning do you detect in this summary?

III

On Friday, July 4, I had a particularly trying day with our adopted teenage daughter, who is going through what seems to be a typical period of resenting parental control—in short, rebellious teenager in today's difficult environment of drugs, drink, sex, and general permissiveness.

We find it small comfort that many of our friends are having similar problems with their teenagers, but we also have to contend with the added dimension of our daughter's adoption, of which she has quite naturally become more conscious in these adolescent years, whereas when she was little she disregarded it.

Up to a point we sympathize with her desire to know her original background and have plainly told her that if there seems real emotional need for her to do so when she is more mature and older, then we will help her. But right now, when she is cross with us and resents any parental discipline or advice, she gets angry and undoubtedly uses as forms of emotional blackmail the fact of her adoption and the threat to run off and find this "real mother" (whom she undoubtedly visualizes sitting waiting ready to indulge her every whim). It is all very upsetting for all of us, and very unrealistic.

Also unrealistic, and sensationalist, was the glaring headline in the *Sun*'s You section on that Friday, July 4 (Dear Daughter: Where Are You?), and it was just about the last thing I wanted to see in my house on that bad day. The only lucky break was that I got to the paper before my daughter did and managed to hide it from her—one reading of that sentimental trash and she'd have been on the phone to Parent Finders, as she was patently urged to do by the article, and who knows what havoc would have been wrought in how many lives.

Did anyone stop for one minute to consider any of that sort of thing before the article was so blatantly published? Did anyone ponder the sentimental nonsense, to say nothing of the selfishness of the so-called "mother" of Cornelia, whom she felt she had a right to claim after 30 years? The ultimate was reached when the mother was reported to have said she would recognize 30 year-old Cornelia anywhere even though she hadn't seen her since she was born. How absurd.

I asked several non-partisan friends for their views on the article and all said unhesitatingly that they were angered and appalled by it and consider it sheer sensationalism without any considered backing—some were men and some were women and none has an adopted child.

But we have an adopted child whom we love dearly. We also have a natural child. To us there is absolutely no difference between them, and of course we would wish that our adopted child felt that way too. We feel very strongly that if we can steer our adopted daughter through this emotionally stormy period of adolescence she will not give another thought to finding her "mother." We feel very strongly that she should leave well alone.

We fully understand her curiosity and wonder, but we do not want her to go to emotional lengths to find this other woman only to be met with disappointment if she is unable to find her—or possibly rejection again, or plain dislike.

When the Berger Commission was considering the advisability of legislation permitting parent-child reunion in cases of adoption my husband and I attended every possible meeting and so fully understand the pros and cons.

Did the *Sun's* July 4 article in any way consider us, the adopting parents? The answer is clearly no. Do we not have any rights as parents who lovingly brought up our child through a great deal of sickness and trauma, laughter and tears, a child who is every bit as much "ours" as is our natural daughter?

We are dealing here with the exchange of human beings and their emotions, not goods and chattels, and are we not entitled to some security with our much-loved children? Why, in heaven's name, is there suddenly such a proliferation in the media of stories that discuss, and promote, the so-called "rights" of the natural child and mother to be reunited, with explicit details on how to go about it? And just where are the adopting parents' rights to protection?

It has always been possible, and rightly so, for any emotionally disturbed adopted child to apply to the courts for the right to find her natural parents *if real need can be proved.* But it should never be the norm, and it should not be made so easy that any momentarily unstable or emotionally upset teenager can run off by picking up the phone—more than probably to meet with rejection that will only confuse him or her more. That could be tragic.

As for the rights of the natural mother, she chose to give up her child—whether willingly or not is not relevant now. She waived all rights to that human life when she signed the adoption papers and she has no claim whatever on that child who now belongs with her adoptive parents who in most cases, have had all the care, joy and expense—all that parenthood implies—in bringing up that child.

If I had made a bad investment some years ago I might well regret it, but I could hardly expect to be able to recoup my losses. I would have to accept it, and I'm afraid that is how it should be and has to be with those selfish women who more and more are seeking to disrupt our lives and hearts and take our children from us—for it is utter nonsense, human emotions being what they are, to talk of "sharing" under such circumstances, as so generously offered by Cornelia's mother in your article.

Finally, I must tell you that I also endorse all that has been said against the irresponsible and ridiculously permissive answers our teens are receiving weekly in the *Sun*'s Youth Clinic column, which I frequently hide from my teenagers rather than let them read such trash. Your so-called experts should try suggesting self-control which leads to self-respect and the use of a seldom used word, "No."

—Anonymous
The Vancouver *Sun*

IV

GREENPEACE

Who Are We?

Greenpeace is a movement of concerned people who recognize that the human species on this earth is just one part of a vast, interdependent life system. This system is based on balances of food supply versus population, life and death regeneration cycles, and diversity for survival. If the ecological balances are upset, a chain reaction begins to happen all over the living world. These balances have existed for millions of years, until recently, when humans have grown to be a much larger factor in the ecosystem than before.

This rapid population growth and increasing reliance on technological development has had disastrous effects on the life system of our planet. It is accepted that even if we were able to stop the ecological destruction happening now, we will already have lost 1/6 of the life forms on the earth, forever. Our survival is ultimately at stake.

Greenpeace is dedicated to drawing attention to these problems around the world, so we can learn to live more responsibly on this planet. We do public education, and mount campaigns against ecological offenders, such as the whaling industry killing off the last whales of the earth to make lipstick (and money). WE NEED HELP, in our offices, on the campaigns, and everywhere—raising consciousness. We also need your direct financial support. Join Greenpeace today, and help make it a more green, and peaceful world for all of us.

Save The Whales

Over the last century mankind has been killing off the great whales of the world, to the point where only 10% of the original whale population remains alive. Most whaling is done with fleets of killer ships which track down the whales and kill them with 200 lb. [91 kg.] exploding harpoons. The whales are then towed to a huge factory ship, where they are completely butchered in less than 20 minutes.

Why should we hunt and destroy the last remnants of a great and gentle family for pet food, shoe polish and lipstick? Whales are being killed for short term economic gain, when there are cheap synthetic substitutes for all whale products. Behavioural work has indicated that whales have a highly developed intelligence and anatomical evidence supports this. Are we allowing mammals with an intelligence possibly similar to ours to become extinct?

In 1975 Greenpeace first set sail to intercept the whalers. Greenpeacers, in high speed inflatable dinghies (zodiacs) positioned themselves between the killer boats and the whales to stop the killing. Thousands of whales have been saved this way during that first summer, and in confrontations each year since then. This direct-action opposition to the whalers spread to the Atlantic as well as the Pacific Ocean, as Greenpeace groups spread around the world.

Finally, in July 1979 the International Whaling Commission placed a complete ban on deep sea whaling, except for the small, more abundant Minke whales. **After 4 years of work, public pressure and deep-sea confrontations we have succeeded in stopping more than 1/2 of the whaling industry around the world.** Some whales are still not protected from coastal whaling operations, and from the pirate whalers who roam the seas, killing every whale they can find. For the 1980s, Greenpeace is continuing to fight for the lives of the world's whales and dolphins, and to assure a healthy environment for future generations.

Save The Seals

The annual slaughter of Harp Seals off the coast of Newfoundland has, according to government statistics, resulted in a 60% decline in the population in the last 25 years. A recent United States Marine Mammal Commission report released in February 1980 has revealed the fact that 50 000 fewer seal pups are born each year than the Canadian Government's statements indicate.

The reports that Newfoundland needs the seal hunt are largely exaggerated. The whole hunt accounts for less than 1/5 of one per cent of the Newfoundland economy; 60% of the seal hunters earn less than $100 during the 3-6 week season. Most of the real proceeds from the hunt go to the Norwegian economy where the processing of the furs takes place.

It is ecological nonsense to suggest that seals compete with Newfoundland fishermen for fish. The presence of seals in the marine ecosystem **maintains** fish stocks, by contributing to the balance of nature through their excrement feeding lesser life forms, which in turn feed the fish through the food chain.

Brian Peckford, Premier of Newfoundland, has maintained that the seal slaughter is more cultural than economic. Surely this is no better a reason to support the slaughter of walruses on Canada's east coast. This "cultural" practice has now come to an end, for the simple reason that there are no walruses left on Canada's east coast to kill.

The 180 000 seal quota threatens the species with extinction while the government often extends the season in an effort to reach the quota. For the past several years hunters have not been able to find enough seals to meet the quota. Greenpeace opposes the commercial hunt which is conducted by large ocean-going ice breakers. There is absolutely no justification for continuing this senseless destruction of a species to feed the whims of a fashion fur industry.

"We have arrived at a place in history where decisive action must be taken to avoid a general environmental disaster. With nuclear reactors proliferating and over 900 species on the endangered species list, there can be no delay, or our children will be denied their future."

Declaration of Interdependence
Greenpeace Foundation

Discussing the Persuasion Papers

1. What is the tone of the student composition and of the professional writing samples? Do the writers seem to recognize a "moral obligation to support their arguments by adequate evidence and reason?"
2. Do the writers somewhere "state a proposition?" That is, do they clearly state what they are trying to persuade the reader to do?
3. Do the papers show evidence of research? Have the writers looked up facts and figures? Have they looked up *enough* facts and figures?
4. How interesting is the writing? Do the issues (the questions being argued) seem important?

Topics for Persuasion Papers

For your Major Writing Assignment for this chapter you may choose a subject important in your school, your community, your province, or the country. To be worth writing about, the subject must be of interest and concern to readers. To be appropriate for an argumentation and persuasion paper, it must be a subject about which there are at least two points of view. It must also be a subject you know enough about (or can find out enough about) to be able to take an intelligent position.

(Activity 8B)

Choosing a Persuasion Topic

Either in class or outside of school with your friends and family, make a list of subjects that are being discussed in your school, your community, your province or the nation at large.

In the preliminary stages, do not criticize any of the topics as being too broad, too narrow, too difficult, or too controversial. Instead, focus on getting as many ideas as possible. Then go through the list and judge each topic as to its suitability for a persuasion paper.

Following is a list of major issues which face Canadians. Perhaps this list will help you select a subject for your paper.

1. Establish an equitable tax system, eliminating tax preferences and loopholes.
2. Eliminate wasteful federal government programs and subsidies gained by special-interest groups.
3. End unemployment by creating public service and public works jobs.
4. Develop enforceable programs for energy conservation.

5. Curb government spending caused by a growing civil service, unwise Canada Council grants, and just plain waste.
6. Strengthen conflict-of-interest and open meeting requirements.
7. Overhaul the laws concerning the power of multi-national corporations.
8. Protect our physical health and natural resources by defending environmental standards.
9. Establish a federal consumer protection organization.
10. Intensify action against discrimination based on sex, race, or ethnic background.
11. Introduce measures that will decrease regional economic inequalities in Canada.
12. Create an independent office to prosecute cases of political corruption.
13. Protect the free press by guaranteeing the journalist's right to confidentiality of news sources.
14. Introduce a better national minimum wage.
15. Reform current abortion laws.

After you have done your data collecting, either by interviewing people, reading, performing an experiment, distributing a questionnaire, or any other way, you should come to the point where you can make a statement similar to this: "I believe strongly that _____." Then after you have filled in the blank with the position you believe in, you can simply cross out the first four words and what is left is the thesis statement you will support.

The Structure of Persuasion

By looking at the examples of persuasion given in this chapter, you can see that persuasion comes in as many patterns as there are people writing. Not only do the writers differ, but their subjects require different presentations, and their audiences must be approached in different ways. Nonetheless, many writers use a kind of general pattern which they adapt as they write. Knowing this pattern may help you.

A PATTERN FOR PERSUASION

I. Introduction
   A. Begin by arousing interest, identifying the subject, and indicating its importance.
   B. State or imply your position on the subject.
II. Body
   A. Indicate one or two of the more important arguments *against* your position.

B. Refute the positions you have just stated.

C. Present additional arguments in support of your position. Develop each point sufficiently and use effective transition as you proceed from paragraph to paragraph.

III. Conclusion

A. Restate your position on the issue.

B. Present an emotional appeal for your position, perhaps warning what might happen if your position is not accepted.

Here is a persuasion paper written by Pierre Trudeau to promote French Canadian involvement in the life of our country. Notice how the writer follows the pattern for a persuasion paper. Do you agree with the arguments? Perhaps you might be interested in taking the opposite point of view for your persuasion paper.

If Canada as a state has had so little room for French Canadians it is above all because we have failed to make ourselves indispensable to its future.

If we make an exception of Laurier, I fail to see a single French Canadian in more than three-quarters of a century whose presence in the federal cabinet might be considered indispensable to the history of Canada as written—except at election time, of course, when the tribe always invokes the aid of its witch-doctors.

An examination of the few nationalist 'victories' carried off at Ottawa after years of wrangling in high places will reveal probably none that could not have been won in the course of a single cabinet meeting by a French Canadian of the calibre of C.D. Howe. Let's face it: all our cabinet ministers put together would barely ever have matched the weight of a bilingual cheque or the name of a hotel.

The Anglo-Canadians have been strong by virtue only of our weaknesses. This is true not only at Ottawa, but even at Québec, a veritable charnel-house where half our rights have been wasted by decay and decrepitude and the rest devoured by the maggots of political cynicism and the pestilence of corruption. Under the circumstances, can there be any wonder that Anglo-Canadians have not wanted the face of this country to bear any French features? And why would they want to learn a language that we have been at such pains to reduce to such mediocrity at all levels of our educational system?

No doubt, had English-speaking Canadians applied themselves to learning French with a quarter of the diligence they have shown in refusing to do so, Canada would have been effectively bilingual long ago. For here is demonstrated one of the laws of nationalism, whereby more energy is consumed in combating disagreeable but irrevocable realities than in contriving some satisfactory compromise. It stands to reason that this law works to greatest ill effect in the case of minority nationalism: in this case—us.

We have expended a great deal of time and energy proclaiming the rights due our nationality, invoking our celestial mission, trumpeting our virtues, bewailing our misfortunes, denouncing our enemies, and avowing our independence, and for all that none of our workmen is the more skilled, nor a civil servant the more efficient, a financier the richer, a doctor the more advanced, a bishop the more learned, nor a single solitary politician the less ignorant. Now, except for a few stubborn eccentrics, there's probably not one French-Canadian intellectual who hasn't spent at least four hours a week over the last year discussing Separatism. That makes how many thousand times two hundred hours just flapping our arms? And can any one of them honestly say he has heard a single argument not already expounded *ad nauseam* twenty years ago, forty years ago, and even sixty years ago?

Now this is what I call *la nouvelle trahison des clercs:* this self-deluding passion of a large segment of our thinking population for throwing themselves headlong—intellectually and spiritually—into purely escapist pursuits.

A nationalistic government is by nature intolerant, discriminatory, and, when all is said and done, totalitarian. A truly democratic government cannot be 'nationalist', because it must pursue the good of all its citizens, without prejudice to ethnic origin. The democratic government stands for and encourages good citizenship, then, never nationalism. Certainly such a government will make laws by which ethnic groups will benefit, and the majority group will benefit proportionately to its number; but that follows naturally from the principle of equality for all, not from any right due the strongest. In this sense one may well say that educational policy in Québec has always been democratic rather than nationalistic; I would not say the same for all the other provinces.

We must separate once and for all the concepts of State and of Nation, and make Canada a truly pluralistic and polyethnic society. Now in order to do so, the different regions within the country must be assured a wide range of local autonomy, such that each national group, with an increasing background of experience in self-government, may be able to develop the body of laws and institutions essential to the fullest expression and development of its national characteristics. At the same time, the English Canadians, with their own nationalism, will have to retire gracefully to their proper place, consenting to modify their own precious image of what Canada ought to be. If they care to protect and realize their own special ethnic qualities, they should do it within this framework of regional and local autonomy rather than a pan-Canadian one. On this point the record of Québec's treatment of its minorities can well stand as an example to other provinces with large French, German, Ukrainian, and other minorities.

I have no intention of closing my eyes to how much Canadians of British origin have to do—or rather, undo—before a pluralistic State can become a reality in Canada. But I'm inclined to add that this is *their* problem. The die is cast in Canada: there are two main ethnic and linguistic groups; each is too strong and too deeply rooted in the past, too firmly bound to a mother culture, to be able to engulf the other. But if the two will collaborate at the hub of a truly pluralistic State, Canada could become the envied seat of a form of federalism that belongs to tomorrow's world. Better than the American melting-pot, Canada could offer an example to all those new Asian and African States who must discover how to govern their polyethnic populations with proper regard for justice and liberty. What better reason for cold-shouldering the lure of a Canada annexed to the United States?...Canadian federalism is an experiment of major proportions; it could become a brilliant prototype for the moulding of tomorrow's civilization.

If English Canadians cannot see it, so much the worse for them; they will be subsiding into a backward, short-sighted, and despotic nationalism. Lord Acton, one of the great thinkers of the nineteenth century, described, with extraordinarily prophetic insight, the error of the various nationalisms and the future they were preparing. A century ago he wrote:

A great democracy must either sacrifice self-government to unity or preserve it by federalism...The co-existence of several nations under the same State is a test, as well as the best security of its freedom. It is also one of the chief instruments of civilization... The combination of different nations in one State is as necessary a condition of civilized life as the combination of men in society... Where political and national boundaries coincide, society ceases to advance, and nations relapse into a condition corresponding to that of men who renounce intercourse with their fellow-men... A State which is incompetent to satisfy different races condemns itself; a State which labours to neutralize, to absorb, or to expel them is destitute of the chief basis of self-government. The theory of nationality, then, is a retro-grade step in history.

It goes without say that if, in the face of Anglo-Canadian nationalism, French Canadians retreat into their own nationalistic shell, they will condemn themselves to the same stagnation. And Canada will become a sterile soil for the minds of its people, a barren waste prey to every wandering host and conquering people.

If Québec became a shining example, if to live there were to partake of freedom and progress, if culture enjoyed a place of honour there, if the universities commanded respect and renown from afar, if the administration of public affairs were the best in the land—and none of these presupposes any declaration of independence!—French Canadians would no longer need to do battle for bilingualism; the ability to speak French would become a status symbol, even an open-sesame in business and public life. Even in Ottawa, superior competence on the part of our politicians and civil servants would bring spectacular changes.

Such an undertaking is immensely difficult, but possible; it takes more guts than jaw. And therein, it would seem to me, is an 'ideal' not a whit less 'inspiring' than that other one that's been in vogue for a couple of years in our little part of the world.

For those who would put their shoulders to the wheel, who would pin their hopes for the future on the fully-developed man of intelligence, and who would refuse to be party to *la nouvelle trahison des clercs,* I close with a final word from the great Lord Acton:

Nationalism does not aim either at liberty or prosperity, both of which it sacrifices to the imperative necessity of making the nation the mould and measure of the State. Its course will be marked with material as well as moral ruin, in order that a new invention may prevail over the works of God and the interests of mankind.[5]

—Pierre Trudeau
"Canada and French-
Canadian Nationalism"

Activity 8C

Experimenting with the Structure of Persuasion

1. Select one of the topics you listed for Activity 8B. Gather appropriate information and then build an outline for an argument supporting a position regarding that topic. Follow the outline on pages 172-173.

2. After you have worked through an outline, select one of the other topics you have listed and work out a rough outline to support a position on that subject. Remember that you cannot do a satisfactory job on such an outline unless you either already know something about the topic or do some research to get information. Choose a topic suitable for your Major Writing Assignment in this chapter. Working out the outline now will help you later.

3. After you have finished working out your outline, either in class or outside of school, talk through the outline with another person. Discuss the sequence of your ideas and the support you have provided for each point. Talk also about whether or not making such an outline is effective for you before you begin writing your paper. People differ, and some students find it hard to think through a paper in advance of writing it. Others believe that thinking a paper through and developing an outline saves time and effort later.

Tone

The following jingle emphasizes some people's attitude on argumentation:

In matters controversial
My perception's rather fine.
I always see both points of view:
The one that's wrong, and mine.

Whenever you attempt to convince or to persuade, you are, in a sense, asking your listener or reader to abandon a "safe, secure position" and emerge into a world of conflicting ideas and values. You must use a tone that will convince readers that you respect them and their point of view and that if they come to agree with you, you will not feel, or make them feel, that you have triumphed and they have lost. Above all, you must convince them that they will be "safe and secure" in the new position. By using a calm, reasoned, confidence-inspiring tone you can convey this assurance. You achieve such a tone by being logical, fair, and open, and by choosing appropriate words and sentences.

The consequences of using the wrong tone can be very costly. Socrates, one of the greatest philosophers of all time, once used the wrong tone—with fatal consequences. He had been charged with undermining the beliefs of his city and with "corrupting the youth" by encouraging them to ask questions. He was called before the Senate, tried, and convicted. No one really took these trials very seriously. They were looked upon as a warning when someone had stepped out of bounds. Most people, when warned in this way, apologized, received a light punishment, and were careful to conform more closely to the city's customs.

But even though Socrates had been convicted by 281 to 275 votes, and even though the charges were severe enough to deserve death, the great philosopher remained as firm, as haughty, and as confident as ever—a tone that the Senate resented. When the members asked him to suggest his punishment, he suggested that he be fined twenty-five drachma, a very small sum, and also suggested that he be given a pension for life! When the judges voted on his punishment, 361 of them—80 more than had voted him guilty—voted for his death!

According to *Anthon's Classical Dictionary*, "... he would not have been condemned to death if he had not provoked the anger of the court by a deportment (a tone) which must have been interpreted as a sign of profound contempt or of insolent defiance."[6] Most people believe that Socrates deliberately used this tone because he believed that his death would broaden his influence and increase the impact of his ideas. Choose the tone which will best accomplish your purpose.

(*Activity 8D*)

Examining Passages for Tone

Read each of the following selections carefully and then write a generalization about the tone and about a reader's probable reaction to the tone. Be concrete as you support your generalization. Develop each generalization into a short paper.

1. To put it baldly, I have no hair. There's a monk's halo that grows a milligram or two, but the part has less coating than most people's tongues. I regard my condition as a triumph for evolution. Charles Darwin would say I had arrived.

As I understand it, nature provided animals with hair to protect them against the elements, but human animals can protect themselves. Hair is a nuisance. It gets in your eyes when you swim and wind makes it quiver and dance. The advanced members of the species need no hair.

My reason for bragging this way is that most people blush and squirm when they permit their eyes to dwell on my happy state.

The other evening, a lavender-type lady, who takes my night-school course, observed: "Pierre Berton would look much better on television if he wore a hair-piece." Then she broke into gaggling sounds and waxed a delicate pink. Within seconds she felt the social need to assure me that I had a handsome head, baldness suited me, and I was indeed a good-looking guy. (I wouldn't repeat her statements, except I am under oath to speak the truth.)

One day I was dallying with my coffee cup in a restaurant, when a pre-school child sauntered to my table, fixed his gaze on my dome, and squealed: "Look Ma! He has no hair." The mother scrambled down the aisle, seized her social delinquent by the wrist, and wrenched him to his chair. I assured the young matron that her child had done nothing more than make an accurate scientific observation and he did not deserve the opprobrium of the entire cafe. She blustered that she would smite her offspring when she got home. What a pity.

Even my barber blushes. I know I need a haircut when my neck itches. Nothing is more unkempt than an uncut neck. I now keep track of this need by going on paydays: the ninth and the twenty-fourth. My barber snips for three or four minutes, massages my neck (my concept of sheer luxury), but refuses to accept payment. "I couldn't," he says, blushing. "I didn't do anything."

One of my journalism students observed: "If you would wear a wig, you'd look twenty-five." Who wants to look twenty-five? Except twenty-one-year-olds.

When I emerged from the swimming pool at the university, other members of the graduate club search for combs. (One man said: "If you don't mind communicating bacteria, you can have mine," which sounded erudite, I thought.) Not me. I don't even smooth my hair with my hands.

The only place I regretted being bald was in Southern California. I had been basking in the sun for seven weeks, and my head acquired the lustre of teak. The night before my departure, the apex of my head began to itch. In satisfying the itch, six square inches of suntan peeled off and I returned to Canada a blushing pink.

Hair does nothing for people and is a nuisance. I pity men who are on the lower scale of evolution.[7]

—Ted Schrader

2. **Dear Ann Landers:** So you think today's teenagers are just great? You must be living in an air-tight capsule, completely isolated from the real world.

I'm enclosing a clipping from the *Denver Post,* but I'll bet this incident could have happened in any of 200 other cities in the United States.

I quote: "A 15-year old girl was arrested about 2.30 p.m. Wednesday on suspicion of damaging seats aboard a bus on which an off-duty policeman was riding.

"Police said Det. Edward Roy was working off duty for the transit system and riding a bus in East Denver. A group of youths began tearing up a rear seat, pulling out pieces of foam rubber padding and throwing them around. One youth tried to ignite the foam rubber with a cigarette lighter.

"The bus driver was instructed to drive to the East Denver police station, where the girl was arrested. Four other suspects, all boys, escaped through the back door and windows of the bus."

What do you have to say for American teen-agers, now, stupid?

—Tip of the Iceberg

3. **Dear Ice:** Do you think it's fair to put all teen-agers in the same bag with those Denver hooligans? At the very moment those kooks were tearing up the bus, thousands of teens were riding public transportation and behaving themselves—some even offering their seats to the aged and the infirm, although many people insist such things don't happen anymore.

Unfortunately, it's the troublemakers who make news. Who wants to read that half a million kids rode buses today in 200 cities and not one of them tried to set fire to the seats? Decent conduct gets very little press because it's not exciting. Sorry, but these are the facts, friend.[8]

4....(An) example of cop-out "realism" is the way some communities are dealing with cigarette-smoking by teen-agers and pre-teenagers. Special rooms are now being set aside for students who want to smoke. No age restrictions are set; grade eight students have the same lighting-up privileges as graduating students. It is felt that since the youngsters are going to smoke anyway, the school might just as well make it possible for them to do it in the open rather than feel compelled to do it furtively in back corridors and washrooms.

Parents and teachers may pride themselves on their "realism" in such approaches. What they are actually doing is finding a convenient rationalization for failing to uphold their responsibility. The effect of their supposedly "realistic" policy is to convert a ban into a benediction. By sanctioning that which they deplore, they become part of the problem they had the obligation to meet. What they regard as common sense turns out to be capitulation...

The school has no right to jettison standards just because of difficulties in enforcing them. The school's proper response is not to abdicate but to extend its efforts in other directions. It ought to require regular lung examinations for its youngsters. It ought to schedule regular sessions with parents and youngsters at which reports on these examinations can be considered.It ought to bring in cancer researchers who can run films for students showing the difference between the brackish, pulpy lungs caused by cigarette smoking and the smooth pink tissue of healthy lungs. The schools should schedule visits to hospital wards for lung cancer patients. In short, educators should take medical warnings about cigarettes seriously.[9]

—Norman Cousins

5. Yossarian looked at him soberly and tried another approach. "Is Orr crazy?"

"He sure is," Doc Daneeka said.

"Can you ground him?"

"I sure can. But first he has to ask me to. That's part of the rule."

"Then why doesn't he ask you to?"

"Because he's crazy," Doc Daneeka said. "He has to be crazy to keep flying combat missions after all the close calls he's had. Sure, I can ground Orr. But first he has to ask me to."

"That's all he has to do to be grounded?"

"That's all. Let him ask me."

"And then you can ground him?" Yossarian asked.

"No. Then I can't ground him."

"You mean there's a catch?"

"Sure, there's a catch," Doc Daneeka replied. "Catch-22. Anyone who wants to get out of combat duty isn't really crazy."

There was only one catch and that was Catch-22, which specified that a concern for one's own safety in the face of dangers that were real and immediate was the process of a rational mind. Orr was crazy and could be grounded. All he had to do was ask; and as soon as he did, he would no longer be crazy and would have to fly more missions. Orr would be crazy to fly more missions and sane if he didn't, but if he was sane he had to fly them, if he flew them he was crazy and didn't have to; but if he didn't want to he was sane and had to. Yossarian was moved very deeply by the absolute simplicity of this clause of Catch-22 and let out a respectful whistle.[10]

—Joseph Heller

Exposition Within Argumentation

Most of the techniques used in writing good exposition are also used in writing argumentation and persuasion. Most argumentation or persuasion papers make an attempt to interest the reader, explain their intention in a thesis statement near the beginning, and support generalizations with specific, concrete details.

In addition, they provide helps for a reader (transitions, definitions, summaries) and they present information in an order that is both understandable and effective. These expository techniques are used in other modes of writing, including analysis, process papers, opinion papers as well as argumentation and persuasion.

Recognizing Expository Techniques

Look for at least two examples of argumentation or persuasion articles and prepare a one-page report on the expository techniques you find in them. The preceding section may help you identify them, but you may wish to look over the activities in the preceding chapters for more specific techniques, such as those used in analysis, process, or opinion papers.

You can find brief articles of argumentation or persuasion in many places. Try the editorials in your newspaper or such magazines as *Saturday Night, Maclean's* or *Time*. Look at published speeches in your newspaper (if it provides complete texts of speeches). Examine "Letters to the Editor," which appear in your local newspaper when an important issue is pending.

End your analysis with a comment on the writer's tone. Does he or she indicate a respect for the opposition and a note of honest inquiry?

Sentence Length

Students beginning junior secondary school average about 17.3 words per sentence. First year university students average 19.9 words per sentence. Professional writers average 20.9 words per sentence (depending upon their subject, their audience, and their purpose). These figures are based on a recent study.

Average sentence length alone, however, does not tell the whole story. Mature writers may *average* about twenty words per sentence, but to get variety in their work, they consciously try to write sentences of different lengths. One study reveals that out of every ten sentences, six were of about average length (eighteen to twenty-two words), two were extra long (more than twenty-five words), and two were short (fewer than twelve words).

(*Activity 8F*)

Checking Sentence Length

1. Take three of the compositions you have written this year and determine the following:

   A. What is the average length of your sentences in each paragraph?

   B. What percentage of the sentences in each paper have under twelve words? What percentage of sentences are over twenty-five words?

2. Choose a relatively long paragraph (about 250 words) and revise it. Try to get the 2-6-2 ratio for long, average, and short sentences. Try to include one or two questions, imperatives or inversions.

3. After you have analyzed your own sentences, choose two modern writers whose work you have enjoyed, and analyze a number of sentences from their writing. Note to what extent variations in sentence length differ for each. Try to come to some conclusions regarding the effect of sentence length on style.

   You might wish to look at paragraphs from such writers of fiction and nonfiction as Ernest Hemingway, William Faulkner, Margaret Laurence, Thomas Wolfe, F. Scott Fitzgerald, John Updike, Winston Churchill, Margaret Atwood, Ray Bradbury, Shirley Jackson, Kurt Vonnegut, Ralph Ellison, Robertson Davies, Lorraine Hansberry, Saul Bellow, Langston Hughes, Bernard Malamud, John Steinbeck, Ethel Wilson, or W.O. Mitchell.

You'll never get anywhere with all those damned little sentences.

—Canadian humourist Gregory
Clark to Ernest Hemingway
when both worked for the
Toronto *Star* in the 1920s.

Supporting Your Position

Before attempting to persuade an audience or a reader to adopt your point of view, it is essential to gather your facts. They are the ammunition in your campaign. For example, a concerned teacher recently conducted a study in order to show, contrary to popular assumption, that women authors are really very poorly represented in Canadian secondary school English courses. She states her case by detailing the number of women authors represented in various literary genre studied in forty-two different English courses:

> However, statistically significant differences in proportions of male/fe-
> male authorship do occur between the different genres of writing. Novels
> showed the best proportion of women as authors: women were outnumbered
> by men by a mere five to one. In the short prose selections, women were
> outnumbered nine to one. Very few plays by women were listed. Male dram-
> atists outnumbered females nineteen to one. Where timelines were shown
> on course-of-study outlines, drama and novels were commonly given the
> bulk of the class study time and also the major emphasis in student inde-
> pendent essay assignments. More recent works often received less em-
> phasis than the classics in both genres.[11]
>
> —Priscilla Galloway

This is an instance where a person with a legitimate interest in the
content of secondary school English curricula used time and energy to
make her position known to those who make decisions in the field of
education and to the public.

Her use of facts puts the onus on those who would argue a contrary
position to prove her wrong. The use of verified facts makes it very difficult
for your opponent to destroy your credibility.

Dealing with Controversial Issues

It is important to remember that in argumentation and persuasion the
purpose is not to "win" at all costs, but to present facts and opinions in
a sincere effort to arrive at truth. In presenting one side in a discussion,
writers must give due consideration to opposing points of view and practice
diplomacy in presenting their own.

Often writers of argumentation or persuasion are aware that they are
taking positions that are unpopular. They must offer facts and opinions
in a calm, reasonable manner—otherwise they will alienate those in opposition and fail to persuade any who might be neutral. In order both to
be fair to those who hold other opinions and to get a hearing themselves,
they must proceed diplomatically. Often writers acknowledge the value of
the alternative ideas and, sometimes, borrow them and build on them.

(*Activity 8G*)

Practicing Diplomacy on Controversial Issues

1. Choose some current issue in your school and prepare a very brief talk
   in support of what you believe is the *unpopular* side. Concentrate on the
   introduction and on your manner of revealing your position.
2. Appoint a class recorder to list some of the techniques that different
   students use to present their material diplomatically.

These neighbours decided to present both sides of the controversial sovereignty association issue in Québec at the time of the referendum in 1980.

Students in other classes have spoken on such ideas as the following:

Why the number of required compositions should be doubled.
Why football should not be played at the secondary school level.
Why a dress code is necessary.
Why school dances should be opened to dropouts and to students from neighbouring schools.
Why censorship in school publications is desirable.

Activity 8H

Revising and Editing a Persuasive Paper

Working as your teacher directs, revise the following draft of a persuasive essay according to the guidelines for effective persuasive papers you have studied in this chapter. As you revise, consider effectiveness of ideas presented and of the method of development used as well as the quality and quantity of supporting evidence. Edit effectively, eliminating any existing errors in sentence structure, point of view, usage, vocabulary or mechanics (spelling and punctuation).

That more stringent and workable guidelines for the application of censorship laws to television programming are necessary is obvious. Why, just look at your television schedule for any night this week. Violence fills the so-called "adventure dramas" and distasteful sexual innuendo is all that is left of the once noble situation comedy. Only clearer and consistently applied censorship can improve the quality of entertainment viewers expect and need from television.

You need only to turn to any show involving the police to realize the degrading depth to which television drama has descended. Using their badges as a kind of licence T.V. police mistreat, maim or shoot it out with criminals who are equally intent on returning the complement. If the public were to write en masse to government, to T.V. networks and complaining to sponsors of such programs, demanding more stringent censorship from the former and a higher quality of programming from the latter, we would achieve our goal of finer quality viewing.

And what about the comedies. How long can you suffer with the ribald sort of rude innuendo that tears apart or at least mocks family, moral values and the marriage vow? Surely we all agree that what this country needs is a reaffirmation of family and moral values—not a public ridiculing of them. As famous men have said: "all that is needed for the triumph of evil is for good men to do nothing." Let's not be counted among those who do nothing about the downgrading of the family through insidious television comedies.

Write your Member of Parliament and the Minister in charge of the Canadian Radio and Television Commission now! Let them know how that vast majority of Canadians feel about the flagrant misuse of the media that we are daily subjected to. Now is not the time to sit back. Let's help clean up television by urging more workable guidelines for censorship. We can change things if we will only make the effort.

Major Writing Assignment

A Persuasion Paper

Reread the examples of persuasion papers in this chapter and note the organization of each. Choose a real subject. You may use one of those you listed for Activity 8B or one of those you outlined in Activity 8C. For that topic complete this sentence:

I believe strongly that ＿＿＿＿＿＿＿＿.

Now cross out the first four words. You will be writing in the more formal third person.

Then, if you have not already done so, work through a possible outline following the pattern in Activity 8C.

As you begin writing your paper, keep in mind your moral responsibility to use evidence and logic and your practical need to maintain an acceptable tone.

As you develop your argument, work on variety of sentence structure by using different sentence patterns and by varying your sentence length.

Feel free to depart from the "Structure of Persuasion" outline given to you on page 172, but be sure that you have a valid reason for doing so.

Be sure to allow enough time in writing your paper to take advantage of the techniques described in Chapter 2.

9

Writing Letters, Memos, and Reports

Harry, my boy, never write a letter if you can help it, and never destroy one.
> —Sir John A. Macdonald to
> H.R. Smith, Sergeant-at-Arms

Before 1900, letter writing was a very important part of most businesses. Men wearing green eyeshades and black pull-on sleeves to protect their white shirts sat on rows of high stools and wrote endlessly. Charles Dickens' Bob Cratchit in "A Christmas Carol" was such a copyist, and so was Bartleby in Herman Melville's "Bartleby the Scrivener."

Personal letter writing was also important at that time. Many people kept personal secretaries to prepare and file their correspondence. In Canada today, numerous collections of letters are available for reading. Many of these are letters written by people who are outstanding for some reason. The letters that survive of Lord Byron, for example, number over three thousand and fill ten volumes; they provide a vivid insight into the character of this famous poet. Other collections of letters are simply interesting for their descriptions of the life and times of various people.

Some people say that letter writing has declined in importance, in grace and precision, and in volume. It's true that many people depend on the telephone and on greeting cards to communicate with friends and relatives, and that businesses often have their own Telex machines and special discounted long-distance telephone arrangements.

◄This drawing, done in 1884, shows a typical clerk, seated at a high desk, working on an office account book.

Nonetheless, letter writing remains important. From 1963 to 1978, the volume of letters mailed has increased sharply. Because of this volume, large postal systems, like that in the United States, for example, are considering making a system of microfilming available. During the Second World War, over one billion letters were reduced to 1.6 square centimetre microfilmed pictures, flown to their destinations, and then printed full-size once more. Instead of weighing 23 kilograms, a bag of eighteen hundred letters on microfilm would weigh only 198 grams. This method would save a great deal of cost and labour.

Soon you will be writing some of the most important letters of your life. Here are two letters similar to those you may be writing.

```
                2132 Jasper Avenue
                Edmonton, Alberta
                T5N 3K9

                80-11-12

                Director of Admissions
                University of Saskatchewan
                Saskatoon, Saskatchewan
                S7N 0W0


                Dear Director:


                I am a grade 12 student at Pearson Secondary School in Edmonton,
                and I plan to enter university in the fall of 1981.  In
                particular, I hope to enroll in the College of Engineering.  I
                am a good student with a grade point average of 3.2 on a 4-point
                scale and a current standing of about 56 in a class of 523
                students.

                I would be very grateful if you would send me a copy of your
                current calendar, together with admissions information and
                application forms.

                Because I shall require living accommodations, I would also
                like information regarding on-campus residence.

                Sincerely yours,

                Elizabeth Smith


                Elizabeth Smith
```

Elizabeth does not have personal stationery with a letterhead. Note that she provides her home address and the date in her typewritten heading.

How does Elizabeth avoid the problem of not knowing whether she is writing to a man or a woman?

Elizabeth has chosen to use *block style* for her letter. That is, all lines are "flush left"—beginning at the left-hand margin. She doublespaces between elements of the letter (heading, inside address, salutation, body, and complimentary close) as well as between paragraphs. Notice that Elizabeth has allowed enough space between the complimentary close and her typed name to write her signature.

Not too long ago, the heading, complimentary close, and signature began two-thirds of the way across the page. The electric typewriter influenced the more modern placement. Why?

Roy Williams answered this advertisement from the classified section of his local newspaper.

> INVENTORY CONTROL CLERK. High School grad. Some experience helpful. Able to work with minimum supervision. Accurate with figures, able to prepare readable reports and accept responsibility. Good starting salary, company benefits. Apply in own handwriting to Safety Equipment Co. 1404 Dansey Ave., Coquitlam, B.C. V3K 3H8

3314 Kelsey Street
Coquitlam, B.C.
V3K 4H7
81-05-23

Safety Equipment Company
1404 Dansey Ave.
Coquitlam, B.C.
V3K 3H8

Gentlemen:

    I have just read your advertisement for an Inventory Control Clerk in the Herald, May 22, and I would like to apply for the job.

    I am a grade 12 student graduating this year from Beckett Secondary School, and I will be available to start work after 81-06-27. Actually, if you need me sooner, my counsellor has informed me that the school will make arrangements for an early release these last few days.

    I have taken a vocational program in school concentrating on metal working. For the last two years I have served part of the time as tool-room manager and part of the time as assistant foreman for my instructor, Mr. Phelps.

    You can request information about me from

MR. LYNN PHELPS   MR. ELWOOD PETERSON
INDUSTRIAL EDUCATION TEACHER   PRINCIPAL
BECKETT SECONDARY SCHOOL   BECKETT SECONDARY SCHOOL

    I will be happy to send you any additional information you would like and to authorize release of my school records to you. I can come for an interview at your convenience.

    I do not plan to attend college, and I am looking for the kind of position you are offering — a permanent job with responsibilities, satisfaction, and an opportunity for growth.

Sincerely yours,

Roy Williams

Handwritten letters are usually written in *indented style* (slanted) because it is very hard to get the neat, accurate block of the typewriter in handwriting.

Roy uses as his inside address the exact address given in the advertisement.

Although the masculine "Gentlemen" is still common in writing to a company, many people object to the fact that it ignores the increasing number of women in the work force.

Notice that Roy specifies how he knows about the job and immediately tells why he is writing.

Roy must prove that he has had experience, can work with minimum supervision, is accurate with figures, can prepare readable reports, and can accept responsibility.

Which of these does he do well? Which might he improve on? How?

Would including the exact address of the school be an additional courtesy? Why or why not?

Roy can assume that the company will know it can reach him at his home address or through the school. What else might he have included to enable an official to reach him more easily?

Why does Roy mention that he doesn't intend to go to college? Why will this not count against him?

This is the letter Elizabeth received from the University of Saskatchewan.[1]

UNIVERSITY OF SASKATCHEWAN

REGISTRAR'S OFFICE

SASKATOON, CANADA
S7N 0W0

80-11-18

Ms. Elizabeth Smith
2132 Jasper Avenue
Edmonton, Alberta
T5N 3K9

Dear Ms. Smith:

We were pleased to receive your letter of November 14 in which you requested information regarding the requirements for admission to the College of Engineering.

Students from Alberta applying to the College of Engineering must have completed Grade 12 with standing in English 30, Mathematics 30, Chemistry 30, Physics 30 and one other acceptable Grade 11 or Grade 12 subject with an average of 65% on the compulsory subjects and an overall average of 65%.

Under separate cover we are forwarding a copy of our 1980-81 University calendar to you. The new calendars will be available on request to this office approximately the middle of April. An application form is enclosed.

We have forwarded a copy of your letter to the Residence Office for a reply to your question regarding on-campus accommodation.

If we can be of further assistance to you, please do not hesitate to write.

Yours truly,

Emily Farnham

Emily B. Farnham
Director of Admissions

EBF/ep

Encl.

Notice how the letterhead makes it unnecessary for the writer to provide anything except the date of the letter.

This is the usual placement for the inside address. Some writers place the inside address at the end of the letter for two reasons: 1. It puts first things first—that is, the message at the beginning; and 2. It makes the inside address easier to find for filing and retrieval purposes.

Note that this writer double-spaces between paragraphs and uses block style. What are some advantages of block style?

These initials remind the reader (and the writers, too, in case it is necessary to fix responsibility for a decision or an error) that Emily B. Farnham (EBF) wrote the letter and that a secretary with the initials "ep" typed it.

The word "Enclosure" reminds the secretary to be sure to include the enclosure as promised and it enables Elizabeth to be sure that she received everything that Ms. Farnham intended to send.

Activity 9A

Exploring Various Kinds of Business Letters

Job application letters and university or college entrance application letters are two kinds of letters that you are going to find most important in the near future. However, there are dozens of other kinds of letters. Working either alone or with a group, try to collect from your family, friends, and relatives a number of different kinds of letters. Write examples of different types of letters if you can't find real letters.

This is the letter Roy received from the employment manager of Safety Equipment Company.

SAFETY EQUIPMENT COMPANY

1404 Dansey Avenue
Coquitlam, B.C.
V3K 3H8

Your Safety-Our Concern
604-936-9069

81-05-25

Mr. Roy Williams, 3314 Kelsey Street, Coquitlam, B.C.   V3K 4H7

Dear Roy:

Ordinarily, my partner and I would prefer to have someone older and more experienced as our Inventory Control Clerk, but both Mr. Phelps and Mr. Peterson gave you the highest recommendations when we called them.

We would like to have you come to our main office at 324 - 20th Street on 81-06-06 at 1600 h. so that we can both take a look at you.

We're both pleased with the way you express yourself and with the record you've made in school, so we're looking forward to meeting you.

Cordially,

Ben Swenson

Ben Swenson

BS/nc

cc. Bennett

This form of inside address is relatively new, but think how much time it saves a secretary.

Many people think business letters are cold, detached, objective, and formal. Nonsense! They *can* be, but they can also project an image of friendliness, cordiality, and interest. What are the signs in this letter that Mr. Swenson wanted to project such an image?

The cc: indicates that a carbon copy has gone to the person indicated; in this case, the partner.

Try to include these types:

Letters of complaint
Letters of inquiry
Sales letters
Letters of application for jobs
Letters requesting adjustments or explanations
Letters of application for college, university or technical school

Letter to an editor explaining a point of view
Letter to an editor challenging a statement
Letter to an elected official
Letter to a government agency requesting information or service

Letters of application for membership

Letter to a radio or television program requesting air time to present a point of view

Letter to an organization requesting a speaker or program

After each example or model letter, list some situations in which you or other people in your age group might want to write such letters.

(Activity 9B)

Exploring Opportunities for Letters of Application

1. If you are planning on working after secondary school, skim the want ads of your local newspaper and find several jobs which you think you would like and which would require letters of application. (Some firms discourage letters. They require the person to appear for an interview.) Discuss with your friends or a small group the information you would give and how you would organize such a letter. Actually write one or more such letters and submit them to the group for editing, proof-reading, and judging.

2. If you are planning on going to university, discuss with your parents, teachers, and guidance counsellors the kinds of schools in which your interests and talents could be best developed. Get the addresses of such schools from the Guidance Office or the library.

   Write and mail your letter to the one or two colleges or universities in which you are truly interested. It is not fair to ask a university to send you an expensive calendar if you do not plan to apply.

Form and Content in Business Letters

At one time, most schools taught a single form—or at most, two forms—for the business letter. Even at that time, however, individuals and businesses used several different forms. The important consideration is that the letter be neat, clear, and functional. The four model letters at the beginning of this chapter indicate some of the variety you can find in modern business letters. Your scrapbook collections will indicate additional varieties.

Your teacher may let you experiment with various forms. However, many businesses and almost all publishing houses develop a *style sheet* to ensure that their correspondence projects a consistent image. The skeleton letter pictured here shows the six parts of a conventional business letter—heading, inside address, salutation, body, closing, and signature. Notice their placement and how they are punctuated.

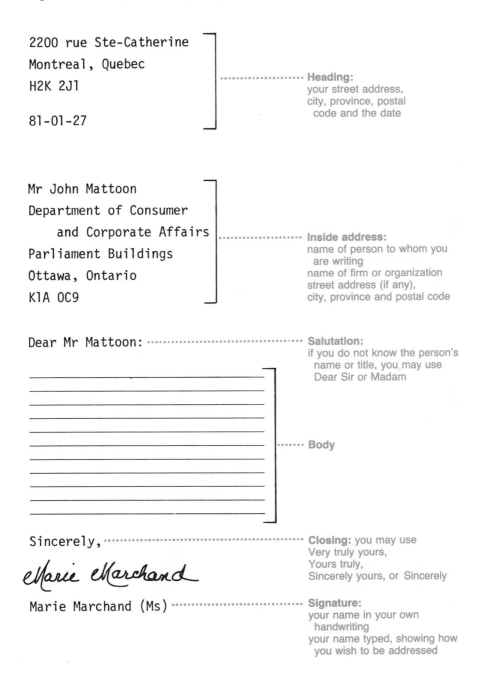

2200 rue Ste-Catherine
Montreal, Quebec
H2K 2J1

81-01-27

Heading:
your street address,
city, province, postal
code and the date

Mr John Mattoon
Department of Consumer
    and Corporate Affairs
Parliament Buildings
Ottawa, Ontario
K1A 0C9

Inside address:
name of person to whom you
    are writing
name of firm or organization
street address (if any),
city, province and postal code

Dear Mr Mattoon:

Salutation:
if you do not know the person's
    name or title, you may use
    Dear Sir or Madam

Body

Sincerely,

Closing: you may use
Very truly yours,
Yours truly,
Sincerely yours, or Sincerely

Marie Marchand (Ms)

Signature:
your name in your own
    handwriting
your name typed, showing how
    you wish to be addressed

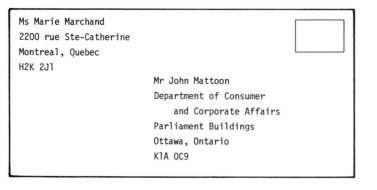

Ms Marie Marchand
2200 rue Ste-Catherine
Montreal, Quebec
H2K 2J1

          Mr John Mattoon
          Department of Consumer
                and Corporate Affairs
          Parliament Buildings
          Ottawa, Ontario
          K1A 0C9

Stamp

Return address:
your name and address

**Name and address of person
to whom you are writing.**
Include proper title—Miss,
Mr., Mrs., Ms., Dr., Professor,
etc.

Guidelines for Writing Business Letters

Unless your teacher specifies a certain form, refer to the models at the beginning of this chapter and to the skeleton business letter on page 193. Observe the following guidelines for writing business letters.

1. Use appropriate stationery. In most cases you will choose standard, white, business size (21.5 cm × 28 cm) sheets. Brightly coloured stationery attracts attention, but it makes a poor impression on some people. Small or over-sized sheets are easy to lose and hard to file.

2. Type, if possible; if not, use blue or black ink. Use one side of the page only.

3. Centre your letter horizontally on the page, leaving at least three cm margins on each side. Estimate the probable length of your letter and begin far enough from the top of the page so that the letter will also be centered vertically on the page. If you must use more than one page, allow at least four cm at the bottom of the first page. Plan ahead, so that several lines of the body of your letter can be written on the second page.

4. Use one style—either block or indented (slanted)—throughout the letter. Block is more often used in typed letters; indented, in handwritten letters.

5. Using one of the patterns in the models, include this information:
   a. Your address (including the postal code).
   b. The date.
   c. The exact name and address (including the postal code) of the person to whom you are writing.
   d. Your signature. Below your handwritten signature, type your name, showing how you wish to be addressed in a return letter.

6. Double-space between elements in the letter (heading, inside address, salutation, complimentary close, and signature) and either double-space between paragraphs or indicate their beginning by indenting.

7. For a letter written on 21.5 cm x 28 cm stationery, use a long envelope. Place the return address in the upper left and the main address in the lower centre of the envelope.

8. Fold the letter up from the bottom about a third of the way, then down from the top. Place the letter in the envelope so that it will be right side up when taken from the envelope and unfolded.

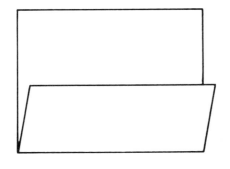

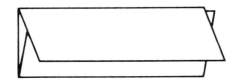

In planning the content of your business letter, follow these suggestions:

1. Be clear.
2. Be accurate.
3. Be brief.

Organize your material in such a way that you answer these three questions:

1. Why am I writing?
2. What will the reader need to know in order to understand and be willing to act on my request?
3. What is my request? What do I want the reader to do?

Remember that in today's business world, these letters often function simply as confirmation of information obtained over the telephone.

(*Activity 9C*)

Planning Business Letters

Consult this list of possible places to write to, and think of situations in which you write to such places. Plan the contents for the letter, answering in a separate paragraph each of the three questions above. Write the letter and follow the procedures for editing and proofreading.

If your letter performs a real function, prepare a final draft and mail it.

ORGANIZATIONS YOU CAN WRITE TO

Here are some places to which you can write a business letter and expect a reply:

1. Write to the National Film Board of Canada, P.O. Box 6100, Montréal, Québec H3C 3H5, requesting a current film catalogue.
2. Write to the Philatelic Service, Canada Post, Ottawa, Ontario K1A 0B5, requesting information on how to receive First Day Cover stamps.
3. Write to the Department of Consumer and Corporate Affairs, Parliament Buildings, Ottawa, Ontario K1A 0C9, requesting recent information on the Cost of Living Index, or on the possibilities of solar heating for Canadian homes.
4. Write to the Canadian Cancer Society, 200 Melrose Ave., Ottawa, On-

tario K1Y 4K7, asking for information on the relationship between smoking and cancer.

5. Write to the Canadian Advisory Council on the Status of Women, 151 Sparks St., Ottawa, Ontario K1P 5E3, requesting information on government legislation dealing with the status of women in Canada.

6. If you have doubts about a charity or other organization which is collecting money, write to your local Better Business Bureau. The address will be listed in your telephone directory.

7. Write to your local Greenpeace Foundation office, requesting information on conservation activities in your area.

8. Write to your Member of Parliament, Parliament Buildings, Ottawa, Ontario, giving the birthdate of a person over eighty or the wedding anniversary of a couple married for fifty years in order to receive an official greeting card from the Governor General. Be sure to allow four or five weeks for delivery.

9. Write to your provincial Hydro and Power Authority, requesting information on insulating your home in order to cut down on fuel costs.

10. Write to the Toronto Stock Exchange, Commerce Court East, 234 Bay St., Toronto, Ontario, requesting information on how the stock market works.

11. Write to the Canadian Film Institute, 611-75 Albert St., Ottawa, Ontario K1P 5E7, requesting information on film-making in Canada.

12. Write to the Canadian Dairy Commission, 2197 Riverside Drive, Ottawa, Ontario K1H 7X3, requesting information on careers available in the Canadian dairy industry.

Writing a Résumé

Sometimes you need to tell more about yourself than you can conveniently include in the body of a letter of application. Refresh your memory by rereading the letter of application on page 189.

After all, such letters should be brief, and by the time you explain why you're writing, give a little background, and make your request, there's little room for a lengthy discussion of yourself. Instead of including such material in the body of the letter, enclose a résumé.

A résumé is a summary of facts about yourself. These facts include your personal situation, your education, your work experience, and any appropriate information about events in your life, your interests, and ambitions.

The contents of a résumé can be organized and presented in different ways. Depending upon your purpose in preparing it, you may include different information or stress different ideas. The résumé on page 199 follows a format suggested by Canada Manpower.

The required elements of a résumé are these:

1. It should present you in the best possible light. Avoid errors in grammar and spelling.
2. It should be concise and direct.
3. It should be organized so that the nature of the information in each section is clear.
4. It should be neat and attractive. Usually résumés are typed, with headings underlined or in capital letters, and with lots of white space.
5. It should be factual and honest.

Events which occur over a period of time, such as schooling and employment, are usually listed in reverse chronological order, with the most recent experience listed first and working backward to the earliest.

Usually, the information most relevant to the purpose for which you are sending a résumé is listed at the beginning. For example, if you are applying for college, you would probably place your educational background and school honours first. If you are applying for a job, you would probably place your work experience first.

You can list people who will recommend you, together with their addresses, but if you do so, be sure that you have obtained their permission first.

More information on résumé writing is available at any Canada Manpower office. A good reference for writers of résumés and job application letters, recommended by Canada Manpower, is *What Colour is Your Parachute? A Practical Manual for Job-Hunters and Career Changers*, by Richard Bolles, Ten Speed Press, 1977.

(*Activity 9D*)

Writing a Résumé: Focus on Purpose and Audience

John Jacobs is twenty-seven years old, is married and has two children. He has practiced law for three years, but the firm with which he was employed is to dissolve soon. John attended Dalhousie University for seven years. He spent four years in the Faculties of Arts and Education, and three years in the Faculty of Law. He is both a qualified school teacher and lawyer. He is also an accomplished pianist and has done some acting. In fact, one of his majors in the Faculty of Arts was acting. He also acted in secondary school productions at Dartmouth High School while he attended

```
                    PERSONAL DATA SHEET

                          FOR

                    DALE G. ROBERTSON

                Box 2481, Quesnel, B. C.

                        V2J 3J5
```

JOB OBJECTIVE   To work with a company concerned with preparing
                 food for commercial and domestic use.

WORK HISTORY

May 1980   Position: Labourer, Quality Building Supplies,
                 1286 Quesnel Lake Road, Quesnel, B.C. V2J 3J5

                 Work Performed: Unloading trucks, piling lumber,
                 cleaning up yard.

                 Supervisor: Mr. J.L. Lohnes, Yard Foreman

October 1979 -   Position: Labourer, Poole Construction,
                 864 Cranbrook Road, Fernie, B.C. V0B 1M0
March 1980
                 Work Performed: Sweeping pavement base before
                 paving, clearing rocks, directing traffic.

                 Supervisor: Mr. K.L. Knickle, Foreman

                 Reason for Leaving: Paving Contract was completed.

April 1979 -   Position: Taxi Driver, Yellow Cab Company,
                 864 Northill Road, Kamloops, B.C.
August, 1979
                 Work Performed: Driving Passengers to and from
                 airport.

                 Supervisor: Mr. M. K. Wilson

                 Reason for Leaving: Temporary position

EDUCATION   Completed Algebra, Physics and Chemistry 12 at
                 Cariboo College, Kamloops, B.C. 1980.

                 Completed Grade 11, Quesnel High School, Quesnel,
                 B.C. 1979.

PERSONAL   Age: 19   Interests: Travelling, skiing, hunting

                 Marital Status: Single

                 Health: Excellent Memberships: Secretary, Minor
                                                  Hockey Association

REFERENCES   Will be supplied at interview.
```

there (1966-1968). He was captain of the school's debating team for those two years, and played on the rugby team.

While working his way through university, John was employed as a clerk in a legal office for two summers (1973 and 1974) and as a summer playground coordinator in Halifax (1975 and 1976).
```

Creating any other details you think necessary, develop two résumés for John. The first one will be directed towards a number of law firms where he would like to work. The second will be directed towards school board officials since John, who holds a Nova Scotia Teaching Certificate, would like to teach elementary school if he cannot get an immediate job with a good legal firm.

You may vary the form of the résumé to suit John's different purposes and audiences. Present John in the best light in each situation. For ideas on résumé form, see the outline already presented on page 198 and the one following Activity 9D on page 199.

(Activity 9E)

Writing a Personal Résumé

Collect the information necessary to write a résumé. Discuss your material with someone who knows your background, and then write the résumé, varying the form, if necessary, to suit your purpose. Before submitting your finished résumé for editing and proofreading, prepare a cover letter that tells why you are submitting the résumé and what you are requesting. Base your résumé on the model presented on page 199 and check the following outline developed by Canada Manpower.

RÉSUMÉ OUTLINE

A résumé is sometimes called a Qualification sheet, a Data sheet, or a Brag sheet. Most people are overly modest about their personal achievements, and a well prepared résumé enables them to reveal their best points to the prospective employer in the first five minutes of a job interview.[2]

1. Your name—address—telephone
2. Objective: Statement explaining position sought
3. Work experience—month—year—(start with most recent
         work experience)
         Name of company:
         Position: (title)
         Duties: (give detailed description of work done)
         Employees supervised if any: How many?
         Reference: (name of supervisor, manager etc.)
         Reason for leaving:
4. Work experience: Same as above
5. Work experience: Same as above
6. Related experience: List related experience in short sentences

7. Equipment I can operate: (group various kinds of equipment)
8. Education: High school graduate, college, degrees, special courses etc.
9. Miscellaneous information (if pertinent) (optional)
10. Hobbies: List a few only.
11. References: List three work and/or character references.

Preparing Memos

Memos, or memoranda, are simple notes, usually on a single subject, to be circulated *within* an organization, rather than between organizations. They are used to communicate information, to summarize oral agreements so that all participants are certain of exactly what was decided, and to record decisions so that at some later time there will be a notation of exactly who was responsible for a particular action. Notice the differences and similarities between memos and business letters.

```
                          M E M O


To:  Everyone Concerned with "The Tiger's Cry"

From:  Wilma Schuerer, Student Director   W.S.

Subject:  Dress Rehearsal Schedule

1.  At a meeting with Dr. Smith in her office on Tuesday, October 20,

    the Board of Advisors agreed on a rehearsal schedule limited to

    2 ½ hours per night, three nights a week (Monday, Wednesday, and

    Friday) from 7-9:30 p.m.  The band room has been reserved for

    these rehearsals beginning October 27 through November 12.

2.  Because we need to set up and practise in the gymnasium but

    cannot do so after school when the basketball team is practising,

    Dr. Smith has agreed to excuse everyone in the production from

    12:30 p.m. to 3:00 p.m. for dress rehearsals on Thursday,

    November 13, and Friday, November 14.  The homecoming performance

    will be on Saturday, November 15.

3.  Mrs. Schubert, band director, and Mr. Rice, basketball coach,

    have accepted this arrangement.
```

Here, for example, is a memo, or memorandum (note the plural form in previous paragraph and the singular form in this sentence). As the director of the school play, Wilma talked with Dr. Smith, her principal, about the rehearsal schedule. When Dr. Smith gave her permission to have dress rehearsal on school time, Wilma wrote a memo, duplicated it, and sent it to everyone involved. Her memo satisfied all three reasons that memos are written:

1. It communicated information.
2. It summarized the oral agreements of the conference so that everyone would know exactly what was agreed upon.
3. It fixed the responsibility on Dr. Smith for releasing students from class. (Obviously, Wilma wouldn't want to be held responsible for that decision.)

Note that Wilma simply initialed the line on which her name appears, rather than signing the memo formally. Note also that a memo is much simpler than a business letter. What elements of the business letter does it leave out? How does the form differ? Why can a memo, which is prepared for *internal* circulation (circulation *within* an organization) afford to take short cuts forbidden in a letter, which is usually prepared for *external* circulation (circulation *between* organizations or between organizations and individuals)?

(Activity 9F)

Listing Situations Calling for Memos

You probably belong to several different school, church, or community organizations. List several situations in which a memo to one or more members in one of these organizations would be an appropriate communication. Write one or more memos. Submit your memos for editing and proofreading. Here are some examples to get you started:

1. The Science Club circulates information about a trip to a local planetarium.
2. The Debating Club arranges a special gift and recognition for Mrs. Herrick, the adviser.
3. The Sports Council must change the date of the homecoming basketball game.
4. The Creative Writing Club agrees on a method of choosing the judges for the annual contest.
5. The student council plans the annual canned goods collection for Thanksgiving.

Writing Reports

At times, people refuse to accept and believe what they see with their own eyes. According to Vesalius, a famous doctor in the 1500s, another doctor in an anatomy class once told his students as he dissected a body, "The great teacher Hippocrates said that there is a vein in this spot right here." But as he dissected the body, he found no vein. However, instead of challenging the statement of Hippocrates, he said, "Unfortunately, this body, too, is wrong. In thirty years of teaching, I have never found a body which has the vein where it is supposed to be." Because people ignored their own observations and depended upon the pronouncements of ancient authorities, many incorrect and harmful beliefs continued for centuries. Fortunately, Vesalius was willing to challenge the scientific assumptions of his day.

Consider the accountant trying to improve efficiency in a business office, the industrial engineer working to solve a problem in the design of a machine, or the argicultural scientist studying ways to increase a crop's yield. In almost every field, observing carefully and reporting those observations are very important in trying to make a present situation better.

Let's consider a very simple kind of observation that can result in a worthwhile report. A media critic, Karl E. Meyer, was bothered because he felt that television is not treated as seriously as it should be by modern magazines. He said that some live plays, seen at most by a few people, are taken more seriously than a TV mini-series that will be viewed by tens of millions.[3]

Was Meyer correct in his opinion? Was he right in being disturbed? The only way to know would be to do some research and find out. Here is the kind of study he devised in order to find out whether or not he was correct. He took thirteen consecutive issues of a widely read news magazine and recorded the number of columns devoted to books, cinema, music, art, theatre, show business, and television. Then he could say for certain that he was right. In thirteen issues, the magazine devoted one hundred and two columns to books, fifty-two columns to movies, forty-two and a half columns to music, thirty-nine columns to art, twenty-five to theatre, twenty-seven to show business in general, and only six to television.

If Meyer had been writing a report for business, industry, or science, he would have organized his paper in this way:

Part I   —Why this question occurred to me and why I thought it important enough to research.

Part II   —What I did to reach a conclusion.

Part III —What I specifically observed (that is, how many columns were devoted to each medium).

Part IV   —What I concluded as a result of what I observed (that this magazine, at least, devotes much more space to media which have less influence than television).

Part V   —What I recommend as a result of what I observed and what I concluded. (Mr. Meyer is probably not in a position to make recommendations that will result in action, but someone writing a report to stimulate action might recommend: 1. That readers demand a more balanced allocation of space for reviews; 2. That editors increase the amount of space for television reviews and reduce that for less influential media.)

The report pattern just presented is useful in science, industry, business, education, and every other field in which people benefit by observing and reporting accurately. Chances are you will someday be called upon in your career to prepare some sort of report.

This kind of purposeful observation has played an important part in every area of human endeavour. Here is an example of a report by Benjamin Franklin of an experiment he conducted in England in 1765. He knew that the ancient Greeks had learned that oil spread on water would calm waves.

Part I—Why I wanted to find out something

Recollecting what I had formerly read in Pliny, I resolved to make some experiments of the effect of oil on water, when I should have the opportunity....

Part II—What I did

At length, being at Clapham (London), where there is, on the common, a large pond, which I observed one day to be very rough with the wind, I fetched out a cruet of oil, and dropped a little of it on the water.... I went to the side where they [the waves] began to form....

Part III—What I observed

I saw it [the oil] spread itself with surprising swiftness upon the surface.... and there the oil, though not more than a teaspoonful, produced an instant calm over a space several yards square, which spread amazingly, and extended itself gradually till it reached the lee side, making all that quarter of the pond, perhaps half an acre, as smooth as a looking-glass.[4]

Thus Franklin demonstrated the benefit of "pouring oil on troubled waters." Franklin did not finish his report with Part IV—What I Concluded and Part V—What I Recommend. It is easy, however, to imagine what he might have said:

Part IV—What I concluded

I concluded that Pliny and the ancients were indeed correct and that a minute quantity of certain kinds of oil will calm the waves.

Part V—What I recommend

I therefore recommend that all naval vessels be required in the future to carry at bow and stern, port and starboard, four barrels of specially prepared oil to jettison into the sea in case of bad weather threatening to sink the ship. I further recommend that shore installations such as lighthouses, ports, and gun emplacements likely to be threatened by severe storms likewise store barrels of oil for discharge into the water.

Here is a student's report of a simple investigation.

After Mr. Carruthers explained Gresham's Law and showed how "Bad money drives good money out of circulation," I saw what he meant and how people would "hoard" their good money—gold and respected currency—and spend their "bad" money, which might lose its value. When he casually said that the same thing applies to television and that bad programs drive out good, I disagreed with him.

Part I—Why I Wanted to Find Out Something

To see whether he was right or not, I had Miss Lane and Mr. Barrett, two English teachers, rate the six different programs that came on our local channels last night at 9.00 p.m. as either "good," "bad," or "indifferent." The "classic" movie on Channel 3 and the Masterpiece Theatre play on Channel 10 rated "good." The PG-rated movie on Channel 8 rated "bad," as did the Channel 7 sit-com. The travelogue special on Channel 13 rated "indifferent" as did the ancient movie on Channel 5.

Part II—What I Did

Then I asked 46 students in two of my classes what they watched. This is what I found:

Part III—What I Observed

Channel		Number Watching
3	(good)	0
10	(good)	2
8	(bad)	24
7	(bad)	0
13	(indifferent)	1
5	(indifferent)	0

(19 students were not watching TV)

If this little poll is any indication, students from this school who watch television are overwhelmingly interested in "bad," rather than in "good" or "indifferent" programs. And with television programs depending on ratings for their existence, I guess I would have to agree that bad programs drive out good ones.

Part IV—What I Concluded

Although it seems to be an insurmountable problem, I think English and social studies teachers should

Part V—What I Recommend

keep on trying to get their students to watch quality programs, rather than bad ones. Perhaps there ought to be some way to reward producers of good programs and the stations that keep them on the air, in spite of ratings. Maybe we could have a subsidy for good programs, or just more support for educational public broadcasting. Maybe, too, we could try to turn the networks and the advertisers away from the ratings race.

—Matthew Burke

(*Activity 9G*)

Gathering Ideas for Research Reports

Working as your teacher directs, use each of the following headings as ideas for possible research and report projects. After you get a list of at least five projects, spend some time devising an investigation or experiment to help you learn about each subject.

1. What the people in our town (school, club, neighbourhood, church, other) think about a current issue.
2. How certain people act when confronted with a certain kind of situation.
3. How people value different things, programs, ideas, activities.
4. Who supports a certain program.
5. What kinds of career objectives certain student groups hold.
6. Where our school draws its teachers from.
7. What books, films, magazines, and programs are most popular among certain groups.
8. What characterizes a certain author's style.
9. How people feel about certain highly emotional words, such as Commie, scab, cheat, and so on.

When you have worked out a possible experiment or observation for a number of different subjects, choose one, carry it out as thoroughly as possible, and prepare a written report following the form you have learned. In actual business and industry, the headings used are usually:

1. Background
2. Procedure
3. Results (or Observations)
4. Conclusions
5. Recommendations.

For short periods, the headings need not be used. Do as your teacher directs.

King Edward VI of England was not quite ten years old when he wrote this letter to his uncle, the Duke of Somerset. In this letter, Edward congratulated the Duke on his "good courage and wise foresight" in a battle against the Scots.

Social Notes and Gracious Communication

Up until now, you have been concentrating on business letters of various kinds, résumés, memos, and reports. There will be many occasions in your life when you will find it useful to know these business forms. There will also be occasions that will call for another kind of letter, a friendly letter or social note.

Whole volumes have been written about how to plan and write various kinds of social notes. It is rather unfortunate that modern technology has now simplified life to such an extent that few of these are necessary any more. At one time, almost everyone was very careful to send personally written notes concerning:

Invitations of various kinds (lunch, dinner, special occasions, weekend visits, and so on)

Acceptance or refusal of invitations

Birth announcements

Christening announcements

Engagement announcements

Wedding announcements

Thank-you notes for gifts

Apologies for broken appointments

Congratulations on various events (graduation, promotion, new job, new home)

Birthday greetings

Get-well notes

Letters of introduction (presenting one of your friends to another)

Sympathy for a death

How would you reply if a friend from your graduating class wrote to invite you to her engagement party? Here is a sample of one student's reply to such an invitation.

---

24 Avalon Street
St. John's, Newfoundland
A1C 4P7

1980 09 23

Dear Sandy,

Congratulations! You wouldn't believe how happy I was when I read of your engagement to Tom. Right now you must feel like the luckiest girl in the world.

I was honoured to receive an invitation to your engagement party; however, with things as they are now, I can't quite afford to come over for a weekend. I really wish I could, for I miss all my friends and I'd like to see everyone again. But, what I am doing now is saving extra money so that I can make it for the wedding.

I hope the party will be wonderful, and although I won't be there, my blessings reach out to you both.

A friend always,

Janet

— Janet Michel

Many people solve most of these communication problems by sending commercial cards that express the appropriate sentiment. Although these are quite acceptable, a simple personal note conveying your own sincere sentiments is both less expensive and usually more highly regarded. Rather than memorizing a set form, just express your own thoughts in your own way. If you feel the need for guidance, you can find it in "The Correspondence Guide" in the back of many dictionaries, such as *The Reader's Digest Great Encyclopedic Dictionary*, in such books as *Amy Vanderbilt's Guide to Modern Etiquette*, and in many library reference sources. Various suppliers of services (florists, stationers, wedding shops) will also provide expert, but somewhat expensive, guidelines. It is probably better to visit your library reference room, ask the librarian for help, and prepare your own social note, using the sentiments and form that you are most comfortable with.

> *...the tested formula for becoming rich as an author is to write regularly to an uncle who is dying from a surfeit of oil wells.*
> —Eric Nicol

Personal Letters

One of the most famous letters of all time was written by Lord Chesterfield to his son, telling him to write a personal letter.

My dear Boy,

When you read my letters, I hope you pay attention as well to the spelling as you do to the histories. You must likewise take notice of the manner in which they are written: which sets out to be easy and natural, not strained and florid. For instance, when you are thinking about sending a billet-doux, or love letter, to Miss Pinkerton, you must only think of what you would say to her if you were both together, and then write it; that renders the style easy and natural; though some people imagine the writing of a letter to be a great undertaking, and think they must write abundantly better than they talk, which is not at all necessary....

Nothing is more requisite than to write a good letter. Nothing in fact is more easy. Most persons who write ill, do so because they aim at writing better than they can, by which means they acquire a formal and unnatural style. For instance, if you want to write a letter to me, you should only consider what you would say if you were with me, and then write it in plain terms, just as if you were conversing.

Affectionately,

(Lord Chesterfield, 1789)

Lord Chesterfield's ideas are excellent. This is the order in which he presents them. Rearrange them in what you consider to be the order of importance:

1. Pay attention to spelling.
2. Pay attention to the ideas (histories).
3. Write in an easy, natural manner.
4. Write as you would speak personally to the one to whom you are writing.
5. Avoid a formal and unnatural style.

At the present time, Canada is far more relaxed and informal than England was in the time of Lord Chesterfield. Personal correspondence is similarly relaxed and informal. In writing to a close friend you may be as informal as you wish. When writing a friendly letter to a person whom you do not know or do not know well, you should use the standard form as in the letter that follows.

The usual form of a friendly letter is identical with that of a business letter with one exception: it has no inside address. There are two reasons for putting an inside address on a business letter: 1. It assures the sender that the letter will reach the proper person within the company; 2. It assures the sender that the letter will be filed properly for retrieval. Since a friendly letter goes directly to an individual, it needs no inside address.

Whether your letter is casual or a bit more formal, you owe it to yourself and your reader to write interestingly and correctly. Besides the message of its content, every letter carries another message. It tells a lot about the character of the writer. A careless, messy, ungrammatical letter is not only hard to read, it creates a negative impression about the writer. A neatly written letter that is dull and uninteresting creates an impression too. Think about what kind of person you are and make your letters reflect that person.

Two Model Letters

In 79 A. D., just south of Naples by the Sarno River, Mt. Vesuvius suddenly erupted, burying Pompeii and some of its people under nine metres of ashes and mud. In the book, *Letters from Pompeii*, a professor from the University of Maryland and his wife tell, in a series of letters to nieces and nephews, about several visits to Pompeii almost nineteen hundred years after the disaster. No heading was given for this letter. Can you supply one that would be suitable?

II

Dearest Sally, Jimmy, Ruth, and Kathy,

Yesterday was another exciting day. Something happens every day that I know you would like to hear about—but it seems there is little time for writing letters.

"Come with us to the new excavations near the south wall," we were told yesterday morning when we stopped at the *Scavi* office. We knew what that meant! Several days ago we had been shown some mounds of hardened volcanic dust that had been left untouched during the excavation of a large garden. When we examined the mounds, we saw two skulls partly exposed in one of them. The archaeologists knew there would be cavities in the mounds, just the shape of the human bodies that perished there.

The workmen were almost ready to make the casts. We watched them mix plaster of Paris and water and carefully pour it into the cavities. Soon it began to harden. Finally they were ready to pull away the volcanic dust that had smothered these people. It was a dramatic moment.

They began to scrape away the ashes very carefully, for, of course, they didn't know just where the plaster casts would be, and they didn't want to injure them. First the head and back of an adult came out—next a hand, then a foot—finally the second foot. It was obvious that this unfortunate person had fallen on his stomach, turning his face sidewise as he fell.

They continued to remove the rest of the volcanic dust—first at one place and then another. Finally, they located a second cast. Gently they pulled away more of the covering of earth-like volcanic dust. We watched for nearly three hours. It gave us a queer feeling when we saw a small foot come into view. "A *bambino*," we said. They continued to uncover the little body. "How old?" I asked.

"Seven years," one of the experts estimated.

All at once it became clear. A parent fleeing with a child had not been able to make it to safety as so many did.

Nearby are two other mounds in which we can see cavities and human bones. Who else perished here? Perhaps the rest of the family? Do you suppose they will find other children? We will tell you when they pour the casts.

Love to you all,

Aunt Mina and Uncle Stanley

P.S. You can see in the picture, under the temporary roofs, the exact spot in the garden where the bodies were found! Apparently these people did not try to escape until the ashes began to cover the second story of their home. Then they fled out of the upstairs window, but they did not get far.[5]

For a number of years, novelist Malcolm Lowry lived in Dollarton, a small community on Burrard Inlet north of Vancouver. In this letter to his brother, Lowry, in an intimate and informal way, shares some of his successes and heartaches.

III

Dollarton, B.C.
Canada
—or perhaps I should
spell it Dolorton
(Fall, 1950)

Dear old Stuart:

A towering sea is bearing down upon me. Gulls are balancing in the gale. A black cormorant is struggling low over the waves against the wind. All around me is a thunderous sound of breaking, smashing, trees pirouetting and dancing, as a full gale smashes through the forest. What is this? A seascape—or a suggestion for program music, as for Sibelius or Wagner. No: this is the view out of our living room window, while we are having our morning coffee. What I see is quite unbelievable, even for you, unless you have seen it—and where else would you see, but here, a house that is built in the sea and where the problems—and noises—are those that beset the mariner rather than the normal householder? It is wonderfully dramatic—too dramatic, even for me, for us, in some respects, for we now live under the shadow, at any moment, of losing it. This I've told you before. We only live here by grace of being pioneers, and Canada, alas, is forgetting that it is its pioneers who built this country and made it what it was: now it wants to be like everyone else and have autocamps instead of trees and Coca-Cola stands instead of human beings. In that way, for it has little culture at all, it could destroy its soul: that is its own business, no doubt—what we mind is that it threatens to destroy us in the process, an eventuality that it now becomes my duty to try and avoid. Have I mentioned that this is supposed to be a begging letter, even if addressed to one who can do naught, and is hamstrung even as I? One of those letters that you see, or may see one day, under a glass case in a museum—just as this house that we fear to be thrown out of someone may make money out of one day—for I am the only Canadian writer ever to be placed in the *Encyclopedia Britannica*—a sort of begging letter at least, though I don't know on what moral grounds I am presumed to be begging for what upon one plane of reasoning would certainly seem to have been once at least intended to be mine; begging being something I understand that even the tycoons of Canada may be driven to from their neighbouring country as an alternative to stealing, a practice I am inhibited from less on moral grounds than fear of the consequences and plain incompetence.

All this, in my usual direct fashion, you may take to refer to the crucifical position of a writer in Canada.

First I shall give you—an important item in the technique of such letters even when one understands perfectly well the utter fruitlessness of it—a list of my accomplishments, immediately followed of course by a similar list of catastrophes.

Have written and completed in collaboration with Margerie a detailed movie script—adapted from a novel you won't have heard of—upon which we worked, sometimes with the temperature below zero in the house, some fourteen hours a day—it was so cold at one point we couldn't take off our clothes for a fortnight.

Succeeded in having the *Volcano* published in translation in Norway, Denmark, Sweden and France—in the first and last countries put into an edition with the classics of the world.

Seen it hailed as the greatest masterpiece of the last ten years in the French translation in Paris.

Been put in the *Encyclopedia Britannica*. (For how long? Are you comfortable there, Malcolm?)

Well I could go on with these, but I think it's time now for a few catastrophes.

Operation for a chronic condition of my legs. Successful and expensive.

Continued anxiety—partly responsible for condition when you met me—of thinking one had T.B. Tests showed I have had T.B. at some time or other—when?—and am liable to it: but have it no longer. Have conquered anxiety neurosis on this score.

My monthly income is now little more than $90—that has the purchasing power of little more than a fiver in the old days, and I am not exaggerating. Rent makes sympathetic and contradictory fluctuations of course, but you would be lucky merely to rent anywhere these days for $90 a month, without food—let alone live.

A notice of eviction that seems final, but with just a bare possibility of reprieve in it: but it scarcely seems possible it can last more than a few months.

Margerie ill—with ourselves still in the dark as to what is really wrong with her: x-rays, brain tumor still suspected, treatment that must be continued, begins to put us into the category of the starving. Much may be done with oatmeal. I begin even to think of the saying, 'Home is the place where, when they have to, they take you in.' But where indeed is that, unless here? Her mother lives 2000 miles [3200 km] away in America, mine 10 000 [16 000 km]. And we have no friends in Canada save three fishermen in like case, a cat, five wild ducks, two seagulls, and, of course, a wolf.

In my case the possibilities of work are or were three: teaching, radio, newspaper work. The first requires at least a year's negotiation and a complete rededication of one's life—and probably going to the Prairies, since the English are hated in B.C. The second pays starvation wages and moreover requires a car, while the third not only does that but would be senseless because what I do anyway to attempt to augment the income makes more money and comes into the category of free lancing. In short there is no possibility of a job where we live—short of turning sailor again or working in a sawmill—for taking one would mean abandoning the really practical hope we cling to in regard to our serious work, and also our house: and indeed at the moment we haven't got money even to *move* anywhere else. Even if I could get a labourer's job the cost of transportation would swallow the money we save by living in the house. And writing is a whole-time job or nothing, so it would mean quitting. Margie can't augment matters by getting a job herself because she's not well enough: besides we do our work together. And for the same reason, however willing to turn my hand to anything, I couldn't leave her long enough in the wilderness by herself. In short, it's better to stick to one's guns: only it seems that begging is a standard part of writing, or is about to become so. You may therefore count this as work, for it's my all too valuable time, not counting yours. It may interest you to know that there is a long broadcast tonight or tomorrow night on the subject of Malcolm Lowry, Canada's greatest, most successful writer, which we can't listen to because our radio has run down and we can't afford to replenish the battery. The unkindest cut of all. Despite our love I have been warned that for Margie to live another winter under these conditions is very dangerous during the coldest part.

Losing the house under these callous conditions—and they are totally callous and selfish—would be a blow considering all the others—having lost it by fire and rebuilt it ourselves—of such psychological importance that if we had our way we wouldn't live in Canada at all any more. Well, we don't expect our way. The object is to live at all.[6]

(*Activity 9H*)

Discussing the Models

Either in small groups or with the entire class, discuss the following questions:

1. What are the elements of the form of these friendly letters?
2. Why are these letters interesting?
3. Notice how both writers have drawn on their everyday life experiences in their letter writing. What kinds of things that happen to secondary school students might be worth writing about?
4. How do the letters communicate the personalities of the writers? Compare and contrast their purpose, tone, and points of view.
5. What narrative and descriptive techniques do the writers use that you can use in your own letter writing?
6. Discuss the extent to which a letter should cover many subjects as opposed to focusing on one main event or a very few.
7. Make a list of life experiences related to school and community events which are interesting or important enough to include in a friendly letter.

(*Activity 9I*)

Fleshing Out an Empty Letter

Sometimes letter writers simply list ideas without developing them. The following letter is an empty letter. Using its content as a starter, flesh out the details by using your imagination. For example, specify where the writer visited Charlie, who his friends were, and what kinds of things they did together.

175 Warden Avenue
Scarborough, Ont.
MIN 2Z5
81-01-08

Dear Charlie,

It seems a lifetime since I visited you last summer, and yet it's only been seven months. Did'nt we have a great time, though? I haven't had such a good time for years, and I certainly enjoyed meeting all of your friends. You certainly have a fine bunch of friends, Charlie. I don't know when I have met such a great group. I'll never forget them, and I'll never forget what we did together.

In the seven months since I saw you, though, I haven't been letting any grass grow under my feet. I've been doing lots of interesting things. I've really been living it up, and I can't wait to tell you about it.

I guess about the most important thing is that I've found a new girlfriend. We have many things in common. I would like you to meet her. You would really like her.

I'm planning a great summer next summer. You know its only six months until school is out. I can't wait. I've really decided to do a lot of interesting things. It's going to be the best summer of my life. I hope you can join me for part of the time.

I hate to break off a letter to a friend, but duty calls. One of my teachers just gave me a big assignment, so I'd better get at it.

I hope I'll see you soon.

Yours truly,
Al

Major Writing Assignment

A. Write a letter to a friend or relative, which communicates both your personality and your interests to your correspondent. Follow these suggestions:
   1. Follow the form of the models just presented.
   2. Write as if you were speaking to the person.

3. Focus on a few ideas and develop them with description, details, and figures of speech.
4. Include events and your reactions to those events.
5. Edit and proofread your work before you submit it.

B. Three months ago, you purchased a new car. While you were out of town with the car, it developed a problem with the fuel line and had to be towed into a garage. When you returned home you reported the problem to the company from which you purchased the car, but the service-manager refused to reimburse you, claiming that the warranty does not cover such out-of-town situations. You feel that the $165 involved should be covered by the dealer's warranty.

Write a letter of complaint to the president of this dealership, Better Cars Ltd., explaining your situation and requesting that he look into it.

1. Adopt an appropriate format and tone for a letter of complaint.
2. Expand the details of the situation given here. Include the names of the people involved and proper addresses also.
3. After appropriate revision and editing, prepare a final draft, proofreading carefully before you submit it.

C. The following newspaper advertisement has aroused your interest. Write a letter to the personnel director, Ms. S. Fitch, in which you request an interview for this position. Indicate in your letter that you are enclosing a full résumé for her consideration. Remember to carry out appropriate editing and final proofreading tasks before you submit your letter.

Management Trainees

Applications are welcome from bright, ambitious secondary school graduates to enter Douglas Inns management trainee program. Good training courses; good starting salary. Write to Ms. S. Fitch, Personnel Manager, Douglas Inns Inc., 5325 24th Ave., Regina, Sask. S3S 4E6

D. You have been appointed chairperson of your student council's annual Christmas Hamper Food Drive. Write a memo which will be posted in each classroom. Include the following information:

1. The dates for the Food Drive.
2. How collection of donations will be handled.
3. How decisions will be made concerning who gets the hampers.
4. A request for volunteers to help you carry out the job; give time and place for a meeting of volunteers.

10

The Library Resource Paper

Sometime near the middle of the semester, your English teacher, your history teacher, or your science teacher may say, "Now, your term paper will be due on...."

In your school such a major paper may be called something else— research paper, semester report, major thesis, or senior research project— but the results of the announcement are the same: Panic!

Actually, you shouldn't be as disturbed as the regular student ritual encourages you to be. Prepare yourself for writing such a paper by 1. making sure you understand the assignment, 2. proceeding systematically, and 3. allowing yourself sufficient time. In this chapter, you will be given insights into what a library resource paper is and you will be shown how to proceed. It will be up to you to proceed systematically and to allow sufficient time to do your best work. Since the major writing assignment at the end of this chapter assumes you are working on a research paper, this chapter should be studied during the completion of such an assignment. Your teacher will relate such an assignment to some current issue of class study.

◀ This engraving shows the library of the University of Leiden in the Netherlands as it appeared in 1610. William of Orange built the university to reward the citizens for their heroism in defending the city.

What a Library Resource Paper Is

Of all the terms used to describe the major paper some courses require, perhaps the best name is "library resource paper." Very simply, in writing such a paper, you take some subject you know about and are interested in and make a statement about it. Then you try to convince or persuade a reader that your statement is correct. As one of your techniques for convincing or persuading your reader, you frequently refer to what other writers or speakers have said on the subject. In short, you borrow—always using the regularly accepted, customary procedures—the ideas, statistics, reasoning, research, history and so on that other writers have previously presented. By adding this material to your own ideas, you increase the chances that the reader will accept your thesis. He or she is bound to be impressed with the information you've collected, with the prestige of the people who agree with you and with the work you've done in supporting your idea.

Reasons for Learning to Write Library Resource Papers

The ability to write a library resource paper is both a "school skill' and a "life skill." Most students are assigned a library resource paper at some time during their high school careers, and all those who go on to university—no matter what field they choose to major in—must, at some time or another, write a paper in which they use the standard customary procedures in citing the works of other writers to support their own ideas on a particular subject. This is, obviously, an important "school skill."

But how is the ability to write a library resource paper a "life skill?" Will students who do not go to university ever use such a skill after graduating from secondary school? Actually, they may never use all of the formal techniques of arranging footnotes and preparing the bibliographies that list sources of information. However, they will use the skills of finding, arranging, and presenting material to convince or persuade someone that they are right about a certain idea. They may, for example, become active in local politics. In that case, they may need to get information to convince the town council or the voters that city planning pays off, that privately-owned utilities are (or are not) cheaper than city-owned power and water plants, that parking meters are worthwhile, or that closing a street to make a pedestrian mall will help the merchants. If they become active in a service club or a P.T.A., they may need to find material to prove that a certain kind of fund-raising drive is (or is not) a good idea. If they work in a church group or a neighbourhood improvement association, they may need to convince others, by finding, arranging, and presenting information, that certain kinds of businesses should be banned from an area, that groups in other places have found certain procedures successful, or that tax reductions (or raises) will benefit the residents. If they run their own businesses, they may find themselves using these skills frequently.

The purposes of this kind of paper, then, are to make a careful search for information about a particular subject, and then to present and interpret what has been found. A research or library resource paper should *not* be a mere report of reading or a hodgepodge of quotations and summaries.

An effective research paper is an orderly, systematic study undertaken for a specific purpose. To turn out a good library resource paper takes time. It is a task that cannot be done hastily or postponed until the last moment.

Most people believe that high school graduates should know how to write library resource papers for these reasons:

1. The skill is both a school skill and a life skill.
2. You learn other important English skills, including library resource procedures, paragraphing, and logic, as you do the library resource paper.
3. The skill is important for success in high school.
4. Many university professors—both of English and of other subjects—simply assume that beginning students have the skill and assign resource papers without teaching the procedures.

Library Resource Paper Procedures

Writing a library resource paper involves these steps:

1. Deciding on a subject, an area, or a field.
2. Acquiring general information, background, or experience.
3. Narrowing the subject to a specific topic and making a statement you believe in about the topic (stating your thesis).
4. Searching for information to support your thesis statement.
5. Recording your sources of information.
6. Recording *usable* material to support your thesis statement.
7. Preparing a tentative outline.
8. Writing your first draft complete with footnotes and bibliography to fit your thesis statement and outline, revising where necessary.
9. Getting someone to edit your draft and make suggestions.
10. Preparing your final draft and front matter (title page, outline and possibly an introduction).
11. Proofreading and submitting.

The following sections will explain each of these steps. Each of the next eleven sections is a separate activity for you to do as you prepare your library resource paper. Because you can combine some of the steps and handle others in different ways, they are not listed for you as "Activity 10A," "Activity 10B," and so on. Nonetheless, you should consider them as helpful and necessary as you prepare your paper.

Before you begin this section, work out with your teacher both a schedule of when you will be undertaking each step and an indication of how much time, both in and out of class, you ought to be spending on each one. For example, for Step 2, your teacher may advise you that to write a good paper you will probably need to browse in the library at this point for three or four hours.

To write a well-developed paper, you should probably allow from three to five weeks, but, of course, you will be doing other kinds of writing assignments at the same time.

1. Deciding on a Subject[1]

The most important step in writing a library resource paper is the first: choosing a topic that is interesting to you, important enough to be worth your time, defined enough for you to handle, and significant enough to matter.

Student-teacher consultations can be a very useful part of this selection process—and of your whole research process. Some teachers like to set up a schedule of consultations during the writing of a library resource paper. In any case, make sure you understand what is wanted and then use your teacher as a sounding board as your paper develops. Initially, be sure to observe any limitations your teacher imposes. An english teacher, history teacher, or science teacher may limit you to a specific range of topics and then expect you to work within the boundaries established. Remember, a *topic* is a very broad term for a subject. Once you have identified a subject or topic area, it must be narrowed down to a more specific purpose. Discuss the assignment with friends, other teachers, or experts in the field as well as with your subject teacher. Browse among library books in the appropriate field and review appropriate encyclopedia entries. Begin to develop a focus by defining the possibilities of your chosen topic area.

2. Acquiring General Information, Background, or Experience

Often, after you've decided on a topic area and even focused in on some of its possibilities, you still don't know enough about the area to be able to specify an idea about which you might successfully develop in a research paper. For example, a secondary school student named Kal Gill knew, after going through the first step, that he wanted to write about "the Vietnam conflict," but until he moved to step 2, he had no idea of the range of possibilities of this rather large subject. Kal's paper will be used as a model for this chapter and you will follow his procedure step by step.[2] By consulting with his teacher, talking to others and skimming appropriate books, encyclopedia entries and periodical indexes, he began to narrow the field. He discarded such aspects of the topic as the involvement of the United States in the Vietnam conflict (a popular subject which Kal felt students had already over-worked) and the significance of the conflict in terms of the Cold War. Instead, he decided to focus on "French colonial involvement in Vietnam (Indochina)" during the period in which preceded what we usually think of as "the Vietnam War."

3. Making a Thesis Statement

After Kal limited himself to the topic of "French colonial involvement in Vietnam," he began to look for an appropriate thesis statement—the next step in giving focus to a topic.

> The thesis of a research paper expresses an opinion about the topic boiled down to one arguable statement.

The reason a topic or subtopic alone is not enough for a library resource paper is this: If you have just a topic, all you can do is collect facts, statistics, information—as much of these kinds of data as possible—and present them wholesale, similar to the way an encyclopedia presents a lot of ideas on a topic. A library resource paper is not strictly a presentation of information; it is rather, a persuasion or argumentation paper that tries to get a reader to accept an opinion or point of view.

Everything in the paper depends upon the thesis, for the entire purpose is to explain, clarify, defend, and illustrate it—and thus, to persuade the reader of its truth. It is the ONE MAJOR POINT that is made with everything else stripped away. It is the result of selective thinking: the narrowing of a broad topic to a specific judgment.

A few simple guidelines will help you to formulate an effective thesis statement.

1. Select a thesis which can be adequately treated in the space available.
2. Select a thesis about which enough information is available.
3. Select a thesis which is interesting but not overly technical or specialized.
4. Formulate a thesis which provides a clear purpose as to what will be demonstrated, proven, or concluded by the research. Note the following examples:
   (a) Solar energy is the answer to Canada's long range energy problems.
   (b) A successful Gallipoli Campaign (1915) could have altered both the course and consequences of World War I.

(c) T. S. Eliot's poetry reflects a concern with the absence of strong spiritual values in twentieth century western society.

(d) Proper application of wage and price controls could help eliminate inflation and economic stagnation in Canada.

Kal, after considering a number of possibilities concerning his focus on the French in Vietnam, finally settled on the following tentative thesis statement: "It was not possible after World War II for France to retain Indochina." He decided that such a thesis was specific enough and workable in terms of time and resources available. Notice, though, that this was Kal's *tentative* thesis statement. The word "tentative" means "not definite" or "subject to change." If, as Kal learned more about his topic, he had decided that he wished to alter the focus of his paper, he would have changed his thesis statement and selected and reorganized his material to fit the new thesis.

If you can select your tentative thesis statement before you begin to write, your task is made easier for you. Sometimes, however, you might have to begin to read, organize, and write in order to discover a supportable position about a subject. In that case, you do your best to select information, organize, and write logically, even though you may have to redo some of your work when you formulate your thesis statement.

4. Searching for Information to Support Your Thesis Statement

Information, in its broadest sense, is any kind of knowledge capable of being transmitted. The task of the researcher is to gather from the world of information that which is related to his or her own investigation. Information is stored in persons or things. At any given moment every person is a storehouse of insight, observations, experiences and understandings. These kinds of information may be recovered through a personal interview. "Things" which store information include books, periodicals (magazines), pamphlets, newspapers, maps, charts, drawings, letters, records, tapes, films, microforms (microfiche and microfilm), artifacts, etc.

Libraries store many of these kinds of information. Information stored in a library is organized in a certain way; the information thus stored can be retrieved only by knowing the particular system for that specific form. For example, there are two systems of cataloguing for books: the Dewey Decimal and the Library of Congress. Become familiar with them if you are not already. Your librarian can explain them to you.

Your main tools for finding information in the library are the Card Catalogue which lists books (either on paper and filed in drawers or on microfiche), and the various indexes or abstracts which list serial holdings (periodicals and newspapers). Two widely used indexes are the *Reader's Guide to Periodical Literature* and the *Canadian Periodical Index*.

Kal first wanted to locate books related to his thesis, so he found the appropriate subject cards in the Card Catalogue.

Here is one of the subject cards that Kal used in researching his topic:

SUBJECT CARD

```
    959
    H183                    Indo-china
        s

            Hammer, E.J.
                Struggle for Indochina, 1954
```

Besides subject cards, author cards and title cards are also included in the Card Catalogue. The author and title cards for Kal's book look much like the subject card, except for the first heading.

AUTHOR CARD

```
    959
    H183
        s
                    Hammer, Ellen Joy
                    Struggle for Indochina, 342p.
                    with a preface by Rupert Emerson
                    maps    1954
                    Stanford Univ. Calif.
```

TITLE CARD

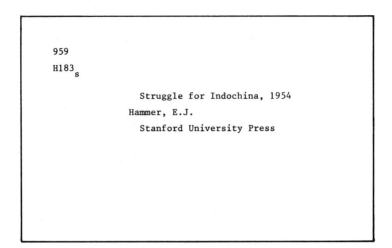

After locating appropriate books, Kal turned his attention to serials. He located an appropriate periodical index and began a systematic search. He checked the index to determine the time span it covered, checked the inside front cover to see which periodicals were indexed in it, used appropriate subject headings he found in the index ("Indochina," "Vietnam," "Vietnam War") and then recorded any potentially useful entries. Here is one entry Kal found useful that indicates the way most periodical indexes are organized:

INDOCHINA—French Involvement . . .
entry heading   subject

| Indochina | Newsweek | 43 | 37-38 | Mar. 15, 1954 |
| *title of article* | *name of periodical* | *volume* | *page numbers* | *month and year of publication* |

Entries in indexes like those in the Card Catalogue may be listed by subject, title or author, and Kal was able to figure out the meanings of most of the entries he consulted. When he was puzzled by an abbreviation, he looked it up in the list near the beginning of the index. He also found a model entry that explained all the abbreviations. He also took care to limit his search to the periodicals the library subscribed to ("serial holdings"). Their names were posted near the indexes. Larger libraries convey this information through a "library has" card in the Card Catalogue or through up to date computer print-out lists.

In order to cover other potential sources of information, Kal next consulted the library's index of newspaper holdings. He found that the library had several newspapers stored on microfilm. He also checked the library's vertical files for relevant pamphlets, news clippings, documents, drawings, etc. Material here is filed alphabetically by subject.

5. Recording Your Sources of Information

A key to efficient research is effective noting of your information sources. For each book, magazine, newspaper or pamphlet which he thought would be helpful, Kal prepared a separate bibliography card, or "bib card." He chose to use 3" x 5" pocket size cards. Cards are easier to handle than stacks of paper and they also play a very special role in collating the information to be included in the paper.

On each "bib card," Kal listed all of the information he would need to find that book or periodical in the library and to record the book properly in his footnotes and bibliography. Kal's bib cards for books looked like this:

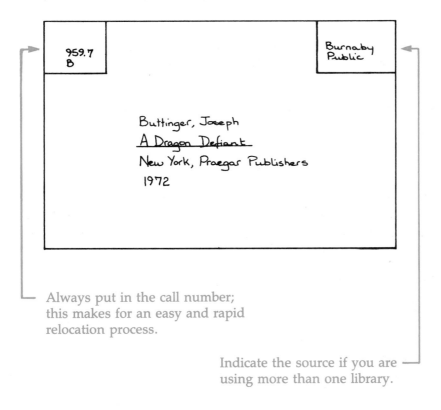

Always put in the call number; this makes for an easy and rapid relocation process.

Indicate the source if you are using more than one library.

His bib cards for articles in periodicals were similar:

```
Microfilm                                    S. F. U.


     Agreement Ending Vietnam and Laos Fighting, signed
     New York Times - July 21/54
     Page 1   Col. B
```

After preparing a separate card for each book or magazine he might use, Kal alphabetized them according to the last name of the author or editor and then placed a number in the upper right hand corner of each. As he prepared note cards while reading or skimming each source, he would be able to write on each note card the number of that source for easy cross referencing.

6. Recording Usable Material to Support Your Thesis Statement

Kal now began his in-depth research. Beginning with the most promising source, he skimmed rapidly, slowing down only when he noticed something important he might be able to use. During this process, his "full bibliography" became his "working bibliography" as he dismissed unavailable or useless materials. Cards for these materials were destroyed.

When he began taking notes, he tried to limit himself to several different kinds:

1. Direct quotations of statistics, details, or even stylistically satisfying sentences he might want to quote directly. (These he *always* indicated with quotation marks.)
2. Brief notations (often abbreviated), paraphrases of ideas and passages too long to quote, key phrases to remind him of entire ideas.
3. Short outlines of complicated thought processes.

Two of Kal's note cards looked like this:

Indochina Tragedy - Hammer   I
P.7 French policy towards Indochina was indicated at the conference of the French Committee for National Liberation at Brazzaville in January, 1944. General de Gaulle said, "The aims of the work of civilization which France is accomplishing in her possessions exclude any idea of autonomy and any possibility of development outside the French Empire Bloc. The attainment of 'self government' in the colonies, even in the most distant future, must be excluded."

New York Times Jun.16/54

P.6. France's "world mission" was to accumulate territories outside of Europe under the French flag. This position was jeopardized by Indochina. If the French lost Indochina, her relationship with her other colonies would become tenuous.

The heading on the top left of each card identifies the source of its content. Each card is limited to one item of information to make it easier to sort the cards and arrange them in the order Kal will eventually use while writing the paper.

The first card has quotation marks around the material that is quoted exactly as it appears in the original source. If Kal were to omit some words from the quote, he would use an ellipsis (three dots...); this device can be used at the beginning of a sentence ("...---"), in the middle of a sentence

("---...---"), or at the end of a sentence ("---..." or ----...?"). If he were to insert his own explanatory information in the quote, he would set that off with square brackets ([ ]).

In order to keep his reading and notetaking in the proper perspective, Kal practiced the idea of "focus reading." He began with the sources that looked most general in relation to this thesis and proceeded to more specific items:

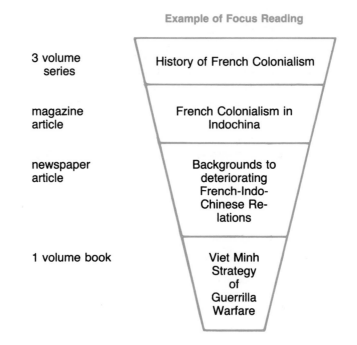

Example of Focus Reading

3 volume series	History of French Colonialism
magazine article	French Colonialism in Indochina
newspaper article	Backgrounds to deteriorating French-Indo-Chinese Re-lations
1 volume book	Viet Minh Strategy of Guerrilla Warfare

Focus reading helped impose an order on note cards and facilitated the next step in writing the paper.

7. Preparing a Tentative Outline

Kal was now ready to prepare a tentative or "working" outline. As he read, he recorded information he would use to support his thesis. He found that the information he was gathering suggested some natural divisions of his topic area:

These major divisions of information became major sections of Kal's outline. These in turn were further subdivided into equal parts: for example...

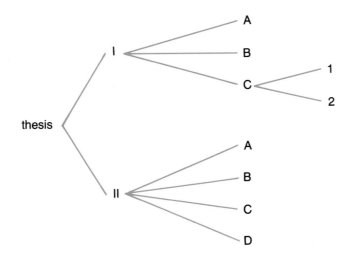

The first part of Kal's working outline looked like this. His complete finished outline—very similar to the working one—can be found on the specimen pages near the end of this chapter. Check it to get an idea of the format of a full outline.

Thesis: It was not possible after World War II for France to retain Indochina.

    I. The growth of independence movements in Indochina indicated increasing resistance to French rule.

        A. An anti-Communist Vietnamese nationalist front known as the Dong Minh Hoc was created in China in 1942.

        B. The Viet Minh, a Communist-backed independence league formed in 1941, emerged as the most powerful independence movement.

        1. The Chinese and Americans relied on the Viet Minh for intelligence information about the Japanese in Indochina.

        2. Weapons were received by the Viet Minh from the American O.S.S. for anti-Japanese work inside Vietnam.

        3. The Viet Minh initiated the attack on the French.

As you can see, while writing his outline Kal remembered that there can be no "A" without a "B" or no "1" without a "2", etc. Although the outline—like the tentative thesis statement—was subject to revision, he wanted to impose as much logic and order on it as possible in order to create a "tight" effective argument.

Kal now went back to his note cards and shuffled them into related groups according to divisions suggested by the working outline. This procedure is known as "collating." After collating he checked his outline to ensure that it and the information on the cards accurately reflected each other.

8. Writing Your First Draft to Fit Your Thesis Statement and Outline.

Kal now began to write, having only four items present beyond pen and paper: the outline, the note cards, the bibliography, and his dictionary-thesaurus. If your research has been adequate, these resources are all that you need as you proceed from the prewriting to the writing phase of the library resource paper. Do not do any more reading at this point as you are at a "strictly writing" stage of your work. Furthermore, aim to have this draft as complete as possible—including footnotes and bibliography. Because he had kept careful bib cards and note cards, the task of preparing footnotes and bibliography was easy. Kal wanted to lend authority and credibility to the facts and ideas in his paper and to avoid the charge of plagiarism (the attempt to pass off another person's ideas or words as one's own) so he was conscientious about acknowledging his sources. He knew that he should use footnotes in these situations: 1. to indicate that he had borrowed an idea, judgment, or information from an author even though he had used his own words; and 2. to show that he had borrowed an author's exact words as well as ideas. He put quotation marks around directly borrowed passages. He knew that he did not have to use footnotes for information that is common knowledge.

Kal's bibliography, made with the help of his bib cards and note cards, listed complete information about the sources he used in preparing the paper. Each item in the bibliography included the author, if given, the title of the article or book, the place of publication, the publishing company, and the year of publication. As Kal made up his footnotes and bibliography, he kept in mind the function of these two parts of his paper.

FOOTNOTES	BIBLIOGRAPHY
1. A number slightly above the line in the paper signals a footnote. The number refers the reader to extra information at the bottom of the page. (Or the information may be grouped together at the end of the paper before the bibliography.)	1. The bibliography always comes at the end of a research paper.
2. A footnote gives the source of a specific idea, fact, quotation or judgment.	2. The bibliography lists the sources (books, magazines, pamphlets, etc.) used in writing the paper.
3. Footnotes are always in the order in which they occur in the paper. They are numbered consecutively.	3. The sources in the bibliography are listed alphabetically by the last name of the author or by title, if no author is given.
4. Each footnote is begun with the name of the author, first name first.	4. Each entry is begun with the last name of the author first (if the name of the author is given).

As Kal prepared his footnotes and bibliography, he used these models for guidelines.

FOOTNOTE	BIBLIOGRAPHY
For a book—one author:	
¹Sam J. Lundwall, *Science Fiction: An Illustrated History* (New York: Grosset & Dunlap, 1977), p. 48.	Lundwall, Sam J. *Science Fiction: An Illustrated History.* New York: Grosset & Dunlap, 1977.

For a book—more than one author:

2Sherman Hines and Ray Guy, *Outhouses of the East* (Halifax: West House Publishers, 1978), pp.64-6.

Hines, Sherman and Ray Guy. *Outhouses of the East.* Halifax: West House Publishers,1978.

For a book compiled by an editor:

3Robert Weaver (ed.) *Canadian Short Stories* (Toronto: Oxford University Press,1960), p. 35.

Weaver, Robert, ed. *Canadian Short Stories.* Toronto: Oxford University Press, 1960.

For a book—only one chapter used:

4R.E. McConnell, "Language and Dialects," in *Our Own Voice: Canadian English and How It is Studied* (Toronto: Gage Educational Publishing, 1979), p. 101.

McConnell, R.E. "Language and Dialects," in *Our Own Voice: Canadian English and How It is Studied.* Toronto: Gage Educational Publishing, 1979, pp. 95-107.

For a magazine article—author given:

5John N. Cole, "It's Not Safe To Be An Eagle," *National Wildlife,* December-January 1979, p. 13.

Cole, John N. "It's Not Safe To Be An Eagle." *National Wildlife,* December-January 1979, pp. 13-17.

For a magazine article—no author given:

6"Warning ... Danger ... Loaded Words Ahead!" *Senior Scholastic,* March 11, 1966, p. 6.

"Warning ... Danger ... Loaded Words Ahead!" *Senior Scholastic,* (March 11, 1966), pp. 6-11.

For an encyclopedia article—signed:

7*Funk & Wagnalls Standard Reference Encyclopedia,* 1967 ed., s.v. "Cervantes Saavedra, Miguel de," by E.F.

Funk & Wagnalls Standard Reference Encyclopedia, 1967 ed., s.v. "Cervantes Saavedra, Miguel de," by E.F.

For an encyclopedia article—unsigned:

8*Encyclopedia Canadiana,* 1970 ed., s.v. "Alberta."

Encyclopedia Canadiana, 1970 ed., s.v. "Alberta."

(Note: s.v. means "sub verbo," or "under the word." Encyclopedia articles are cited by the title of the article rather than by volume and page number.)

For a pamphlet—no author given:

[9]*How do you apply for a Social Insurance Number?* Ottawa, Employment and Immigration Canada, 1979, p.5.

How do you apply for a Social Insurance Number? Ottawa, Employment and Immigration Canada, 1979.

For a newspaper article—unsigned:

[10]"Saving Medicare," *The Province,* 21 December 1980, sec. B, p.B1.

"Saving Medicare," *The Province,* 21 December 1980, sec. B, p. B1.

Your teacher may require that you use a particular form of footnoting and bibliography format which differs from the format given here. For example, the Modern Language Association Style Sheet is often used for research papers. Colleges and universities usually specify a particular style sheet they wish students to use.

When Kal was writing his paper and preparing his footnotes, he decided he would use only *reference* footnotes and not *content* footnotes. Content footnotes provide additional information not included in the text; they are rarely used in library resource papers. They may confuse readers, who must jump from the text to the foot of the page and back again. Reference footnotes, on the other hand, merely indicate where the writer found specific facts, opinions, and direct quotations included in the text.

As Kal discovered that he was referring to the same sources in several footnotes, he found the following abbreviations useful in saving time and trouble.

Ibid.—The abbreviation Ibid., which is capitalized, underlined, and followed by a period, means "in the same place." If the third footnote in a paper comes from the same source as the immediately preceding reference, simply put Ibid. and the new page. The entry would look like this:
Ibid., 5.
Do not use Ibid. if some other reference comes between the new reference and the earlier one from the same source.

Op.cit.—The abbreviation Op. cit., which is also capitalized, underlined, and followed by a period, means "in the work cited." It is used to refer to a source used a second or subsequent times, but which cannot be referred to by Ibid., because another reference comes in between. But to be sure a reader doesn't become confused, the author's name must be repeated. Such a footnote looks like this:

Harper, op. cit.,

In this case, op cit. is not capitalized, because it does not come at the beginning of the footnote.

The first page of Kal's paper (included in the specimen pages) shows the finished appearance of one of his footnotes.

In preparing his bibliography, Kal chose the title "Selected Bibliography" because he knew he had not used all the sources available on his topic. If he had limited his bibliography to works mentioned in footnotes, he would have labelled it "Works Cited." If he wanted to indicate that his bibliography included both works he mentioned in footnotes and works he merely read, he would have used the heading "Sources Consulted." For every source mentioned in a footnote, Kal was careful to have the work listed in his bibliography. He also remembered that a bibliography includes *only* those sources actually read and consulted. Kal's bibliography can be found near the end of the chapter. Note that it is a *critical* or *annotated* bibliography which demands that the researcher evaluate his or her sources by means of a short commentary. This evaluation may be positive, negative, or mixed. It is *not* necessary, even in a critical bibliography, to comment on each source.

9. Getting Someone to Edit Your Draft and Make Suggestions.

A library resource paper should go though the same cooperative editing procedures that were described in Chapter 2. Just as a professional writer uses the insights of others in making a publication as nearly perfect as possible, you should take the advantage of the insights of other students and adults. The difference is that the professional writer is usually aiming only at improving the selection. You are aiming both at improving your paper and at learning something yourself. Kal met with a group of four students, and each person contributed his or her insights to improve the work of all the others. As they worked they were to pay attention both to matters of form (style) and substance (content).

10. Preparing Your Final Draft and Front Matter

In preparing his final draft, Kal paid close attention to matters of format, following the suggestions in the approved style guide. Since he could type proficiently, he decided to type his final draft. Kal noted in the style guide that his library resource paper must contain a title page and his final outline as well as the body pages (with footnotes) and the bibliography. Specimen pages from different parts of Kal's finished paper are presented here for your guidance.

title page:

Note that Kal's title excludes the thesis, but accurately reflects the scope of the topic:

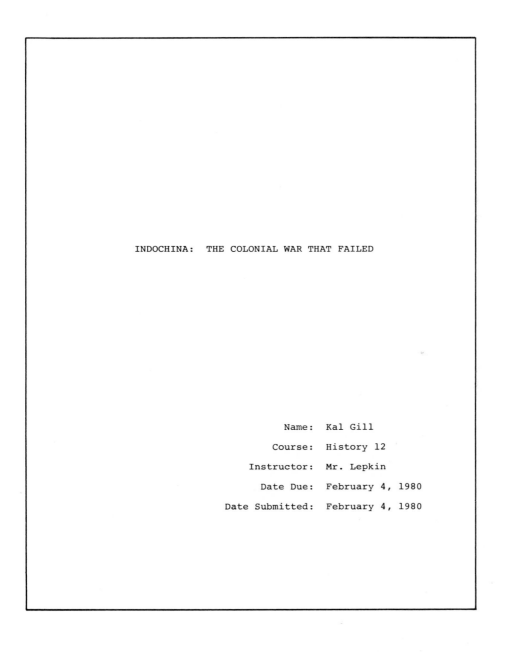

INDOCHINA: THE COLONIAL WAR THAT FAILED

Name: Kal Gill

Course: History 12

Instructor: Mr. Lepkin

Date Due: February 4, 1980

Date Submitted: February 4, 1980

outline:

Note that Kal has placed his thesis statement at the top and has indicated primary divisions of the thesis by Roman numerals, secondary divisions

Thesis: It was not possible post World War II, for France to
         retain Indochina.

I.   The growth of independence movements in Indochina
     indicated increasing resistance to French rule.

     A. The anti-Communist Vietnamese nationalist front
        known as the Dong Minh Hoi was created in China
        in 1942.

     B. The Viet Minh, a Communist-backed independence
        league formed in 1941, emerged as the most
        powerful independence movement.

        1. The Chinese and Americans relied on the Viet
           Minh for intelligence information about the
           Japanese in Indochina.

        2. Weapons were received by the Viet Minh from the
           American O.S.S. for anti-Japanese work inside
           Vietnam.

        3. The Viet Minh initiated the attack on the French.

II. France was not prepared for a long war.

     A. The army was mismanaged.

     B. France was facing revolt in another overseas territory.

     C. As the war dragged on, there was mounting opposition
        within France to the military effort.

     D. The war was draining France's economy and human
        resources.

by capital letters and tertiary divisions by Arabic numerals. Successive divisions are indented to give a step-down appearance.

III. Various factors helped to make victory possible for the Viet Minh.

    A. The establishment of a Communist regime in China in 1949 created a pro-Viet Minh regime.

        1. China was available as a base.

        2. The Chinese, along with the Soviets, provided economic and military aid and thus allowed the continuation of the war.

    B. The organization of the Viet Minh made them more powerful than they were.

        1. There was an extensive Viet Minh political structure based on participation by the population.

        2. Viet Minh strategy of guerilla warfare was very effective.

    C. Failure of the French-Bao Dai solution removed the only threat to the power of the Viet Minh.

IV. The French suffered the major military defeats.

    A. The French lost the Chinese border posts.

    B. When the French appeared to be gaining strength under de Lattre, they were defeated at Hoa Binh.

    C. In a desperate attempt to win the war, the French were defeated at Dien Bien Phy.

first two body pages:

Notice how the title is identical to the one on the title page. Never underline the title. Centre the title at the top and leave three lines between

INDOCHINA: THE COLONIAL WAR THAT FAILED

During the mid-nineteenth century, France, like Great Britain and Germany, embarked on a campaign to acquire the unclaimed territories of the world. This resurgence of imperialism brought many different nationalities into the French empire. The rigid control of those foreign people by the French laid the seeds for a power struggle. The French-Indochina conflict from 1946 to 1954, which was a colonial war, exemplified such a struggle. France, which had controlled Indochina since the 1850s, sought to re-establish her dominance in the area. World War II had not only inter-rupted French rule, but also spawned nationalist movements in Indochina. In an era when imperialism was yielding to nationalism, France remained steadfast in her position of maintaining colonies. France's attempt to put down by force a nationalist movement and later to justify the war under the guise of fighting Communism, ultimately shaped her defeat. In essence, France just did not have the resources to under-take a costly war in order to maintain her grip on Indochina.

The French policy towards Indochina was very clear. This policy was expressed at the conference of the French Committee for National Liberation held at Brazzaville in January, 1944.

it and the first line of the opening paragraph. Kal has used a lengthy quote on these pages. Note how he has indented it and has used single spacing.

2

General de Gaulle said:

> The aims of the work of civilization which
> France is accomplishing in her possessions
> exclude any idea of autonomy and any
> possibility of development outside the
> French Empire bloc. The attainment of
> "self-government" in the colonies, even [1]
> in the distant future, must be excluded.

The British, however, adopted a different policy towards

their colonies and dominions. By 1945 they had recognized

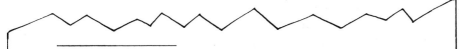

[1]Robert J. O'Neill, <u>Indochina Tragedy</u>, (New York:
Frederick Warne & Co. Ltd., 1968) p. 7.

three subsequent body pages:

Notice that subsequent body pages are numbered using Arabic nu-

---

3

the pressure of nationalism and as a result they had put into
effect plans for national governments in Malaya, Burma and
India. The British showed that they were willing to settle
disputes by discussion instead of force, even if it meant
that nationalist governments would be created more quickly
than the British wanted. Had French foreign policy been
patterned along British lines, the Indochina war might have
been prevented.

With the outbreak of World War II in Europe, the French
tried to prevent potential uprisings in Vietnam. Nationalists
and Communists were arrested, but the key leaders escaped to
southern China. Nguyen Ai Quoc joined the exiled Communists
and nationalists in China and organized them into a resistance
movement. He held a meeting involving the Indochina Communist
Party Central Committee, some Communist associations and splinter
groups from nationalist parties at Chingsi in May 1941. There
the Viet Nam Doc Lap Dong Minh Hoi (League for Vietnam Independence) was formed. This group became known by its abbreviated
name of the Viet Minh. The Viet Minh was a front organization
which concealed Communist activities by having representatives
of national groups. Members from nationalist parties were
bribed or threatened into joining. After the formation of
the Viet Minh, Vo Nguyen Giap, a senior Communist, was sent
to organize and operate guerrilla forces in Vietnam.

The governor of Kwangsi, Chang Fa-k'uai, persuaded the
Vietnamese nationalists to form their own organization to

merals in the upper right hand corner. Numbers should not have a period after them.

4

oppose the Viet Minh. Thus, in October, 1942, the Viet Nam
Cach Dong Minh Hoi (Vietnamese Revolutionary League), better
known as the Dong Minh Hoi, was formed. By this time, Nguyen
Ai Quoc had been imprisoned by Chinese authorities for the
crimes he committed against the nationalists. For the Allies,
the Dong Minh Hoi failed to produce accurate intelligence of
the Japanese who had occupied Vietnam during World War II.
In return for his release from prison, Nguyen Ai Quoc offered
the services of his Communist organization. The Chinese
Governor released Quoc in 1943 to carry out intelligence work.
Since there were records of Nguyen Ai Quoc in China's security
services, his name was changed to Ho Chi Minh. The word Ho
means "he who seeks after intelligence."[2] After being released
from prison, Ho began to work on the destruction of the Dong
Minh Ho. He used Chinese funds meant for the Dong Minh Hoi
to improve the Viet Minh and strengthen the Indochina Communist
Party. The Viet Minh were further strengthened when Giap's
guerrilla forces received arms and supplies from the American
O.S.S. (Office of Strategic Services) for anti-Japanese work
in Vietman. These arms were stored for later use against the
non-Communists and the French.

A Dong Minh Hoi congress set up a provisional Vietnamese
government at Luichow in March, 1944. Ho, who had long since
been enrolled in the Dong Minh Hoi to destroy it from within,

---

[2]P. J. Honey, Genesis of a Tragedy, (London: Ernest Benn
Ltd., 1968), p. 519.

5

was given a portfolio. The provisional government was
ineffective and was nothing more than a body on paper.
Ho exploited the government by creating a legal cover
for his guerrillas, thereby giving them a better image
amongst the uneducated Vietnamese. He arrived at Tongking
to personally direct operations in October, 1944, and set
up his headquarters at Thai-nguyen.[3]

---

[3]_Ibid_., p.611.

You have now had an opportunity to read the first five pages of Kal's
paper. Match their content to the first part of his outline in order to see
how his paper reflects that outline.

bibliography:

SELECTED BIBLIOGRAPHY

Books:

Buttinger, Joseph. <u>A Dragon Defiant</u>, New York,
        Praegar Publishers, 1972. Chapter five was the
        most relevant to the topic and offered a general
        overview of the French-Indochina war.

Hammer, Ellen J. <u>The Struggle for Indochina</u>, Stanford,
        Stanford University Press, 1954. An in depth analysis
        of the Indochina war. The politics of the pre-war
        and war years were handled excellently.

Honey, P.J. <u>Genesis of a Tragedy</u>, London, Ernest Benn Ltd.,
        1968. This work mainly concentrated on the history of
        Vietnam prior to the French-Indochina war. Thus, only
        the last few chapters were significant. It dealt with
        only the highlights of the conflict.

McAlister, John T. Jr. <u>Vietnam, The Origins of Revolution</u>,
        New York, Alfred A Knopf, 1969. McAlister attempts
        to define the universal characteristics of all
        revolutions and apply them to Vietnam. He thoroughly
        covers the politics involved in a revolution. However,
        sometimes it is difficult to find pertinent material
        on Vietnam.

O'Neill, Robert J. <u>Indochina Tragedy</u>. New York,
        Frederick Warne & Co. Ltd., 1968. Covers both
        the military and political aspects of the war extremely
        well. Thus, it was very useful.

Periodicals:

Ennis, T.E. "Indochina: The Aftermath of Colonialism."
        <u>Current History</u>, Vol. 23 (Aug. 1952), pp. 92-96. A
        well-presented look at the economic, political and
        military components of the Indochina war.

Gillie, D.R. "France and Indochina." <u>Spectator</u>, Vol. 189,
        (Dec. 12, 1952), p. 802.

Hammer, E.J. "Struggle for Indochina." <u>Nation</u>, Vol. 178,
        (May 8, 1954), pp. 406-8.

Heath, D.R. "France is Fighting the Good Fight."
    Life, Vol. 35, (Sept. 21, 1953), p. 62. American
    propaganda on the French position of fighting Communism.

Menken, J. "Military Aspects of Indochina." Spectator.
    Vol. 192, (June 4, 1954), p. 674.

Werth, A. "The French Must Choose." Nation, Vol. 174,
    (Jan. 26, 1952), pp. 76-78.

White, T.H. "Indochina, the Long Trail of Error."
    Reporter, Vol. 10, (June 22, 1954), pp. 8-15.

"Central Issue in Indochina." America, Vol. 89
    (June 27, 1953), p. 331.

"Face of Defeat and the Face of Victory." Life, Vol. 37,
    (Aug. 2, 1954), pp. 10-15.

"Fall of Dien Bien Phu." Time, Vol. 63, (May 17, 1954)
    pp. 34-35.

"France Calls it Quits in Indochina." Business Week,
    Vol. 10, (July 24, 1954), p. 110.

"How Staunch the Stand?" Newsweek, Vol. 44, (Oct. 4, 1954),
    p. 42.

"Indochina Danger." Newsweek, Vol. 43, (Mar. 15, 1954),
    pp. 37-38.

"Indochina, France and the U.S." Life, Vol. 35
    (Aug. 3, 1953), p. 28.

Newspapers:

"Agreement Ending Vietnam and Laos Fighting Signed."
    New York Times, 21 July, 1954, p. 1, col. 3.

"Failure of Policy." New York Times, 16 June, 1954,
    p. 6, col. 3.

"French Attitude." The Times, 21 July, 1954. p. 6, col. 3.

"Problems Caused by the Indochina Truce." New York
    Times, 15 Aug. 1954, p. 10.

"Viet Minh Attitude." The Times, 26 July, 1954, p. 8,
    col. 3.

"Vietnamese Attitude to Peace." The Times, 12 July, 1954,
    p. 8, col. 1.

11. Proofreading and Submitting

Proofread carefully with the dictionary and style manual close by. Eliminate all mechanical errors. Use the guide under "Major Writing Assignment" as both a progress check and a final check of your paper before you submit it—on time, of course! Kal's completed research paper was 29 pages, including title page, outline, body of the paper with footnotes, and selected bibliography. Your paper may be shorter or longer than Kal Gill's, but like his it should display these qualities: neat margins, consistent format, sound facts, clear progression of ideas, and thorough documentation of information.

Major Writing Assignment

An Evaluation of Your Library Resource Paper

This chapter assumes that you are working on a research paper. You are now nearing the end of that process.

Before you put your paper in final form and submit it to your teacher, ask yourself these questions to see if you have followed through on each stage of writing the library resource paper.

1. Is my topic important to me and others and suitable for the assignment?
2. Have I acquired enough facts and ideas on my topic to qualify me to say something significant about it?
3. Is my thesis focused and stated in terms that make it persuasive, argumentative, easily discussed, and easily supported?
4. Have I consulted appropriate indexes and card catalogues in search of a variety of material to support my thesis?
5. Have I prepared my bibliography cards carefully, including all the necessary information, such as the author, title, volume, date, publisher, and call number of each source?
6. Have I done the right amount of in-depth research and have I gathered enough usable material to make a good case for my thesis? Have I been accurate in my recording of direct quotations, in my paraphrases, and in my outlines of thought processes?
7. Have I followed the outline I prepared before my first draft, or have I revised this preliminary organization to be more effective and logical?
8. Does my thesis fit the material in my paper? Does every section and idea in the paper derive from the thesis and support the thesis?
9. Have I found and corrected all mistakes in content, structure, grammar, and spelling?
10. Are my footnotes and bibliography neat, accurate, and complete so that anyone could find my facts and information in the sources?
11. Are my title page, outline or table of contents, and introduction in the correct form? Does my introduction capture the reader's interest and prepare for the discussion of my thesis?

11

Narration

For the writer, one way of discovering oneself, of changing from the patterns of childhood and adolescence to those of adulthood, lies through the exploration inherent in the writing itself. In the case of a great many writers, this exploration at some point— and perhaps at all points—involves an attempt to understand one's background and one's past, even sometimes a more distant past which one has not personally experienced.[1]

—Margaret Laurence

Everyone loves a story, and that's all a narration, or a narrative, is— a story. It can be a story based on something that actually happened, as in a biography or an autobiography (nonfiction), or it can be a story that the writer has made up (fiction). In both fiction and nonfiction, the writer uses many of the same techniques to make a series of related events come alive for readers.

In learning to write narration, a good place to begin is with your own personal experiences. After all, you were there. You know what happened better than anyone else. You know how warm it was, how the sun felt on your shoulders, and how the conversation went. More than that, you know better than anyone else how you felt as the event was taking place. In addition, personal experience narrations are the stuff of which history and literature are made. They are also the raw material you will use as you go on to write fiction. You can even combine personal narrative and fiction by imagining that you are some other person and then writing a fictional account of events that might have happened to you as that person. You will then narrate the events as in a personal narrative. ("I stepped carefully around the fallen tree.")

◀ This is an Oglala Sioux pictograph telling the story of the last moments of the Battle of the Little Big Horn, June 25, 1876.

Sometimes your personal life may be changed by events completely beyond your control, such as a war or a volcanic eruption. Being only one of many people who are affected in such cases, you may feel helpless and incapable of telling the whole story. An account of your personal experiences, however, will be a unique record of these events as one individual saw them. It will help others who are not involved to understand the human element.

The Depression of the 1930s was an event of this magnitude. During the ten years the Depression lasted, many people went through dramatic changes in their lives. Barry Broadfoot recorded their stories in *Ten Lost Years,* a collection of stories about the Depression as told by people all over Canada. Their stories paint a portrait of Canadian life during the Depression.

These personal narratives prove that everyone experiences events and emotions worth describing and preserving. It isn't just professional writers who can handle narration; you have within you hundreds of stories worth exploring and writing, if only you take the time to do so. The great short story writer O. Henry named one of his books *The Four Million* because there were that many residents in New York City at the time and he believed that each of them had a story to tell.

Why should anyone want to write narration? One of the best reasons is simply that writing stories is fun, just as reading them is fun. Another reason is that writing narration lets you either relive your own experiences or create a whole new life. Writing personal narratives based on your own experience gives you an opportunity to reexamine, reshape, relive, and interpret your life. Writing fictional narratives gives you an opportunity to create a whole new world with events occurring and characters acting just as you wish them to.

Here are some examples of narratives. The first one is taken from *Ten Lost Years.*

I

Teaching from Eaton's Catalogues

I graduated from normal school and I was 18, not at all too young in those days for teaching, and it was 1935 and you know what that meant? Well, I'll tell you. It meant I would be lucky to get a job, but I did, in a one room school in Saskatchewan, south of Wynyard.

The school secretary wrote me the district had been hit hard and he wrote and said they could not stick to the schedules, the graduated scale they paid teachers, but they would pay me $30 a month. I knew the government grant was $300 a year for each room, so this district was just paying me the government grant. My mother told me to take it, it would be experience.

The first night I slept in the cloakroom with a horse blanket and my coat until the board could meet and figure out who would take me for that year.

I got into a house of the farmer nearest, practically across the road, and I think, as I recall, the others paid their share of my board by working for him two or three days, ploughing or haying. No money changed hands. There was none. Hah!

I liked teaching, the children were a pleasure and the farm family I stayed with were nice people. Everybody tried to help each other, and I put on a Hallowe'en dance in the school and a Christmas concert, and the last day of school there was a picnic with races, old shoe races, egg and spoon races, things like that. They were hard times, but good times too, in a way.

I remember one thing. I had this terrific inspiration. The school books were practically useless, in tatters, and I thought, what will I do? Then I had this brain wave. I told every child to bring to school next day the Eaton's catalogue. The one at home, you see. Of course, some families had two and three children in school, but you know what I mean. I thought these would make wonderful texts for the older children. And they did too. But this is what happened. I'd be doing the grade sevens and eights together, and they had the catalogue and I'd let one child pick out to read what he wanted to. The girls would read aloud from the clothes section or the kitchen things, china sets, curtains, things like that, and the boys would read the harness section or guns or such and the younger ones would turn right to the toy section. I believe the Shirley Temple doll section was read two dozen times.

It was study, it was learning, it was fun. In other words it wasn't like school. But I began to notice that when one class, say the grade fives, and there might be four or so in that, when they were doing their reading from the catalogues, everybody else stopped their own lessons and listened. I began to watch and I found out that no work except the catalogue reading was being done in that little red schoolhouse on the Saskatchewan plains.

Everybody listened, everybody knew what everybody else wanted or liked, and no work was being done. I had to put a stop to that, send them home with their catalogues and go back to the old readers. It was too bad because it was such fun, for them and me too.[2]

II

As It Happened

In Miss Farthing's room in Laura Secord everyone sat very straight, knees tucked under the desk, feet flat on the floor.

"No slouchers in Room 5," Miss Farthing said, whacking her ruler on the desk. "Not when we're taking up Alfred the Great."

Miss Farthing printed ALFRED THE GREAT in big chalk letters on the blackboard. Then she whirled round.

"What are you waiting for? Out with your notebooks. Copy this down. No one wastes time in my class."

We chewed the end of our pencils, shaped our letters, pressed hard to make everything clear. Billy Bunt, who sat at the back of the room, put up his hand. He wanted to know if we should underline. Mary Love waved her hand. Should we use two lines to make everything stand out? Harry Barclay had his hand up. He was telling Miss Farthing he had an uncle named Alfred who drove a bus only everyone just called him Alfie.

At the front, near Miss Farthing's desk, Benny Brewster let go with some put-put sounds. Betty Smith who sat behind Benny held her nose and pointed at Benny staring innocently out the window.

Miss Farthing's face turned a beet red.

"I'm not taking any more nonsense from you, Benny," she said sternly. "You can leave. Right now. Tell Mr. McArthur in the office what you've been up to."

Miss Farthing marched over to the door and held it open. Benny shuffled out and headed down the hall to the office.

From my seat near the pencil sharpener about all I could sniff were Billy's old running shoes and the rain-soaked windbreakers in the cloakroom. And I could hear the slip-slop sounds of Mr. Berton, the janitor, hurrying down the hall with his mop and pail. But I was also wondering about Benny and if I should try out my new red pencil for the underlining.

Miss Farthing was taking a tour up and down the aisles making sure we were on the right track. She said Mary Love's idea about the underlining was an excellent one. She bent over my desk. I could smell her rose water perfume and see the chalk dust on her long fingers. Miss Farthing liked my printing and the way I made my Gs. I felt a glow of pride and showed her my new red pencil. She said it would do a better job for the underlining than an ordinary crayon.

At Harry Barclay's desk Miss Farthing stopped abruptly and made tut-tut sounds. Harry had drawn a face with a big moustache, which he was saying was his Uncle Alfie. Miss Farthing hovered over him impatiently until Harry dug out his eraser from his pencil box. Some elastic bands fell out on the floor. Harry showed Miss Farthing his eraser. It was a brand new one. Then he rubbed very hard at his drawing. Soon he had a big hole in his paper. Miss Farthing ripped out the page and told Harry to take those elastic things up to her desk and stay after school.

Down the hall we could hear scuffling sounds and Benny's voice trying to make a point. I dropped my new red pencil and watched it roll under Harry's left foot. I decided to leave it there for a moment. I didn't want to miss what was going to happen to Benny. Harry was concentrating on the sounds and rubbing his hands on his knees. His foot tapped gently up and down on my pencil.

The first thump of the strap was always a practice one. Everyone knew that Mr. McArthur was just warming up and checking his aim. There would be a short pause for adjustments, as usual, and then came the first stinging strap sounds, which now cracked down the hall like backfires in my Dad's old Ford. Everyone in Room 5 was beginning to count, silently of course, and just barely moving his or her lips. Two, three, four, five, six... Mr. McArthur never stopped until you let out a yell... seven, eight, nine... Benny was going for a new world record. I wanted to let go with a cheer. Benny made it to 11. And then we heard a wail, not a big one, but just loud enough to do the trick.

Everyone in Room 5 began to relax. Mary Love gave a little sigh. Harry was smiling to himself the way it is when it could have been you, but isn't. Miss Farthing who had been standing at the back of the room looking up at the ceiling was now saying we'd all make a good start on our printing.

There was a knock on the door. Benny came in and took his seat. He looked fine except his hands were in his pockets. Miss Farthing picked up her ruler and carefully underlined ALFRED THE GREAT twice. Benny slipped into his seat and held up his hand. He wiggled and twisted his fingers. His hand looked like a bright red tulip.

"Yes, Benny, you have a question?" Miss Farthing's voice was a little shaky. "Did I miss anything important when I was out?" Benny asked.

Before Miss Farthing could answer there was a loud knock and Mr. McArthur strode in. He was beaming and smiling.

"Good morning, Miss Farthing. Good morning, class."

Miss Farthing dropped her ruler.

Mr. McArthur swooped down and picked it up. He examined it carefully.

"One of our new issues, Miss Farthing," he said. "Hard to break these new ones."

Mr. McArthur looked us over. His eyes bored into your heart. Made you automatically straighten your back. Get your feet flat on the floor. He slapped the ruler against his legs and strode up and down the aisles looking at our notebooks.

Harry Barclay put up his hand.

"Yes, my boy?" Mr. McArthur said.

Harry got slowly out of his seat and stood up very straight.

"We're studying Alfred the Great sir," Harry said. "I've got an Uncle Alfie..."

Before Harry could finish, Mr. McArthur was saying Alfred the Great was one of his favourite heroes. One of the great men in history. Then his eyes glided up and down the rows.

"Tell me, lad. Yes, you. The boy in the black sweater. What do you know about Alfred the Great?"

I looked down at my sweater. It was black all right. For a moment I wished I'd worn my old yellow one. Just my luck to have the black one on today.

"Me sir?" I asked.

"Of course, you," Mr. McArthur said. "You're the only one with a black sweater, aren't you?"

I looked around to check the other sweaters. I stared at Harry's green one. And there was Benny with his red jumper, and Billy Bunt was wearing his usual sweat shirt.

"Well. Up on your feet, Mr. Black. Up on your feet."

I shot up like a jack-in-the-box and stood straight as a soldier facing the firing squad.

"Now, Mr. Black. Tell me what you've learned today about Alfred the Great?"

"We're just printing out his name on a new page," I said. "And we're waiting for the lesson so we can get started on the history part."

Mr. McArthur said something about trying someone else and I sat down feeling confused and flustered.

Mary Love was waving her hand.

"Yes, young lady. What have you to say about Alfred the Great?"

Mary Love was up on her feet explaining her ideas about the underlining.

Mr. McArthur looked upset. He turned to Miss Farthing who was standing behind her desk. Miss Farthing looked tiny and unimportant. Her lips trembled.

Mr. McArthur's voice was cold.

"Miss Farthing. Is this your good class?"

Miss Farthing stared around the room as though she didn't recognize a soul. I thought she was going to burst into tears. I wanted to shout out for her to tell that bully McArthur we were the greatest... we worked hard... our class won the paper drive...last week we had perfect attendance two days in a row...it was Room 5 that cleaned up the playing field only yesterday...Mary Love got 8 out of 10 on her spelling test...I was right behind with 7...Benny won the 50 yard dash at the track meet...

Miss Farthing shook her head and stared down at her shoes.

Mr. McArthur slapped his legs with the ruler and he was saying in this game we have to take the good with the bad.

Everyone in Room 5 was now twisting and squirming in his seat. Mary Love shook her head in disbelief and sniffed into her handkerchief. Benny got up and started to fiddle with the sharpener. Harry's foot crunched down hard on my new red pencil. Somebody mumbled who cares about Alfred the Great anyway. Billy Bunt was whispering it was all a big double cross and what's the use of trying.

At the bell for recess we charged out of the room. On the playing field we gathered around Benny to ask him what it was like this time. We stared at his hands. He said it was nothing and he could have made it to 20 only McArthur ran out of steam.

Just then Miss Farthing hurried down the school steps. She had her coat on and was carrying her big brief case and heading full speed for the bus stop.

"I guess something happened," Mary Love said.

The bus rolled up to the corner and Miss Farthing climbed aboard. Then Harry yelled that his Uncle Alfie was at the wheel. Everybody ran over to see Uncle Alfie and listen to him giving his old bus the gun and revving her up.

Harry yelled and waved at Uncle Alfie.

In the front seat Miss Farthing stared straight ahead. Her face was white as chalk. Uncle Alfie let the old bus idle wide open and Harry was still waving and yelling at Uncle Alfie who was too busy checking his tickets to look around.

Suddenly Miss Farthing turned her head to take a last look at the old school. But when she saw Harry waving like mad her face lit up as though she couldn't believe her eyes. She tried to give a little wave back. Then the bus jerked forward and Uncle Alfie shifted gears and wheeled down Second Avenue towards the station.[3]

—Sam Roddan

Student Composition 11A

IMPRESSIONS

Everything about my grandmother's death seemed quick and abrupt. We found out she had lung cancer on the fourteenth of September, and then, only sixteen days later, it was all over, and she was dead. Just that fast, she was gone.

I didn't realize until weeks later how very bravely Nana died. She knew towards the end that she was about to die, but she never cried or felt sorry for herself or even complained when the pain grew worse. She accepted everything quietly and peacefully and only once said a word about her death. Only a few days before she left us, she suddenly said to my Aunt Sue,

Which of the 5 W's and an H (Who, What, When, Where, Why, and How) are answered in the first paragraph? If so much is revealed, how does Wendi make you want to read on?

Is this narration basically about Wendi or about her grandmother? Explain your answer. What seems to be the point, or purpose, of the narration?

"I want to be cremated." And nothing more was said between them about the matter.

When I found out that Nana was to be cremated, it bothered me because I could not understand why she had wanted such a thing. It made her death seem even more final to me. Then our pastor took me aside, and he reminded me that the Bible says, "Out of the ground were you taken; you are dust, and to dust shall you return." He explained that cremation was just a way of speeding up the natural process of returning to the earth from which we come—ashes to ashes and dust to dust, only much faster. Because he took the time to discuss it with me, I began to accept it.

The ashes were stored at the funeral home for three months, not forgotten, just left there because we didn't know what to do with them. It was difficult to get the family all together at one time, and Nana had not instructed just where she wanted her ashes to be scattered. We finally decided upon the woods of my Aunt Sue's ranch. So, on December 31, the last day of 1977, we took my grandmother's ashes to the place where they would mix back into the earth.

We walked to a large clump of tall, ancient pine trees, and they looked like great wooden pillars supporting a roof of boughs and branches. The open space inside and the upward curving slope of the trunks formed a natural cathedral, and we knew that this sanctuary was the perfect place.

Each of us stood there, silent and deep in our own private thoughts and loving memories as my father said a prayer. Then I watched as Uncle Hunter carefully and lovingly began scattering handfuls of ashes around the trees and into bushes. The last ashes gracefully floated into powdery clouds before finally settling on the ground, and we burned the plastic bag. Then it was all done.

As we walked away, it began to sprinkle lightly, and I knew that the ashes had begun their journey back into the earth.

—Wendi Jordan

In much narration, emotions are overstated rather than understated. How would you criticize Wendi's writing in this respect? What does that contribute to the mood and tone of her piece?

What details help you visualize the place the ashes were scattered?

What might the sprinkling of rain in the last paragraph symbolize? Discuss the effectiveness of the very short final paragraph.

Student Composition 11B

A DIFFERENT OUTLOOK

Finished at last. I placed my pen on the desk and stretched. Why did Mr. McKewan seem to give exams only on days when the classroom felt like a sauna? I glanced at my watch. There were still ten minutes left

Some narratives are made more exciting because the writer begins in the middle of the story—often near the climax. This is really a story about till the bell. I sighed, and once again checked over my work.

Looking around the class, I noticed that I was the only one finished. Not even Jamie Dickson, a good friend of mine and the school brain, was done. I made a mental note to give him a ribbing about being so slow.

I watched through the window as the P.E. students ran around the track, and then disappeared into the gym. The field seemed strangely vacant, sort of like it was resting before the inevitable rush the bell was sure to bring.

"And just what do you think you're doing?"

The sound of the teacher's voice brought my attention back to the classroom.

"Mr. Dickson, I asked you a question!"

"Uh, nothing, sir," Jamie replied, obviously startled. "I mean, I was doing my test."

"You mean you were..."

He was cut short by the bell. Jamie stared at his paper, trying not to see that the entire class was looking at him.

"Leave your exams on my desk as you go." Mr. McKewan motioned everyone to leave. "Jamie, I'd like a word with you."

I tapped him on the shoulder. "Do you want a ride home? I'll wait."

"Yeah, thanks." His eyes asked for help but there wasn't anything I could do.

"The car's in the normal spot." I left, feeling as though I was deserting someone in need.

I was listening to the car radio when Jamie got in. He didn't seem any better than when I'd last seen him. Shaking his head silently, he looked up and somehow managed a wry smile.

"Who'd have believed it? Me, the supposed intellect, caught cheating."

"Why'd you do it?" I felt dumb for asking, but my curiosity needed to be satisfied.

"To tell you the truth, I really don't know." Jamie shrugged his shoulders, still somewhat shocked by what had happened.

"I don't want to be pushy or anything," I searched his face, looking for a sign that would tell me I was going too far, "but you're getting straight A's, why risk it?"

"I guess I panicked. You see, I never got a chance to study and I knew I'd already missed a few questions, then one thing led to another..."

"I still don't understand." I'd been friends with Jamie since grade three, and in all the time I'd known him, he'd never even got the answers for homework from anyone else. "You can afford to get one lousy test mark without dropping a letter grade!"

understanding others, not writing a test. Where else might the narrator have begun the story? What would he have included in a flashback?

How would you rewrite the sentence beginning "The field..." to make it more effective and interesting?

How realistic do the speeches of Jamie and Mr. McKewan sound? How has the narrator tried to communicate the feelings of each speaker?

In writing narration, authors can make time pass as rapidly as they want to, just as long as they make clear the time and sequence of each event. Instead of breaking off the story to show the passage of time, how else might the narrator have shown that a certain period of time has passed?

What do we learn about Jamie's character and attitudes from his conversation here? How can we tell that the narrator does not really understand Jamie at this point?

Is the kind of language used here appropriate for these characters?

"It's just that...oh, forget it. You wouldn't understand." Jamie looked out the window and shook his head. "Let's go."

I started the car and drove him home in silence. When we got to his place, he thanked me for the ride and opened the door to leave.

He stood for a moment lost in thought. "I've never failed before," he said, "not ever." He slammed the door shut and walked into his house.

As I drove home, I kept wondering why he had done it. Why someone like him would ever resort to cheating was beyond me, yet something must have happened.

It took a chance comment by Jamie later that year before I finally was able to put things into perspective. We'd been talking about how school had been going lately, and he mentioned that since people had stopped expecting so much of him, he'd been enjoying school a lot more. It was only then that I fully realized what he had gone through.

Ever since, I've thought twice before kidding people, who, in my mind, tend to study too hard. Not only do they have to contend with marks, but they've also got to live up to other people's expectations. And trying to maintain an image is a lot tougher than you might think!

—Gregg Sewell

The writer says that he finally realized what Jamie had gone through. What does he mean by this? How does the narrator change by the end of the story?

How effective is the ending? Can you suggest any ways the writer could get this idea across to the reader without stating it directly?

Reacting to the Narrative Models

Two of the models were written by professional writers, and two of them were written by students. None of the models is perfect, of course, but you can learn from them. After reading the models, discuss the following questions.

1. Of all the personal experiences the writers must have had, something has caused each one to write about one particular incident. What seems to have influenced each writer's choice? (There may be several influences.) How will recognizing these influences help you select your subjects?

2. Rudyard Kipling, who was a newspaper reporter as well as a writer of stories and novels, once wrote a verse that names the elements of both news stories and narratives:

I have six faithful serving men
They taught me all I know.
Their names are what and where and when
And why and how and who.

Where does each of these elements occur in the selections? Is any element ever omitted from a narrative? To what extent are most of them included in the introductory paragraphs of these models?

3. How closely do the selections follow natural chronological order? What advantages, if any, result from using out-of-order incidents (flashbacks)? What dangers does using them entail?

4. What are the differences between *showing* an event and *telling about* it? Which is more interesting and exciting? Why? (You will learn about these later in this chapter.)

5. How important are concrete descriptions and appeals to the senses? How can you make the readers smell, taste, touch, hear, and see objects and incidents?

6. How are the various paragraphs connected with each other? What helps thought flow smoothly from one to the next?

Elements of Narration

In order for a narration to be interesting and meaningful, it must have the following elements:

1. *Emotion.* Writing is really such hard work that people ought not to bother writing something with which they are not emotionally involved. What emotions are apparent in each selection? How strongly is the narrator involved? What indications are there in the models of strong emotional involvement?

2. *Action.* Something happens; that is, tension increases and conflict intensifies as various events occur. In simple stories, the action is very often physical—fights, calamities, contests—but in more subtle stories the action may be emotional or intellectual. The action, however, whether it is exterior and visible or interior and invisible, causes the situation to change so that conditions are different at the end of the story from the way they were at the beginning. This movement, or development, is important.

3. *Suspense.* Each passage suggests that something is going to happen so that the reader eagerly anticipates the outcome of these events. To build suspense, you plant seeds that hint at conflicts, problems, mysteries. You promise the reader that you will show the plants in bloom and that all conflicts, problems, and mysteries will be solved at the end of the story. Suspense is a vital factor in building and retaining the interest of the reader.

4. *Structure, or order.* Events in real life happen in a definite order—the order of time. But in discovering meaning in the events or in imposing a meaning on them, the writer may need to arrange them differently from the order in which they originally occurred. Whether writers use straight chronological order or determine a new order, they are giving structure to

their narrative in order to heighten suspense and make incidents and events more meaningful.

5. *Point or purpose.* Although everyone loves a story and thousands of narratives are written and read only for entertainment, the best stories have a purpose or meaning of some kind. Indeed, even those written and told for their own sakes, often make some kind of statement on human beings, human values, or some aspect of life. To get the most satisfaction from the effort that goes into writing a narrative, select an incident in which you can discover a meaning or an event on which you can impose meaning. Sometimes the meaning is an overall impression or attitude. At other times it is an idea that can be expressed in a single sentence. What are the meanings of the models?

6. *Point of view.* In every narrative, someone (or something) tells the story, and this person or animal or thing marks the story with his or her personal imprint. Imagine how much different the story of the "Three Little Pigs" or of "Little Red Riding Hood" would be if, in each case, the wolf told the story! If you write a personal story about one of your own experiences, you will probably use "I" or "we," which is called *first-person narrator.* Occasionally, you may write a first-person narrative when you are relating events in the life of a fictional character, rather than yourself. In those cases, you have "assumed a *persona*," or taken on the role of another person, much as an actor does. You then speak consistently from that person's point of view—seeing things as he or she sees them, reacting as that person would, and even using the language appropriate for the character. Sometimes, when you are reading narratives, it is difficult to separate the author from the persona he or she is "speaking through." For example, Ernest Hemingway really did participate in the Spanish Civil War and go on safaris in Africa. Yet sometimes when one of his characters tells about those experiences, it is a persona, or imagined character, rather than Hemingway who is speaking. Knowing who is speaking is sometimes important in getting the meaning of a narrative. *Third person* is another point of view often used in narration. When telling a story from that point of view, you relate events as though you were an onlooker, and you use the pronouns "he," "she," "it," or "they." Of course, you already know that when you are telling a story that is really true, you are presenting nonfiction. If, however, you are making up a story, then you are presenting fiction.

7. *Effective description.* Concrete details create images, or pictures, in the readers' minds and make the events in the narrative come alive.

Preparing to Write

The first step in preparing your narrative is either to recall or invent some situation which excites you emotionally. It is better to recall an actual event if you can, but there is nothing wrong with inventing a situation, provided it is realistic and you can become emotionally involved with the events.

Getting an Idea

Everything you learn comes to you through your senses. You experience life through seeing, touching, tasting, smelling, and hearing. Your senses are the sources of all your ideas.

Of course, you can experience life vicariously—at secondhand—by reading, listening to the radio, and watching television and films. By using these secondary sources well, you can find out about anything you choose, and you can write on thousands of subjects you have never experienced firsthand. But the most vital writing you will do will be the writing in which you are emotionally involved with your subject.

Using an emotion to stimulate an idea.   Think. Remember. Feel. Go back to your storehouse of personal sensory experiences. Dredge up the details and emotion of some half-forgotten event. Perhaps you can remember the anguish of a moment long ago when others seemed for some reason to forget you. Perhaps you still feel loneliness or fear or pain or delight from some experience you once had. From this memory you can begin to write about the experience.

Of course, as you examine some previous experience in your life, you will see a difference between real life and stories that you read. In life, events are not crisp and clear and precise with a definite meaning and emotion. As one writer declared,

> One thing that makes art different from life is that in art things have a shape; they have beginnings, middles, and endings, whereas in life, things just drift along. In life somebody has a cold, and you treat it as insignificant, and suddenly they die. Or they have a heart attack, and you are sodden with grief until they recover to live for thirty petulant years, demanding you wait on them.... In other words, in life one almost never has an emotion appropriate to an event. Either you don't know the event is occurring, or you don't know its significance.... Feelings are large and spread over a lifetime.... Anyway, that is a thing art does for us: it allows us to fix our emotions on events at the moment they occur, it permits a union of heart and mind and tongue and tear.[4]
>
> —Marilyn French

As you begin to think about your experiences, the chances are that the emotion-laden events will at first have little meaning or importance to you. As you think about them more and more, however, you will be going through an artistic shaping and exploring process.

When Gregg Sewell first thought about the events he described in "A Different Outlook," he was probably somewhat bewildered by his friend's behaviour. Yet as he examined, explored, and, above all, organized the experience, he found new significance and many additional meanings in the event. Many events without additional insights might not be worth reading about, but with the action sharpened and highlighted and with the meanings explored, they become interesting and important.

(Activity 11A)

Exploring Areas of Personal Experience

In anticipation of the Major Writing Assignment for this chapter, be prepared to discuss in class the areas in which you have had important personal experiences. List these areas on the blackboard. Then begin listing under each of these categories possible subjects that you might write on. Does the following list include most of the significant areas of your experience?

Family and home	Mass media	Friends
School	Clubs	Travel
Work	Hobbies	Reading
Church	Boy-girl relationships	People

Creating imaginary events to portray real emotions.   Working with a partner, describe a situation that you remember and an emotion that you still feel. Then decide whether or not your writing about the situation would cause a reader to feel as you felt. If you decide it would not, discuss what imaginary situation you could create to communicate the feeling you wish to convey. For example, if a favourite uncle promised to take you to a movie and forgot to come for you, your pain and disappointment might be very real to you, but the incident is so slight that a reader might not be moved. What imaginary incident might communicate the same pain and disappointment? Perhaps readers would be touched by the story of a fatherless child who was heart-broken when plans for a rare visit to the circus fell through. Or perhaps they might feel the hurt of a girl who is all dressed up for her first dance and learns that her date is not coming.

(Activity 11B)

Writing about Real and Imagined Events

Write a brief description of an event you experienced and of the emotion it generated. Then write a brief description of an imagined event that would convey to a reader the same emotional reactions even more vividly.

These Egyptian hieroglyphics, carved in stone, give an account of the career of Thetä, a royal adviser who lived four thousand years ago.

Giving Order to Your Narrative

Reading novels and short stories will convince you that there is no single pattern for a narrative. Each writer chooses the organization that seems appropriate to the story. Nonetheless, each narrative must have a beginning, a middle, and an end. As you understand how each part functions, you will be able to develop distinctive patterns for your own narratives.

The beginning.   The beginning of any narrative is important for these reasons:

1. It establishes the relationship between writer and reader.
2. It hints at why the narrative is worth reading. It suggests the significance of the events.
3. It reveals the background for the events. It often defines the *who, what, when, where,* and hints at the *why* and *how*.

The middle.   The middle section develops the narrative.

1. It narrates selected events, often in the natural order but always in the order best calculated to hold the reader's attention and create suspense.
2. It explains, comments on, and interprets the events when explanation, comment, and interpretation are necessary.
3. It provides guides to time, place, sequence, and significance, so that the reader doesn't get lost.

The end.   The end contributes to the final impression left with the reader.

1. It brings the sequence of events to an interesting close.
2. It comments on, reaffirms, or simply clarifies the meaning or significance of the events.

Reread the narrative compositions to see whether each fits this pattern. This outline of a narrative is so simple that most writers follow it automatically. This chapter should help you gain additional insight into your own most effective means of using such an outline. Even professional writers differ from one another in their use of the standard pattern.

Some outline a story before they begin to write.
Some prepare a simple list of events in the order of occurrence.
Some prepare a simple list and then experiment with different orders of presentation.
Some plunge right into the rough draft, ignoring any kind of standard pattern.
Some plunge right into the rough draft following a kind of standard pattern they have internalized so that they follow it automatically.
Some—usually the ones who have planned ahead most carefully—do little revising.
Some—usually the ones who have plunged ahead most quickly—revise extensively.

How do you work best? With what procedures are you most comfortable and most productive?

Adapting the Inverted-Pyramid Style to Narration

Have you ever heard someone ruin a joke by telling the punchline first? How frustrating it is to be on the verge of hearing a fresh, new joke, only to have it spoiled because the narrator gives you too much too soon. The same is true in writing or telling a story: you want to give your reader or listener just enough of the who, what, where, and when to arouse interest and make the story understandable. Then, with interest aroused, you want to reveal more details, one at a time (especially those about the why and the how of events) to intensify interest and build suspense right to the climax of the story.

Newspaper writers have a different purpose from storytellers. They organize their articles to give a complete summary of their story in the first paragraph. Consequently, they use the inverted-pyramid style and include in the opening the who, what, when, where, why, and how of the story. Then they fill in the less important details.

The inverted-pyramid style developed during the American Civil War, 1861-1865, when correspondents on battlefields began using the newly invented telegraph. Because the telegraph was unreliable and might fail at any time, reporters sent their most important information first: the who, what, when, where, why, and how. Busy people seemed to like this order of presentation, possibly because it allowed them to skip the less important details that came at the end of the story. And so, inverted-pyramid style has become standard newspaper form.

You may find it helpful to be aware of the 5 W's and an H as you think through your narrative and plan your beginning. Determine which of them will help arouse interest and make the rest of the story easy to understand. Avoid including information in your opening that will destroy suspense.

(*Activity 11C*)

Studying Introductions

1. Discuss how the writers of the following story openings 1. borrow from journalistic inverted-pyramid style, 2. provide background information, and 3. include a "narrative hook" to get the reader interested.

    a. There was a cheerful atmosphere in the gym the night of the parent-teacher basketball game, and the teachers enjoyed a seven-point lead midway through the second quarter. My dad was playing along with the other parents, and they all seemed to be enjoying the game. Suddenly a big man on the parents' team drove for the basket and missed the shot. He slammed his fist against the protective mat under the basket and snarled like a savage animal.

    b. If you have been blessed with a perfect set of thirty-two teeth, impeccable speech, and a charming smile, you have been luckier than I. I don't remember ever having straight teeth, being able to say the word "statistic" without lisping, or smiling without feeling like a stand-in for Bugs Bunny. And, somehow, when I was in the sixth grade, I realized that my teeth were not going to correct themselves. My mother realized it, too, for she took me to a well-known orthodontist in our area.

2. From the list of subjects you prepared for Activity 11A, choose two or three and write an introductory paragraph for each. Come to class pre-

pared to exchange papers and to evaluate the introductory paragraphs of other students in terms of 1. background provided, 2. interest aroused, 3. concreteness, and 4. suspense.

Giving Meaning or "Point" to an Experience

One day a young mother carefully cleaned the refrigerator, piled seven-year-old Brian into the car, and went grocery shopping. Upon their return, just as she started to put the food away, the telephone rang. After a long conversation, she was delighted to find that the child had continued storing the food in the pantry, cupboard, and refrigerator.

Then she opened the refrigerator to find egg all over the back, sides, and shelves, and all over the food inside as well. She was furious.

Suddenly, she stopped and thought. Why did he do it? Her first reaction was to think that he was angry and frustrated at being left alone. Then she looked at the little oval-shaped compartments for storing eggs on the inside of the refrigerator door. They were full. There was no room for the extra eggs. Brian, wanting to be helpful by keeping like foods together, had piled the six extra eggs on top of the eggs already stored. When he closed the refrigerator door, the six precariously perched eggs were thrown all over the inside of the refrigerator.

What was the mother's interpretation: that her son was careless and stupid, or that he was eager to help but inexperienced?

One of the differences between life and art is that anything that is included in a poem, a painting, or a drama is significant. It's there for a reason. In life, however, some events or objects seem to mean absolutely nothing. Other events or objects might have several different meanings. For example, a star might be interpreted as a symbol for the Soviet Union, the rank of brigadier general, or the brand of a certain cattle ranch. If the writer intends only one meaning, a setting or context must be provided to limit the interpretation to that one meaning. In some cases, events can have several different meanings or interpretations. We know that, especially in poetry and painting, such *ambiguity* (the condition of having more than one meaning) is prized very highly. For example, when A. E. Housman thought of the friends he had in his youth who had since died, he wrote, "With rue my heart is laden." The word "rue" has two meanings: "regret, remorse, unhappiness" and "a strong-scented woody herb whose bitter leaves are used in medicine." Both meanings are appropriate, and the ambiguity enriches the poetry.

As you write narratives, you must not leave things frustratingly ambiguous. You must omit anything that is completely meaningless, you must clarify anything that could have more than the one meaning you intend, and you must be sure that ambiguous objects or events are presented so that all possible meanings are appropriate and enrich your narration.

Here are some simple examples of situations in narratives in which the writer had to guide the reader to the correct interpretation.

1. In Joseph Conrad's novel *Lord Jim,* an officer on a ship full of pilgrims abandoned them when he thought the ship was sinking. He was the only officer who was eventually tried in court. Later, he left Western society to live in Malaysia. Was he ashamed and afraid to face his people, or was he determined to find his true nature and prove himself in another emergency?

2. Philip Bentley, in Sinclair Ross' novel *As For Me and My House,* seemed unhappy in his role as minister in a small prairie town and spent a great deal of time alone, drawing and sketching. Until the end of the novel, however, he refused to listen when his wife pleaded with him to leave the church and become an artist. Did he stay with the church for so long because he felt some responsibility for his congregation and his family or because he was afraid to start a new life?

3. In Gabrielle Roy's novel *The Tin Flute,* set in Québec during the Depression, the protagonist was a girl named Florentine, the oldest daughter in a very poor family, who married a well-to-do young man from an upper class family. Was her marriage the result of genuine affection for him or a desperate grab at happiness for herself?

These are examples of situations in which you must impose meaning on a sequence of events. Whenever any event or series of events makes an impact on you, you must analyze, interpret, and impose a meaning or "point" on the events. Can you see how the young mother in the incident on page 265 might spank her child because of one interpretation or hug him because of another?

(*Activity 11D*)

Imposing Meaning on Events

For each of the following briefly described incidents, determine one or more interpretations. Working as your teacher directs, take one of the incidents and flesh it out with real people in a real situation. Use description and conversation, and make clear, either through implication or direct statement, the interpretation you want your readers to make.

1. A respected citizen dresses up in a costume and mask and dumps sewage and motor oil in the office of the president of a company that has been polluting the environment.

2. A new girl at school sits by herself, refuses to speak to anyone, and ignores attempts of others to be friendly.

3. A family with the finest home, the most beautiful lawn, and the best car in town has always been very careful about appearances in all situations. Suddenly, the lawn goes to seed, the house needs painting, the car's fenders, bent in an accident, have not been repaired, and the children go to school in soiled clothes.

4. A brilliant, outgoing exchange student from Montréal suddenly becomes quiet and withdrawn, even with the friendly family which has given him a home during his stay.

5. At an auction, a student bids casually on an oil painting and gets it for practically nothing. Shortly afterwards, a well-dressed, apparently wealthy stranger bursts into the room and declares that he owns the painting.

Point of View

It is most important, as you think about the narrative you will write, to decide from what point of view you will tell your story. When you are reading or writing a narrative, the person who is telling the story makes a difference in how much you believe and how much you will accept. One basic point of view is the first-person narrator, in which the person telling the story says, in effect, "I did this" or "This happened to me." The narrative "As It Happened" on pages 251-254 is an example of a story told in the first person.

Sometimes, of course, the I-narrator is an imaginary, or fictional persona who tells the story as though it had happened to him or her, even though the reader recognizes that the events never actually happened and the person never existed.

In Chapter 12 you will read a character sketch (page 300) in which the author, Charlotte Brontë, uses a fictional persona.

Another common point of view is the omniscient author, in which a kind of superhuman all-seeing narrator tells the story.

This point of view allows you to enter the mind of any of your characters. You can shift the focus from one character to another. You can interpret the actions of your characters or explain their innermost thoughts.

There are other variations on these two basic points of view. The narrator may distort the truth, and the reader must decide what to believe and what not to believe. In some stories, the narrator is a character in the story who does not perceive or understand anything beyond his or her own experiences.

(*Activity 11E*)

Experimenting with Point of View

Following is a brief narration from a point of view that is rarely used in storytelling, second-person point of view. (First-person narration uses the pronoun "I"; second person uses the pronoun "you"; third person uses the pronoun "he" or "she.") Working as your teacher directs, discuss which point of view would be most effective for this story. Rewrite this second-person narrative using first-person or third-person point of view.

> You walk from the locker room to the dark, dirty minehead. Overhead and in the distance you can see the tipple and hear the clank, clank, clank of the conveyor belt. You wait with the other men for about two minutes until you hear a sharp, metallic screech, the bar to the elevator lifts, and the lunge of about fifty other miners carries you onto the scarred wooden platform with the steel cage surrounding you. You hear the bell ring, smell the mouldy air from the deep shaft, reach to your helmet to flick on your light, and feel the wooden bar once again clunk into place. Then you grip the sides of the cage as the platform drops suddenly from beneath your feet, and you plunge at breakneck speed into the darkness. At intervals, you pass dimly lighted transverse shafts until you are a mile [1.6 km] below surface and the cage slows screechingly and stops with a jerk. Now you're at work level, a mile [1.6 km] down, and the hot, moist air wraps around you as you leave the elevator. You're ready to work.

Using Narration to Support Exposition

In writing exposition, a writer will often present a topic sentence or a thesis statement and then tell a story to demonstrate or illustrate the idea. Locate the topic sentence in the following paragraph and notice how the narrative that follows illustrates the idea.

> Electric automobiles may be the answer to the pollution of the internal-combustion engine. Inventor Ray Boeger established Electrodyne, Inc., as a manufacturer of three-wheeled golf carts and electric prams for factory messengers and beach vacationers. Then he got the idea of developing Mark II, a four-wheeled vehicle weighing 426 kg, able to range sixty-five to eighty kilometres without recharging, and adding very little to the average family's electric bill. Boeger set up sales offices and an assembly plant in California. He now sells about four Mark II's a week but he believes that with little trouble he could set up to produce ten to fifteen a day. Anyone who purchases a Mark II must be satisfied travelling silently at forty kilometres an hour, and he must be prepared to be towed home if the six heavy-duty batteries lose their charge.

Activity 11F

Using Narratives to Support Expository Ideas

Read the following selections. For each one, locate the topic sentence, and identify the supporting narrative example. Think of some other narrative you could use to support the main idea. It may be fact (an actual instance) or fiction (an imagined instance).

1. Sometimes the name given to a group of people is entirely wrong, and its continued existence perpetuates a misconception about them. For example, in the American northwest and the Canadian southwest is a group of native people commonly known as the "Gros Ventres," which is French for "big bellies." These people are now, and for many years have been, slim, trim, neat, and attractive. When they were first discovered by the old French voyageurs however, they were in the throes of a long and devastating famine. Suffering from hunger and malnutrition, their bellies had become distended and swollen, and their limbs were shrunken. For this reason the voyageurs called them "the big bellies." This led other explorers for two hundred years to think of them as wastrels and gluttons, when nothing could have been further from the truth.

2. Jenny Pike, a 27-year-old Toronto nurse, was pregnant and still smoking a pack of cigarettes a day. She knew vaguely that her smoking might cause her baby to be smaller than average, but was confident that there would be no other significant ill effects on the fetus. Then, in her seventh month, she began attending prenatal classes and found out that her smoking could even kill her unborn child. The guilt and anxiety she felt until the moment she delivered a baby that happily was alive and normal made the last two months of her pregnancy the most unpleasant of her life. And yet she didn't give up smoking: "It made me angry rather than positive about quitting."

The experience of Jenny Pike—not her real name—is not unusual. Thousands of Canadian women may be inflicting irrevocable damage on their unborn children for no reason other than ignorance. If nothing else, the case of Jenny Pike clearly illustrates the wall that exists between scientific knowledge and its translation into public information that could prevent disease and disability.[5]

Activity 11G

Writing and Developing Topic Sentences

1. Prepare a list of ten sentences that you might use as topic sentences. You will support one of these topic sentences with a narrative paragraph similar to that in Activity 11F. Working as your teacher directs, develop a list of acceptable ideas. Begin with the following:

a. Noise pollution is one of the most destructive problems of life in any large city. For example...

b. Getting involved in the community, through such activities as sports leagues or volunteer programs, can result in major changes in a person's attitude to life. For example...

c. Gun control is essential to the well-being of our society (or is a violation of the individual's rights). Support for this viewpoint is...

d. Television commercials can affect our values and our ideas about our relationships with other people. To illustrate this...

e. Young people influence the fads and fashions of many other groups in society. For example...

2. Take about fifteen to twenty minutes of class time to develop one of the topic sentences by writing a narrative paragraph in support of it. You may need to use your imagination to create a fictional narrative for this purpose. Then work on your rough draft as your teacher directs.

3. Be prepared to spend about half a class period discussing your narrative paragraphs and the ideas that give them purpose. As other students read their work, take notes so that you can react to such questions as these:

a. Is there a meaning or point in the paragraph? Is this hinted at or expressed in the first sentence?

b. Is the rest of the paragraph tied to the topic sentence?

c. Is this a narrative; that is, does it tell of an event or a sequence of events?

d. Is it fairly concrete? Does it present real people in a real situation doing real things? Does the description appeal to your senses?

e. Is each sentence tied to the preceding one so that thought flows smoothly, without shift of focus?

Enriching Your Narrations

So far in your study of narratives, you have looked at first-person and third-person narratives written by both professional and student writers. In addition, you have examined ways of getting ideas and making use of experiences that evoked emotions. Next, you examined ways of organizing your narrations by emphasizing suspense, by adapting the journalistic inverted-pyramid style to your openings, by finding or imposing on your experiences, by selecting and using consistently an effective point of view, and by shaping your narrative to support an expository idea.

Even with all of these techniques mastered, however, you might find yourself with a carefully organized but lifeless narrative unless you enrich it and flesh it out by describing the sensory experiences which cause real-

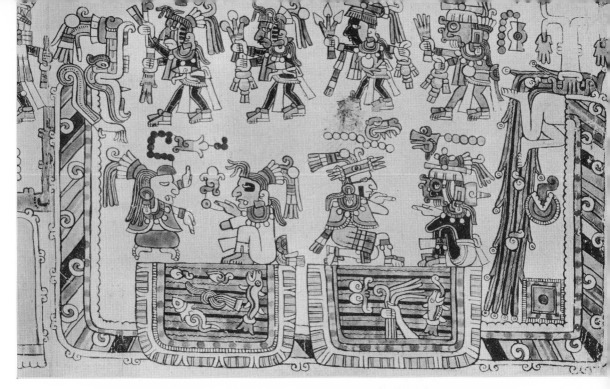

This pictograph was painted on deerskin. It probably tells the story of the creation of the Mixtecs, a people who lived in Mexico before the coming of Columbus.

life incidents to register details on your consciousness. In addition to adding sensory experiences and descriptive details to your writing, you have the opportunity to select, focus, and organize details that will heighten the impression you want to make. In a real-life situation, your mind may select a few from the thousands of impressions that surround you, but it's a rare person who can focus to the extent that only the details appropriate to one preconceived mood or attitude enter the mind. In art—and writing narration is an art—you can determine in advance the impression you want to create. Then you can select only the sensory details that will reinforce that impression, and focus and organize them for the most powerful effect. No wonder art focuses and heightens experience.

Selecting Details That Convey Meaning and Add Concreteness

Suppose you are sitting in English class when a baseball suddenly shatters a window. Your senses are bombarded. You *hear* the smashing of the glass, the thud of the ball on the floor, the tinkle of the shattered fragments, the gasps of your classmates. You *see* the flash of the ball, the quick, fluttering reflections as the fragments of glass catch the sun, the jagged hole, the skinned horsehide of the ball. At the same time your senses of taste and smell and touch are providing subconscious impressions of the total situation. (You *taste* the remnants of the beef stew the cafeteria served at lunch; you *smell* Janie's perfume, the chalk dust from the blackboard, the burst of fresh outdoor air; you *feel* the desk with your elbows, the floor with your feet.)

Yet, when you tell a friend about the incident, you may say simply, "A ball broke the window in our English class." Just think how much of the complete experience you have left out!

Recreating experiences by selecting details.   Anyone who wants to write an interesting narrative tries to include the details of the total experience to reinforce an idea and communicate an experience to the reader. Writing can never communicate the whole experience, but it is important to be aware of all the aspects of the situation so that you can select the details that support the idea or impression you are stressing. Then, by using a specific word instead of a general word, by using modifiers, and by using comparisons, you can come closer to communicating the experience or the idea.

Omitting details.   It is just as important to omit some aspects of an experience as it is to stress others. Just as your mind consciously perceives only a small portion of a total experience, so you must transmit only a small portion of your total perception to your reader. To include all the details would result in a fuzzy, confused, purposeless narrative. Choose, instead, the incisive, important details, and make them clear and memorable.

(*Activity 11H*)

Three Ways of Achieving Concreteness

1. *Exact words.* Be prepared to discuss in class why the sentences on the right are better than those on the left.

a. The plant grew higher than the other plants.	a. The milkweed towered above the tomatoes.
b. The clock sounded.	b. Big Ben boomed.

2. *Modification.* Be prepared to discuss in class why the sentences on the right are better than those on the left. Note that in English sentences single-word modifiers ordinarily come before the word they modify (the *heavy* book, the *tired* dog) but that phrasal and clausal modifiers ordinarily follow the word they modify (the book *of Roman myths,* the dog *who was so tired he couldn't move*).

a. The milkweed towered above the tomatoes.

a. The blown milkweed, its pods shivering in the breeze, towered above the young tomato plants.

b. Big Ben boomed.

b. High above the Houses of Parliament, Big Ben boomed over sleeping London.

3. *Comparisons.* Be prepared to discuss in class why the sentences that follow may or may not be better than those on the right above.

a. Looking like a captured queen, the blown milkweed towered haughtily above the young tomato plants.
b. High above the houses of Parliament, Big Ben laboriously hoisted his hands to the hour and boomed noisily above sleeping London.

Activity 11 I

Expanding Sentences to Achieve Concreteness

1. Prepare a list of simple sentences like those in the first set of examples in Activity 11H. Perhaps these will help you get started:
   a. The thing came into the room.
   b. The group gave the boy a present.
   c. Amy thought the present nice.
   d. The official seemed puzzled.
   e. The message inspired the action.
2. After you have listed fifteen or twenty sentences, be prepared to participate in a class discussion during which your teacher lists on the blackboard the most stimulating sentences of the class. Then you may choose five to rewrite. First, replace general words with exact words. Next, add modifiers. Finally, insert, where appropriate, a figure of speech or a comparison.
3. The following day, bring to class the rewritten sentences, recopied in good form. Working as your teacher directs, note how students have developed the same basic sentences in different ways. Discuss which sentences are particularly well done and which sentences lose effect because they are overdone.
4. The following passage is written in very general terms. In order for it to be effective narration, it would need to be fleshed out with the sensory impressions that can be added by using exact words, modification, and comparison.

Working as your teacher directs, rewrite this passage to include more sensory impressions. Use the three operations you have examined above: substituting exact words, adding modifiers, and including comparisons.

> The parade is the most exciting event in the town during the whole year. For a while before the date, all the townspeople work as a team. They sew things. They build things. They create things. They practice things. A publication holds an election for the parade couple.
>
> No one knows the winning couple until the day of the parade. The two winners wear unusual robes with things on their heads. When the people see the winners, they usually make a lot of noise. Next come the men in funny clothes, then the things people have been working together on all year, then the vehicles from the various divisions. Finally the boys and girls from local schools come by with musical instruments. It is a big day for the town.

Linking Narration and Description

Everyone loves a good story, but not many people enjoy long descriptive passages. In the past, when life moved more slowly than it does today, people who read books for pleasure were not distracted by television and other entertainments easily available today. With more time and fewer distractions, readers were happy to read more slowly and to spend more time on savouring description. Today, description is usually presented in the context of various kinds of writing, such as narration, exposition, and argumentation rather than as a separate and distinct kind of writing. Since, however, it is absolutely essential in narration, the art of writing description is presented in this chapter.

Despite some people's preferences for watching television, skimming magazines and newspapers, or simply listening to records, a larger group of people than ever before reads and enjoys good description. Their tastes, however, have been influenced by the activities that compete with reading, and the style of description today reflects those influences. As you read the following examples of descriptive writing notice the techniques used by the writers.

I

> A yellow sun always broils Southern Italy in August. But on this morning in the Roman pleasure resort of Pompeii, the earth steams. The heat is almost unbearable. Springs and wells already have dried up mysteriously, and for four days the ground has rumbled and growled. Along the shore, the Bay of Naples sizzles like a massive devil's cauldron. Dogs strain at their leashes and birds fly away.[6]
>
> —M. W. Newman

II

I think the next ten miles [sixteen kilometres] were the most exciting I have ever traveled in a train. We were on the coast, moving fast along a spit of land, and on either side of the train—its whistle screaming, its chimney full of smoke—white sand had drifted into magnificent dunes; beyond these dunes were slices of green sea. Sand whipped up by the engine pattered against the carriages behind, and spray from the breakers, whose regular wash dramatized the chugging of the locomotive, was flung up to speckle the windows with crystal bubbles. It was all light and water and sand, flying about the train speeding towards the Rameswaram causeway in a high wind. The palms under the scudding clouds bowed and flashed like fans made of feathers, and here and there, up to their stupas (dome-like mounds containing Buddhist shrines) in sand, were temples flying red flags on their crooked masts. The sand covered the track in places; it had drifted into temple doorways and wrecked the frail palm-frond huts. The wind was terrific, beating on the windows, carrying sand and spray and the whistle's *hooeeee,* and nearly toppling the dhows (single-masted ships) in full sail at the hump of the spangled horizon where Ceylon lay.[7]

—Paul Theroux

III

It was noon before the wind let up a little and the rain slowed to a drizzle. I pushed open the door and leaped out. The wind snatched off my rain cap and sent it whirling across the highway, jerked open my raincoat and spread it like wings, lifting me completely off the ground.

Clasping my hands below my knees, I collapsed the wings, flopped like a wounded turkey and stumbled toward the entrance. Ann Cullen flung the door open, letting in a blast of wind, a gush of rain—and me.

My raincoat looked as if it had been peppered with buckshot; my arms and legs were spotted with blood where pebbles had struck; and the car had a severe case of freckles, bare metal glistening where paint had been chipped by flying debris.[8]

—Gene Plowden

IV

The sun dipped behind the hills across the river and the windows of the bungalow ceased blazing with evening sunlight. At once you felt the cool air as if it were the earth's cool breath. Anybody looking out of the front windows of Mrs. Dorval's bungalow could look down on to the racing Thompson River. Perhaps the water was emerald, perhaps it was sapphire. It is both. It is neither. It is a brilliant river, blue-green with lacings of white foam and spray as the water hurls itself violently along in rapids against hidden or projecting rocks, a rapid, racing, calling river. The hills rise high and lost on each side of the banks. These hills are traversed hardly at all. There is no reason to climb, to scale to the top, to look down. In the sunlight the dun-coloured gorges of the blue-green river look yellow and ochreous, and in some places there are outcroppings of rock that are nearly rose red. Large dark and solitary pine trees give landmark and meaning. Here and there in a gully an army of these dark pointed pine trees marches up an ancient waterway of the hill-side, static. How do they grow on stone? A figure of man or beast crawling distant across the great folds and crevasses of these sprawling hills would make you stop, look, point with surprise, and question. One is accustomed to their being empty of life. As evening comes on, the hills grow dove grey and purple; they take on a variety of surprising shapes and shades, and the oblique shafts of sunlight disclose new hills and valleys which in daylight merge into one and are not seen. It is the sage-brush that covers nearly everything, that helps to transform everything, and that in the mutations of sunlight and moonlight helps to change the known hills to the unfamiliar. Because the hills are so desolate, strange and still, without movement, the strong brilliant water in headlong motion at their base holds your eyes with its tumult.[9]

—Ethel Wilson

V

The building has been turned inside out, with all the intestines, normally hidden from public view, hanging on the outside. What's more, the pipes are in a riot of colors: blue for air conditioning, red for elevators, and green for water. The whole mass is suspended from a giant metal scaffold that displays its bare metal bones, too. Escalators, enclosed in tubes of Plexiglas, make their way up the outside walls like giant, inquisitive caterpillars creeping along.[10]

—Horace Sutton

Here are some characteristics of modern description you can observe in the preceding examples.

1. *Single tone, mood, and atmosphere*—Everything in a description should add up to one feeling or impression. Anything that would weaken or change that feeling should be omitted.

2. *Action*—Many of today's readers refuse to spend time reading a description for its own sake. They want movement and action even in descriptive passages.

3. *Many sensory impressions*—Writers include words and phrases that appeal to all five senses to make the reader feel what they are describing.

Reread the selections and notice the mood and atmosphere of each. In the first writing sample the writer uses several verbs that appeal to your sense of hearing. Can you hear the Bay of Naples sizzling, the ground rumbling? What are the words in sample two that give you a feeling of action and speed? Notice the images in sample three. First you see the narrator flying through the air like a bird then flopping about like a "wounded turkey." Sample five also makes good use of figurative language. The writer speaks of the "intestines" of a building and compares the escalator to "inquisitive caterpillars."

Though you are studying description in connection with narration, good description is important in all kinds of writing, even in the writing of technical and scientific reports.

Distinguishing Between Showing and Telling

At the beginning of a silent movie, a printed title might say, "Oliver Hardwick was a stern and heartless man. His greatest joy was to foreclose on the homes of widows and to turn them out." Then Oliver Hardwick would rub his hands in glee.

Today, movie directors avoid *telling* the audience what a character is like. Instead, they *show* the characters in action and let the audience form their own ideas about them. The finished film reveals the character and background of each person by showing details of behaviour, mannerisms, actions in relation to other people, and many other revealing features. These are not told by narration.

Comparing methods.   Writers can either tell what they want readers to believe about a character or they can show a scene or an incident and let the readers draw their own conclusions. Similarly, in description, a writer can tell that a road is a scary place after dark or show it through details and mood.

Here are examples of each method, taken from the same short story.

TELLING

"Don't come back till you have him!" the Ticktockman said, very quietly, very sincerely, extremely dangerously.

They used dogs. They used probes. They used cardioplate crossoffs. They used teepers. They used bribery. They used stiktytes. They used intimidation. They used torment. They used torture. They used finks. They used cops. They used search & seizure. They used fallaron. They used betterment incentive. They used fingerprints. They used Bertillon. They used cunning. They used guile. They used treachery. They used Raoul Mitgong, but he didn't help much. They used applied physics. They used techniques of criminology.

And what the hell: they caught him.

SHOWING

Once more, in anticipation, the elfin grin spread, and there was a tooth missing back there on the left side. He dipped, skimmed, and swooped over them; and then, scrunching about on the air-boat, he released the holding pins that fastened shut the ends of the home-made pouring troughs that kept his cargo from dumping prematurely. And as he pulled the trough-pins, the air-boat slid over the factory workers and one hundred and fifty thousand dollars worth of jelly beans cascaded down on the expresstrip.

> Jelly beans! Millions and billions of purples and yellows and greens and licorice and grape and raspberry and mint and round and smooth and crunchy outside and soft-mealy inside and sugary and bouncing jouncing tumbling clittering clattering skittering fell on the heads and shoulders and hardhats and carapaces of the Timkin workers, tinkling on the slidewalk and bouncing away and rolling about underfoot and filling the sky on their way down with all the colors of joy and childhood and holidays, coming down in a steady rain, a solid wash, a torrent of color and sweetness out of the sky from above, and entering a universe of sanity and metronomic order and quite-mad coocoo newness. Jelly beans![11]
>
> —Harlan Ellison

In the first example, Harlan Ellison gives a motion-picture montage impression of a rapid-action search for the independent clown who refuses to fit into a timed and scheduled daily world. Because the impression of the rapid-action search is more important than the realistic details that would make it slower, but more real, he simply tells, rather than shows.

In the second example, which appears earlier in the story, Ellison shows the audience the crime of which the Harlequin is guilty: floating on an airboat, he gummed up the machinery and the time schedule of a modern factory by dropping millions of jelly beans into the moving sidewalk carrying workers to their jobs. This time he shows the event in full detail.

Both showing and telling are legitimate and useful techniques. Each should be used where appropriate.

(Activity 11J)

Recognizing Showing and Telling

Number your paper 1 to 10 and (a) write Showing or Telling to indicate which method predominates in each of the following passages; then, (b) if the passage primarily *tells*, write two or three good sentences with some concrete information that would show the same thing. If the passage primarily *shows*, write a single sentence that tells or summarizes what the passage shows. An example follows. (Since the telling-showing distinction applies in forms other than description, many of the passages are not descriptive.)

TELLING

> There was something gallant in his carriage and something fearless in his manner.

SHOWING

> The soldier swaggered into the room and bowed elaborately. As he looked at the twenty pairs of hostile eyes, he smiled coldly, and his right hand sought the hilt of his sword.

1. She was one horse, and she was all horses. Thundering battle chargers, fleet Arabians, untamed mustangs—sitting beside her on her manger I knew and rode them all. There was history in her shapely head and burning eyes. I charged with her at Balaklava, Waterloo, scoured the deserts of Africa and the steppes of the Ukraine. Conquest and carnage, trumpets and glory—she understood, and carried me triumphantly.

To approach her was to be enlarged, transported. She was coal-black, gleaming, queenly. Her mane had a ripple and her neck an arch. And somehow, softly and mysteriously, she was always burning. The reflection on her glossy hide, whether of winter sunshine or yellow lantern light, seemed the glow of some fierce, secret passion. There were moments when I felt the whole stable charged with her, as if she were the priestess of her kind, in communion with her deity.[12]

—Sinclair Ross

2. Although many South Pacific islands are beautiful, perhaps none matches the television picture of paradise.

3. The temperature on the prairie rose as high as 43 degrees, but none of the hunters could be seen to perspire. The thirsty air greedily absorbed the moisture and left only whitened salt stains on the fading homespun. On both sides of the trail lay husks of broken wagons and the bleached bones of oxen. An occasional rude cross, fashioned from the only wood available—a broken singletree, the slats of a barrel, the tortured rocker from a prized chair—marked a human resting-place.

4. At the first whoop of the destroyer's alarm siren, the slender craft knifes to the south and bends its wake into a sudden bow. In less than fifteen gale-tossed minutes it hovers above the suspected shoals, now lighted with blinkers, searchlights, and white parachute flares. Then, where the huge oil slick ironically traps the rainbow hues of the flares and calms the sullen waves, we see the flotsam of the sunken sub: a mattress, some life preservers, a battered briefcase. A strong smell of diesel oil pervades the atmosphere.

5. A grimy little door at the very top of the stairs stood ajar. A very poor-looking room about ten paces long was lighted by a candle-end; the whole of it was visible from the entrance. It was all in disorder, littered up with rags of all sorts, especially children's garments. Across the furthest corner was stretched a ragged sheet. Behind it probably was the bed. There was nothing in the room except two chairs and a sofa covered with American leather, full of holes, before which stood an old deal kitchen table, unpainted and uncovered. At the edge of the table stood a smouldering tallow-candle in an iron candlestick.[13]

—Fyodor Dostoyevsky

6. She was so old that her face no longer held any trace of how she had looked when she was young. Only her eyes had no dustiness of age about them. The years that had washed away their colour seemed to have disclosed an original brightness. Neat, bright, delicate: that pattern was repeated everywhere—in the white hair caught back into a tight bun; in her hands, her feet; even in the black dress she wore, with the white piping at the neck. Her clothes had always stayed neat and clean, even if she had been transplanting cabbage plants on a wet day. She was the sort of woman whose daughters, if she had any, are delicate like herself, but who bears incredibly sturdy sons.[14]

—Ernest Buckler

7. Dogs often wander into the classrooms at schools, and always cause an uproar. Kids cannot contain themselves when dogs appear in the midst of Egypt lesson, for what reason no one seems to know. Why couldn't they, the kids, just let the dog be in the class, wandering around, sniffing here and licking a few hands there, quietly, moseying about in the style of dogs while the class continued with the most important part of the lesson about Egypt? But no, they can't. They got to rush the dog, they got to pick him up and drop him, they got to offer the dog candy and pieces of sandwich, they got to yell and scream and act like they never saw any dog before in their whole lives.[15]

—James Herndon

8. Chimo Park in the centre of town may once have been as inviting and pleasant as the garden around a small town's municipal hall, but all that is changed today. Whether it's because there are too many people for the little space, because people are too careless, or because taxes no longer will support the care that such a park requires, Chimo Park has changed. It's no longer inviting. It's no longer safe. It's no longer comfortable. It's dirty, crowded, littered, and dangerous.

9. Two great concrete parabolas intersected, seeming to float in the sky 30 metres above the runway, capturing the billowing of a parachute or perhaps the half-imaginary lines of a Leonardo da Vinci flying machine. On the front of the building, an acre of vertical smoked glass filled the void from ground to roof and showed the visitor the floors, offices, and floating stairs within. The great glass expanse half mirrored the parking lot and highway behind the visitor and made him think himself indeed into the fourth dimension.

10. Sometimes in winter the cold air from the far north made a pool over the Namko Country. It drifted down slowly, a breath, a sigh, over the patchwork of meadows and pine and swamp and lake that lay just inside of the Coast Range. Then the land groaned as the weight of the cold settled upon it. Two days before there had been two sun dogs riding right and left of the pale sun. Within twenty-four hours the cold air had seeped down and on Puntlakuntlet Lake the two-foot-thick [61 centimetres] ice began to split in long, jagged, lightning-shaped cracks, with the appropriate noise of thunder. The previous night an old dog coyote had lain down and tucked his grey nose into his thin tail beside the Russel fence of Smith's Home Place and in the coldest hour, just before the dawn, he had died. Man is supposed to be the only animal who spends his adult life anticipating death but it would be easy to believe that the old coyote had some sense of futility of it all when he had lain down in the poor light of a young moon that night.[16]

—Paul St. Pierre

More Meanings of Point of View

On page 259, you learned that point of view refers to the writer's choice of the narrator to tell the story. The term "viewpoint" may also be used to refer to the way the narrator perceives the story. As you recall, the writer may decide to tell the story with no limitations on what the narrator knows about the characters, about their actions, and about their thoughts. If, however, the writer has chosen a character in the story as narrator, that person will have some restrictions on what he or she can tell. Obviously, if Uncle Jimmy is telling the story and Uncle Jimmy has been isolated in a cabin in the Yukon for ten years, he simply cannot narrate what happened in New Brunswick last month. He has no way of knowing about it. Similarly, if Uncle Jimmy is a natural-born optimist who always looks on the bright side of things, it would not be consistent to have him narrating the aches and pains and miseries of the world. We know that most people, depending upon the mood they happen to be in at a given time, will either not perceive or will deliberately ignore details that don't fit that mood. Also, personality is a determinant of a person's response to a situation. Uncle Jimmy can reveal to the reader only what he feels, suspects, or knows.

Choosing your point of view, then, is like deciding which camera to use. Here are additional meanings of point of view. They can be compared to deciding where to place your camera (physical viewpoint) and selecting a filter to put over the lens (psychological viewpoint).

Choosing a physical viewpoint.   If photography is your hobby, you know how important it is to focus your camera carefully. You know also, that by changing your position in relation to your subject, you get a completely different picture. For an unusual perspective, you may aim from overhead in a tree or from a prone position on the ground. Similarly, a writer chooses a physical viewpoint for a story. Just as a camera cannot take a picture of anything out of its range, so a writer, once the viewpoint has been established, cannot reveal anything beyond that limited viewpoint. In many stories, the narrator maintains the same physical viewpoint throughout. A writer may, however, decide to allow a shift in the narrator's viewpoint. This is something like shifting from a still camera to a moving-picture camera. In such cases, the writer must let the reader know that this shift is deliberate and there must be some explanation to account for it.

Choosing a psychological viewpoint.   Writers may also choose a psychological viewpoint, selecting and emphasizing the details that would be seen if one were in a particular state of mind. Just as a camera lens may be covered with a filter to screen out undesirable lights or shadows, so writers can "cover the lens of perception" by adopting a certain attitude or mood. For example, a narrator might describe the hall of a school immediately after receiving an A on a test. Or, the narrator might describe the same scene after receiving a failing grade. The mood "filters perception" so that different objects might be recorded, different colours emphasized, and different comparisons used. In the first case, the engraved list of valedictorians might be described as "a modest plaque gently reminding students of the accomplishments of their predecessors." In the second case, because of anger, disappointment, and frustration, the plaque might be called "a garish brass tombstone mocking students' aspirations."

Changing a viewpoint.   In Ray Bradbury's novel, *Dandelion Wine*, twelve-year-old Douglas Spaulding, his younger brother Tom, and their father were picking fox grapes and wild strawberries when suddenly Doug experienced a revelation. "I'm alive!" he thought.

When he expressed it to Tom, the younger boy wasn't impressed.

I

"I'm alive."

"Heck, that's old!"

"Thinking about it, *noticing* it, is new. You do things and don't watch. Then all of a sudden you look and see what you're doing and it's the first time, really. I'm going to divide this summer up in two parts. First part of this tablet is titled: RITES AND CEREMONIES. The first root beer pop of the year. The first time running barefoot in the grass of the year. First time almost drowning in the lake of the year. First watermelon. First mosquito. First harvest of dandelions. Those are the things we do over and over and over and never think. Now here in back, like I said, is DISCOVERIES AND REVELATIONS or maybe ILLUMINATIONS, that's a swell word, or INTUITIONS, okay? In other words you do an old familiar thing, like bottling dandelion wine, and you put that under RITES AND CEREMONIES. And then you think about it, and what you think, crazy or not, you put under DISCOVERIES AND REVELATIONS.[17]

—Ray Bradbury

With his increasing maturity, Douglas Spaulding had experienced a shift in his psychological point of view. He realized that he was no longer a child, content with just experiencing life. From that point on, he would think about life and interpret it.

Not all shifts in psychological point of view are so all-encompassing and so long lasting. Nonetheless, your particular psychological perspective at any given time can have a profound effect on the way you see things and the way you react to them.

As you tell a story from a character's psychological point of view, you must always consider how such a viewpoint makes the character look at the scene or events. By explaining any changes in that point of view you make your story more believable.

(*Activity 11K*)

Analyzing Paragraphs for Physical and Psychological Viewpoint

Read the following pairs of descriptions to see how changes in physical and psychological viewpoints can completely alter a description. Write a short paragraph discussing how the change in viewpoint changes the selection and presentation of ideas. What techniques in these examples can you use in your own writing?

PHYSICAL VIEWPOINT

1. From the back of the auditorium the stage set for the school play looks like the proverbial desert island on which the cast of *The Admirable Crichton* is supposed to be stranded. Tall, graceful palm trees frame the stage and their fernlike fronds meet above the centre front. A row of exotic marsh plants extends across the stage front so that the viewers seem to be peering from a dense forest into a tiny clearing, in the centre of which is the bamboo shelter of the castaways. To stage right of the hut, casting flickering shadows as high as its palm-thatched eaves, a cheerful fire warms the actors. Directly behind the fire, a path curves up and around behind the hut, leading, the audience knows, to the great signal fire dimly visible in the distance.

2. When viewed from the first few rows of the auditorium, the set for the school play is theatrically fake. The second act is supposed to occur on an island on which the Loam family, some of their friends, and their butler, Crichton, have been cast away. The palm tree trunks on each side of the stage are actually painted strips of muslin. The edges curl slightly, and when an actor walks nearby, they wave and sway in the breeze. Overhead are painted fronds cut from wrapping paper and pasted on a kind of scrim, or cheesecloth. Across the front of the stage, a row of dried cattails cut from Turkey Creek almost hides the footlights, and completely hides some of the important action. In the centre of the stage, cardboard tubes collected from carpeting stores have been painted to look something like bamboo and wired together to make a two-dimensional hut. But as one looks into the windows or through the door, it is evident that only two walls have been finished. The fire to stage right of the hut quite obviously consists of piled sticks, red and yellow cellophane, a few strips of red cloth tacked to the floor at one end, a pair of light bulbs, and a small fan. Not only does the "fire" look like what it is, but the faint hum of the fan reminds the audience that civilization is not too far from this particular desert island. Behind the fire, a papier-mâché hill built on a set of narrow steps leads to a "distant" signal fire painted on the cyclorama. Unfortunately, however, as the actors reach the top of the hill which is supposed to be behind the hut, the audience can see them stoop and clamber down a little step-ladder.

PSYCHOLOGICAL VIEWPOINT

1. That first day of basketball practice, the locker room had been a mass of eager, shouting, half-dressed boys chortling about the coming season.

As Stan burst through the second set of swinging doors, he saw the traditional benches where only members of the first string sat and dressed. With its short row of taller lockers and wider, more comfortable benches, the first string's section of the locker room radiated dignity and security. With a special heartskip, Stan pictured himself there next season. Walking past the first string's benches to join the crowd of other hopefuls who had come to try out for the basketball team, Stan saw the cheerful, glassed-in office where Mr. Rice and Mr. Newman, the coaches, were discussing strategy. From the shower room behind the coach's office came the pseudo-operatic, reverberating voice of a singer from the last gym class. Stan smiled confidently as he pushed his coat into an empty, khaki-coloured locker, and began to undress. The faint mist from the shower room put rainbow halos around the lights.

2. After the third week of practice Mr. Newman announced who had made the basketball team and who had been "cut." Stan could hardly believe his ears. Some of the others who were no longer on the squad elected to complete the two-hour practice session—their final session on the team—but Stan and three others moved gloomily toward the locker room. When the last boy pushed through the swinging door, it flapped mournfully slower and slower. The only sound in the locker room was a minor echo of an off-key tune from the nearby showers. Stan slowly opened the dull, scratched, khaki-painted locker door, which was stained with adhesive-tape marks where he had stored the strips he had used to bandage his sprained ankle. He could see only with difficulty; the room was half in shadows because the tall lockers shut out the light. Even the light from the coach's office seemed to shine reluctantly through the smudged and steam-clouded windows. The mist from the nearby shower room caused the overhead bulbs to radiate many coloured sunsets, "the same sunsets you see when your eyes are full of tears," thought Stan.

(*Activity 11L*)

Using Point of View

1. After you have discussed the examples in Activity 11K, write two similar pairs of contrasting paragraphs. Choose a single scene and describe it from two different locations. Then choose another scene and describe it from two different psychological viewpoints. Perhaps the following will suggest some possibilities:

PHYSICAL VIEWPOINT

a. A racetrack from the point of view of a jockey and as seen from the grandstand.

b. The deck of an aircraft carrier from the point of view of a pilot and of the deck crew.

c. The highway as seen from a motorcycle or from inside a bus.

d. Your classroom as seen from a desk in the back row or from the teacher's desk at the front of the room.

PSYCHOLOGICAL VIEWPOINT

a. A moving train from the viewpoint of passengers aboard the train and of a girl who has just missed it.

b. A school election from the point of view of a winner and of a loser.

c. A school track team practice outside in a cold, blustery wind, described from the point of view of a member and of an outsider.

d. The toy department of a store as seen by a six-year old child and by one of the clerks.

2. After you have written the viewpoint paragraphs, work with them as your teacher directs. Discuss the difference that the change in point of view has made. A partial list of the differences in the physical viewpoint paragraph on page 283 follows:

FROM THE BACK OF THE AUDITORIUM	FROM THE FRONT OF THE AUDITORIUM
a. Graceful, swaying palm trees	a. Painted strips of muslin to represent tree trunks
b. Overhead fronds	b. Wrapping-paper fronds pasted on cheesecloth
c. Exotic marsh plants	c. Dried cattails that hide the action and fail to hide the footlights

Subordination of Ideas

The skill of subordinating ideas is an important one for you to use in your writing. The word "subordination" means "placing below in order or importance." A reader will follow your story more easily if you indicate the relative importance of your ideas. Here are two ideas presented as if they were of equal importance:

Steve collected old newspapers and glass for recycling and he was interested in ecology.

The writer should have provided "thought connections" for these two ideas. Study the examples which follow. You will find a series of sentences using different structures to combine the two ideas. The words which illustrate each kind of structure are enclosed in parentheses.

ADVERBIAL CLAUSE   beginning with *after, although, because, before, if, in case, provided, since, when, while, unless, until* or several others.

Steve collected old newspapers and glass for recycling (because he was interested in ecology.)

or

(Since Steve was interested in ecology,) he collected old newspapers and glass for recycling.

PARTICIPIAL PHRASE   beginning with an -ing verb

(Being interested in ecology,) Steve collected old newspapers and glass for recycling.

PARTICIPIAL PHRASE   beginning with an -ed or -en verb

Steve, (interested in ecology,) collected old newspapers and glass for recycling.

PREPOSITIONAL PHRASE

Steve collected old newspaper and glass for recycling (because of his interest in ecology.)

INFINITIVE PHRASE

(To show his interest in ecology,) Steve collected old newspapers and glass for recycling.

RELATIVE CLAUSE   beginning with *who, which, that*

Steve, (who was interested in ecology,) collected old newspapers and glass for recycling.

Activity 11M

Experimenting with Subordination

Here are some sentences that might appear in your writing. Working as your teacher directs, see how many of the preceding patterns you can use to subordinate one idea to the other.

1. The little boy sat on the patch of grass, and the petunia border made a picture frame around him.
2. Kim couldn't believe the applause, and she returned to the stage for an encore.

3. The shadows of the ancient cypress trees began to lengthen, and the sun began to merge with its reflection on the water.

4. The prairies suffered severe drought and erosion of topsoil during the Depression, and farmers now make greater use of measures such as irrigation and crop rotation.

5. The sound of the television announcer's voice filled the room, and the news of the plane disaster stunned the listeners.

6. The students drifted slowly into the auditorium, and the program didn't appeal to them.

7. The company announced a new policy of hiring inexperienced workers for a training program, and many teenagers were quick to apply.

8. The prairies of Saskatchewan and Manitoba are sweeping and beautiful, and the coastal rain forests of British Columbia are green and lush.

9. The little garden with the crystal pool is crowded into the apartment-house patio, and the little garden seems out of place in the middle of all that concrete.

10. Sara was concerned about the seal hunt, and she wrote to her Member of Parliament.

Eliminating Dead Wood

Some writers think that lots of words, especially long words, improve a piece of writing. Actually, good narrative writing, like all good writing, uses only the words required to accomplish the task at hand. Effective writing is achieved through use of precise, expressive words. Each word should contribute to the author's intention. If your ideas are complex, or if you are aiming at a special emotional tone, you may need to use many words, but the rule still holds: Always use the fewest words that will do the job.

(Activity 11N)

Removing Dead Wood

Read the following paragraph in class. Decide which words and phrases are repetitious. Cut the paragraph down to a minimum number of effective words. Write out your revised version and be prepared to discuss it with your classmates.

In my opinion, I think it is essential for me to recognize that my best friend is the one person whom I know who can amuse me and make me laugh and entertain me completely at the same time that she is irritating and bothering me a great deal. I can't help but smile because when she is feeling in a humourous mood and wants to make me laugh, she reminds me of a particular kind of monkey which I think is very funny, the Rhesus monkey. When I look at her and try to picture what she is like, the first thing I see at first glance is a balloon of red fuzz that when closely examined by looking intensely at it can be seen and thought of as hair. Then her sharp little nose, which is in the middle of her face struggling under a pair of huge glasses, comes into view, closely followed by her wide-open mouth which is usually open so as to show her teeth because she is talking and giggling and laughing so much. I have never gotten a good look at her body because it is always active and moving so that she is never still long enough for me to form an impression of what it is like. She darts over here and then darts over there and then whirls around to reach for something she forgot in the first place when she darted over there. While jumping up and down at a fast pace she is doing all this darting. She is so funny to watch that after a time I can't stand to look at her because she is so funny and active that as I look at her I become tired and want to stop looking out of sheer exhaustion. The thing, however, that irritates me most is her habit of being so completely agreeable and pleasant all the time. No matter what I suggest, she agrees to do, but if I change my mind because I no longer want to do the thing I originally suggested that we do, she changes her mind just as I did and agrees immediately to the new idea by saying, "Oh, no, I wouldn't think of doing anything like that." When moments before she was gung-ho for that activity, she is still willing to change her mind just because I have changed my mind and she wants to be agreeable. But she is still my friend because, no matter how much she irritates me, I realize that her silliness is just her way of showing that she is an individual and this is her way of showing that she is a person different from all other people.

Major Writing Assignment

A Narration

Refer to the "storehouse of materials" that you developed in connection with Activity 11A, page 261. Think of some specific event you experienced in one of the areas you selected. Impose a purpose or meaning on the event; give it the significance that will make it worth writing about.

You may write a personal narrative; recounting this actual experience in the first person. Or you may tell the story of an imagined event. Another choice you have is to write an account of another person's experience, using a third-person narrator.

Whether you choose to write about an actual experience or an imagined event, be sure you take into account these elements:

point, purpose or significance   emotion
structure or order   action
point of view   suspense
effective description

Before you begin to write, try to think through this outline. If you cannot use the outline in this way, plunge ahead with your first draft and then reread the outline to see if you can add anything from it to improve your narrative.

GENERAL NARRATIVE PATTERN

      I. Introduction

           A. Introduces the *who, what, when,* and *where*—with a mystery (for suspense) about the *why* and *how.*

Optional   B. Reveals any necessary background.

Optional   C. Suggests importance of the subject.

Optional   D. Provides a point, or purpose, for the narration. (This may be saved until the end, or even omitted entirely so that it is left to the reader's imagination.)

     II. Body

           A. Explains and describes selected events, usually in order of time.

           B. Explains, comments on, and interprets the events, when necessary.

           C. Provides guides to time, place, sequence, and significance so reader doesn't get lost.

    III. Conclusion

           A. Ends interestingly as soon as possible after the climax.

Optional   B. Comments on, reaffirms or simply clarifies the meaning.

12

The Character Sketch

The artists tell us what they think we are. They help us to hear our own voice, recognize our own shape, laugh at our own follies, rejoice in our own powers. Accepting or rejecting the artist's views, we become more thoroughly ourselves.[1]
—Elizabeth Waterston

When the editor of a small country newspaper was able to double the circulation of his publication after several previous editors had failed, he was asked to explain the secret of his success.

"It's easy," he said. "All I have to do is mention the name of every single person in town at least once each month. They all want to see their own names in print, and besides that, they're curious about everybody else."

Successful newspaper and magazine editors have all learned this rule for building readership: Names are news.

Perhaps you've thought of the character sketch as a classroom exercise—something that teachers assign, but that doesn't exist outside of school. Well, think again! Almost every magazine, journal, and newspaper runs character sketches of one kind or another. Is it a magazine catering to hotel managers? Then the readers are interested in outstanding, successful, and colourful people in the hotel business. Is it a magazine emphasizing science? Then the editor will present a character sketch of an outstanding scientist. Whatever the publication, it will publish character sketches of men and women who will be interesting to its particular audience. Some successful magazines consist entirely of brief character sketches of well-known people.

◄ From what point of view would you write a character sketch of this girl? Who is she and what is she doing?

There are three things to consider in writing a character sketch: the subject, the point of view, and the method you will use to present your subject. The subject must be worth writing about for some reason. That reason will be the focus of your sketch. Do not attempt to describe every aspect of the character's life. Instead, select the traits that will make the character "live" on the page. Another pitfall to avoid is the use of stereotypes, stock characters, which lack both individuality and realism. As you write your character sketch select the details that make your subject unique among all others. The best way to avoid stereotypes is to become more sensitive to the people around you, noticing the qualities that make each person distinct and individual.

As you read the character sketches that follow, keep in mind the differences between individualized characters and stereotypes.

I

She met us at the train yesterday, officially, and took us home with her for dinner. There's one at least in every town, austere, beyond reproach, a little prim with the responsibilities of self-assumed leadership—inevitable as broken sidewalks and rickety false fronts. She's an alert, thin-voiced, thin-featured little woman, up to her eyes in the task of managing the town and making it over in her own image. I'm afraid it may mean some changes for Philip and me too, for there's a crusading steel in her eye to warn she brooks no halfway measures. The deportment and mien of her own family bear witness to a potter's hand that never falters. Her husband, for instance, is an appropriately meek little man, but you can't help feeling what an achievement is his meekness. It's like a tight wire cage drawn over him, and words and gestures, indicative of a more expansive past, keep squeezing through it the same way that parts of the portly Mrs. Wenderby this afternoon kept squeezing through the back and sides of Philip's study armchair. And her twelve-year-old twins, George and Stanley, when they recited grace in unison their voices tolled with such sonority that Philip in his scripture reading after dinner sounded like a droney auctioneer. Philip at the table, I noticed, kept watching them, his eyes critical and moody. He likes boys—often, I think, plans the bringing-up and education of *his* boy. A fine, well-tempered lad by now, strung just a little on the fine side, responsive to too many overtones. For I know Philip, and he has a way of building in his own image, too.[2]

—Sinclair Ross

II

Becker, the first time you see him, is at the mainland terminus waving your car down the ramp onto the government ferry and singing to your headlights and to the long line of traffic behind you that he'd rather be a sparrow than a snail. Yes he would if he could, he loudly sings, he surely would. In his orange life-jacket and fluorescent gloves, he waves his arms to direct traffic down that ramp the way someone else might conduct a great important orchestra—a round little man with a sloppy wool cap riding his head and a huge bushy beard hiding all of his face except the long turned-down weather-reddened nose. He'd rather be a forest, he sings, than a street.

Follow him home.

Ride the ferry with him on his two-hour trip across the Strait of Georgia, while the long backbone ridge of the island's mountains sharpens into blue and ragged shades of green, and the coastline shadows shape themselves into rocky cliffs and driftwood-cluttered bays; then follow him up the ramp, the end of his shift, as he sets out through the waiting lines of traffic and gusts of rushing passengers on foot. No longer the serenading conductor, he is a short stump of a man walking the full length of the waterfront parking lot and then up the long slow hill towards the town, his black overcoat hanging down past the top of his rubber boots suggesting the shape of a squat crockery jug. He stops to explore the rain water running through the limp grass in the ditch, and to talk for a while with someone leaning over a front-porch ledge, and to buy a pocketful of candy in a corner store. But eventually he gets into his old fenderless green Hillman parked in one corner of the shopping-centre lot, and drives down the long slope to the beach again, and along past the bay, and north beyond town altogether on a road that twists around rock bluffs and dips through farm valleys and hemps through second-growth timber until he turns off suddenly and rattles downhill on a gravel lane to his log cabin where it stands with others near the water's edge.[3]

—Jack Hodgins

Student Composition 12A

GRANDDAD

I awoke to the clanking and rumbling of my antiquated radiator as the frantic steam gushed from the heater through the rusty pipes. I burrowed deeper into the warm blankets and lay quietly, listening contentedly to the sounds of the winter dawn. From the hall bathroom came the gurgling of hot water as it filled the chipped, narrow basin, and I could hear a muffled voice humming like a giant bumblebee. Granddad was up already and was preparing to shave. I smiled and resisted the impulse to go and watch him. I loved to watch his leathery hands, his methodical strokes, and his steady patience, and I couldn't remember ever seeing him shave differently. And as I let my mind wander back to my childhood, I realized that Granddad's habits and moods changed little over the years.

"Aye, lassie," Granddad said to me once, "I like things the way they are, and I canna' be changed now." Granddad was a cooper in the local brewery when the whole family lived in the Scottish village of Coldstream. He took pride in the neat, sturdy wooden ale kegs he created. His job demanded that he be up at sunrise and ready for a long day. I can still remember Granddad singing in a lusty tenor as he washed and shaved while

How does the writer tie the beginning and end of this paper together? What do they have in common?

What sensory images does the writer provide in her opening paragraph?

How does the writer communicate her emotional relationship with her subject?

What do Granddad's actual words add? Why is their flavour particularly strong and effective?

What natural connections does the writer make between life in Canada and life in Scotland? How do these connections help shape the paper?

I lay in my cot waiting for the breakfast porridge to be cooked. He would leave for work, dressed in coarse overalls and leather cap, just as I came down to the parlour, and his greeting was the same nearly every day. "Good mornin' to you wee'un," he would call, "it's a fair sight to behold at the morn, you are!"

One midday Granddad came home with a frown creasing his brown face. "Mary," he said to my grandmother, "I'll tell you directly. The other coopers have been listening to the union men from Edinburgh, and now the lads themselves want a union. It would mean better pay and less work. It would mean pay benefits during sickness." He stopped abruptly and looked from Grandmother's face to the rough flagstone floor. Then he said, slowly, "And it would mean team construction on the kegs, an end to the individual's work." He looked up again into my grandmother's startled eyes and spoke, defiance crackling in his voice. "And I'll tell you, Mary, I'll never let that happen. I'll work for my day's earnings and care for mysel' when I'm sick. And for sure I'll build the kegs alone without anyone else's advice!"

Granddad didn't even stay for his dinner that day, but returned to his work. But despite his warnings and protests, the unions did come to the Coldstream brewery. Granddad refused to join. Many times he threatened to leave altogether and move the family to Islay where the larger breweries were located, but time and again he was persuaded to stay. Soon he was the only cooper who worked alone, bending the taut fresh slats of wood into barrels and fastening them with black iron rings and seals. He remained the only cooper to brand his initials, as was tradition, onto the bottoms of the kegs.

Granddad resisted unions, but he could not stand against the waves of progress that flooded even the smallest breweries. Aluminum kegs were being cast in large Edinburgh factories for the transportation and storage of ale. The cooper no longer had a job. Gradually the Coldstream coopers left the brewery to accept jobs elsewhere. But Granddad was adamant. "Even the best stout will rot in those silver caskets." He encouraged his mates not to leave town. "These manufacturing fools will soon realize their mistakes. I, for one, will not go near the damned things. I canna' change my mind about quality, progress or no progress." Granddad never did go near the "damned things," for he retired from the brewery as other coopers were fired.

Despite the fact that the Coldstream village no longer held the promise of work for Granddad, he stubbornly refused to leave his home when my father suggested a move to Canada.

What does the use of the word porridge add to the picture of Scottish life?

How does the writer get tension and suspense into her paper? What is the conflict about whose outcome you are uncertain?

Why does the writer put Granddad's absolute position on the side of individual work at the end of the paragraph, rather than earlier in it?

What adjective would you use to describe the writer's attitude toward her grandfather's lone labour?

In what ways has the writer increased the pressures on Granddad and the suspense of the reader?

"I canna' change this old body to fit a new place. You don't seal new iron rings to the wood with worn and rusted clasps. So leave me here in my own home." But eventually Granddad did leave for Canada with us, and although he adapted to the new environment, he never really changed.

Granddad finished shaving by now, I could no longer hear water splashing or a Lowland country song being hummed. I smiled and climbed out of bed to get my breakfast, thinking of Granddad's latest problem.

The doctor had forbidden him to smoke cigarettes and to eat starchy foods. The young doctor had also warned Granddad about getting rest and dressing wisely for winter. I passed Granddad's door on the way downstairs. Everything was in order: the Bugler cigarettes, which Granddad rolled himself, were stacked neatly in a biscuit tin on the night stand; the remains of three slices of toast and jelly lay on a sticky plate atop the alarm clock.

Chuckling softly, I ran down the stairs to the kitchen. There was Granddad, sitting sweaterless in the drafty room, cheerfully reading the sports page.

"Good morning, Granda."

"Mornin' to you, wee'un." He smiled. "You're a fair sight in the mornin', lassie."

—Robin Wilkening

How do Granddad's words and images reinforce his personality and character? What connections have they with his work?

How does the ending echo the opening paragraph?

In what way are Granddad's actions symbolic of his character? What does his disregard of the doctor's orders indicate?

How does the repetition of Granddad's words affect the reader? Why do they make an effective ending? What do they tell you about his adjustment to Canadian life?

Student Composition 12B

MR. BRICCETTI

Mr. Briccetti raised his baton and collapsed in laughter. "I've just gotta tell you this joke about Stravinsky," he gasped. He lowered his baton and proceeded to tell the almost pointless anecdote with generous Italian gestures. The story wasn't particularly funny, but Mr. Briccetti could make anything seem hilarious.

Maestro Thomas Briccetti is short and thin, but wiry. His longish hair is coarse, straight, and black. Beneath his thick, expressive brows, his big black eyes constantly crinkle with amusement. And even though his complexion is too sallow and his nose is a bit too large, his appearance is dashing.

His flamboyance carries over into his style of conducting. He dances across the podium, stooping and leaping, his face frowning, then smiling. But his showmanship is supported by a deep knowledge and understanding and love of music. Briccetti demanded a great deal from all of us in the Youth Symphony, and we worked as hard as we could for him. Frequently he

In what ways is the texture of this opening thinner and less interesting than the opening of the preceding composition?
Do you think this character would use "I've just gotta...."

What order does the writer use in describing Mr. Briccetti? What additional details would you like to have?

Have you felt a need to know who Mr. Briccetti is and why he is worth writing about? How might this information have been presented earlier?

called extra rehearsals for each instrument—I played cello—so he could explain the music and help us struggle through the more tortuously constructed passages. These trials were punctuated by jokes, admonishments, reassurances, and individual workouts.

Mr. Briccetti tried to make each person feel important. He could focus all of his vast supply of charm on an individual to make even the least gifted person feel like a virtuoso. Every player had a vital part in the overall sound of the Symphony; each person had to feel necessary.

Mr. Briccetti was too wonderful to last. He lost his job with the Symphony Orchestra when a bigwig conductor was flown in. Many of us in the Youth Symphony quit when he left town. I don't even play the cello any more, but I still have vivid memories of Mr. Briccetti. He was a surging, innovative, tolerant, colourful personality, and he was fantastic with young people. While so many other adults were impatient and condescending, Mr. Briccetti stressed our uniqueness and individual importance.

—Susan Hicks

What is another form of the word "admonishments?"

How might the writer have ended her paper if Mr. Briccetti had not left town?
How do you feel—how does the writer feel—about her not playing the cello any more? Is Mr. Briccetti responsible for her quitting? Why?

Elements of a Character Sketch

As was mentioned earlier, three things to consider in writing character sketches are: the subject, the point of view, and the method.

1. *The subject.* Who will the subject be? The subject of a character sketch may be real or imaginary. There should be some outstanding quality, feature, accomplishment, or trait that will make the subject interesting to the reader.

2. *The point of view.* If the subject of your character sketch is a real person, you will probably write from your own point of view. You may, however, decide that your sketch could be more forceful or more effective if you wrote from another point of view—that of a close friend, a son or daughter, even a pet dog. In such a case, even though your subject is a real person, your viewpoint is fictional.

If the subject of your character is imaginary, you may write from a third-person point of view or you may assume the point of view of a "persona," a voice other than your own. There is no limit to the possible points of view you may assume in writing a character sketch.

3. *The method.* There are a number of methods a writer can use to reveal character. Some of them parallel quite closely the ways we build up impressions of the people we meet in everyday life. Others are techniques that belong only to writing. The subject you have decided upon and the point of view you have chosen will help you to determine what method or combination of methods you will use.

Evaluating the Character Sketches

With the three elements of a character sketch in mind, reread the professional models and the student compositions. Evaluate the choice of subject, determine the point of view, and notice the way the writer presents the character in each case. Discuss and evaluate each sketch in the light of these questions:

1. Is the subject real, interesting, and worth writing about?
2. What details selected by the writer focus the reader's attention on an important quality of the subject?
3. What method has the writer chosen to reveal or develop the character? What other method could have been used?
4. One of the methods of revealing character is the use of words, that is, dialogue (conversation) or monologue. Two people speaking to each other may shed light on a third character, or they may tell the reader something about themselves. A monologue is a convenient device for revealing character. It lets you "read the mind" and learn the inner thoughts of the character. Does the writer use dialogue or inner monologue effectively?
5. How does the setting affect your perception of the character?
6. What incidents, actions, or reactions reveal traits of the character?
7. What use is made by the author of imagery (figures of speech, vivid language) or symbolism?

As you work on the activities and as you do your regular literature assignments, be thinking of a subject for a character sketch. Students usually find it easier to write about people they have known, rather than about characters from fiction or drama. You may enjoy researching a currently popular figure, collecting information from several sources, and then writing a vivid character sketch based on the information. If you decide to write about a real person, try to choose someone who has been influential in your life or who has made a great impression upon you.

Selecting a Subject for a Character Sketch

The first thing you must do is to choose a subject—someone interesting enough to be worth your time and your readers' time. Following are several character sketches taken from various sources. Discuss the kinds of people chosen and possible reasons the writers selected them. Then begin making up lists of people about whom you might write.

I

He lay in his bed at Georgetown University Hospital, looking so drawn and tired, the intravenous needles feeding his right arm and hand. He motioned for me to come up on the left side of his bed. I went up to him and squeezed his hand, trying to say without words all the things I wanted to say, how much I had learned from him, how grateful I was, how much I loved him.

"Ouch," he said. "Don't break my hand."

And Vince Lombardi grinned, that grin that could lift you or warm you or dazzle you, that grin I had seen so many times in locker rooms and on sidelines, in meeting rooms and at banquets. That grin didn't belong in a hospital room. He didn't belong in a hospital room. If anyone had ever suggested to me that there was one indestructible man in this world, I would have thought it was Vince Lombardi.[4]

—Jerry Kramer

II

He gave us a dream as big as our country.

Now this man—22 years old, maybe 150 pounds [68 kilograms], with the map of Canada on his T-shirt—was trying not to cry because, he said, he owed us that much.

The doctors at Port Arthur General Hospital read the shadows on the x-rays Tuesday and told Terry Fox what he already knew: The cancer was back, this time in his lung, and the Marathon of Hope must end.

He asked when he might run again, and then he tried to walk across the street and he knew. It was time to go home. His wide, wonderful world shrank to the metal walls of a Thunder Bay ambulance.

His mother, Betty, sat at the front, eyes staring, streaming. Behind her was Bill Vigars, loveable, wise-cracking Bill, the unofficious official from the Canadian Cancer Society, suddenly quiet and perfectly still. Alongside Terry, clutching tight a paper bag of food and with the tears just a breath away, was his father, Rolly.

Terry was on the stretcher, wrapped in a soft blue blanket.

He looked very small. His face was deeply tanned, broken only by a red, raw patch of sunburn on the left cheek. His hair was the colour of dark honey, his lashes and brows bleached white.

He was having trouble breathing. Every once in a while, when it hurt very much, he put a hand to his chest and coughed, a tiny sad cough.

A big Northern Ontario fly buzzed in his face.

He flailed at it a few times, brushing it away, and then he left it alone, and it walked on his upper lip, just below the beads of sweat, and he closed his eyes.

He forgot about the fly, the run the day before was so important, the best parents ever, the funny, stocky official who had become his friend— forgot about anything that would diminish the single-minded iron will that carried him more than 5300 kilometres.

Alone with the cancer, Terry Fox geared up for battle.[5]

—Christie Blatchford

III

Steve brought home a dog today. A big, rawboned, houndish brute, with sad running eyes and a ratty tail. He's black except for a little fleck of white round his face and chin that gives him an ancient, monkey-look of grief and wisdom; but even though his back comes up to Philip's knee there's a gangling awkwardness about the way he brings his big feet down to show him up as an overgrown and still self-conscious pup.

He limps, and smells, and has fleas. While Steve and I held him Philip examined his foot, and finally cut out a pebble imbedded between the toes. Then we bathed his eyes with boracic acid, spent eighty cents on a bottle of mange cure, and topped it off with a thorough scouring in the washtub.

He was too frightened to struggle, and when it was over and he stood dripping and bony and drowned-looking Philip named him. El Greco—be- cause El Greco was an artist who had a way of painting people long and lean as if they'd all been put on the rack and stretched considerably, and if he had ever painted a dog, Philip says, it would have been just such a one as ours.[6]

—Sinclair Ross

IV

Something in the general drift now has John Kauffmann on his feet and off to the river. He assembles his trout rod, threads its eyes. Six feet three, [191 cm] spare, he walks in his determination, tilted forward, ten degrees from vertical, jaws clamped. He seems to be seeking reassurance from the river. He seems not so much to want to catch what may become the last grayling in Arctic Alaska as to certify that it is there. With his bamboo rod, his lofted line, he now describes long drape folds in the air above the river. His shirt is old and red. There are holes in his felt hat and strips of spare rawhide around its crown. He agitates the settled fly. Nothing. Again he waves the line. He drops its passenger on the edge of fast water at the far side of the pool. There is a vacuum-implosive sound, a touch of violence at the surface of the river. We cheer. For two minutes, we wait it out while Kauffmann plays his fish. Adroitly, gingerly, he brings it in. With care, he picks it up. He then looks at us as if he is about to throw his tin star in the dust at our feet. Shame—for our triple-hooked lures, our nylon hawsers, our consequent stories of fished-out streams. He looks at his grayling. It is a twenty-five ounce [709 g] midget, but it will grow. He seems to feel reassured. He removes the fly, which has scarcely nicked the fish's lips. He slips the grayling back to the stream.[7]

—John McPhee

V

John Reed was a schoolboy of fourteen years old; four years older than I, for I was but ten; large and stout for his age, with a dingy and unwholesome skin; thick lineaments in a spacious visage, heavy limbs and large extremities. He gorged himself habitually at table, which made him bilious and gave him a dim and bleared eye and flabby cheeks. He ought now to have been at school; but his mama had taken him home for a month or two, "on account of his delicate health." Mr. Miles, the master, affirmed that he would do very well if he had fewer cakes and sweetmeats sent him from home; but the mother's heart turned from an opinion so harsh, and inclined rather to the more refined idea that John's sallowness was owing to overapplication and, perhaps, to pining after home.

John had not much affection for his mother and sisters, and an antipathy to me. He bullied and punished me; not two or three times in the week, nor once or twice in the day, but continually: every nerve I had feared him, and every morsel of flesh in my bones shrank when he came near. There were moments when I was bewildered by the terror he inspired, because I had no appeal whatever against either his menaces or his inflictions; the servants did not like to offend their young master by taking my part against him, and Mrs. Reed was blind and deaf on the subject: she never saw him strike or heard him abuse me, though he did both now and then in her very presence; more frequently, however, behind her back.

Habitually obedient to John, I came up to his chair: he spent some three minutes in thrusting out his tongue at me as far as he could without damaging the roots: I knew he would soon strike, and while dreading the blow, I mused on the disgusting and ugly appearance of him who would presently deal it. I wonder if he read that notion in my face; for, all at once, without speaking, he struck suddenly and strongly. I tottered, and on regaining my equilibrium retired back a step or two from his chair.

"That is for your impudence in answering mama awhile since," said he, "and for your sneaking way of getting behind curtains, and for the look you had in your eyes two minutes since, you rat!"[8]

—Charlotte Brontë

Activity 12A

Choosing Character Sketch Subjects

1. Put these headings either on the blackboard or on your paper: Real People I Know, Real People the Class Knows, Fictional People from Literature, Celebrities. In a group, prepare a list of five or six people for each of the last three headings, and then, by yourself, prepare a list of five or six for the first heading. Don't forget the possibilities within your own family and circle of friends.

2. After you have prepared your list of people, select five whom you find most interesting. Next to each of these five characters, jot down the reason for your interest and, in a few words, the outstanding aspect of the character.

This is a page from the only surviving manuscript of *Beowulf*, the Anglo-Saxon epic poem. It was written on sheepskin a thousand years ago.

Selecting a Dominant Impression

At every moment of every day, thousands of sense stimuli bombard your nervous system. If you perceived all of these and gave them equal consideration, you would be unable to "make sense" out of the world. From long experience you have learned to ignore thousands of these stimuli, to group others into meaningful patterns, and to concentrate on a few significant impressions.

As you describe a character, you must do the same thing. Even if you could perceive and write down every single thing about a character, your reader would expect you to single out and focus on the important, meaningful and striking aspects.

Activity 12B

Restating the Dominant Impression

Review your list of five characters and the aspect you singled out for each one in Activity 12A. Now, rewrite that characteristic in a more subtle manner as it might appear somewhere in the introduction or conclusion. The following is an example of how this is done.

BLUNT STATEMENT

The most outstanding aspect of Milton Foster's personality is his stinginess.

MORE SUBTLE STATEMENT

Milton Foster smiled happily as he realized that the homeroom teacher was not going to ask him for a contribution to the class Christmas fund after all. He felt the change in his pocket and thought how pleasant it was not to have to part with a penny.

Be prepared to discuss your rewrites in class.

Experimenting with Point of View

The next thing to consider in writing a character sketch is point of view. Character sketches may be written from a kind of neutral, distant, third-person point of view; from the writer's own point of view; or from an imaginary point of view. If you move from nonfiction to fiction by assuming the point of view of a persona or character or voice other than your own, you must make up insights, events, conversations, and relationships which exist only in your imagination.

If you choose to write your character sketch from a fictional point of view, you should make full use of the special advantages such a point of view offers:

1. It enables you to report details which an outside observer could not know. For example, a politician might make comments in front of her cat that she would never make in public! An actor who is courteous and charming in public might act and speak before his family in ways no outside reporter could imagine.
2. In enables you to include judgments, explanations, emotions, attitudes, and reactions to the character. These should all be consistent and clearly recognizable as fiction, coming from your assumed persona, or voice. Such comments can be humourous, ironic, surprising, or awe-filled.

3. It enables you to experiment with a style completely different from your own. If you wrote from the point of view of the politician's cat, you are faced with the question, "How would a cat express itself?" Could you write from the point of view of a Martian? Or a doting mother? Assuming a persona, or voice, can be fun for the writer.

(*Activity 12C*)

Experimenting with Point of View in a Character Sketch

Working as your teacher directs, think of three or four different points of view you might assume if you were writing about each of three different characters. Prepare to tell a group of other students how you would make use of the three special advantages described above.

Multiple Ways of Showing Character

When you have chosen your subject and decided on your point of view, you will then consider the best way of revealing the character to your reader. Writers create characters by:

1. Letting the characters reveal themselves.

   a. Their own actions, words, and thoughts may reveal the kind of persons they are. (A skillful writer may heighten interest by having a character's actions contradict his or her words.)
   b. The reader may be told quite specifically what minor characters are like. Then the writer describes the main character's *reactions* to other characters, and thus reveals much about the main character.

2. Letting other characters shed light on the main character.

   a. They give the reader an idea of what the character is like by what they *say* to and about the main character as well as what they *think about* and how they *react to* the main character.

3. Showing the way the writers themselves perceive the characters.

   a. They may describe the appearance of the character.
   b. They may make interpretive comments about the thoughts, words, actions, and reactions of the character (explanations, analyses, hypotheses).
   c. They may compare the main character with other characters.

4. Using miscellaneous techniques.

    a. They may describe (in a way that sheds light on the characters) a setting in which the character appears.

    b. They may give the character a name that reveals something to the reader (Scrooge, Becky Sharp, Apeneck Sweeney, Casper Milquetoast).

    c. They may relate the character to a symbolic object or action.

    d. They may present a series of scenes that reveals some change in the character.

(*Activity 12D*)

Recognizing Character Technique

Which of the techniques described above have been used to reveal character in the following examples? Read each one carefully, and decide what the author has done to help you get a picture of the main character.

1. Every day after he got home from work, Mr. Tibbles spent most of the evening watching television on the little set in his bedroom. As grainy pictures flickered across the screen, grey light from the set lit up the room, picking up the faded green chenille bedspread, the sagging maroon plush armchair, and the TV tray holding an empty glass and the remnants of a defrosted lasagna dinner. In the dimness, Mr. Tibbles himself looked a little like a large mushroom sprouting before the television set.

2. "Wouldn't you know it," Mrs. Blake thought, and her mouth tightened as she watched Donald struggling to pick up the books he had just dropped. "Never mind," she said aloud, "I'll pick them up. I suppose you did the best you could." She snatched the books away and pushed the little boy aside.

3. "Just look at her," Marg whispered to Emily, and they both stared across the room at Lisa. Lisa reached up to flick back a strand of her smooth blonde hair as she smiled at the two sales representatives who had stopped beside her reception desk. "From the way she acts," Marg went on, "you'd think she was the only one around here who knew anything. She took all the credit for that report we wrote together last month, but yesterday when Accounting discovered a mistake in the budget, she certainly kept quiet."

4. Pleased with what the mirror revealed, Lorna studied the effect of her clinging sweater and red velvet skirt. She tugged the sweater lower over her heavy hips and swung this way and that before the mirror, poised

on stubby feet strapped tightly into high heeled shoes. In the dim light, her swinging earrings looked almost like gold, and her carefully made-up face might have passed for forty again.

(*Activity 12E*)

Analyzing Professional Techniques

Choose one character from a short story and examine all the passages in which the author develops that character's personality. Make a list of phrases that describe the character, list under each phrase the words or events that support that phrase, and then determine which of the techniques listed in the preceding section your author has used. Come to class prepared to discuss the different techniques and their relative effectiveness.

Using Action to Reveal Character

As you prepare to write your character sketch, you should observe your subject closely or else do some research to gather information. If your subject is a real person find some actual situations in which behaviour communicates a dominant impression about the nature of your subject. Notice how the writer of the following selection accomplishes this.

Gordon Lightfoot will be 40 this year, and he has spent more than 20 of those years in the music business. He has won every award available to a popular singer, from a clutch of Junos for being an outstanding Canadian recording artist to a Vanier Award for being an "outstanding Canadian." He's a millionaire many times over and lives in a spacious 100-year-old home in Toronto's old-line money section of Rosedale.

It's a house that might pass for a men's club: woody, comfortable, masculine and very, very private. It's a house that hides secrets and, for this very reason, a house you might expect to find Gordon Lightfoot living in. For, despite the millions of words written about him over the years, despite the several hundreds of songs he's written and recorded, despite the fact he has concertized constantly throughout his career—despite, in short, his constant presence in our lives—he remains a remote individual. He'll let you see the craggy surface of his life, but beyond that—nothing. He is alone.

And this is not the kind of aloneness that is the prerogative of any public figure who wishes to keep separate his public and private lives. With Lightfoot, you sense it goes much deeper: that it's not just a product of his life but a requirement of his survival. This, of course, is something he never talks about.

When he celebrated his 20th year in show business last year, I asked him what he felt he'd achieved. He growled a bit, embarrassed by the question and mumbled something about "a bunch of songs, pretty good ones I think." A little later, though, remembering the sheer breadth and consistent quality of this "bunch of good songs," I realized just what his achievement was—that, like a good craftsman, he has never wavered from what he has set out to do: to write popular music with good singable melodies. It's music that never strays too far from the popular sound of any particular period, but it remains unalterably his own creation.

There is greatness in his achievement, not just through what he has written but through the loneliness it has cost him to write it. It's a unique kind of greatness, too, for a celebrity dealing with our hyperactive media.

Hence, his reliance on his craft and why some of his finest songs, such as *The Wreck of the Edmund Fitzgerald,* deal with events, people or even ideas that don't touch him directly. And hence, too, his need to work so hard—he has just come back from Hawaii where he enjoyed his first vacation in 20 years. And also, for the first time in nearly 20 years, he has no definite plans for this spring and summer, aside from his annual stint in Toronto's Massey Hall, where he'll be appearing March 17 to 25, and work on a new album, his 14th.

This is not to suggest he avoids dealing with his own feelings. On the contrary, I suspect he deals with them so often and with such agonizing introspection that a retreat into his craft or into hard work are his escapes. Watching him when he's not on guard, you suddenly come to understand what T. S. Eliot meant when he wrote, "I am moved by fancies that are curled / Around these images, and cling: / The notion of some infinitely gentle / Infinitely suffering thing."

Years ago, CBC-TV did a documentary on Lightfoot, and at one point during the show, the camera followed him into the small room in which he wrote, and watched him outline a song on the old fragile desk he used. He was, I remember, in his bathrobe. The show had been breezy enough up to that point, but the moment he sat down to write, everything became silent. It was as if just being at that desk had removed him from everything else around him. And he was isolated, out of necessity.[9]

—Peter Goddard

Writing imaginary incidents.   In some instances, over a long period of time you may have formed a dominant impression of a person, but you may not have observed any single specific action that you can use to present your dominant impression in a dramatic and effective way. Is it acceptable, then, to make up an imaginary incident that communicates this impression of your character? You can, if you wish, make up an incident to support your dominant impression, but in doing so you change from writing fact to writing fiction. For your character sketch, you may write either fact or fiction, but don't err by claiming fiction to be fact.

Activity 12F

Suggesting an Incident to Reveal Character

1. Working with a partner whom you know well and with whom you may have many acquaintances in common, make a list of several of the people

you know and try to agree on a dominant impression for each. Consider such character-revealing adjectives as friendly, courageous, intelligent, altruistic, selfish, domineering, generous, confident, foolish, and helpful. Try to recall an incident you have observed in which the individual did something to reveal such a nature. Write a brief description of the incident to share with the class.

2. For any person for whom you could not provide an actual incident to support your dominant impression, create an incident that might have revealed the characteristic you listed for that person. Note clearly at the bottom of your page which items are fictional.

Using Conversation to Reveal Character

Almost everything people say reveals something about their characters. In the following passage, a mother and daughter are discussing the daughter's plans. Notice how their words reveal something about the character of each.

I

The first time I ever went to a movie with a boy, I was fifteen. The adult price wasn't charged until sixteen. The boy was sixteen. I stood beside him on the winter street, outside the ticket window, shivering, obsessed with one thought—how would I ever walk past the ticket girl and face the usherette if he bought a child's ticket for me? He didn't, of course, so I had upset myself needlessly.

'Where are you going, Rachel? Are you going somewhere?'

'Yes.' I should have told her before, I know. 'I'm going to a movie.'

'Oh, what's on? Maybe I'll come along.'

'I mean I'm going—with someone.'

'Oh, I see. Well, you might have said, Rachel. You really might have told me, dear.'

'I'm sorry, Mother. I just—'

'You know how glad I am, dear, when you go out. You might have mentioned it to me, that's all. It's not too much to ask, surely. After all, I do like to know where you are. I would have thought you could have said, Rachel.'

'I'm sorry.'

'Well, it's quite alright dear. I'm only saying if you had let me know, it would've been better, that's all. I could have invited one of the girls in, maybe. Well, never mind. I shall be quite fine here by myself. I'll just slip into my housecoat, and make some coffee, and have a nice quiet evening. I'll be just dandy. Don't you worry about me a speck. I'll be perfectly all right. If you'd just reach down my pills for me from the medicine cabinet. As long as they're where I can get them handily, in case anything happens. I'm sure I'll be fine. You go ahead and enjoy yourself, Rachel.'[10]

—Margaret Laurence

Activity 12G

Analyzing Character Through Conversation

Without telling you directly about the characters in the previous selection, Margaret Laurence lets them tell you certain things about themselves. How would you describe the character and personality of Rachel and of her mother?

Does either Rachel or her mother remind you of anyone you know?

In the following passage from a short story called *Cress Delahanty*, the main character reveals something about herself in a conversation with her parents. Read the message carefully and be prepared to discuss what it is about Cress that is revealed by the conversation.

I

"You have a perfect right to say, 'I told you so' now if you want to, Mother," Cress said. "You told me I was getting to be a character and I was, all right."

"What do you mean, Cress?" her father asked.

"I mean I'm a Character," Cress said bleakly. "I'm 'Irresponsible Delahanty.' I'm that 'Crazy Kid.' If I said I was dying, people would laugh." Water ran out of her hair and across her face and dripped off her chin, but she scorned to wipe it away.

"I made a good speech to the Student Council, and they laughed at every word I said. They laughed and held their sides and rolled in their chairs like loons."

"What speech was this, Cress?"

"The speech everybody who is a candidate for an office has to make to them. Then if they like you, they nominate you. I was a candidate for freshman editor. What they nominated me for was *Josh* editor. *Josh* editor. A two-year-old can be *Josh* editor. All you need to be *Josh* editor is a pair of scissors to cut out jokes with. I wouldn't be *Josh* editor if they shot me for not being. It's a silly job."

"Take off your coat, Cress," Mrs. Delahanty said, and Cress, not ceasing to speak, began also to unbutton.

"I would've been a good editor, and I told them the reasons—like I was responsible, knew the meaning of time, would see that the assignments were in on time, and so forth. They laughed like hyenas," she said, not bitterly but reflectively. "They said, 'This is the richest thing yet. Delahanty is a real character.' So they nominated me for *Josh* editor and I'm branded for life."

She threw her raincoat, which she had finished unbuttoning, onto the floor, said "I have ruined my life," and walked out of the room, no longer trying to hide the fact that she was crying.[11]

—Jessamyn West

Planning Conversations That Reveal Character

1. Think of several dramatic situations in which one or more characters reveal more about themselves in their words than they intended to. The following situations are possibilities for you.

   a. A girl who has just celebrated her eighteenth birthday tries to register to vote. A local election official tries to discourage her and, in doing so, reveals some attitudes about youth, politics, democracy, and change.

   b. The owner plans to sell a tract of land opposite a historic landmark. During his interviews with a manufacturer of chemicals, a low rental housing official, and a representative from a foreign embassy, he reveals his own biases.

   c. Two students discuss a recent, highly-rated motion picture treating an important human theme. One student reveals either failure to understand the theme or inability to accept its values.

   d. An instructor from a nearby community college reveals, as she speaks to Grade 12 students at your school, that her ideas about a good education differ from those of some of the students.

2. After you have worked out several situations, write one or two pages of the conversation in rough form. If you have not thought of a better situation of your own, you may use one of those suggested in the first activity above.

3. In order to write conversations into your character sketch, you need to know the mechanics of organizing, punctuating, and capitalizing them. Refer to the Style Sheet to determine how you punctuate dialogue when:

   a. Introductory words such as *he said* or *she replied* precede the actual words of the speaker.

   b. Such words interrupt the actual words of the speaker, coming in the middle of the direct quotation.

   c. Such words follow the actual words of the speaker. You may also wish to refer to the selections by Margaret Laurence and Jessamyn West on the preceding pages.

4. After you have checked the conventional mechanics of writing conversations, review and rewrite the pages you prepared in the second activity. Be prepared to discuss the kinds of details that make your dialogue sound natural.

Using Description to Reveal Character

Writers often use a straightforward descriptive passage to make their readers "see" the subject of a character sketch. In an essay called "On Stephen Leacock," Robertson Davies describes the famous humourist this way:

I

Only an artist could write like Leacock at his best. And only a man who thought of himself consciously as an artist would have undertaken to explain how he did it. And only a man who yearned for popularity would have thought it desirable or wise to do so.

I have stressed his desire for popularity because I want to call your attention now to the extraordinarily successful public personality which Leacock created for himself. There may be some among you who remember that personality—the strikingly masculine impression created by the big figure with the big head and the rough mop of grey hair; the rugged face alight with intelligence and merriment, the twinkling eyes and the infectious laugh, the deep voice, which he used as skilfully as a fine actor—for Leacock was a fine actor, and perhaps the finest that Canada has ever produced. Do you really suppose that there was not calculation in the impression which he gave, in his expensive, though rumpled clothes, his dress tie usually untied, and his great watch-chain fastened to his waistcoat with a safety-pin? He was a great man; he looked and behaved like a great man; and he knew that he was doing so.[12]

—Robertson Davies

In her story, "The House on the Esplanade," Anne Hébert's description of the main character not only paints a vivid picture of the woman, but lets you know how she lives and what her philosophy of life might be.

II

Stephanie de Bichette was a curious little creature with frail limbs that seemed badly put together. Only her starched collarette kept her head from falling over on her shoulder; it was too heavy for her long, slender neck. If the head of Stephanie Bichette looked so heavy, it was because all the pomp of her aristocratic ancestors was symbolized in her coiffure, a high up-swept style, with padded curls arranged in rows on her narrow cranium, an architectural achievement in symmetrical silvery blobs.

Mademoiselle de Bichette had passed, without transition period, without adolescence, from the short frocks of her childhood to this everlasting ash-grey dress, trimmed at neck and wrists with a swirl of lilac braiding. She owned two parasols with carved ivory handles—one lilac and the other ash-grey.

When she went out driving in the carriage she chose her parasol according to the weather, and everyone in the little town could tell the weather by the colour of Mademoiselle de Bichette's parasol. The lilac one appeared on days of brilliant sunshine, the ash-grey one whenever it was slightly cloudy. In winter, and when it rained, Stephanie simply never went out at all.[13]

—Anne Hébert

Activity 12I

Writing Description That Reveals Character

In Activity 12G you worked out several dramatic situations and made up conversations to reveal character. Choose one of the subjects of those sketches and write a paragraph of description. Choose details of appearance, mannerisms, facial expressions, and gestures that make your subject different from anyone else.

Finding Insights into the Characters of Real People

Have you heard anyone talk about "roughing it in the bush?" This slang expression refers to more than just a weekend camping trip; at an earlier time in Canada, it summed up pioneer life for early immigrants like Susanna Moodie, who emigrated to Canada with her husband in 1832. In her book *Roughing It in the Bush,* Susanna Moodie describes their experiences homesteading in the backwoods of Upper Canada, where she had to spend the winter alone in their cabin in the bush while her husband served in the militia to help put down the Rebellion of 1837. Today her book is a fascinating picture of the hardships endured by people who left the cosmopolitan cities of Europe for the backwoods of pioneer Canada.

There are many such fascinating people in Canadian and world history. By looking through the reference books in your library, you can find thousands of such stories of real people in interesting situations. After skimming some of the reference books, you may have to do additional research to flesh out your character sketch.

Here are some books in which to begin your search:

A Standard Dictionary of Canadian Biography: The Canadian Who Was Who. Edited by Sir Charles G.D. Roberts and Arthur Tunnell. 1934-38.
Prairie Portraits. R. St. George Stubbs. 1954.
The Macmillan Dictionary of Canadian Biography. 1963.
Canadian Writers: Ecrivains Canadiens. Edited by Brandon Conron, Carl F. Klinck, and Guy Sylvestre. 1964.
Flamboyant Canadians. Edited by Ellen Stafford. 1964.
Dictionary of Canadian Biography. 1966.

The Oxford Companion to Canadian History and Literature. Norah Story. 1967.

Supplement to the Oxford Companion to Canadian History and Literature. Edited by William Toye. 1973.

Exploring Library Resources for Your Character Sketch

Spend at least an hour browsing in your school or community library to find the kinds of resources that would be available to you if you decided to write your character sketch on a celebrity or a historical figure. Look especially at the reference section, the section on "collective biography" in which the lives of several people are presented in one volume, the vertical file, and the magazine and periodical collection.

Major Writing Assignment

A Character Sketch

Reread the sample character sketches at the beginning of this chapter and review the techniques the professional and student writers used. Then choose a subject and begin to work on your character sketch. To write an effective character sketch you must:

1. Observe as many aspects of a given character as possible.
2. Taking into account the audience who will read the character sketch, decide which aspects of character to emphasize and which to ignore.
3. From the material selected, decide on a *dominant impression* and try to put it into words.
4. Choose the appropriate point of view. Is the character described by someone who is intimately acquainted with that person or by someone who has only limited knowledge and insight?
5. Write down the description, interpretation, dialogue, and action that seem to support the dominant impression.
6. Compare the material written down with the dominant impression you decided to focus on.
7. If necessary, revise either the dominant impression or the material.

Just as in other kinds of writing, a character sketch has a beginning, a middle, and an ending. You may wish to begin your sketch by showing your subject engaged in a significant action. Fill in the descriptive details that will make the sketch come alive for the reader. One technique is to indicate your dominant impression indirectly. Choose the most appropriate method for supporting your dominant impression and for revealing or developing your character. Be sure the setting is appropriate for the subject. If you have decided to use conversation to reveal character, write it, read it, and rewrite it. Sometimes reading a dialogue aloud helps you to spot any false or artificial notes. Provide careful transitions to make your sketch move along smoothly. One interesting way to end a character sketch is to have the subject perform an action that symbolizes or reinforces the dominant impression that was the focus of the sketch.

13
Imaginative Writing

No matter how much experience we may gather in life, we can never in life get the dimension of experience that the imagination gives us. Only the arts and sciences can do that, and of these, only literature gives us the whole sweep and range of human imagination as it sees itself.[1]

—Northrop Frye

All writing is creative in the sense that it involves "the originating, the making, and the bringing into being" of a new communication. The kind of writing most people think of when they use the term "creative writing," however, differs from the kind of writing that explains, analyzes, or persuades. The creative writer is a poet in the Greek sense of the word *poietes*, "one who makes." Creative writers create or recreate an experience and stamp it indelibly with unique marks of their own personality, background, experience, and perception. When the work is successful, the reader and the writer are joined through the sharing of an experience and of a response to that experience.

Essential Aspects of Creative Writing

As you write your next major composition (and perhaps others that you will submit), you will want to emphasize these aspects of your writing:

1. Sincerity
2. Emotion
3. Originality
4. Recreation of an experience

◀ Margaret Atwood is one of Canada's outstanding writers of poetry and imaginative prose. Much of the appeal of her poems, stories and novels stems from their vivid imagery and Atwood's engaging use of point of view.

Sincerity.   An absolute essential of creative writing is sincerity. No matter how beautiful and how technically perfect a work of art is, if it lacks sincerity—and, amazingly enough, professional critics can almost always tell—it is worth little. In his poem "Andrea Del Sarto," Robert Browning emphasizes the need for sincerity. Andrea Del Sarto was a Renaissance painter whose draftsmanship was so perfect that he was called "The Faultless Painter." In the poem, Del Sarto, while boasting of his skill, acknowledges that he lacks a spiritual quality—part of which is sincerity—and without it he cannot create great art. He says:

> No sketches first, no studies, that's long past:
> I do what many dream of all their lives,
> —Dream? strive to do, and agonize to do,
> And fail in doing.
>   * * *
> Well, their less is more, Lucrezia! I am judged.
> There burns a truer light of God in them,
> In their vexed beating stuffed and stopped-up brain,
> Heart, or what'er else, than goes on to prompt
> This low-pulsed forthright craftsman's hand of mine.
> Their works drop groundward, but themselves, I know,
> Reach many a time a heaven that's shut to me....
>
>   —Robert Browning

Some students, when trying their hand at creative writing, forget that above all they must be sincere in what they are trying to express. They make the mistake of including an off-the-subject idea that will pad their paper and make it look more impressive, or they dash off a line which, though it may be nonsensical, has the desired rhythm and rhyme.

In a parody of Edgar A. Guest's poetry, Louis Untermeyer satirizes the problem of the hurried or insincere writer. Edgar Guest was for many years a popular, syndicated-newspaper "versifier" who had to write at least a poem a day to meet the ever-pressing deadlines. Mr. Guest was conscious that in writing hastily for a large audience he was at times less effective than at other times, and he insisted that he should not be called a poet. Though he was never so unconcerned with meaning as Louis Untermeyer's parody suggests, the parody nonetheless emphasizes how ridiculous verse can be if the poet lets rhythm and rhyme dictate content.

EDGAR A. GUEST
SYNDICATES THE OLD WOMAN WHO LIVED IN A SHOE

> It takes a heap o' children to make a home that's true,
> And home can be a palace grand, or just a plain, old shoe;
> But if it has a mother dear, and a good old dad or two,
> Why, that's the sort of good old home for good ol' me and you.[2]
>
>   —Louis Untermeyer

Notice how Untermeyer sacrifices logic, sense, and sincerity, simply to fill out a line and make a rhyme.

Emotion.   Most of your writing so far has been expository; that is, it has been the kind of writing that communicates facts or ideas. Creative writers, however, are usually less interested in communicating facts than they are in communicating attitudes and emotions. Expository writing is important for what it *contains*; creative writing is important for what it *is*. In his article "What Does Poetry Communicate?" Cleanth Brooks is writing specifically of poetry, but he might be speaking of all art when he says, "The poem communicates so much and communicates it so richly and with such delicate qualifications that the thing communicated is mauled and distorted if we attempt to convey it by any vehicle less subtle than that of the poem itself."[3] In other words, creative writing communicates attitudes and emotions that cannot be communicated in any other way. It's relatively easy to communicate an expository idea—you can use a hundred different methods—but in expressing an emotion or an attitude, no two pieces of writing will do it in exactly the same way. Expository writing tends to make readers think; creative writing tends to make them feel.

Originality.   Every human being is unique. Nobody like you has ever existed before. No one has had your particular physical and mental makeup, your individual background, and your special experiences. Because you are unique, you have ideas and emotions that no one else has ever had, and if you respect your own uniqueness you will write sincerely and originally about what only you can write about. As Emerson said, "Envy is ignorance and imitation is suicide!"

Recreation of an experience.   Of course, words can never actually recreate an experience. Words are simply symbolic sounds—sounds that stand for something. Yet they can convey the impression of an experience. Notice how D. H. Lawrence in *Sea and Sardinia* communicates, with the rhythm and sound of his sentences, the movement of a ship:

> And so we steam out. And almost at once the ship begins to take a long, slow, dizzy dip, and a fainting swoon upwards, and a long, slow, dizzy dip, slipping away from beneath one. The q-b (Mrs. Lawrence) turns pale. Up comes the deck in that fainting swoon backwards—then down it fades in that indescribable slither forwards. It is all quite gentle—quite, quite gentle. But oh, so long, and so slow, and so dizzy. [4]
>
> —D. H. Lawrence

In writing creatively, then, you create or recreate an original experience as vividly as possible. To accomplish this, you use concrete words that appeal to your reader's senses. You include actual conversations. You choose your language so that your images summon up the effect of the original experience.

Finding Ideas for Creative Writing

If a five-centimetre line could represent all the possible ideas and experiences suitable for expository writing, then it would take a metre-long line to represent all the possible emotions and experiences suitable for creative writing, for the range of ideas takes in all of human feeling and experience. The problem, therefore, is not in finding enough ideas but in selecting the right idea. First of all, you must recall and isolate an emotion and experience you feel strongly about; and secondly, you must figure out some way to communicate it. Ideas suitable for exposition consist of subjects which, by definition, can be expressed in words. Ideas suitable for creative writing, by definition, cannot be expressed in simple, ordinary words. Artists of all kinds—painters, dancers, composers, sculptors, poets—are always searching for new ways of communicating emotions and experiences.

As you do the activities in this chapter, think of an emotion, an attitude, or an experience from your own background, and think about the form that you will want to write it in. You may write a short story, a poem, a prose poem, an essay, or even the impressionistic description of an event, perhaps in the "stream-of-consciousness" style. This is a style in which the writer records all the thoughts flowing through the mind of a character at any given moment.

Some students will want to know: "Is it all right to write on a purely imaginary subject? How about science fiction or a war story? Or how about a poem on something that we haven't experienced yet, such as death?"

The decision will be up to your teacher. Certainly, many creative writers have never experienced some of the things they write about. It is possible to write good, honest, creative material on subjects outside of your own experience, but it is more difficult.

Student Composition 13A

WHILE

This morning while my mother
was yelling at my brother
go get up for school
and my father was mumbling
about the tragedies in
the eight-o-clock news
i saw your ring
that you forgot on my night table
smiling like a golden eye.

This poem does not rhyme or have a regular rhythm. Why can it be considered a poem?

Who is the speaker in the poem? How can you tell whether or not the poet is writing in her own voice?

and while my mother complained
about the way i drink coffee
and while my father said
that you looked like a hippie.
and while my brother ate
his third bowl of cornflakes
i remembered that last night
you said you loved me.

and while my mother screamed
that the bus was waiting
and while my father sighed
that he didn't know what would become of me
and while my brother looked at me
like i was crazy
i clutched your precious ring
in secret anticipation.

—Trudi Woods

How does the speaker feel about the person she addresses as "you?" What details are significant in showing the reader these feelings?

Point out lines in which the poet appeals to the various senses—sight, sound, touch, taste, smell.

How would you describe the *tone* of the poem?

Poets must select carefully from objects and events in reality. Suggest some objects and events the writer hints at but leaves out.

Student Composition 13B

The moist sands run along the beach
and winds play
havoc with my hair.
The waves splash up—
leaving dry-white salt
on my legs
that I will wash off
later, when i must
dress and be
beautiful for
your examination.

—Linda Price

The previous poem was a kind of narrative poem. (It told a story.) What makes this a lyric poem—one expressing personal feelings or emotion? Paraphrase the poem (put it in your own words). Which is more interesting to read, your paraphrase or the original poem?

Student Composition 13C

THE ACCIDENT

Two words hidden
somewhere in my
mind racing impa-
tiently towards
my imagination,
collide head on
and explode into
a new idea.

—Madonna Hamel

This poem depends on a single image for its impact. What other image, or picture, might you use to communicate the feeling the writer is describing?

Student Composition 13D

THE FAMOUS TREE

The tree with its sweeping arms
Standing alone in the golden clearing
With the sparkling sun dancing on its
Floor of fallen leaves, crunchy and
                                    spotted.

A rope hangs from a jutted branch
Still and undisturbed
Where children once swung
                    back and forth

Laughing and shouting
Tarzan they were or the lady, Jane.

—Charlene Sears

A number of details in this poem seem to convey a deeper meaning than the one on the surface only. What is significant about "the floor of fallen leaves" and "where children once swung/back and forth?" What do you think the tree represents?

What terms describing the tree also seem to reflect the mood and character of the poet?

Student Composition 13E

THE DRUM

The drum is sacred
for it has life
for life is a circle
for you were nothing
then you were born
you grew into adult-hood
then back to whence you came.

The drum is sacred
for it has the four seasons
the flowers of spring
the greens of summer
the colours of autumn
the snow of winter.

The drum is sacred
for it has the four directions
west, where the thunder beings live
north, where the giants live
east, where the sun continually shines
south, where you always face.

The drum is sacred
for it has everything
and everywhere
the drum is in the centre of the circle.

The drum is sacred.

—John Keeshig

To what senses does this poem appeal?

This poem uses a great deal of repetition, either repetition of the same structure ("the flowers of spring/the greens of summer") or of the same words ("the drum is sacred"). What effect does this repetition create?

What are the tone and atmosphere of the poem? Point out some specific words that create the tone and atmosphere.

What is the dominant picture, or image in the poem?

Student Composition 13F

WE GIRLS FROM MISS WATSON'S CLASS
(On Our Return to Greece)

Hopefully we return
to the place
of our early love rituals

His body stood there
proud and ripe,
tender curls and an aquiline nose,
brave bee-stung lips and kind eyes
seeing
us twittering girls
in floating pink voile dresses
dance before him
oh, so long ago.

On our return
we silly old ladies in tweed Dior suits

found him,
his head bespattered
with bird excrement
and body chiselled
by rain and wind.
Once again he looked down on us,
kindly this time, his lips pruned to a
cheshire grin.

—Catherine Maudsley

The first three-line stanza is vague about the specific details of setting. To what extent might the poem be improved if more specific description had been added? What information would be helpful? What kind of images might you add?

You've probably heard the word *irony* before. Look this word up and discuss how it relates to the poem.

What comment do the last three lines make on the speaker as a young girl and as a grown woman? Why has the description in stanza two changed from "brave bee-stung lips" to "a cheshire grin" in stanza three?

Student Composition 13G

ABRUPTLY

You like
short
things:
Sudden summer rain storms
that
begin, reach a climax, and end
in
one
breath...
Two-lined passionate love notes
written
on a corner scrap of the newspaper...
Impromptu picnics

The poem mixes very short lines of only one or two words with longer lines such as "begin, reach a climax, and end." How does this mixture of lines build up the central idea of the poem?

What symbolic meaning does the reference to "sudden summer rainstorms" have in the poem? What other words or details have the same meaning?

on
a sun-warmed blanket...
Quick glances...
Hasty embraces...
And so,
a
brief
"good-bye"...[5]

—Heather Nast

Student Composition 13H

WHATEVER HAPPENED TO UNCLE MARTIN

My uncle was the most obstinate man in Alberta. If you know Albertans, then that means he was the most obstinate man in the world, and for some reason, he had the power to disbelieve things out of existence. Let me tell you how he got that power.

It all started when I got a telegram from Aunt Edith that said, "MARTIN STRUCK BY LIGHTNING. COME AT ONCE." There was a sound of alarm in those seven words which scared me. I caught the first train to Lakeside. Zeke Hanson, who was also town constable, met me in his beat-up taxi. I asked him how Uncle Martin got hit by lightning.

"Got hit by his own stubbornness. If I told him once, I told him a thousand times, don't get under a tree during a thunderstorm. Trees draw lightning. Well he got under the oak tree. Guess he figured he could ignore that lightning. Well, lightning hit that tree, split it, knocked Martin 6 metres."

"Did it hurt him?" I asked Zeke.

"No," he said, "Guess it's because he had such prime good health. Ain't been sick a day of his life, except that time he fell off that horse and thought he was a farm machinery salesman named Walt Morrison from Edmonton. Actually I think it helped him. He walks like he's on springs and he seems to give off electricity from every pore."

From the train station, we passed through town, and I noticed a group of people standing and staring at something. The something they were staring at was an empty marble pedestal that had formerly held a large bronze statue of a local politician named Arnold J. Quantly, an individual whom Uncle Martin had always held in the utmost contempt.

Who is the narrator? How would you describe him?

Sometimes writers use *flashbacks* to provide background information in dramatic form. Point out some flashbacks in this story. Why are they effective?

Uncle Martin absolutely refused to admit that any-one would erect a statue to anybody like Quantly. He actually refused to admit there was any such statue in the village square, but there had been, and now it was gone.

I leaned forward and asked Zeke what had hap-pened.

"Stole," he replied, "Yestiddy afternoon, 'bout five. Yessir, in plain view, took between two winks of an eye. We was all in Charlie's store—me 'n' Charlie 'n' your Uncle 'n' your Aunt Edith 'n' some others. Somebody said as how somebody ought to clean that statue, 'come plumb pigeonfied past few years.

"'What statue?' Martin wanted to know. 'There ain't no such thing as a statue to a blubbery-mouthed fool nincompoop like Quantly in this town!'

"So I knowed it wasn't any use, he wouldn't believe in that statue if he walked into it an' broke his leg. Never met as obstinate a man as Martin Carabiener for not believing in something he don't like—anyway, I turned to point at it and it was gone. Minute before it was there, now it wasn't. Stolen between one look an' the next."

I asked him if maybe being struck by lightning had softened Uncle Martin's obstinacy.

"Made it worse," he said. "Most obstinate man in Alberta, your Uncle Martin. Dad blast it, when he says a thing ain't, even though it's right in front of him, blamed if he don't say it so positive you almost believe him."

Zeke dropped me off at Uncle Martin's gate. Uncle Martin wasn't in sight, but I headed around back and Aunt Edith came scurrying out of the kitchen.

"Oh, Joseph!" she cried. "I'm so glad you're here. I don't know what to do, I simply don't. The most dread-ful thing has happened to Martin and ..."

"If you didn't know the truth, you'd think it actually did him good to be hit by lightning, but here he comes. I'll tell you more after dinner. Oh I hope nothing dreadful happens before we can stop it."

Uncle Martin walked over and shook my hand, and my arm tingled as if from an electric shock. We strolled over and sat on the front porch and started looking at the old rotting barn which spoiled the view.

Looking for something to talk about, I mentioned it was too bad the storm two days before hadn't knocked down the barn and finished it.

"Barn? What barn? No barn there, boy!" said Uncle Martin. "Nothing but the view—finest view in Alberta. If you can see a barn there, better get to a doctor as fast as you can hike."

Like Zeke said, he spoke so convincingly that I looked again to be sure. I stood looking for a long time,

Many writers begin stories in the midst of the action, rather than near the climax. They then provide the back-ground through flashbacks. Put the events in this story in chronological order—in the order of the time in which they happened. How near to the climax does the writer begin the story?

because Uncle Martin was telling the truth. There wasn't any barn—NOW.

Aunt Edith only sighed when I told her about the barn.

"Yes," she whispered, "I knew yesterday when the statue went. Yesterday, we were in Charlie's store. I was looking at the statue when Martin said what he did, and then it was gone, right from under my eyes. That's when I sent you the telegram."

"You mean," I asked, "that since Uncle Martin was struck by lightning his stubbornness has taken a new turn, that before he just didn't believe in things; and now because of a huge heightening of his stubbornness, that now he can just disbelieve things right out of existence?"

Aunt Edith nodded. "They just go!" she cried almost wildly. "When he says a thing's not, now it's not."

Suddenly Uncle Martin came in, "Listen to this," he said, and read us a short item that told about Martin's step-brother, Seth Youngman, who owned Marble Hill. Seth somehow got Marble Hill away from Martin and since then Martin refused to believe in it. When he finished, he said, "What are they talking about? There's no hill around here by that name."

Then we heard a far distant rumble, like stones being displaced. Aunt Edith and I both looked out the window and looked at Marble Hill, or where it had been.

Uncle Martin turned and walked away. As he passed the doorway, he caught his foot in the turned-up linoleum and fell the full length of the hall and hit his head on the table. He was unconscious when we reached him. We picked him up and put him on the sofa. Soon he opened his eyes and blinked at us without recognition.

"Who're you?" he asked. "What happened to me?"

"Martin," Aunt Edith cried, "I'm your sister. You fell and hit your head. You've been knocked out."

Uncle Martin stated at us with deep suspicion. "Martin?" he repeated, "My name's not Martin. Who do you think I am anyway?"

"But it is Martin!" Aunt Edith wailed. "You're Martin Carabiener, my brother, and you live in Lakeside, Alberta. You've lived here all your life!"

Uncle Martin's lip stuck out obstinately. "My name's not Martin," he declared rising, "I'm Walt Morrison. I sell farm machinery. I'm from Edmonton. I'm not your brother. I've never seen you before, either of you. I've got a headache and I'm tired of talking."

Uncle Martin's amnesia had come back, just like twenty years ago when he fell off the horse and thought he was Walt Morrison from Edmonton, for a whole week.

The writer knows that a reader enjoys recognizing events, incidents, and even phrases from earlier in a story. Point out some of the repetitions from the early part of the story.

He turned and stomped up the stairs.

Aunt Edith and I followed him up and watched him slam the door. We heard the bedsprings squeak as he sat down and the sound of a match being struck, then the smell of cigar smoke. He always allowed himself one cigar before bed.

"Martin Carabiener," we heard him mutter to himself and one shoe dropped to the floor. "Nobody's got such a name. It's a trick of some kind. Don't believe there is such a person."

Then he was silent. The silence continued. We waited for him to drop the other shoe. When a full minute had passed, we gave each other a horrified look and then slammed open the door. The window was locked from the inside. A cigar in the ashtray was sending a curl of smoke upwards. There was a hollow in the bed covers slowly smoothing out where someone might have been sitting. One shoe was on the floor where Uncle Martin had dropped it.

But Uncle Martin, of course, was gone. He had disbelieved himself out of existence.

—Paul Soukup

One editor thought the last two lines of Paul's story should be cut. Do you think they are necessary? Would removing them provide more impact—or less?

Student Composition 13 I

It's all in the ...

POINT OF VIEW

Bernie sat stiffly on the edge of the bed, his finger poised over the telephone dial.

I just know she won't go, he thought. She's probably not home and her mother won't like me. He clenched his fist and watched the knuckles whiten. No, wait—it's now or never. If she says "No," it won't be the end of the world. So let's get on with it! It was a steady finger that dialed the seven digits.

Oh, no, it's ringing! His confidence vanished in a flash. Maybe if I hang up now, she'll never ...

"Hello?"

Julie slumped into the green beanbag chair, her eyes staring blankly in the general area of the television set. She absent-mindedly twirled a lock of auburn hair with her right hand and thought, What's wrong with me? I haven't been out for three weeks and I'm bored. Lonely. I try to be nice to everybody, but ...

The phone jangled, and she shuffled over to answer it.

"Hello?"

There was a slight pause on the other end, then, "Julie?"

Calm now. Just take it easy, he mouthed silently. "Julie?"

"Yes?"

"This is Bernie Potter. There's a great movie on at the Palace and I thought maybe if you weren't doing anything ..."

Boy, you're dumb, he thought. You sounded too eager. Make her think you don't care. Oh well. Too late now.

"Sure, Bernie, that'd be great."

He let out a great sigh of relief and leaned back on the flowered bedspread. No sweat, he thought. I knew I'd knock her dead.

"I'll pick you up at eight, then," he said, tapping casually on the clock radio beside his bed.

"All right. 'Bye."

"So long."

He stood up and strode from the room, a broad smile on his face. "Never any doubt in my mind," he muttered. "I knew she'd go. I *knew* it."

What's this all about? she thought. C'mon, now, Babe, don't blow it.

"Yes?"

"This is Bernie Potter. There's a great movie on at the Palace and I thought maybe if you weren't doing anything ..."

She thought, Wow, this is like something out of a grade-B movie, me lying around thinking about it and ...

"Sure, Bernie," she said. "That would be great."

How dumb, she thought. Make him think it's all the same to you. Oh well, it's done now.

"I'll pick you up at eight then."

"Sure. 'Bye."

"Okay. So long."

Julie gently set the phone on the hook, turned slowly and did a forward flip on the green and orange shag carpet.

—Bill Post

Activity 13A

Critiquing *It's All in the POINT OF VIEW*

1. This story narrates only a simple and almost universal experience shared by most young people. In a brief paragraph, explain what makes it worth reading.

2. Writers used to be advised to write short stories from one point of view only. What do you think of such advice? Explain when it would be appropriate.

3. Writers often capitalize on the fact that there is pleasure in recognizing parallels in the experiences of different people. Using two columns, jot down the parallels in this selection and compare them. To what extent has the writer been very careful to make them identical?

4. Discuss how irony contributes to your enjoyment of this story. Can you identify with either speaker in the selection?

5. Notice the way the writer handles the dialogue in the story. How has he saved words and yet kept the identity of his speakers clear? Rewrite some of the dialogue yourself to reveal more about the speakers.

6. In several places the writer *shows* the emotions of the speakers. What are some of the ways he communicates the emotions without simply stating what they are? Go through the selection and *state* the emotion being shown in each case.

Discussing the Student Creative Writing

1. To what extent do the examples measure up to the four criteria for creative writing given in the introduction to this chapter (sincerity, emotion, originality, and recreation of an experience)?
2. Do the selections appeal to your senses, present vivid images, and use special techniques to help you experience the actual emotion the writer wishes to communicate?
3. What is the emotion expressed in "While?" How do you react to the viewpoint it projects?
4. Poetry often tries to deal with attitudes and emotions in terms of things and events. How effective are the figures of speech in "The Accident" and "The Drum" in revealing the writer's inner feelings? What do they communicate to you?
5. Do the stories have point or purpose, meaningful structure and order, and carefully selected details that support the intended effect or meaning? Do they express emotion? Provide concrete details? Contain suspense? Deal with action (external or internal)?
6. Is the tone of the stories maintained throughout? Do they succeed in presenting a mood or character consistently? What is the attitude of the writer in each case toward the characters?

Collecting Materials for Your Writing

I write basically to communicate joy, mystery, and passion...not the joy that naively exists with knowledge of pain, but that joy which rises out of and conquers pain. I want to construct myths.

—Gwendolyn MacEwen

When you read an absorbing short story or an emotion-filled poem, you become aware of the wealth of experience the writer has packed into the language. Poets, particularly, seem to be more perceptive and to react more deeply than other people. It may be true that poets are more sensitive, but you too can increase your awareness and begin to collect and store the raw materials that will enrich your own writing.

Throughout his entire life, James Joyce, one of the greatest Irish writers, collected and stored away details, information and sensory impressions to use in his books. One of his friends observed the way he worked in preparing to write *Ulysses*.

I

I have seen him collect in the space of a few hours the oddest assortment of material: a parody on "The House that Jack Built," the name and action of a poison, the method of caning boys on training ships, the wobbly cessation of a tired unfinished sentence, the nervous trick of a convive [one who eats and drinks in festive fellowship] turning his glass in inward-turning circles, a Swiss music-hall joke turning on a pun in Swiss dialect, a description of the Fitzsimmons shift.

In one of the richest pages of *Ulysses*, Stephen, on the seashore, communing with himself and tentatively building with words, calls for his tablets.... [Like his character, Stephen] Joyce was never without them. And they were not library slips, but little writing blocks specially made for the waistcoat pocket. At intervals, alone or in conversation, seated or walking, one of these tablets was produced, and a word or two scribbled on it at lightning speed as ear or memory served his turn. No one knew how all this material was given place in the completed pattern of his work, but from time to time in Joyce's flat one caught glimpses of a few of those big orange-colored envelopes that are one of the glories of Switzerland, and these I always took to be storehouses of building material. The method of making a multitude of criss-cross notes in pencil was a strange one for a man whose sight was never good. A necessary adjunct to the method was a huge oblong magnifying glass. [6]

—Frank Budgen

Like Joyce, many writers use notebooks, journals, or diaries to record fragments of experience from which to build their work.

(*Activity 13B*)

Building a Storehouse of Ideas for Writing

Create a list of the different kinds of ideas, emotions, and information you might collect from your daily experiences to help you with your writing. Then decide on a way to record and store this material. Spend three days making an intensive effort to build a storehouse of materials to use in your writing. Include your experiences, impressions, and reactions, as well as images, passages you read, or phrases you hear. If you are finding the recording and storing process helpful, continue it indefinitely beyond the three days.

Thinking in Pictures

Several of the student models that you read earlier include vivid pictures to reflect the meaning, feeling, or psychological situation the writers are describing:

> In "While," the speaker "clutched your precious ring," holding on to the ring physically just as she holds on to thoughts of her boyfriend to block out the hostility around her.

> In "The Accident," the speaker pictures her stroke of inspiration as the shock of a collision between two speeding cars.

> In "The Drum," the speaker uses the image of a drum to represent the rhythm of life itself, beating out the changes in seasons and the cycles of nature.

> In "The moist sands...," the wind, sea and sand are free and spontaneous, the direct opposite of what the speaker sees in her usual way of life.

Sometimes a poet will build an entire poem around a single image such as each of these. Here are some examples by professional writers of such single-image poems.

I

Serve me a slice of moon
on a hot summer day.
A
nice
ice
slice
that rustles like taffeta
against my teeth—
and trickles winter through me
drop by drop.
Serve me a slice of moon
on a hot summer day—
with just a dab
of deep,
dark
shivery shadows
on top.

II

Rain
polished the night—
then,
over patent-leather streets,
cars moved
on narrow stilts
of
light.

III

I saw a man
murdering flowers—
a long parade of marching
flowers
in giddy-bright happy-hats.
He pushed into the parade
with a steel mower.
The blades bit.
The flowers shrieked
and fell,
their giddy-bright happy-hats
askew.
And as their green life
trickled out
the
murderer
sang.[7]

—Marcie Hans

IV

THE TOASTER

A silver-scaled Dragon with jaws flaming red
Sits at my elbow and toasts my bread.
I hand him fat slices, and then, one by one,
He hands them back when he sees they are done.[8]

—William Jay Smith

In your reading of poetry you will find many images. Poets have compared a train crawling across the countryside to a dragon puffing smoke and flames, the headlights of two cars passing at night to the lances of two duelling knights, and traffic lights to glowing emeralds and rubies.

The choice of images reveals a great deal about the poet's vision of life. Canadian poetry often tells of the sea, mountains, or prairies, and through this choice of images, suggests such themes as man's feelings of insignificance when confronted by the untamed natural world. Consider carefully the underlying meanings suggested by the imagery in the poems you read.

(*Activity 13C*)

Looking for Metaphors (Implied Comparisons)

1. Both in poetry and in prose, writers create vivid pictures by imaginatively comparing one thing with another. Think of metaphors (comparisons), images, or pictures for each of the following:

typewriter	frightened deer	long, boring class
night light	dog in a car	feeling of triumph
garbage disposal	unjust scolding	class bell
bridge game	a disappointment	sound of a crowd
concert	flat tire	vicious grin
soiled wallpaper	lightning flash	unforgettable melody
unexpected cry	bashfulness	conflict

2. This time, begin by making a list of objects, events, and emotions that most students will have experienced. Then create word pictures to represent them.

Letting Sound Reinforce Meaning

Early in this chapter you saw how D. H. Lawrence let the sound of his language reinforce the motion of the waves he was describing. The poetry in Chapter 14 demonstrates how emotion and tone can be conveyed through the choice of words, the length of lines, the selection of details, all uniting to transmit meaning through sound.

There are two useful techniques for letting sound echo sense. First is the use of *onomatopoeia*—the use of words that sound like what they mean. Examples of onomatopoeic words are "swish," "murmur," "crackle," "whiz," "zip," "trudge," "buzz," "drizzle." These words are very expressive. The second technique is the arrangement of words (as in the passage from D. H. Lawrence) to recreate the mood and experience.

Activity 13D

Creating Mood Through Sound

1. Choose a situation in which a certain mood, emotion, or kind of activity is dominant. Then write a brief paragraph or a poem in which you reinforce the sense with the sounds you use. (Your poem does not have to rhyme.) Remember that the primary requirements of creative writing are sincerity, emotion, and originality. Above all, do not write nonsense sentences in which the words, chosen for their sounds alone, are meaningless or inappropriate. Perhaps the following subjects will suggest some ideas to you:

a storm	an empty church	a roller coaster	a locker room
a seashore	a waterfall	a street corner	a kite in flight
a cave	a concert	a cafeteria	a mountaintop
a cemetery	a zoo	a pep rally	a typing room

2. After you have written your paragraph or poem, prepare to read it to the class. As each person reads, note where sound has been used with particular appropriateness. Be prepared to discuss changes or additions you might make.

Borrowing from Your Reader's Experiences

In Chapter 5 (page 108), you reviewed several common figures of speech. When writers wish to convey many impressions in few words, as in poetry, they often use figures of speech—they "borrow" from impressions that are stored in the reader's mind. For example, in the sentence "The guard sullenly *croaked* his refusal," the reader immediately transfers to the guard all his impressions of a frog: unpleasant, stupid, dull-eyed, slimy.

With figures of speech, the writer draws the reader into an experience. The reader's own background and conditioned emotional responses fuse with those of the writer.

Some figures of speech you may wish to try in your own writing include the following types:

a. **Simile**—one of the most common figures of speech. A simile is a comparison between two objects using "like" or "as." For example, "the road was as straight as a line drawn with a ruler" or "he was as green as grass when it came to understanding other people."

b. **Metaphor**—a more complex comparison between two objects without using "like" or "as." A metaphor often implies that the two are somehow closely associated. "The road was a ribbon of moonlight" is a fairly simple metaphor. More complex is the poet Yeats' metaphor about an old man who is "a tattered coat upon a stick."

c. **Personification**—parts of nature or inanimate objects are represented as persons, feeling human emotions or doing human actions. For example, "the wind moaned and howled around the old house" or "the huge boulder crouched on top of the cliff, as if deciding when to plunge down into the valley."

d. **Hyperbole**—exaggeration to create an effect or emphasize a mood. For example, "the heart-broken child cried a river of tears."

e. **Synecdoche**—naming a part of something to represent the whole object or person. For example, "hired hand" refers to the entire human being.

f. **Metonymy**—substituting an object that is closely related to a person or an object for that person or object. For example, using "crown" to refer to the king or queen. "The crown is respected by the people."

(*Activity 13E*)

Using Figures of Speech

Rewrite each of the following sentences to include a figure of speech that borrows from your reader's storehouse of experiences. Try to use several different figures of speech and to vary your sentences. After you have rewritten each sentence to include at least one figure of speech, list beneath each the major sensory impressions that you intended to borrow from your reader's previous experience. Avoid sensory impressions that seem inappropriate.

1. The car went by.
2. Charley was surprised.
3. The ball went into the stands.
4. The team ate supper.
5. The college gave him the diploma reluctantly.
6. Frightened, the boy used his sister as a shield.
7. Everyone seemed ready.
8. The pencil was the prize.

Developing Expressive Forms

In addition to using figures of speech and onomatopoeia, some writers try to make the *form* of their selection express the meaning they wish to communicate. Here is an anecdote that makes the concept of "expressive forms" clear.

In *The Sacred River,* L. A. G. Strong tells of a revealing conversation between James Joyce and Frank O'Connor. The scene is Joyce's flat: O'Connor has just touched the frame of a picture on the wall.

I

"What's this?"
"Cork." (The city of Cork in Ireland)
"Yes, I see it's Cork. I was born there. But what's the frame?"
"Cork."

This anecdote illuminates one of Joyce's major artistic techniques.... The technique—to which I have given the name "expressive form" [borrowed from Yvor Winters]—seeks to establish a direct correspondence between substance and style. The form "expresses" or imitates qualities of its subject.... Thus an episode which takes place in a newspaper office is cast in the form of a newspaper, or a section on sentimental girlhood is written in a "namby-pamby ... style." [9]

In short, to emphasize the fact that the name of the pictured city was Cork, Joyce framed the picture with a cork frame! To emphasize the fact that an episode took place in a newspaper office, he wrote the passage as though it were a newspaper article. Here are some examples from Joyce and others in which the writers have used expressive form to reinforce their content.

In *A Portrait of the Artist as a Young Man,* James Joyce begins at the beginning—when he was a baby. Notice how his style in this passage is mostly baby talk to reinforce the subject he is writing about. (As the artist matures in the story, the style, too, "grows up.")

II

Once upon a time and a very good time it was there was a moocow coming down along the road and this moocow that was coming down along the road met a nicens little boy named baby tuckoo....

His father told him that story: his father looked at him through a glass: he had a hairy face.

He was baby tuckoo. The moocow came down the road where Betty Byrne lived: she sold lemon platt.

> *O, the wild rose blossoms*
> *On the little green place.*

He sang that song. That was his song.[10]

—James Joyce

In *The Sound and the Fury,* William Faulkner uses expressive form to emphasize his theme—that life is meaningless. To make the point, he tells the story through Benjy, a young man who is retarded. This is the way

Benjy sees a golf game. The caddy, Luster, removes the flag from the cup and searches for lost balls in the rough. Benjy, of course, doesn't understand what is going on.

III

Through the fence, between the curling flower spaces, I could see them hitting. They were coming toward where the flag was and I went along the fence. Luster was hunting in the grass by the flower tree. They took the flag out, and they were hitting. Then they put the flag back and they went to the table, and he hit and the other hit. They they went on, and I went along the fence. Luster came away from the flower tree and we went along the fence and they stopped and we stopped and I looked through the fence while Luster was hunting in the grass.

"Here, caddie." He hit. They went away across the pasture. I held to the fence and watched them going away. [11]

—William Faulkner

In poetry, too, writers sometimes use expressive forms to reinforce the content. The poet e e cummings is well known for his unusual forms and his departure from customary spelling, punctuation, and sentence structure. (Notice the way his name is printed.) In this poem, cummings uses expressive form to represent the ugly skyline of suburbia. (The word *ecco* is the Latin word for "behold" and the spelling *ts* is sometimes used to express the sound of disapproval.)

IV

e
cco the uglies
t

s
ub
sub

urba
n skyline on earth between whose d
owdy

hou
se
s

l
ooms an eggyellow smear of wintry sunse
t

—e e cummings[12]

Activity 13F

Experimenting with Expressive Forms

In most of the writing you do, especially in university and in the business world, you will be communicating ideas and information in a straightforward way. Consequently, in most of your writing, the use of expressive forms would not be appropriate. By experimenting with expressive forms, however, you will become sensitive to possibilities of the language that can enrich all of your writing. In addition, for your own enjoyment of effective self-expression and for the occasions when you want to communicate feelings and attitudes and atmosphere in your writing, experience with expressive forms will help you.

1. List words which can be written or printed so that the form expresses the meaning. Here are some examples.

2. Write a concrete poem in which the words actually form the shape of the object you write about, as in the mouse's tale (tail) from *Alice in Wonderland*.

```
                    "Fury
               said to a mouse, That
                    he met in the house,
                         'Let us both go
                    to law: I will prose-
                  cute you.—Come,
               I'll take no denial:
             We must have the
          trial; for really
       this morning I've
       nothing to do.'
          Said the mouse
              to the cur,
                'Such a trial,
                    dear sir,
                       with no
                          jury
                      or judge,
                   would be
                wasting our
             breath.' 'I'll be
             judge, I'll
               be jury.'
                  said cun-
                     ning old
                        Fury: I'll
                       try the
                     whole
                    cause,
                   and
                  con-
                 demn
                you
                    to death'."
```
                                              —Lewis Carroll

Here are some possible subjects for which you might try matching meanings, impressions, sounds, or feelings to the shape:

a question   a bouncing ball
a geyser erupting   a river (or a waterfall)
a religious symbol   a bird in flight

3. Write a brief passage in which you use words that imitate the language or atmosphere of the place you are describing.

a kindergarten classroom	a submarine
a jetport in the future	a church
a gymnasium	a cave
a mountaintop	a bus station

4. Write a brief passage or a poem in which the sound of the words, the rhythm of the language, and the form you use all combine to reinforce the content.

the sound of an echo in a deep, rounded cave
the sound of the sea battering a rocky coast
the sound of a jet taking off

Various Poetic Forms

Over the years, poets have developed many different patterns for expressing ideas and emotions. You can find whole volumes describing these patterns and the uses to which they can be put.

Many poets today create their own forms, but few of the best poets ignore the patterns developed in the past. Often, as they work toward developing their own patterns, they have already internalized earlier forms. The word "internalize" here means that the poets have become so familiar with the forms that they have incorporated them into their own patterns of thinking. Following are explanations of some poetic forms:

Couplet.   A couplet is simply two related lines of poetry. Often they rhyme, but they need not. They may be of any length and rhythm. Here are two examples.

I	II
ON THE ANTIQUITY OF MICROBES	**THE QUARREL**
Adam	The clouds and the wind in
Had 'em.	heated debate
—Strickland Gillilan	Argued on whether to rain
	or wait.

Haiku.   Haiku is a Japanese form consisting of a total of seventeen syllables, with five in the first and third lines and seven in the second. The subject matter is nature, and the lines should contain an image of permanence and an image of change. Usually the haiku makes an indirect comment on life.

III

THE TEMPTER

Plum blossoms swaying:
Here! Here! Steal this one!—is that
What the moon's saying?[13]

—Issa

IV

SILENCE

The sound of the moth
Wings folded on the clapper
Of the temple bell.

—Nishi

Tanka.   Tanka is another Japanese form that begins with exactly the same pattern as the haiku and moves into the *ageku*. The ageku consists of two additional lines of seven syllables each, for a total of thirty-one syllables in the complete tanka.

V

THE FISH

The fish feels water
Squish along his scaly back
And doesn't know it.
He feels the sudden hook yank
And his water world is gone.

—Catherine Clint

VI

MY TRIUMPH

The conversation
Wasted through the dawdling hour.
Subjects like blind worms
Turned upon themselves and nipped
Their tails. I sat in silence.

—Fred Prince

The Chain Haiku (or Chain Tanka).   A series of related verses following the same form—is used to tell a kind of story by revealing little pictures of a sequence of events. For example, how might you develop a series of events around the conversation in the foregoing tanka? Another use is for two writers to write and respond to each other in a series of haiku or tanka.

Cinquain.   The cinquain is a modern form invented by Adelaide Crapsey of Rochester, New York. It has five lines of two, four, six, and eight syllables respectively. The double cinquain may have twice as many syllables in each line. A good way to develop a cinquain is to use a noun in the first line to provide a subject and title; to use two adjectives in the second line describing the subject; to use an *-ing* phrase in the third line expressing an action; to use a sentence fragment in the fourth line communicating a feeling; to use another noun, a synonym for the title, or a symbol for the object named by the title as the fifth line.

VII

Homework
Heavy, pushing,
Pulling deep breaths from me
Marathon runner charging home
Hard grind.

—Leonard Van

VIII

swallows—
swooping, soaring,
ecstasy in motion
across the windswept sky above
the world.

—Barney McDonald

Limerick.   Limericks have been used for hundreds of years for light subjects and word games. Though some people think they were invented by Edward Lear or first developed in Limerick, Ireland, no one knows for sure where and when they originated. They consist of five lines, with the first, second and fifth rhyming, and with the third and fourth lines either not rhyming or having a different rhyme. Limericks do not use the traditional rhythms of most poetry written in English. Instead, they use a system of counting only the primary (very heavy) accents. Lines one, two, and five have three primary accents each, whereas lines three and four have only two. Often such surprise elements as puns, allusions, or plays on English spelling make the verses humourous. The limerick below has been marked to show the typical pattern of syllables and rhymes.

IX

There was a young girl in the choir	(a)
Whose voice rose up higher and higher	(a)
Till it reached such a height	(b)
It was clear out of sight	(b)
And they found it next day in the spire.	(a)

Sonnet.   All sonnets consist of fourteen lines of iambic pentameter; that is, lines such as the following with a ten-syllable accent pattern:

O pardon me, thou bleeding piece of earth,

—William Shakespeare

Beyond the common elements of fourteen lines and iambic pentameter, there are other characteristics that divide sonnets into two groups. The English (or Shakespearean) sonnet consists of three quatrains (four-line groups) and a couplet. The Italian (or Petrarchan) sonnet is organized into an octave (eight-line group) and a sestet (six-line group). Both types display a structured elegance and demand great discipline and skill on the part of the poet. When well handled, the rigid form of the sonnet is submerged in the poem's meaning and goes almost unobserved by the reader. In the examples below, however, the organization and rhyme pattern of both types have been highlighted for purposes of comparison.

X

SONNET 29

(an English sonnet)

	When, in disgrace with Fortune and men's eyes,	(a)
	I all alone beweep my outcast state,	(b)
quatrain	And trouble deaf heaven with my bootless cries	(a)
	And look upon myself and curse my fate,	(b)

quatrain	Wishing me like to one more rich in hope,	(c)
	Featured like him, like him with friends possessed,	(d)
	Desiring this man's art and that man's scope,	(c)
	With what I most enjoy contented least;	(d)
quatrain	Yet in these thoughts myself almost despising,	(e)
	Haply I think on thee, and then my state,	(f)
	Like to the lark at break of day arising	(e)
	From sullen earth, sings hymns at heaven's gate;	(f)
couplet	For thy sweet love rememb'red such wealth brings	(g)
	That then I scorn to change my state with kings.	(g)

—William Shakespeare

XI

ON THE GRASSHOPPER AND THE CRICKET

(an Italian sonnet)

octave	The poetry of earth is never dead:	(a)
	When all the birds are faint with the hot sun,	(b)
	And hide in cooling trees, a voice will run	(b)
	From hedge to hedge about the new-mown mead;	(a)
	That is the grasshopper's—he takes the lead	(a)
	In summer luxury—he has never done	(b)
	With his delights; for when tired out with fun	(b)
	He rests at ease beneath some pleasant weed.	(a)
sestet	The poetry of earth is ceasing never:	(c)
	On a lone winter evening, when the frost	(d)
	Has wrought a silence, from the stove there shrills	(e)
	The cricket's song, in warmth increasing ever,	(c)
	And seems to one in drowsiness half lost,	(d)
	The grasshopper's among some grassy hills.	(e)

—John Keats

Triolet.   The triolet is rarely used today. It is a French form that is delicate and dancing, consisting of eight lines, with the first line repeated as the fourth and the seventh and the second line repeated as the eighth. Although any kind of rhythm is acceptable, the triolet uses only two end rhymes.

XII

THE TRIOLET

Easy is the Triolet,
    If you really learn to make it!
Once a neat refrain you get,
Easy is the Triolet.
As you see!—I pay my debt
With another rhyme. Deuce take it,
Easy is the Triolet,
    If you really learn to make it![14]

—William Ernest Henley

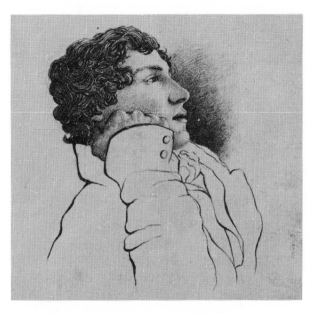

In 1819, just two years after this drawing was made, Keats died at the age of twenty-five.

Blank Verse.   Blank verse consists of unrhymed lines of iambic pentameter. Of course, departures from the rigid pattern are necessary to express ideas naturally, and sentences frequently continue from line to line rather than ending at the end of a line. Shakespeare's plays are in blank verse, except for occasional passages. As a matter of fact, ordinary conversation is spoken, and can often be written in the form of blank verse. Here are some lines from *Hamlet*:

> But look, the morn in russet mantle clad
> Walks o'er the dew of yon high eastward hill.
> Break we our watch up, and by my advice
> Let us impart what we have seen tonight
> Unto young Hamlet, for upon my life
> This spirit, dumb to us, will speak to him.
>
> —William Shakespeare

Free Verse.   Many of the student poems near the beginning of this chapter are in free verse, a form that has no specific requirements for syllables, lines, rhymes, meters or rhythms. But a free verse poem *does* have form, usually a form that matches its content, mood, and meaning. As professional poets know, good free verse is as demanding as any other form and can be written successfully only when the poet has become familiar with other forms and is willing to work hard at polishing each phrase in the poem.

These are only a few of the many, many forms that poets have developed over the centuries. Others are the rondeau, rondel, villanelle, ode, ballade, ballad (two different forms), and epic. If you are interested in these and other forms, go to your library and get a book on "prosody," which will explain and illustrate them.

Various Prose Forms

The usual form most students choose for creative writing in prose is the short story. A short story can be read at one sitting and aims at a single effect. It often begins with an event which leads to complications; these complications increase and intensify the suspense until there is a crisis. After the crisis comes the climax, the point of highest interest in the story. At this time some decision is made that influences the ending of the story. After the climax comes the "falling action," or denouement (which means "the untying of the knot"), and the writer concludes the story quickly.

Many short stories do not follow the "classical pattern" just described. In fact, the only requirements are that short stories be fiction, that they be interesting, and that they have a purpose of some kind—even if that purpose is simply to describe "a slice of life."

You need not be limited to the short story to be inventive and creative in prose. Here are only a few of the forms you might use in writing imaginatively in prose:

1. Tell a story in a series of letters.
2. Tell a story in a series of journal or diary entries.
3. Create a tall tale, a joke, or a legend.
4. Develop a dream or a daydream into a story.
5. Write a fantasy, letting ideas come to you as you listen to music or view a painting or sculpture.
6. Dramatize an event, real or imagined.
7. Tell a story using a series of newspaper clippings.
8. Write a film, radio, or television script.
9. Recreate fictionally a historical event.
10. Extend a short story or a historical event by imagining a sequel.
11. Write a dramatic monologue in which one person recounts and reacts to action as it is taking place.
12. Describe a single incident from various points of view using thoughts that each of several characters would have during the event.
13. Write a serial consisting of several parts, each ending with a "cliffhanger"—an event creating unusual suspense and causing the reader to want to know what happens next.
14. Make up an interview with a real or imaginary person.
15. Write a *pourquoi* (which means "why") story, a fable explaining why something exists ("How the elephant got its tail" or "How Great Bear Lake was created," for example).

Avoiding Clichés

One of the four requirements of creative writing stressed in the introduction to this chapter is originality. You might agree with the writer of Ecclesiastes that "There is nothing new under the sun," and you would, in a sense, be correct. For thousands of years people have been writing on the same themes: *carpe diem* (live for the day), salvation through suffering, ambition and its effect, loyalties, the place of human beings in the universe, among many others. But though they write on age-old themes, they handle them in individual and original ways. Originality, then, may be a new expression of an old idea.

One of the great obstacles to originality is the use of clichés. A cliché is an expression or idea that has been used so often that it has lost its effectiveness. Imagine getting set to take a delicious bite from a savoury hamburger—only to discover you have a mouthful of sawdust! Clichés in writing have the same effect. A reader gets all set to savour an incisive new expression, only to discover a worn-out cliché.

One must also avoid the other extreme, using expressions that are too new or unusual or ridiculous. A great creative writing teacher, Hughes Mearns, published these verses written by one of his students.

XIII

B.C. (BEFORE CLICHÉS)

MORNING

I watched a fluffy cloud drift by
Across the boundless blue of sky
And saw the sun's rays, molten gold,
Upon the dewy earth unfold.

EVENING

I felt my fettered soul uplift
Before the rosy sunset drift
And in the hazy blue afar
I saw the gleaming evening star.

XIV

A.D. (AFTER DISCOVERING 'EM)

MORNING

I saw the sun with battered face
Trying to warm the human race;
I watched a sodden cloud limp by
Like some discouraged custard pie.

EVENING

The sleepy sun in flannels red
Went yawning to its Western bed;
I saw one shivering small star
No brighter than our dishpans are.[15]

—Jewel Martin

Do not be surprised if an expression that sounds new and exciting to you turns out to be a cliché that you have not heard. In a way, earlier writers had an advantage over you since they have already used the images that you might like to use now. Because these expressions were so appealing and vivid, they were used again and again and so became clichés. Robert Burns' "My love is like a red, red rose that's newly sprung in June," and

Shakespeare's "All the world's a stage and all the men and women merely players," were fresh, vital lines when they were written. You, however, must go on to create new and equally effective images of your own.

Activity 13G

Creating New Expressions

1. The following expressions are the beginnings of common clichés. See if you can fill in the standard expression and then see if you can create a new image or a new comparison to replace the old one:

   a. crazy as a _____
   b. dead as a _____
   c. happy as a _____
   d. white as _____
   e. strong as an _____
   f. it rained _____
   g. mad as a _____
   h. clever as a _____
   i. skinny as a _____
   j. eyes like _____
   k. red as _____
   l. cold as _____
   m. black as _____
   n. modest as a _____
   o. full as _____
   p. sings like _____
   q. writes like _____
   r. whimpers like _____
   s. wet as a _____
   t. blind as a _____

2. After you have identified the clichés and created new comparisons, see whether the class can list any additional clichés. Go through both processes with your own list.

Activity 13H

The Creative Editor

Revising and editing a piece of imaginative or creative writing call for you to be sensitive to language in special ways. The style should be fresh and original without leaving the reader confused. Ideas should show insight and imagination, yet they should also be organized in such a way that the reader can easily understand them. Read the passage below and decide what you would like the writer to change during the revising process. You may wish to take note of material stressed earlier in this chapter, such as point of view, imagery, sound effects and clichés. Prepare to discuss your editing and proofreading comments with the rest of the class.

I have never forgotten the day I learned just how important solitude can be. To me, a special peace of mind will always be conjured up by the vision of a sandy, wind-swept beach I explored one afternoon, where the waves washed wetly over the worn, white stones piled in tumbled mounds along the shore. Walking by myself. At times like this, you discover special things about yourself. Walking alone, with nothing much on your mind, you find out more about who you are. Too many people get caught up in the hustle and bustle of the nine to five rat race. If they took the time to feel the wind in their hair and listen to the sounds of nature, they would hear a special sort of music in life. This is how I learned that the grass isn't always greener somewhere else. They might learn, as I did, that special afternoon, that being in tune with yourself adds a special kind of peace to life.

Major Writing Assignment

Creative Writing

Write a short story, an essay, or a poem, keeping in mind that your creative writing must have sincerity, emotion, and originality, and that you should try to recreate an experience. Refer to the storehouse of ideas you gathered in Activity 13B. Make use of the suggestions in this chapter; try to think in pictures, use sound to reinforce your meaning, use images that your reader will respond to, use expressive forms and avoid clichés. After you have written a rough draft, go over your work to look for ways to improve it. See Chapter 2, The Writing Process: An Overview.

The experiences you draw on for your creative writing will play a large part in determining what form you choose to write in. Choosing to write about a person who influenced your life or your values, for example, will probably mean that you find an essay or a story more appropriate than a poem. Selecting a moment of intense emotion, on the other hand, may mean that poetry is the most effective form for you to share your experience with a reader.

14

Criticism of Prose and Poetry

The critic who discusses a flaw in Canadian literature is considered very clever; but the critic who discovers genius in our poetry or prose is immediately taunted with nationalistic prejudice.

—Wilson MacDonald

In the eighteenth century when almost every boy went into an apprenticeship to learn a trade, it was the master's job to criticize whatever the apprentice produced. "Here now," a shoemaker might say, "you've got to leave a little more welt, or you won't have anything to stitch."

Of course, the wise and skillful master knew that criticism should be positive as well as negative, rewarding as well as corrective. "That's a fine window!" the glazier (glass worker) might shout. "The sun will come like fire through those bright colours."

Criticism has always been an important activity in almost every human endeavour. It is, in a sense, a gift of insight from the past to enlighten the future.

In some areas, where the standards are clear and absolute, criticism is very easy. "Water won't flow uphill, unless it's under pressure. You've got to change the angle of that pipe!" There is no room for opinion here. The plumber has based his criticism on a clear and absolute set of standards.

◀ The inscription on this arch was written for a purpose: to extol the virtues of the Roman emperor who built it. Whether the message is true or not is a subject for the critic.

In literature, standards are neither absolute nor so widely accepted as to be clear and uniform. As a result, some writers and critics adhere to one set of standards while other groups accept another. In short, there is no universally accepted, conventional set of literary values. Read, for example, this discussion of Tolstoy's evaluation of Shakespeare.

> Tolstoy felt that Shakespeare was a minor literary figure. Truly dramatic situations, Tolstoy said, do not require easy props like earthquakes, floods, or famines. Nor should they lean on black-and-white characterizations in which absolute good is juxtaposed against absolute evil. The authentic literary product finds its raw materials in everyday situations and in the struggle that goes on inside a man's soul. And it was precisely in these respects, Tolstoy believed, that Shakespeare was most deficient....
>
> Tolstoy's evaluation of Shakespeare ... emphasized three principles:
> 1. The subject had to be significant. It had to be important in the life of the people.
> 2. The treatment had to be authentic. Characters had to speak as people do in real life. The scenes had to be realistic. The plot had to be natural and had to engage the emotions of the audience. Emotion had to be delicately handled.
> 3. The sincerity of the enterprise had to be clearly manifest. The author had to feel deeply about what he was writing.
>
> Measured by this yardstick, Shakespeare was "inconsequential" and his characters "contrived." Pervading the whole of his work was a "premeditated artificiality" in which the author "juggles words." Tolstoy's conclusion: "The sooner people free themselves from the false adulation of Shakespeare, the better it will be." This liberation, he said, would enable them to understand that the "trivial and immoral productions of Shakespeare and of his imitators ... can never be the teacher of life."
>
> It should be apparent by now that Tolstoy's standing in world literature did not rest on the acuity [keenness] of his critical abilities.[1]

That one of the greatest of the Russian writers could so misjudge another great writer proves that criticism is a complex, difficult, and somewhat subjective activity.

Elements of Criticism

Several years ago UNESCO, the United Nations Educational, Social, and Cultural Organization, funded a study to determine a classification system of literary criticism.[2] After reading hundreds of examples of such criticism, the researchers found that when people write about literature, they follow some standard patterns.

1. They explain their own *involvement* in the work. That is, they explain what they felt, how they reacted, how the work related to their lives and the lives of others. In short, they tried to show how the work influenced them, with emphasis on its emotional impact.

2. They discuss their *perception* of the work. They explain its basic pattern, its use of language, literary devices, structure, tone, and techniques for communicating its theme. They classify it with relationship to other works and explain the significance of the classification.

3. They discuss their *interpretation* of the work. They explain the meaning of the work, giving their interpretation of any difficult passages, symbols, inferences, implications. They show what the author seems to be saying about people, about the world, about society, and about the divine.

4. They explain their *evaluation* of the work. They show what they thought the work was worth. Because values are so complex and various, the critics often set forth and explain their standards and then show how the work measures up. Critics differ in the emphasis they place on these elements: the emotion the work generates; the form or structure of the work; the unity and coherence of the work; the theme of the work and the way it comments on life; the tradition it follows; its believability.

This list of "what people say when they write about literature" gives you an idea of the subjects you can use when you write about a poem, a short story, a play, a novel, or any other literary selection. The list can be condensed into a series of questions:

1. How do I feel about the work?
2. What do I think the work means?
3. How did the writer communicate meaning? (What literary techniques, devices, customs, conventions, are used?)
4. How effective is the work? How does it compare with other works?

Sometimes a critic may go beyond the province of art into the areas of ethics, morality, and religion to answer an additional question:

5. Is the message of the work worthwhile?

The ideal review...reflects the personality of both author and reviewer and holds the attention of its readers. It is at once a narrative, an exposition and a judgement: and it is in itself, literature.

—W. A. Deacon

Some Examples of Literary Criticism

The following excerpts from reviews of literature demonstrate how professional writers approach the criticism of fiction, nonfiction, and poetry. Study the technique of each and decide whether or not you would employ similar methods.

Consider these questions as you read the reviews:

Which of the five questions above does each reviewer answer?

Which question or questions does each reviewer emphasize?

Are all the questions equally important in criticizing poetry, fiction, and nonfiction?

I

FAIRY TALES AND AFTER: FROM SNOW WHITE TO E.B. WHITE
BY ROGER SALE
REVIEWED BY CLARA CLAIBORNE PARK

"Children's literature," writes Roger Sale, "is one of the glories of our recent literary heritage." Therefore, he takes it seriously, as he takes any literature that is precious to him—the works of George Eliot, William Empson, or Spenser, for instance, the authors who are for him irreplaceable. So *Fairy Tales and After* is not a casual series of remarks and judgments, of interest to librarians and professors of education who preside over a ghetto called "children's literature," but considered literary criticism, useful to all of us who remember the books of our childhood. "Useful," of course, should be taken to mean "enjoyable"; "seriously" is not at all the same thing as "heavily."

Sale begins with one of the oldest definitions of the function of literature: that it give profit and delight, a definition these days honored chiefly in the breach. He writes—on fairy tales and talking animals, on Lewis Carroll, Beatrix Potter, Kenneth Grahame, L. Frank Baum, *Kim,* and *Charlotte's Web*—in the genial spirit of one wanting to write about very good books that nobody else has been writing about.

For Sale, children's literature is literature, make no mistake. *The Wind in the Willows* is, quite simply, "part of the ongoing emotional equipment of all who love it," and "The River Bank," its first chapter, is "one of the great opening chapters of any reader's reading life."[3]

II

THE NIGHT COUNTRY
BY LOREN EISELEY
REVIEWED BY RAY BRADBURY

Let's clear away dead fact and dry description first. *The Night Country* by Loren Eiseley, professor of anthropology and the history of science, University of Pennsylvania, is 240 pages long. It is a book about rats, birds, bones, spiders, shadows, and time. It can be read, one would imagine, in about three hours.

The vibrations from those three hours, however, might well last the rest of your life.

Because to read Loren Eiseley is to fall instantly in love.

*   *   *

"The Night Country" is the summation of Eiseley's life of turning over rocks, submerging himself in caves, visiting spider dens, ducking bats and puzzling over fossil apeman's bones.

Eiseley is a haunted man, haunted by the shadow of himself on hotel walls, which will be replaced by yet other men's shadows tomorrow. But his heart beats and his hand moves to record past history, gaze steadily at the present which buries itself by the instant, and look to a future where Man, with his odd machines, can hope to toss further, brighter shadows.[4]

III

A REVIEW OF UP AGAINST IT:
CHILDREN AND THE LAW IN CANADA
BY JEFFERY WILSON

Up Against It is a concise and helpful legal handbook. Jeffery Wilson has made a valiant attempt to explain the situation of the child under Canadian law in terms that are comprehensible to interested laymen. He covers the concept of the child as victim and as offender under the Criminal Code, dealing with incest, child abuse, infanticide, arrest and the consequences of being labelled a delinquent.

In the section on family law, Wilson describes several custody cases, including examples where an attempt was made to define the particular talents and interests of an individual child to decide which parent would be best able to nurture these aptitudes. He deals, too, with adoption and with the nightmarish situation where the child is kidnapped by one of his parents.

Wilson uncovers some surprising facts. In the section on learning, he explains that boards of education are obliged under the law to provide only accommodation; no legal definition of the quality of education exists. And it appears that truancy regulations are more stringent for native children in Canada.

Although Canadian law is good in looking after the welfare of children in employment, Wilson cites cases where children are still unfairly treated. He explores the role of the lawyer in representing children and of other professional disciplines in helping them. Wilson calls for change in the present status of children under the law and advocates recognition of the child as a citizen. At the end of the book, he gives a comprehensive list of services available to help children.[5]

—Joan Malcolmsen

IV

A REVIEW OF MADWOMEN: POEMS
BY FRASER SUTHERLAND

Fraser Sutherland is fascinated with people, the strange things they say to one another, the funny places they turn up, the looks that invade their eyes. His poems are about people and *Madwomen* is a portrait gallery. His people talk about what it means to be Canadian, about love, art, literature, about the way men treat women, the way women treat men.

One of Sutherland's strongest points is his blend of satire and wit, as in The New Yorker's Dream of Canada. He's also a master at assuming different personalities, like a makeup artist. The Two Hearts of Frida Kahlo is a character play. When he tells haunting half stories such as On The Beach One Day he mingles rhythm with clean, sensual language.

At times, *Madwomen* falls short. Sutherland is heavily influenced by writers and artists, which is fine, but sometimes they figure too literally in his work and top-heavy, uninspired pieces like Dada 1919-66 ensue. He is capable of writing fine tributes though, most visible in Auden's Face. Also, Sutherland often writes a poem that's obviously been sparked by one meagre fancy. The result (Lessons in French Gender) is amusing, but lacking in depth.

Madwomen, like that portrait gallery, suffers at times from blank expressions, shallowness and unearned wrinkles. But on the whole, Sutherland is a good poet; there's lots to look at and appreciate. *Madwomen,* even in its weakest moments, is entertaining.[6]

—Barry Dempster

V

A REVIEW OF *ALEX DRIVING SOUTH*
BY KEITH MAILLARD

Keith Maillard's second novel, *Alex Driving South,* is a thoughtful and well-crafted book that establishes its author as a mature, accomplished writer. The book is compelling, the pace is expertly set and the result is one of the best novels of the year.

The story concerns Evan Carlyle who returns to his native West Virginia after 13 years of living in Los Angeles and Canada. He meets Alex Warner, his best friend from the old days, and the two begin the job of recalling the past and reconciling it to the present.

Evan Carlyle left the U.S. to come to Canada (as did Maillard) and became a CBC radio producer. His life has changed but his ties to West Virginia prove stronger than he expected. Alex Warner was the hero of Carlyle's youth. He was a star athlete, he stole cars on a whim, and he cultivated a life of risks and frenetic energy.

The intervening 13 years have changed Alex. As the book opens, he is married with two children, owns a failing garage and lives a predictable life in a suburban development.

But the impulse of those wilder days remains, even though it has been twisted and stunted by failure and time. The two men begin a rambling tour of bars and old haunts during which each man tries to sort out what life has become. Neither is particularly content with the answers. Time has changed them and the future is far bleaker than their glory days of the past.

Throughout the book, Maillard shows a steady hand that slowly unwraps the basis of the friendship and analyzes the bonds and tensions between Alex and Evan. The stark, discouraging life of West Virginia provides a powerful backdrop for the interplay of memory and reality. *Alex Driving South* combines surprising acuity with an engrossing style. It's a rewarding combination.[7]

—Paul Hornbeck

Examining the Professional Criticism

In each of the preceding criticisms, the writer seems to begin by suggesting the contents and value of the work being discussed. The first review begins with a quotation, the third review begins with a concise, simple statement of the book's contents. Look at each of the examples and try to discover where the intention of the writer is defined by the reviewer. Are the writers' intentions, summarized below, stated or implied by the reviewers?

1. *Fairy Tales and After* presents serious criticism of children's literature, which is valuable to all who remember the books of their childhood.
2. *The Night Country* pursues the history of man, recording the past, observing the present, and looking ahead to the future.
3. *Up Against It* is a practical handbook which explains the often surprising legal position of children in Canada.
4. *Madwomen* is a collection of poetry about people which blends satire and wit.
5. *Alex Driving South* is a novel about the interplay between the past and the present.

In these reviews, most of the reviewers considered all five critical questions. They differed, however, in their choice of which question to begin with. Look again at the reviews to see which of the questions each reviewer treated initially. If one of the reviewers introduced other information, how do you justify the extra inclusion?

As you read the following student reviews, look at the different ways the reviewers answered the five critical questions.

Student Composition 14A

A REVIEW OF *THE STONE ANGEL*
By Margaret Laurence

The success of any novel depends primarily on the degree to which it accomplished its purpose. Whether the work is simply escape fiction, pulp romance or insightful, serious fiction, the impact on the reader can only be measured in terms of the goals of the novel. In the case of *The Stone Angel*, Margaret Laurence presents what is basically a complex character study within the framework of an interpretative piece of fiction. The author succeeds in engaging the reader's interest as she explores the personality of her detailed central character, Hagar Shipley.

Why does Nicola open with this kind of statement?

How effective is the "outer structure" in arousing interest?

Hagar Shipley is a tough, unyielding woman who is intimately described to the reader through her own actions. In fact, it is this slow revelation of character, mastered by Laurence, which creates the emotional impact, holds the reader's interest and most importantly, creates empathy for Hagar. For despite her apparent coldness and total inability to express her feelings, Hagar is an admirable, courageous woman in whom one sees the pain and humiliation of old age.

The book begins with a memory of childhood and Hagar's hometown of Manawaka. Especially clear in the flashback is the stone angel which stood on the hill in the Manawaka cemetery. Throughout the novel it becomes increasingly clear that the stone angel is actually Hagar Shipley herself, the product of the harsh pioneer life which she experienced. The statue is cold and hard, very expensive—which denotes superficial acceptability—but perhaps most like Hagar in that it is blind!

> She was doubly blind, not only stone but unendowed with even a pretense of sight.
> (p.1).

Only as she approaches death and is physically and mentally deteriorating is Hagar able to see the tragedy of her own life.

The plot structure in which Laurence places her central character is essentially quite straight-forward. Hagar Shipley is ninety years old, living with her son Marvin and his wife Doris. After much consideration, these two decide to place the aging woman in a rest-home. Hagar, however, cannot accept this; she will not, as Dylan Thomas stated, "...go gentle into that good night." Instead, she will "Rage, rage against the dying of the light." Therefore, she runs away and finds herself at a beach resort, but is soon rediscovered by Marvin and Doris. Finally, illness takes its toll and Hagar is forced to enter the hospital. There she dies. It is impossible, however, to judge the novel's plot on the basis of this rather simplistic outline since the use of flashbacks reveals brutal mental conflicts while creating much suspense and an engaging character tormented by a bitter secret.

Hagar's father was a "self-made man" (p.5) and it is from him that she has inherited her almost paranoid concern with appearance and her icy exterior. She was his favourite, and was therefore, alienated from her two brothers, Matt and Dan. The tragedy of her entire life is perhaps most profoundly summarized by the pathetic statement:

> After though, I was sorry I'd witnessed it, and tried to tell them so, but they wouldn't hear me out. (p.6)

Which of the critical questions is Nicola dealing with here?

Why is it important that Nicola discuss the meaning of the book's title?

Note Nicola's use of direct quotations. How effective are they?

Does Nicola "over-summarize" the plot, or is her discussion of plot proportionate and useful? Why or why not?

What critical question is Nicola dealing with here?

She is unable to break out of the constraints of her "stone" personality and when she goes on to marry Bram Shipley she does so chiefly out of a spirit of rebellion against her authoritarian father. Through Laurence's skilled prose, the reader is moved to such an extent that often he is overwhelmed by the desire to shake Hagar and make her understand that it *is* safe to reveal emotions. But it is impossible to simply "shake" away a whole era and all the lessons of the past which bear down upon one's life. Even when Bram turns to Hagar at night in bed, her pride—and perhaps fears—which control her, deny her the ability to reveal love and tenderness for him. To some extent, Hagar finally destroyed Bram after she left their home with her son John. When she returned, Bram was a shadow of a man and she had already started to destroy John through over-protection and stifling love. Hagar never hurt the ones she loved intentionally; it seemed her actions were simply beyond her control. The enormous pain and guilt she feels in her old age, especially about John's death, are well expressed by Laurence's clear, first person narration.

Besides being a precise character novel, *The Stone Angel* is also a stark, realistic statement about the state of the aged. As Hagar deteriorates mentally and physcially, she is not spared any of the indignities which are coupled with old age. She can no longer control her bodily functions, is allowed virtually no privacy and must bear the embarrassment of memory lapses. These normal aging processes are nearly unbearable for Hagar since she is so fiercely independent right until her death. In the moment before she dies, Hagar is still struggling to assert herself and prove that she is capable of making choices:

> I wrest from her the glass full of water to be
> had for the taking. I hold it in my own hands.
> There. There. (p.275)

Hagar does maintain her independence, but then is faced with the ultimate defeat of death without ever having revealed her emotions, or softening her "stone" covering. She has, however, come to terms with her life in a sense, been a dynamic or developing character, since she has finally realized the pain and tragedy of her past. Although this is never admitted, Hagar Shipley has gained a new awareness, ironically, just prior to her death.

The Stone Angel by Margaret Laurence is one of the masterpieces of Canadian fiction. It is not simply a detailed and beautifully crafted character study, but also the vehicle for discussion of the dilemmas faced by old people in modern society. Not all are torn by the personal struggles of Hagar, but each is, in some

Why does Nicola concentrate on a discussion of the character of Hagar?

What does this section add to the review? Which critical question does it address?

Which critical question does this section answer?

sense, a pioneer in Canada and must cope with an age which cannot understand past values and experience. Ultimately, we must all struggle to "be," even in a technological society which easily supplies most of what we think we need in order to live comfortable lives.

—Nicola Marotz

Is the "outer structure" ending appropriate? Could you suggest any changes?

Student Composition 14B

REVIEW OF *ODE TO A NIGHTINGALE* By John Keats

The "Ode to a Nightingale" is a poem of longing, heartache, and yearning for a better existence. This is shown in the first stanza, where Keats is obviously envious of the nightingale as he listens to its song. Yet he claims not to be envious of the bird's happiness, but speaks of himself as "being too happy in thine happiness." He longs for the simple, free, and happy existence of the bird.

Keats speaks in the second stanza of leaving his cruel, hard world completely, perhaps by means of getting drunk and joining the bird in his mind. Reality crushes Keats as he recalls in the third stanza the "weariness, the fever, and the fret" that make up his existence on earth. Keats falls deeper into sorrow as he yearns for a release from this anguish. He wishes to "fade, far away, dissolve. ..."

A burst of energy causes him to release his sorrow and decide he can join the free bird after all. This is to be done through his poetry, his writings, not through a fuzzy, foggy, dreary-eyed drunken state. The fourth stanza shows the joy he felt as he made his decision. It was as if a great weight (of death, perhaps?) had been lifted from his shoulders.

In the fifth stanza, drunk on poetry, he uses his imagination to describe his death, "in embalmed darkness" and his rebirth into the joyous world of the nightingale. Keats makes good use of imagery to show the transition of the imagination to this new environment.

The nightingale sings on in the sixth stanza. Keats has called on death to release him from his tortuous life. He longs for death, true death, as he listens to the songs. An easing of pain and sorrow is what is signified by death, the bird representing a rebirth and carefree new life.

The bird again captures Keats' attention in the seventh stanza, and the poet realizes that his bird is immortal and not born for death, but for eternal life.

This limited critical selection does not attempt to answer all of the critical questions. Which one does it focus on?

The three parallel words in the first sentence lose effect because they are not recognizably parallel. How would you change "longing," "heartache," and "yearning" to make them truly parallel?

The word "this" ordinarily should refer to complete subjects, rather than to whole sentences. To what does the word "this" in the second sentence refer? How might the sentence be improved?

How does the writer keep the reader "on the track" as she progresses through the poem? What is the order of arrangement of the selection?

Again, notice the misuse of the word "this." How would you improve this sentence? How might you avoid the passive voice in the same sentence? Why is the passive not desirable?

How could the writer *show* that Keats makes "good use of imagery" rather than just *telling* that he does?

One problem with interpreting and explaining a poem is that readers differ in interpretations. Unless you include

Sadness fills Keats' heart as he comprehends his inability to join the free flight of the bird, perhaps symbolizing God and eternal life, because he is bound to earth with his forlorn, lethargic life. He refers to Ruth whose story reflects the sadness and yearning for home which he felt. One could almost feel his heart breaking.

The reader feels a release of tension as Keats falls back to his sorrowful life in the eighth stanza. A dazed existence awaits him, in a world where there is no hope, no music.

—Mary Lutgen

exact quotations and reasons for making certain inferences, readers may not accept your ideas. What ideas really need support from the poem?

Look at the poem itself and then suggest an ending for this review that uses a short, telling quotation. Why would such a conclusion be more effective than the present ending?

Discussing the Student Criticism

Whether you study the student compositions individually at home or in class as a group, you should be able to agree on answers to the following questions:

1. To what extent have the writers followed the composition pattern that you learned in Chapter 3? As you recall, that pattern consisted of an outside structure and an inside structure, with the outside structure "wrapping up" the main body of the paper.

2. To what extent have the writers been aware of their audience, their situation, and their purpose?

3. Some beginning critics tell either so little about the work that the comments are meaningless or so much that the review practically repeats the whole story or poem. How effective have the student reviews been in this respect?

4. Have the writers made generalizations, interpretations, or evaluations without supporting them? How have they supported such statements? Some students write concretely about their own experiences but become very abstract when writing about literature. To what degree are the reviews concrete or abstract? What contributes to this quality?

5. Criticism has many different purposes, depending upon the individual writer's approach. It may explain a work; interpret the meaning; place the work in relation to a particular school of ideas, form, or historical development; analyze the artistic techniques used; relate to other works; connect with other works; or evaluate and judge the work. A single criticism rarely includes all these functions. Which of these functions does each of the student compositions perform?

6. Look back at the five questions in the checklist for literary criticism on page 349. How well do the students deal with each question in their reviews?

Examining the Critical Questions

The five questions listed on page 349 can provide a convenient framework for organizing a review. As you have seen in the reviews you have read so far, not all critics use the questions in the same order or give them the same emphasis. Before you can use these questions effectively in your own writing of reviews or criticism, you must become more familiar with the possible implications and development of each.

The First Critical Question: How Do I Feel About the Work?

You probably won't begin your review by answering this question, although that is one possibility for an opening. It is a good idea, however, to begin your analysis of your subject by thinking carefully about your personal reaction to it.

Ask yourself the following questions: Did I like it? Did I not like it? How did I respond to it? Did it make any connections with my past experience? Does it suggest to me any application in my own life? Does it remind me of any other idea or presentation?

Since there is no "right" or "wrong" answer to the question, "How Do I Feel about the Work?" you should certainly be honest with yourself and refuse to deny your own impressions in order to follow those of either another student or of a professional critic. Later, after you are sure of your own reactions, you may want to check them against those of others, but unless you can clearly see a reason to change, trust yourself.

Activity 14A

Determining Your Response

Read thoughtfully each of the poems that follow. When you have finished each, jot down your initial response to the work. (Do not be afraid to say you didn't like one or more.) Then reread each one and note your answers to these questions:

How did the poem make you feel (happy, sad, amused, depressed, nervous, etc.)?

How, if at all, did the poem relate to your own life—to past experiences or to present or future situations?

Did the poem remind you of another idea, emotion, or situation? If possible, compare your responses with those of several other students to see how varied and personal each person's response was.

I

The golf links lie so near the mill
That almost every day
The laboring children can look out
And see the men at play.[8]

—Sarah N. Cleghorn

II

SYMPATHY

I know what the caged bird feels, alas!
When the sun is bright on the upland slopes;
When the wind stirs soft through the springing grass
And the river flows like a stream of glass;
When the first bird sings and the first bud opes,
And the faint perfume from its chalice steals—
I know what the caged bird feels!

I know why he beats his wing!
Till its blood is red on the cruel bars;
For he must fly back to his perch and cling
When he fain would be on the bough a-swing;
And a pain still throbs in the old, old scars
And they pulse again with a keener sting—
I know why he beats his wing!

I know why the caged bird sings, ah me,
When his wing is bruised and his bosom sore,
When he beats his bars and would be free;
It is not a carol of joy or glee,
But a prayer that he sends from his heart's deep core,
But a plea, that upward to Heaven he flings—
I know why the caged bird sings![9]

—Paul Laurence Dunbar

III

WARREN PRYOR

When every pencil meant a sacrifice
his parents boarded him at school in town,
slaving to free him from the stony fields,
the meagre acreage that bore them down.

They blushed with pride when, at his graduation,
they watched him picking up the slender scroll,
his passport from the years of brutal toil
and lonely patience in a barren hole.

When he went in the Bank their cups ran over.
They marvelled how he wore a milk-white shirt
work days and jeans on Sundays. He was saved
from their thistle-strewn farm and its red dirt.

And he said nothing. Hard and serious
like a young bear inside his teller's cage,
his axe-hewn hands upon the paper bills
aching with empty strength and throttled rage.[10]

—Alden Nowlan

IV

EX-BASKETBALL PLAYER

Pearl Avenue runs past the high school lot,
Bends with the trolley tracks, and stops, cut off
Before it has a chance to go two blocks,
At Colonel McComsky Plaza. Berth's Garage
Is on the corner facing west, and there,
Most days, you'll find Flick Webb, who helps Berth out.

Flick stands tall among the idiot pumps—
Five on a side, the old bubble-head style,
Their rubber elbows hanging loose and low.
One's nostrils are two S's, and his eyes
An E and O. And one is squat, without
A head at all—more of a football type.
Once, Flick played for the high school team, the Wizards.
He was good; in fact, the best. In '46,
He bucketed three hundred ninety points,
A county record still. The ball loved Flick.
I saw him rack up thirty-eight or forty
In one home game. His hands were like wild birds.

He never learned a trade; he just sells gas,
Checks oil, and changes flats. Once in a while,
As a gag, he dribbles an inner tube,
But most of us remember anyway.
His hands are fine and nervous on the lug wrench.
It makes no difference to the lug wrench, though.

Off work, he hangs around Mae's Luncheonette,
Grease-grey and kind of coiled, he plays pinball,
Sips lemon cokes, and smokes those thin cigars;
Flick seldom speaks to Mae, just sits and nods
Beyond her face towards the bright applauding tiers
Of Necco Wafers, Nibs, and Juju Beads.[11]

—John Updike

The Second Critical Question: What Do I Think The Work Means?

Answering the question, "What does the work say?" only partially affords an understanding of what a piece of writing *means*. Often what it seems to be saying is not what it really means. For example, in *A Modest Proposal*, written in the eighteenth century, Jonathan Swift advocated that Irish children be fattened and sold for food. Swift didn't really propose that Irish children be eaten; he wanted to say to the English, "You are so brutal and callous to the poverty-stricken Irish that you might as well be eating their children!" In 1932, Aldous Huxley described in *Brave New World* a frighteningly amoral, scientific, controlled society of the future. Huxley was not in favour of the society he described: he wanted to show that if the world continued in the direction in which it was then moving, such a society might result.

When authors intend to convey the opposite of what the words seem to be saying, they are using the literary device called *irony*. Irony, if effectively written, can be very powerful, but it requires that readers recognize the author's intention. If they are not aware of what is going on, readers may think the writer is saying the very opposite of what he or she actually means. In all writing, not only in ironic writing, the reader must be alert to subtle meanings and nuances. Indeed, recognizing and understanding subtle shades of meaning give skillful readers the greatest pleasure.

Tentative interpretations.   Because critics cannot read an author's mind and discover exactly what the author intended, they can only read the work very carefully and then say, "I believe that what the author means is. ..." Note that critics do not say, "The author means. ..." They can only report what the work seems to mean.

Themes in literature.   When critics present a view of what a work of art seems to mean, they are presenting the theme of the work. A theme in literature is the main idea, the interpretation of life, or the truth about human experience that a writer expresses. Everything in a literary work should contribute to the theme. The theme may consist of either a specific idea, which can be phrased in words, or a "general area of exploration," which may be inseparable from the total work of art. (In other words, sometimes you can legitimately say, "I can't put the idea into words.") Only with long experience in reading literature do you acquire the ability to recognize the theme easily; therefore, your initial efforts may be somewhat frustrating. Remember that even highly trained literary scholars may be baffled by a work or may disagree on its meaning. Finally, remember that a work is often richer because it may have many meanings or interpretations.

Interestingly enough, sometimes a work may have more meanings than the author consciously intended. What people derive from a work depends partly on the background they bring to it. Moreover, the same person may find more meaning in a work by reading it again later in life.

Four types of "meaning."   Many works of poetry and prose are difficult in language, in ideas, and in style. Such works, however, are frequently rewarding because they yield greater insight and deeper satisfaction than do works that are easier to grasp.

The meaning of poetry can be especially elusive. Since poetry tends to compress a great deal within a comparatively small space, it often requires rereading and concentration before all of its emotion and its ideas come through to the reader. The meter and the rhyme of much poetry give it a special quality that appeals to the reader but sometimes make the inner meaning more difficult to find.

This special difficulty of poetry was investigated some years ago by Professor I. A. Richards, a literary critic, who found that many of his students disliked poetry and claimed they could not understand it. To discover the reasons for their difficulty, he distributed copies of various poems and asked students to write down the meaning of each poem. He then carefully analyzed the responses and presented his findings in the book *Practical Criticism*. Among other things, he stressed two important factors:

1. Many people fail to understand poetry because they concentrate on *one* kind of meaning in a poem, rather than on the *total meaning*.
2. Before people can understand and appreciate the total meaning of a poem, they must understand its *paraphrasable content*. That is, they must be able to put into their own words the physical event described in the poem.

But a prose statement of a poem is not the poem. (Some critics object to the making of prose paraphrases; but others, like Richards, see the prose paraphrase as simply a first step in getting closer to the poem's total meaning.) Richards says that a poem has at least four different kinds of meaning, and only when readers can recognize all four can they begin to understand and appreciate the poem.

Many modern critics extend Richards' ideas to prose. Both prose and poetry can have four different kinds of meaning.

First meaning. Richards' first meaning is the physical event in the poem—its *paraphrasable content*. Although Robert Frost once defined poetry as "that which gets lost in translation," Richards said that the paraphrasable content leads to an understanding of the other meanings of the work. In other words, it is the *who, what, when, where, why,* and *how.*

Second meaning. The second meaning is the *feeling* of the work—its appeal to the senses, rather than to the intelligence and understanding. Through its language, its style, its imagery, it stimulates an emotional reaction in the reader.

Third meaning. The third meaning is the *tone*—the attitudes shown by the writer toward the material, and the audience as expressed in choice of words, phrasing, and selection of details. It is not enough, says Richards, to understand the "sense" of the poem and to experience its feeling; one must also understand the tone, and the spirit in which the situation is described. Tone will vary according to the effect the writer wishes to produce.

Fourth meaning. Finally, Richards emphasizes *intention*. This is closely related to tone. The subject of the poem (first meaning) is expressed sensually (second meaning) with a certain tone (third meaning) in order to achieve a certain end or intention (fourth meaning). One must always be subjective in discussing intention. A poem or a piece of prose will not have the same intention for each reader.

Most poems attempt to create for the reader an experience that selects certain vivid details from life and intensifies them through rhythm, imagery, and other poetic devices. In this way, the poet increases the readers' awareness by giving them a more vivid glimpse of life than they could ever experience outside of art.

What One Poem "Means"

To see how the four meanings of a poem relate to one another, read the following poem by John Crowe Ransom and discuss one reader's interpretation of the meanings.

V

PIAZZA PIECE

—I am a gentleman in a dust coat trying
To make you hear. Your ears are soft and small
And listen to an old man not at all,
They want the young men's whispering and sighing.
But see the roses on your trellis dying
And hear the spectral singing of the moon;
For I must have my lovely lady soon,
I am a gentleman in a dust coat trying.

—I am a lady young in beauty waiting
Until my truelove comes, and then we kiss.
But what gray man among the vines is this
Whose words are dry and faint as in a dream?
Back from my trellis, sir, before I scream!
I am a lady young in beauty waiting.[12]

—John Crowe Ransom

First meaning: Paraphrasable content.   The speaker in the poem is an old man, or perhaps Death himself. He is struck by the beauty of a young lady seated alone before a trellis of roses on a piazza. He tells her to enjoy life, to live it to the fullest before she gets too old. The line "For I must have my lovely lady soon," suggests—if he is simply an older man—that he would like to court her. If he is Death personified, he has come to warn her that she has not long to live, for "... the roses on your trellis ... [are] dying...."

In either case, the lady is impatient and will not listen. She wants (desires) "the young men's whispering and sighing." She considers the speaker a threat and wants him gone.

Second meaning: Feeling.   The poem is rich in feeling and emotion. Readers can feel the desire of an old man to talk to the young beauty and perhaps to enjoy her beauty even while encouraging her to live her life fully. Readers can also feel the radiance and confidence and impatience of the young lady as she waits for her truelove. They can even sympathize with her uneasiness as the old gentleman approaches her. Underlying the whole poem are feelings of sadness and regret. The man has something the lady should hear; she refuses to listen. She waits confidently for her truelove; he will not arrive in time. The roses are dying, and she refuses to see that so is she.

Notice the images in the poem. Dust coats were worn by fashionable gentlemen driving open touring cars, or convertibles. Here, the term suggests both a rich, antique fashion and, in addition, the fact that all human beings return to dust. The lady's soft, small ears suggest beauty and refinement. The dying roses and the spectral (ghostlike) singing of the moon make the reader feel the melancholy of a summer night.

Third meaning: Tone.   The events described in the poem might really have happened to the poet, but whether or not they are real or fictional, he has a definite attitude toward them. He communicates a tender appreciation of the lady and a sad regret that she will not listen. For the speaker—probably not the poet himself—there is the attitude of quiet acceptance of the inevitable. If she will not listen, it does not matter. The course of the world continues, and the speaker will not be appreciably affected by her actions. The attitude communicated by the entire poem is likewise a quiet acceptance. It is as though the poet were saying, "This is the way life has always been. We are young, beautiful, impatient for a short time. It is understandable that we do not live to the fullest because we look to the future and ignore the wisdom of those who have lived longer. It does not matter much that the end of our dreams—through death—comes all too soon."

Fourth meaning: Intention.   We can never be sure that we have truly received the author's intended comment about life. But the finished poem seems to develop a life of its own and an intention of its own—regardless of what the poet intended. This poem, then, seems to say that one should live now, savouring each moment lest death arrive unexpectedly. At the same time as the speaker gives this advice, the poet seems to be shaking his head a bit sadly about the brevity and shallowness—the blindness—of human life.

Activity 14B

Finding Paraphrasable Content

1. The following brief selections are relatively easy to understand. Read each carefully and answer the following questions:
   a. What is the physical situation described?
   b. Who is speaking? (Be careful. The poet is not usually the speaker, but creates a voice or poetic persona.)
   c. What is happening?
   d. Where is the event taking place?
   e. What is the speaker's relationship to the event?

I

WE REAL COOL

THE POOL PLAYERS.
SEVEN AT THE GOLDEN SHOVEL.

We real cool. We
Left school. We

Lurk late. We
Strike straight. We

Sing sin. We
Thin gin. We

Jazz June. We
Die soon.[13]

—Gwendolyn Brooks

Who are the speakers in this poem? How can you tell?

Many dialects omit linking verbs. What would the title be if the linking verb were included?

How do you know that the poet is not the person speaking?

What is her attitude toward the speakers? Does the fact that she is Black make any difference in her attitude? Should it?

What final sounds are left off words in the third stanza?

What is the effect of the final sentence?

II

30 BELOW

In alberta the antelope
are dying on the C.P.R. tracks
at 30 below zero

Their frozen bodies
lie beside the tracks,
feet pointing
at the passenger train going by.

Who is the speaker in this poem? What is the speaker concerned about?

How do you picture the physical setting of the poem?

This summer the hunters will walk
far north
looking for game.

Chief Charley Horse says
Manitou brought the ice
to punish white hunters
who leave their dead ducks and rabbits
by the side of the road.

But the animals are frozen
carcasses now by every road,
the hunters are warm in lodges
waiting for the big thaw.

They know Manitou
doesn't hold his breath
all winter.[14]

—George Bowering

How is the speaker's attitude towards
the "white hunters" conveyed through
his reference to the Indian Chief?
Why is this an effective technique?

What irony does the speaker wish to
point out here? How does this irony
reveal the speaker's relationship to the
event described?

III

MUSHROOMS

Overnight, very
Whitely, discreetly,
Very quietly

Our toes, our noses
Take hold on the loam,
Acquire the air.

Nobody sees us,
Stops us, betrays us;
The small grains make room.

Soft fists insist on
Heaving the needles,
The leafy bedding,

Even the paving.
Our hammers, our rams,
Earless and eyeless,

Perfectly voiceless,
Widen the crannies,
Shoulder through holes. We

Diet on water,
On crumbs of shadow,
Bland-mannered, asking

Little or nothing.
So many of us.
So many of us!

Who are the speakers in this poem?
How do you account for the fact that
you accept them as speakers?

Translate these "actions" or "events"
into what is really happening. Why
is the poetic form more interesting than
your paraphrase?

What "mushrooms" in people's minds,
insisting on pushing a way into consciousness? What is the figure of
speech in which you talk about one
thing, but are really commenting on
another? What is the figure of speech
in which a long narrative about one
subject really refers to parallel actions
on another subject?

We are shelves, we are
Tables, we are meek,
We are edible,

Nudgers and shovers
In spite of ourselves.
Our kind multiplies:

We shall by morning
Inherit the earth.
Our foot's in the door.[15]

—Sylvia Plath

What is the irony of the meekness of the mushrooms? How does it parallel the meekness of another subject?

IV

"Is my team ploughing
      That I was used to drive
And hear the harness jingle
      When I was man alive?"

Ay, the horses trample
      The harness jingles now;
No change though you lie under
      The land you used to plough.

"Is football playing
      Along the river shore,
With lads to chase the leather,
      Now I stand up no more?"

Ay, the ball is flying,
      The lads play heart and soul;
The goal stands up, the keeper
      Stands up to keep the goal.

"Is my girl happy
      That I thought hard to leave,
And has she tired of weeping
      As she lies down at eve?"

Ay, she lies down lightly.
      She lies not down to weep
Your girl is well contented
      Be still, my lad, and sleep.

"Is my friend hearty;
      Now I am thin and pine,
And has he found to sleep in
      A better bed than mine?"

Yes, lad, I lie easy
      I lie as lads would choose;
I cheer a dead man's sweetheart.
      Never ask me whose.

—A. E. Housman

Who is speaking in this first stanza? What do you know about him or her? What details give you information about the sex, work, and present condition of the speaker?

Who is speaking in the second stanza? Is it the same as the person speaking in the first stanza? How do you know?

Who is speaking in the third stanza? What more does this stanza add to your knowledge of the speaker? What is the significance of the implied past tense of the action?

By this point you have the basic pattern of the poem. What is it?

Are the events, content, and questions arranged in ascending or descending order of importance? Why?

What is the double meaning of the words "thin" and "pine?"

What is the irony in the final stanza?

2. When you have completed the first part of Activity 14B, write a short paragraph explaining the first level of meaning. You may have to mention feeling, tone, and intention, but try to concentrate on paraphrasable content. If possible, try to connect the writer's experience with some experience of your own. Bring your paragraphs to class for group consideration and discussion.

3. After you have written your paragraphs and discussed them in class, try to come to some conclusions about the following questions:

   a. Is it necessary to understand the meaning of every word in a work in order to understand the work? Should one attempt to guess at word meanings from context and only afterwards use a dictionary?

   b. How do writers appeal to your senses of sight, sound, touch, taste, and smell? What words, allusions, or comparisons in the foregoing selections make you "think" a certain sound or smell?

Activity 14C

Understanding Feeling in Literature

You may have understood a work on the first level of meaning, the paraphrasable content, but you must still react to the underlying emotion and feeling that the writer has evoked. The following poems are easy to understand on the first level of meaning, but much depends upon the reader's understanding of the emotional aspect. After reading the poems, choose two and write brief papers in which you 1. explain the paraphrasable content (the first level of meaning) and 2. explain the feeling (the second level of meaning) in each poem. Bring your papers to class for discussion and class evaluation.

I

PORTRAIT BY A NEIGHBOUR

Before she has her floor swept
    Or her dishes done,
Any day you'll find her
    A-sunning in the sun!

It's long after midnight
    Her key's in the lock,
And you never see her chimney smoke
    Till past ten o'clock!

She digs in her garden
    With a shovel and a spoon,
She weeds her lazy lettuce
    By the light of the moon.

Who is the speaker in this poem? When do you suppose this poem was written, or what time period was it written about? Do you know anyone like the woman in the poem?

What image do you have of both the neighbour and the woman being described?

She walks up the walk
    Like a woman in a dream,
She forgets she borrowed butter
    And pays you back cream!

Her lawn looks like a meadow,
    And if she mows the place
She leaves the clover standing
    And the Queen Anne's lace![16]

—Edna St. Vincent Millay

What tells you the speaker doesn't quite understand the neighbour? How are the speaker's life and schedule different from the neighbour's?

What do the details of the last two lines tell you about the neighbour? How does the speaker feel about the neighbour's actions? How do you feel about them? How do you think the poet wants you to feel?

II

THE UNKNOWN CITIZEN
(To JS/07/M/378 This Marble Monument
Is Erected by the State)

He was found by the Bureau of Statistics to be
One against whom there was no official complaint,
And all the reports on his conduct agree
That, in the modern sense of an old-fashioned word,
    he was a saint,
For in everything he did he served the Greater
    Community.
Except for the War till the day he retired
He worked in a factory and never got fired
But satisfied his employers, Fudge Motors Inc.
Yet he wasn't a scab or odd in his views,
For his Union reports that he paid his dues,
(Our report on his Union shows it was sound)
And our Social Psychology workers found
That he was popular with his mates and liked a drink.
The Press are convinced that he bought a paper every
    day
And that his reactions to advertisements were normal
    in every way.
Policies taken out in his name prove that he was fully
    insured,
And his Health-card shows he was once in hospital but
    left it cured.
Both Producers Research and High-Grade Living
    declare
He was fully sensible to the advantages of the
    Installment Plan
And had everything necessary to the Modern Man,
A phonograph, a radio, a car and a frigidaire.
Our researchers into Public Opinion are content
That he held the proper opinions for the time of year;
When there was peace, he was for peace, when there
    was war, he went.
He was married and added five children to the
    population,

What questions do you have about *why* a nation would build a monument "To an Unknown Citizen"?

The poem seems to describe the "ideal" person of this nation. What details of his life do you object to? What things that were a part of his life would you not want as part of yours?

How do you react to the words "saint," "Fudge Motors," "scab," "Greater Community?"

What seem to be the values of the nation? Are they your values? Are they the values the poet holds?

Why is there so much emphasis on "belonging"—on fitting in smoothly with the Greater Community, the job, the Union?

The words and sentences in this poem are very simple and easy to understand. What background must you bring to the poem to understand its feeling?

Which our Eugenist says was the right number for a
    parent of his generation.
And our teachers report that he never interfered with
    their education.
Was he free? Was he happy? The question is absurd:
Had anything been wrong, we should certainly have
    heard.[17]

—W. H. Auden

III

BASE DETAILS

If I were fierce and bald and short of breath,
    I'd live with scarlet Majors at the Base,
And speed glum heroes up the line to death.
    You'd see me with my puffy petulant face,
Guzzling and gulping in the best hotel,
    Reading the Roll of Honor. "Poor young chap,"
I'd say—"I used to know his father well.
    Yes, we've lost heavily in this last scrap."
And when the war is done and youth stone dead,
I'd toddle safely home and die—in bed.[18]

—Siegfried Sassoon

"Base" can have two meanings here: a military base and "low or disgraceful."

How does the poet make you feel about officers who stay far behind the lines?

What is the poet's attitude toward the situation he describes?

IV

ARCTIC RHODODENDRONS

They are small purple surprises
in the river's white racket
and after you've seen them
a number of times
in water-places
where their silence seems
related to river-thunder
you think of them as 'noisy flowers'
Years ago
it may have been
that lovers came this way
stopped in the outdoor hotel
to watch the water floorshow
and lying prone together
where the purged green
boils to a white heart
and the shore trembles
like a stone song
flowers were their conversation
and love the sound of a colour
that lasts two weeks in August
and then dies

except for the three or four
I pressed in a letter
and sent whispering to you.[19]

Pangnirtung

—Al Purdy

Understanding Tone in Literature

After you have written your papers for Activity 14C and discussed them in class, write a brief paper discussing each of the following questions.

1. Every *image*, or picture, a poet puts into a poem should "work," not only in contributing to the meaning of the poem, but also in contributing to the emotion communicated. How does each of these images contribute to the feeling of the poem?

   "Portrait by a Neighbour"—she weeds her lazy lettuce, the light of the moon, like a woman in a dream, she leaves the clover standing and the Queen Anne's lace.

   "The Unknown Citizen"—he paid his dues, he was popular with his mates, his reactions to advertisements were normal in every way, he had everything necessary to the Modern Man, he held the proper opinions for the time of year.

   "Base Details"—fierce and bald and short of breath, glum heroes, guzzling and gulping in the best hotel, youth stone dead, toddle safely home, die—in bed.

   "Arctic Rhododendrons"—the description of the flowers as "small purple surprises," and as "noisy flowers."

2. Each of the preceding poems involves a change of mood, emotion, or attitude. Discuss the change in each and try to determine how the poet brings about the change.

Understanding Intention in Literature

The following selections mean more than they seem to mean. Read them carefully and try to find a meaning in addition to the surface story. Then write a short paper interpreting one of the selections and describing the "clues" that led you to your interpretation of its intention. After you finish, work in a group with students who wrote on the same passage, and criticize one another's interpretations.

I

SOUTHBOUND ON THE FREEWAY

A tourist came in from Orbitville,
parked in the air, and said:

The creatures of this star
are made of metal and glass.

Through the transparent parts
you can see their guts.

Their feet are round and roll
on diagrams—or long

measuring tapes—dark
with white lines.

They have four eyes.
The two in the back are red.

Sometimes you can see a five-eyed
one, with a red eye turning

on the top of his head.
He must be special—

the others respect him,
and go slow,

when he passes, winding
among them from behind.

They all hiss as they glide,
like inches, down the marked

tapes. Those soft shapes,
shadowy inside

the hard bodies—are they
their guts or their brains?[20]

—May Swenson

II

In one of the most famous passages in philosophy, Plato records Socrates' "Allegory of the Cave." Chapter XXV of *The Republic* is concerned with the nature of our perception of the world around us. The following version is considerably abridged and simplified.

Imagine a group of people living in a great cave where no daylight reaches them. Here they have been chained from childhood to face the wall. They cannot even turn their heads to look directly at a fire that is glowing behind them. Between their backs and the fire, puppeteers crouch and manipulate puppets. When the dolls are held up their shadows are cast by the fire upon the wall which the prisoners are facing.

Having never seen anything else but the shadows on the wall, the prisoners believe that the shadows are real. They know nothing of the puppets that cast the shadows. If the puppeteers speak, the prisoners think that the echo coming from the wall is the real sound. Imagine what it would be like if the prisoners, after looking at shadows all their lives, were forced to stand up, turn around, and walk toward the fire. They would probably be so dazzled that they would not even be able to distinguish the puppets whose shadows they had always watched. If they finally did see them, they might think them less real than the shadows they were used to seeing. They would turn from the light and long to return to the shadows.

Suppose someone were to drag some of the prisoners out of the cave into the sunlight. They would be so completely blinded that they would suffer pain and frustration at not being able to see their accustomed shadows.

And suppose, after long adjustment, they finally accepted the reality of the puppets and the light of the sun. What would the other prisoners think if one returned to the cave and tried to tell them that their reality consisted only of shadows?

The Third Critical Question: How Did the Writer Communicate Meaning?

You have now examined a number of literary works in the light of the first two critical questions. You have asked:

How do I feel about the work?
What do I think the work means?

The third major consideration in criticizing a literary work refers to the techniques employed by writers to achieve the desired response. These techniques include the use of expressive words, the flow of sentences, rhythm, emotion, and appeals to the senses. All are common to both prose and poetry. In poetry, however, the ideas and the emotion are frequently compressed, the pattern is more defined, the rhythm is developed in a special, noticeable meter, and the sensuous appeal is frequently heightened by rhyme and poetic imagery. Prose, on the other hand, has its own unique qualities, such as variety in sentence and paragraph length, in-depth analysis of character, exciting or suspenseful action, and extended description. Sometimes a work has the qualities of both genres and might fit into either category. A literary composition of this type may be called a prose poem or poetic prose.

Communicating the theme of a work.   Every piece of prose or poetry has a theme—the core of its thought. Through this theme writers convey their reactions to the world around them, their view of humanity, or their insights into the meaning of what they have experienced.

The methods writers use to convey their themes vary, of course, with their personality, training, experience, and talents. Following is a list of

Criticism should praise as well as instruct. This page from a Gutenberg Bible, printed about 1453, gives a commentary on the Proverbs of Solomon.

some methods authors have used to communicate themes. Read the list carefully and try to recall short stories, novels, narrative poems, and films that use these techniques.

1. A situation in which a limited number of characters in a simplified setting encounter problems that parallel those in the world. (In *Lord of the Flies,* William Golding shows how a band of British boys marooned on an island turn a paradise into a land of horror. He suggests that this parallels what adults have done to the world.)

2. A situation exaggerated until it becomes ridiculous. (In *Catch-22,* Joseph Heller exaggerates the absurdities of war.)

3. One character created to be the author's spokesman. (In *Our Town*, the Stage Manager presents many of Wilder's ideas.)

4. A description of what will happen if current trends continue. (In *1984,* George Orwell suggests what the world of the future may be like if today's trends continue.)

5. The reader identifies with one of the main characters and thus absorbs that character's ideas. (Hagar Shipley in Margaret Laurence's *The Stone Angel* is an engaging fictional character.)

6. Newspaper articles, letters, telegrams, diaries, or even the author's own comments are used to reveal a position or character. (In *As for Me and My House*, Sinclair Ross uses a diary or journal pattern throughout.)

7. Different types of people representing different positions are caricatured. (In his satirical novel *The Incomparable Atuk*, Mordecai Richler caricatures opportunist Canadian businessmen who would even sell their country for personal profit.)

8. Basic ideas or moral principles are presented through a story (called allegory) in which people or things have a hidden or symbolic meaning. (In *Animal Farm*, George Orwell comments on totalitarianism—such as Russian communism—by describing a farm on which the animals revolt and take command.)

9. A significant event, symbol, or scene is repeated at various points in the story. (In Malcolm Lowry's *Under the Volcano*, references to Cabbalistic mystic lore repeatedly bring together plot and theme.)

(Activity 14F)

Working with Theme Techniques

List and discuss in class ten themes about which an author might wish to write. Then select one theme and write a paragraph describing how you would try to convey it in a story. Use not less than three techniques, including, if you wish, techniques not listed.

Other students have suggested the following themes for this activity:

1. The sins of the father are visited on the children.
2. Conflict between generations is inevitable, but it can be advantageous.
3. The bad sport hurts only himself.
4. Every person is a bundle of contradictions.
5. Responsibility brings maturity.

The following paragraph is an example of how a theme might be developed in a story.

If I were attempting to explore the theme that "Responsibility brings maturity," I would set up a microcosm in which various people act in different ways when given a responsibility. I might, for example, borrow the Biblical parable of the rich man who gave each of his servants some talents and charged them to use them well in his absence. With this as the framework of the story, I could use caricature in making clear my dislike of the actions of certain of my characters. In the final scene, I might have the rich man return and deliver a lecture on responsibility. His words would be my words, and they would drive home my message.

Activity 14G

Analyzing Techniques for Communicating

In criticizing a piece of literature, a reader should try to be sensitive to the various technical aspects of that work—the tools with which the writer achieves his or her purpose. Unless readers are aware of and appreciate these techniques, they cannot fully understand or evaluate the work.

Reread the selections in Activities 14C and 14E and write a brief paper (several paragraphs) analyzing the techniques employed in one of these selections. Bring your paper to class and be prepared to take part in a discussion on the various methods by which the writers communicate ideas and emotions.

Activity 14H

Understanding Special Effects

One requirement of good style is that it achieve an intended end simply and economically. Each of the following short passages uses a noticeable technique to achieve some kind of special effect. Examine the technique defined in the question following each passage and write a brief paragraph explaining what the writer may have been attempting to do by using that particular technique.

I

Jack be nimble.
Jack be quick.
Jack jump over
The candlestick.

1. Each of the first two short lines is a complete sentence and ends with a period. Why may the unknown writer have chosen to have the third line continue right into the fourth with no pause?

II

UPON A CHILD

Here a pretty baby lies
Lulled asleep with lullabies.
Tread softly that you do not stir
The easy earth that covers her.

—Robert Herrick

2. Why does the poem not reveal until the last line that the child is dead?

III

FROM ESSAY ON CRITICISM

True ease in writing comes from art, not chance,
As those move easiest who have learned to dance.
'Tis not enough no harshness gives offence,
The sound must seem as Echo to the sense:
Soft is the strain when Zephyr* gently blows,
And the smooth stream in smoother numbers flows;
But when loud surges lash the sounding shore,
The hoarse, rough verse should like the torrent roar:
When Ajax** strives some rock's vast weight to throw,
The line too labours, and the words move slow;
Not so, when swift Camilla† scours the plain,
Flies o'er th' unbending corn, and skims along the main.

—Alexander Pope

*the west wind
**the legendary Greek hero famous for his strength
† legendary woman warrior

3. In four lines of this extract, Alexander Pope demonstrates what he means by making the sound "an Echo to the sense." Choose any two of these lines and explain how Pope matches the sound of the line to the meaning it expresses.

IV

SONNET 130

My mistress' eyes are nothing like the sun;
Coral is far more red than her lips' red;
If snow be white, why then her breasts are dun;
If hairs be wires, black wires grow on her head.
I have seen roses damask'd, red and white,
But no such roses see I in her cheeks;
And in some perfumes is there more delight
Than in the breath that from my mistress reeks.

> I love to hear her speak, yet well I know
> That music hath a far more pleasing sound;
> I grant I never saw a goddess go;
> My mistress, when she walks, treads on the ground:
>   And yet, by heaven, I think my love as rare
>   As any she belied with false compare.
>
> —William Shakespeare

4. Although most poets of his time compared their beloveds' eyes with the sun, their lips with coral, their breasts with snow, their cheeks with roses, their breath with perfume, their voices with music, and their walk with the floating of goddesses, Shakespeare specifically says that these comparisons would be false if applied to his beloved. Why may he be doing so?

The Fourth Critical Question: How Effective Is the Work?

Only by painstaking inquiry into the first three critical questions can you arrive at a balanced and sound critical evaluation of a literary work. Certainly you must recognize the elements of style and understand why the various artistic devices are used before you can judge how successful and effective the work is.

Such judgments are largely subjective; that is, they reflect the reader's personal response to the work of art. But opinions and emotional reactions are not valuable unless they are based on features within the work itself. You must examine the piece of prose or poetry carefully, note what effect it has had on you as an individual, and demonstrate how that effect is produced. Then you can arrive at an appraisal of the effectiveness of the work, frequently by comparing it with other works with which you are familiar.

Supporting opinions in criticism.   Some students do not realize that when they write about literature they must support any generalizations they make. General statements like "This writer's work is very difficult to understand" or "That writer captures the flavour of life in Montréal" may or may not be true. If such assertions are made, the reader wants to know what evidence the writer has as the basis for these statements. In creative writing, a writer deals primarily in concretes—descriptions and accounts of events from which the reader draws generalizations. In critical writing, as in most other expository writing, the writer makes generalizations which require support. Critics supply the strongest support possible when they quote from the work itself.

Activity 14 I

Supporting Generalizations in a Critical Review

Following are some generalizations that might appear in a critical review. Read them carefully. Be prepared to discuss in class the kinds of support a reader would expect for each statement.

Then read again a piece of prose or poetry your class has read recently. Review it and then write five generalizations similar to those listed below. List under each generalization some specific quotations or examples which would help demonstrate or prove your assertion.

1. Margaret Atwood's female characters often experience marked difficulties in their relationships with men.
2. Earle Birney's novel *Turvey* chronicles the misadventures of a young army private during World War II.
3. The poetry of E. J. Pratt pictures man's relationship to the impersonal forces of nature.
4. The reader often feels that a descriptive passage is not quite finished.
5. Shelley often wrote very bad poems.
6. Jack Hodgins' newest novel reflects some of the same thematic concerns that were central to his previous works.

The Final Critical Question: Is the Message or Meaning Worthwhile?

You have examined the work of art to determine what it says, what it really means, what literary techniques were used, and how effective the work is. But you still do not have a complete analysis of that work. What remains is to determine whether that work has value, whether it was worth the writer's trouble to produce it.

Writers may be very skilled in their art. They may be adept at using writing devices that pique curiosity. They may be very ingenious in inventing situations or arousing emotions. But if their works have no genuine worth, if they are superficial or frivolous in conception, they might just as well never have been written. On the other hand, many literary works have been condemned for various reasons (moral judgments, use of language, story line, for example) but have survived because they had special qualities that made them worth reading and rereading.

Special qualities in literature. One of the most common misconceptions about literature is that only the story—the plot—is important. Everyone, of course, enjoys a good story, but perceptive critics read a work on many levels. For example, students today are reading the following books and finding, among others, the values indicated.

> Mordecai Richler, *The Apprenticeship of Duddy Kravitz*—literature as an exploration of growth towards maturity.
>
> Ray Bradbury, *Fahrenheit 451*—literature as a picture of human life, and social comment.
>
> Alvin Toffler, *Future Shock*—literature as social criticism, projection of the future, and invitation to involvement.
>
> Erich Maria Remarque, *All Quiet on the Western Front*—literature as social criticism, eyewitness history, and condemnation of war.
>
> Duncan Pryde, *Nunaga*—literature as an account of adjusting to completely different cultural values.
>
> Stanley Burke and Roy Peterson, *Frog Fables and Beaver Tales*—literature as political satire.

Literature can bring pleasure, expand knowledge, provide new insights, inspire positive action, and promote a more informed approach to life.

(*Activity 14J*)

Finding Values in Literature

Look up (or review in your mind) two books you have studied in school or read on your own this year. Then list the different values in each that have made it worthwhile. Be prepared to take part in a class discussion of your list. Be careful not to confine yourself to a consideration of the plot alone.

Tone in a Critical Review

Although some popular professional critics and reviewers have established their reputations by being opinionated, sarcastic, and even cruel, most critics feel that they best serve both the artist and the reader if they try to maintain a positive approach and an open, searching, encouraging tone. Their job, as they see it, is to help readers by revealing to them what the writer has been trying to do and by describing the techniques the writer has used. They also feel that they help writers by showing them where they have succeeded or failed.

Of course, the critic and reviewer approach any work of art from a personal point of view, but they try to remember that any single point of view is limited. They are inclined to qualify their judgments, to define the point of view from which they are speaking, and to indicate possible additional values for others. They rarely take an omniscient and authoritarian stand.

Examining Tone in a Review

Look up a number of periodicals noted for book reviews, play reviews, and film reviews, such as *Macleans*, *Canadian Theatre Review*, *Atlantic Monthly*, *Saturday Night*, *Harper's*, *Quill and Quire*, *Time*, and *Today Magazine*. From these, choose two reviews and read them carefully, noting particularly the *tone* the writer has used. Then prepare a two or three-minute talk for presentation to the class. After arousing class interest in your subject, follow this order:

1. Indicate the title and author of the work being reviewed and the author of the review, if it is signed, as well as the source. (Which is preferable, a signed or unsigned review? Why?)
2. Tell enough about the work (either from reading it or from information given in the review) to enable your audience to understand your later comments.
3. Discuss the general tone of the review—the reviewer's general opinion, the emphasis with which it is presented, and any qualifications that are made.
4. Discuss how the reviewer sets the tone of the review: word choice, comparisons, suggestions, judgments, irony, sarcasm.
5. Make a judgment as to how helpful the review would be to a reader as well as to the author of the work being reviewed.

Major Writing Assignment

A Criticism of Prose and Poetry

Reread the reviews in this chapter and note the organization of each. Select a short story or poem. Try to choose a selection you know well and feel strongly about. Prepare a critical paper based on the information you have learned in this chapter.

Remember that you will be trying to answer the critical questions listed on page 349. The organization of your paper will probably be as follows:

1. Introduction.
2. Enough description of the subject to enable the reader to understand your comments.
3. Statement of what you think the theme or purpose is. Give evidence to support your interpretation.
4. Some of the outstanding techniques the author uses (citing examples).
5. Your opinion of how successful the story or poem is.
6. Your opinion of its value.

If you choose your literary selection with care, writing a review should give you little difficulty. Remember from Chapter 13 that when a work is successful the reader and writer are joined through the sharing of an experience. Try to communicate your response to this experience honestly. Approach your review as an opportunity both to express your opinion on a work that is important to you and to learn a major writing skill.

Literature is not only a mirror; it is also a map, a geography of the mind.

—Margaret Atwood

Appendix

Style Sheet

A Style Sheet is a form or pattern which the members of a certain group or institution (school, university publishing house, office staff) work out and agree to follow whenever possible. It is entirely possible that your school has its own Style Sheet or that your group will prefer to establish one. If you do not have an accepted Style Sheet, this one will serve.

I. MANUSCRIPT FORM

A. Whenever possible, type your work. For typed papers, use standard business size white paper. Do not use "erasable" paper or onionskin. Always doublespace between lines. For handwritten papers, use standard, full-sized, wide-lined notebook paper.

B. Write or type on one side of the page only. Use wide margins: at least four centimetres on the left and bottom and three centimetres on the right.

C. Place your name, the course and period or section number, the name of your teacher, and the date of your paper in the upper right-hand corner of the first page.

Jo Ellen Scott
English 12, Period 2
Ms. Clark
81-11-14

D. Centre the title about five centimetres down from the top of the page. Leave three lines between the title and first line of the paper.

E. Do not use the term *English* as a title. Use a specific title instead, such as, *Inserting Transitions*. Do not use quotation marks around the title even though you use quotation marks when you refer to the title within a paragraph.

II. CAPITALIZATION

A. Capitalize the first word and all other important words in a title. Do not capitalize prepositions, conjunctions, articles, and unimportant words with fewer than five letters.

B. Capitalize the first word in a sentence.
Capitalize the first word of a quoted sentence following such introductory words as *he said, she replied, Jane wondered*, when the quoted sentence

immediately preceding the explanatory words is complete.

> Preceding quoted sentence is complete: *"Vacation is over,"* she said. *"School starts next Monday."*
> Preceding quoted sentence is incomplete: *"Vacation,"* she said, *"is over."*

C. Capitalize proper nouns and abbreviations of proper nouns.

Buildings: the Graybar Building, the Flatiron Building

Business Firms: Prentice-Hall Canada Inc., MacMillan Bloedel

Churches, religious groups, and their members: First Alliance Church; Mormons, Muslims, Hindus

Days, months, holidays, holy days: Monday, August, Canada Day, Thanksgiving, All Soul's Day, Yom Kippur

Historical documents, events, periods: the British North America Act, Hegira, the Renaissance, the Riel Rebellion

Institutions: Vancouver Vocational Institute, McMaster University

Organizations: Kiwanis Club, Boy Scouts of Canada

People: Paul Anka, Sir Wilfred Laurier, Laura Secord

Places: Alberta, Boston Bar, Gambia, South America

Planets, except when *earth* and *moon* are used with *the*: Mars, Saturn; the earth, the moon

Political Parties and their members: Labour Party, Labourite; New Democratic Party, New Democrat; Progressive Conservative Party

Races, languages: Chinese, Thai, French

Sacred figures, Bible, portions of holy books: Jehovah, Allah, Krishna; Koran, Pentateuch

Names of ships, planes, trains: S.S. Titanic, Concorde, Orient Express, Bluenose

Trade Names: Coca-Cola, Lifebuoy, Xerox, Cheerios

D. Capitalize adjectives formed from proper nouns, but not the words they modify unless they would be capitalized written alone: the French language, Iranian oil, Dutch colonial; *but* Japanese Empire, English Bible

E. Capitalize such words as avenue, building, school, park, river, and so on when used as a part of a name, but not when used alone: Toronto Dominion Bank, Fourth Street, Lee Secondary School, Kirkwood Hotel; *but* the bank, a hotel, our school

F. Capitalize personal titles showing office, profession, or rank when using them either before a person's name or as a substitute for a name:

Senator Davis	"Won't the senator reconsider?"
Mayor Rice	She is the mayor.
Sergeant Lewis	The sergeant spoke.
Doctor Higgins	The doctor is very competent.
"Send me in, Coach!"	The coach is fair.

The title of the nation's highest executive is always capitalized:

> In 1978, Edward Schreyer became the Governor General.

G. Capitalize words showing family relationships when they appear before a personal name or in place of one:

> Uncle Jasper and Aunt Faye live in Edmonton.
> I heard Mother coming down the steps.
> I like to visit my uncle and aunt in Edmonton when my mother takes me.

H. Capitalize such one-letter words as *I* and *O*, which would otherwise tend to disappear.

I. Do not capitalize the following types of words:

- adjectives which no longer remind the reader of the proper noun from which they come: parliamentary law, the china dishes, macadamized road
- school subjects (except for languages and specific, numbered courses): geometry, economics, psychology; *but* Geometry I, Economics 12, English, and French
- names of directions (except when they name sections of the country): north, south, east, west; *but* I live up North. *The* West is quite scenic.
- names of seasons (except when personified): The autumn is beautiful; *but* Winter walks in magnificence.

III. PUNCTUATION

A. Period.   In addition to some conventional uses (after number and in abbreviations), a period marks a pause at the end of a complete thought.

1. Use a period after declarative or imperative sentences and after mild exclamations.

> The sun is very bright today.
> Be careful of your tan.
> How nice the weather is.

2. Use a period after abbreviations and initials.
Inc.   Ltd.   Co.   B.C.   L.C. Smith
(Use few abbreviations in formal written work.)

3. Use a period between dollars and cents when a dollar sign is used and to indicate a decimal point between whole numbers and decimals.
$3.42 $9.98 $.14   3.1416   19.2%

4. Use three periods (these are called *ellipses*) to indicate you have left words out of a quotation. Use a fourth period to indicate the end of your sentence.

> I remembered, "Yea, though I walk in the valley . . . I shall fear no evil."
> He urged us, "Please vote in the coming election. . . ."

5. Place periods within quotation marks when the two come together. Place periods within parentheses when a complete sentence surrounded by parentheses appears between complete sentences. Do

not use periods when such a sentence appears in the middle of another sentence.

> He ate syrup on his roast beef. (He was a little strange.) I soon got used to him.
> He ate syrup (I can hardly believe it) on his roast beef.

B. Exclamation Mark. Use an exclamation mark after any word, phrase, or sentence to show strong emphasis or emotion.

> Help!
> What a day!
> She became a star!

C. Question Mark. A question mark indicates an inquiry, uncertainty, or lack of information.

1. Use a question mark to indicate requests for information.

> Where are they going?
> Were they working this morning?

2. Use a question mark after each element in a series of interrogative words for special emphasis.

> What did the Aldermen say? and the city manager? and the mayor?

3. Use a question mark, usually in parentheses, to indicate doubt or inexactness.

> Toussaint L'Ouverture (1743?–1803) led a slave revolt and liberated Haiti.
> Samuel de Champlain, the founder of Québec, was born in 1570 (?).

4. When using a question mark with other marks follow these general procedures:

   - If the question mark pertains to the entire sentence, place it outside the other marks.

   > Quotation marks: Did she repeat the words, "I do solemnly swear"?
   > Parentheses: How often have you seen Gordon Lightfoot (I mean in person)?

   - If the question mark pertains only to the enclosed part of the sentence, place it inside the other marks.

   > Quotation marks: Dad asked patiently, "Are we finally ready?"
   > Parentheses: I've seen five whales (can you believe it?) in less than an hour.

D. Comma. Use a comma both in conventional uses and where a pause is needed to prevent confusion, uncertainty, or unintended humor.

1. Use a comma before, but not after, the coordinating conjunction (*and, but, for, or, nor, so, yet*) joining independent clauses, unless the clauses are quite short or easily distinguishable.

> We climbed Whistler Mountain, but the wind and weather kept us from enjoying the view.
> I studied hard but she got the *A*.
> Perseus had to save Andromeda, or the monster would kill her. (How might this be read without the comma?)

2. Use a comma to set off interrupting elements. (*I hope, I suppose, do you think, don't they, of course, after all*) unless they are closely connected with the meaning of the sentence. Use a comma to set off introductory words, such as *yes, no, well, oh,* and tag questions such as *isn't it, don't we, aren't they*.

> The cost, of course, is passed on to the consumer.
> Yes, what you see is what you get.
> That's the tragedy, isn't it.
> I suppose you know what you want. (no comma)

Treat conjunctive adverbs, such as *nevertheless, consequently, therefore,* and *however,* as interrupters.

> The investigation, nevertheless, had its humourous sides.

3. Use a comma to set off words, phrases, or clauses in a series. When there is no danger of misreading, a comma before the last item of a series is often omitted.

> That charge is ridiculous, preposterous, and absurd.
> We looked in the basement, in the living room, in the bedrooms, and in the attic.
> Louis Riel went to Montana, he worked as a school teacher and then he returned to Canada.

Do not use a comma at the end of a series.

> Arthur insisted on asking how geometry, algebra, and trigonometry ( ) would help him become a florist.

4. Use a comma after introductory phrases and clauses.

> Participial phrase: Inspired by the art exhibit, Mussorgsky composed *Pictures at an Exhibition*.
> Gerund phrase: By swimming with the Gulf Stream, Gastón almost escaped from Cuba to the United States.
> Prepositional phrase: With little to distract them from their purpose, the Vandals sacked all of Europe.
> Adverbial clause: Whenever I hear that magnificent song, I remember our first date.

5. Use a comma to set off nonrestrictive modifiers. Non-restrictive modifiers can be omitted from the sentence and the subject will still be clear. Restrictive modifiers, which are required to identify the subject, cannot be omitted and must not be set off by commas.

> My brother, who lives in Saskatoon, loves the Prairies.

I have only one brother. The words "who lives in Saskatoon" are nonrestrictive and nonessential, for you would know which brother is intended without them. In this nonrestrictive use, commas are required.

> My brother who lives in Saskatoon loves the Prairies.

I have more than one brother. The words "who lives in Saskatoon" are needed to indicate which brother I am talking about. They are essential (restrictive) and commas must not be used.

6. Use a comma to set off nonrestrictive appositives. An appositive is a noun or a noun equivalent that follows another noun construction and means the same as the first. It is nonrestrictive if it is not needed to identify what the first noun refers to.

> Nonrestrictive: The shoemaker down the street, Ivan, is a gentle man.
> Restrictive: The czar Ivan the Terrible killed his own son.

7. Use a comma to set off direct quotations from the introductory words, such as *he said, he replied, she insisted*.

> He said, "I shall see you very soon."
> "I shall see you," he said, "very soon."
> "I shall see you very soon," he said.
> "I shall see you very soon," he said. "It should be tomorrow."

8. Use a comma for various routine purposes.
   a. Use a comma to set off items in dates and addresses.

   > London, England
   > December 7, 1941 (non-metric date)
   > Georgetown, Great Exuma, The Bahamas
   > Cindy Lee Frick, 7880 Kingston Road,
   > Scarborough, Ontario, M1M 1R5

   b. Use a comma after the salutation in personal letters and after the complimentary close in all letters.

   > Dear Liz,   Sincerely,
   > My dear Mrs. Jacobs,   Gratefully,

   c. Use a comma to set off degrees and titles following a name:

   > Ralph B. Tennant, D.D.S.
   > James Froseth, Jr.
   > The Honorable Booth R. Desmond, Mayor.

9. Avoid unnecessary commas. The parentheses in the examples below indicate the absence of commas.
   a. Do not use a comma between a subject and verb. (It is proper, of course, to set off an interrupting element between the subject and verb with a *pair* of commas.)

   > That school is requiring more of students these days ( ) is hard to dispute.

b. Do not use a comma between the parts of either a compound subject or a compound predicate.

> Compound subject: Many of the people elected to Parliament ( ) and many of the people appointed to the Senate were good friends.
> Compound predicate: We read *The Apprenticeship of Duddy Kravitz* ( ) and then saw the movie starring Richard Dreyfuss.

c. Do not use a comma between a verb and its object or complement.

> The restriction on entering the contest was ( ) that no one related to the judges could enter.

d. Do not use a comma between an adjective and the noun phrase it modifies.

> The entire industry is now the target of a thorough ( ) parliamentary investigation.

e. Do not use a comma between two complete sentences. Such a comma fault, as it is called, results in a run-on sentence, which may confuse readers.

> Comma fault: Few volunteers answered the call, the house burned to the ground.
> Preferable: Few volunteers answered the call; the house burned to the ground.
> Few volunteers answered the call. The house burned to the ground.
> Because few volunteers answered the call, the house burned to the ground.

E. Semicolon. A semicolon signals a pause that is longer than that of a comma but shorter than that of a period. When used between two sentences it indicates a closer relationship between them than a period would.

1. Use a semicolon to join clauses of a compound sentence which do not have one of the coordinating conjunctions between them.

> Grace did not attend the lecture; she went to the museum instead.

2. Use a semicolon to join clauses connected by such conjunction adverbs as *however, moreover, nevertheless, consequently, still,* and *then*.

> Scientists will have to tackle the energy problem head on; still, it will be many years before we have an answer.

F. Colon. The colon designates a pause and points ahead to what follows.

1. Use a colon to introduce a long or formal quotation.

> Lester Pearson said: "It has been said that Canada is the most difficult country in the world to govern. I am perhaps a little more aware of that than I used to be."

2. Use a colon to introduce and emphasize a list of appositives at the end of a sentence:

> He prefers any of four fruits for dessert: strawberries, grapes, pears or watermelon.
> Robertson Davies has written a series of novels known as the Deptford Trilogy: *Fifth Business, The Manticore and World of Wonders.*

3. Use a colon for several conventional uses.

After a formal business letter salutation:

> Dear Sir:
> Dear Madam:

Between hours and minutes written in numbers:

> 01:32 h
> 23:00 h

G. Quotation Marks. In general, quotation marks enclose words the writer has borrowed *exactly* from another source. In addition, they identify titles of short works or portions of longer works.

1. Use quotation marks to enclose the exact words of speakers. Note that whether introductory words such as *he said* or *she replied* come before or after or in the middle of the quotation, they are excluded from the quotation marks.

> Before: Josh Billings said, "The ant takes no holidays and doesn't go on strike."
> After: "They have no loafers among them," he continued.
> Middle: "They get up early," he emphasized, "and work all the time."

- Use only one pair of quotation marks to enclose a direct quotation, even if the quoted material goes on for several sentences. (If the quoted material includes several paragraphs, put a quotation mark at the *beginning* of each new paragraph to remind the reader that the material he or she is reading is still part of a quotation. Do not put quotation marks at the ends of the paragraphs—except for the last one.)

- Put periods and commas inside closing quotation marks and semi-colons outside them.

> "That's my favourite book," she said, "but you can borrow it."
> Woody replied, "Thanks, but I've already read it."
> She snapped, "I suppose you didn't like it"; then she rushed off without waiting for an answer.

- Put a question mark or an exclamation mark inside the quotation mark if it applies only to the material being quoted. Place it after the quotation mark if it applies to the whole sentence.

> Helen heard Jerry ask, "Is it really as bad as they say?"
> Did you hear her reply, "I really don't think so"?
> Neal tried to outshout her, "Of course, it is. It's worse!"
> How strange that Helen calmly said, "You're wrong"!

- Use the single appropriate mark inside the quotation marks when both the sentence and the quotation ending the sentence are either questions or exclamations.

  > Was Lynn being funny when she responded, "Who knows?"
  > How frightening when the charging soldiers yelled, "Banzai!"

- Use new-paragraph indentation along with pairs of quotes, to indicate in a narrative the change of speakers in a conversation.

  > It's hard to believe that dirt could overcome hunger, but it did.
  > "Ma, I'm hungry."
  > "Wash your hands; I'll give you a piece of bread and butter."
  > "I'm not hungry."[1]   —Sam Levenson

- Use single quotation marks (' ') to enclose quotations within quotations.

  > Maynard said, "Our teacher is constantly quoting Patrick Henry's 'Give me liberty or give me death!'"

  (Note that both pairs of quotation marks—both single and double—must be complete.)

2. Use quotation marks to indicate titles of materials shorter than book length.

   > Birney's poem, "David"
   > Your story, "Beware the Ides"

3. Use quotation marks to call attention to technical words, words that need explanation, or words you are defining.

   > The "ampersand" (&) used to be considered the twenty-seventh letter of the alphabet.

H. Apostrophe. The apostrophe is used to form a possessive or to signal that one or more letters have been left out of a word. It is also used in a few specialized cases.

1. Follow these rules for forming the possessive:

   - Add an apostrophe and an *s* to any singular noun to show possession.

boy	boy's pencil
Ross	Ross's idea
Mabel	Mabel's victory

   - Add an apostrophe and an *s* to form the possessive of a plural word not ending in *s*:

     > The children's toys
     > the mice's tracks

   - Add only an apostrophe to a plural noun ending in *s*.

     > the two boys' projects
     > the Burnses' home
     > the three lawyers' offices

- Generally, to show joint ownership, make only the last noun possessive.

  Uncle Ernest and Aunt Daisy's plans were quite different from ours.
  The principal and teacher's decisions were final.

  Note how making both nouns possessive changes the meaning from shared, or joint ownership to individual ownership:

  Uncle Ernest's and Aunt Daisy's plans were quite different.
  Both the principal's and teacher's decisions were final.

- Do not use an apostrophe with relative and interrogative and personal pronouns which are already in a possessive form:

my	our	yours
your	their	hers
his	whose	ours
her	mine	theirs
its		

2. Use an apostrophe to show the omission of one or more letters in contractions, such as: doesn't   shouldn't   wouldn't   they're   it's (it is).

3. Use an apostrophe and *s* to show plurals of numbers, signs, letters, and words discussed as words. (In some cases writers use the *s* alone, when leaving out the apostrophe will not cause confusion.

   How many TV's do you have? (or TVs)
   too many &'s (or too many &s)
   a number of confusing *therefore*'s

I. Brackets [ ]. Brackets are used to enclose comments, explanations, queries, corrections, or directions inserted in quoted material by someone other than the original author.

   1. Use brackets to enclose words you insert in material you are quoting.

      Kuhn reported, "The hawk [an emblem of the soul in ancient Egypt] was pictured throughout the temple."

J. Dash. The dash is an emphatic and attention-demanding mark. Use it sparingly.

   1. Use the dash to show an abrupt change in a sentence.

      We started for the restaurant at ten—why, no, I'm thinking of Thursday night.
      Now, Shakespeare frequently says—yes, here's an example on page thirty-three.

   2. Use the dash to emphasize interpolations or interrupters. Both commas and parentheses perform this function, but the dash makes the interrupter stand out emphatically and dramatically. Be sure not to waste such emphasis on something that isn't worth the attention.

> Pliny the younger—he was actually there—wrote about the eruption of Vesuvius.

3. Use the dash to attract attention to appositives, important modifiers, and emphatic conditional phrases.

4. Use a dash after a list or series before you summarize or comment on it.

> New Democrats, Conservatives, Liberals—the whole House of Commons voted against him.

K. Hyphen. Used between words, the hyphen has the effect of unifying the words and making them act as a single word.

1. Use a hyphen to join words placed before a noun as a single modifier.

> up-to-date almanac   a so-what attitude

2. Use a hyphen between elements of a compound noun and between the prefix and root of various words.

> post-World War II   anti-American   half-truth
> pre-Columbian   self-pity   fourth-grader

Usage is so varied in this area that the surest solution to the problem of hyphenation is to consult a dictionary.

3. Use a hyphen to divide a word at the end of a line. Consult your dictionary to be sure you divide between syllables.

4. Use a hyphen in compound numbers from twenty-one to ninety-nine and within fractions used as modifiers: seventy-eight, five-eighths finished, one hundred forty-nine.

L. Parentheses. Use parentheses to set off and deemphasize nonessential explanatory material. If the material in parentheses appears *within* a sentence, no capital letter or period is used, although other marks, such as a comma, semicolon, or question mark are used as usual.

> The space probe of Venus (only last year) revolutionized theories of the origin of the Universe.

M. Figures. In deciding whether to use numerals or spell out numbers, the nature of the writing should be considered as well as consistent style.

1. Spell out all numbers at the beginning of a sentence and all other figures that require only one or two words.

> *Three* people decided not come. The other *345* indicated that they would come. Perhaps *twenty-seven* were undecided.

2. Use figures for all numbers in a technical or scientific report or in any paper including an unusual number of figures.

> Government spending was $980.5 billion that year.
> Annie Jump Cannon, a famous astronomer, analyzed 286 000 stars.

Credits

Chapter 1   **1** From Margaret Laurence, *Critical Views on Canadian Writers*, by William H. New, McGraw-Hill Ryerson Ltd., 1977.

Chapter 3   **1** Based on Chapter 1, "The Computerized Society," *Elements of Computer Careers*, Northwest Regional Laboratory, © 1978, Fearon-Pitman Publishers, Belmont, California.   **2** From "Lift a Little," by François-Régis Klanfer, *Today* Magazine, July 19, 1980, p. 17.   **3** From "The Land Palimpsest," by Roderick Nash, Sierra Club Calendar, 1979. **4** From "Wild Rose Country," by Paul Grescoe, *Today* Magazine, July 19, 1980.   **5** From Harriet Webster, Christian Science Monitor Service, Tampa *Tribune-Times*, Sept. 17, 1978. **6** From "Miracle Plant/Anyone for Winged Beans?", *Time* Magazine, April 17, 1978. Reprinted by permission from TIME, The Weekly Newsmagazine, © Time, Inc., 1978.   **7** From "What's in a No-Name?", *Saturday Night* Magazine, Jan./Feb. 1980, p. 3.   **8** From "88 Keys to Trouble," by Mervin J. Huston originally published in *The Great Canadian Lover*, Musson Books, 1964. Reprinted in the *Treasury of Great Canadian Humour*, Hurtig Publishers, Edmonton.   **9** From "Learned Friends," by Jane Widerman, *Today* Magazine, July 19,1980, p. 13.   **10** From "In Frock Coat and Moccasins," by Douglas LePan, published in *Canada: A Guide to the Peaceable Kingdom* ed. William Kilbourn, Macmillan of Canada. A Division of Gage Publishing Ltd., 1970.   **11** From *The Great Gatsby*, by F. Scott Fitzgerald, Charles Scribner's Sons, New York. © 1953 by Frances Scott Lanahan.   **12** From *Canada: A Guide to the Peaceable Kingdom*, ed. William Kilbourn, Macmillan of Canada. A Division of Gage Publishing Ltd., 1970. **13** From *Across the Bridge* by Graham Greene. Reprinted from *Twenty-One Stories* by Graham Greene. © 1947 by Graham Greene. By permission of the Viking Press, Inc.   **14** From *Hollywood's Canada* by Pierre Berton, reprinted by permission of The Canadian Publishers, McClelland and Stewart Limited, Toronto.   **15** From *National Geographic*, August 1968, Volume 134, No. 2, p. 219.   **16** From "88 Keys to Trouble," by Mervyn J. Huston, originally published in *The Great Canadian Lover*, Musson Books, 1964. Reprinted in *The Treasury of Great Canadian Humour*, Hurtig Publishers, Edmonton.

Chapter 4   **1** Reprinted from the Toronto Telegram as quoted by Ken Weber in *Prose of Relevance*, Methuen Publications, © 1971.   **2** From *A New England Girlhood* by Nancy Hale. Reprinted by permission of Little, Brown and Company, Boston. Copyright © 1936, 1937, 1940, 1941, 1942, 1954. © 1955, 1956, 1957, 1958 by Nancy Hale.   **3** From The World Book Encyclopedia, Vol. 1, World Book, Childcraft International Inc., Chicago, © 1979.   **4** From *The Little Locksmith* by Katherine Butler Hathaway, Coward McCann Inc., New York, 1943.   **5** From *Notes Toward a New Rhetoric: Six Essays for Teachers* by Francis Christensen. © 1967 by Francis Christensen. Reprinted by permission of Harper and Row Publishers, Inc.   **6** From *Canada North* by Farley Mowat reprinted by permission of The Canadian Publishers, McClelland and Stewart Limited, Toronto.   **7** From *A Civil Tongue* by Edwin Newman. Copyright © 1975, 1976 by The

Bobbs-Merrill Co. Inc. Reprinted by permission of the Bobbs-Merrill Co. Inc.   **8** From *Navajo Slave* by Lynne Gessner, New American Library (A Signet Book). Copyright © 1976 by Lynne Gessner.   **9** From *Wipeout* by Pete Pomeroy, Scholastic Book Services, Four Winds Press, New York. Copyright © 1968 by Pete Pomeroy.   **10** From *Are You in the House Alone?*, Dell Publishing Company, New York. Copyright © 1976 by Richard Peck.   **11** From *Born Innocent* by Bernhardt J. Hurwood, Ace Books Novelization © 1975. © 1974 by Tomorrow Entertainment, Inc., New York. **12** From "The Devil's Driveway" by Franklin Russell, published in *Canadian Writing Today*, ed. Mordecai Richler, Penguin Books, 1970. Reprinted by permission of Virginia Barber Literary Agency Inc., New York.

Chapter 5   **1** From *You May Know Them As Sea Urchins, Ma'am* by Ray Guy, Breakwater Press, St. John's, Newfoundland © 1975.   **2** By Art Buchwald, New York *Post*, December 14, 1968. Reprinted by permission of Art Buchwald as adapted and edited.   **3** "How to Avoid Shark Bite," from *How To*, by Peter Passell. © 1976 by Peter Passell. Reprinted with the permission of Farrar, Straus and Giroux, Inc. as adapted and edited.   **4** From *Reminiscences*, by Douglas MacArthur, McGraw-Hill, New York, © 1964.   **5** From *Time* Magazine, September 11, 1978. Reprinted by permission of TIME, The Weekly Newsmagazine, © Time, Inc., 1978. **6** From *The Story of Mankind*, by Hendrik Van Loon, Boni and Liverwright, Inc., © 1921.   **7** Article by Ellen Goodman in the Tampa *Tribune*, September 12, 1978. © 1978 The Boston Globe Newspaper Company/Washington Post Writers Group. Reprinted by permission of The Boston Globe Newspaper Company/Washington Post Writers Group.   **8** From *The Invisible Pyramid* by Loren Eiseley. Reprinted by permission of Charles Scribner's Sons, New York. Copyright © 1970 by Loren Eiseley.   **9** *Ibid*.   **10** From "The Management Team—Its Selection and Development" by Robert K. Burns, *Yearbook of American Iron and Steel Institute, 1955*.   **11** From "Synthetic Perfumes and Flavors," by Edwin E. Slosson, *Creative Chemistry*, Appleton-Century-Crofts, Inc., New York.

Chapter 6   **1** From *Ford's Insider*. Reprinted by permission of 13-30 Corporation, Knoxville, TN, © 1978, as adapted. **2** By Jack R. Hunt, from *Lighter Than Air Flight: The Watts Aerospace Library*, ed. Lt. Col. C.V. Glines, USAF, Franklin Watts, Inc. New York, 1965.   **3** "Beef Prices: Why so High?", from Everybody's Money/A Guide to Family Finance and Consumer Action, Winter 1978, Volume 18, Number 4. Copyright © 1978, Credit Union National Association, Madison, Wisconsin. Reprinted as adapted.   **4** By Mark Stevens, St. Petersburg *Times*, October 16, 1978.   **5** From *Hollywood's Canada* by Pierre Berton, reprinted by permission of The Canadian Publishers, McClelland and Stewart Limited, Toronto.

Chapter 7   **1** Adapted from "Preface" in The *Mysterious West*, World Publishing Company, by Brad Williams and Choral Pepper. © 1967 by Brad Williams and Choral Pepper. By permission of Harper and Row Publishers, Inc. **2** Summarized from *Dene Nation: The Colony Within*, edited by Mel Watkins, University of Toronto Press, 1977.   **3** From "Come Back Krazy Kat," by Arn Saba, *Today* Magazine, November 26, 1980. Reprinted by permission of the author. **4** From *A Civil Tongue* by Edwin Newman. Copyright © 1975, 1976 by the Bobbs-Merrill Co., Inc. Reprinted by permission of the publisher as edited.   **5** From "Lotoland" by David MacFarlane, *Weekend* Magazine, May 26, 1979. Reprinted by permission of the author.   **6** From "How to Dress Like a Loser" by Alexander Ross, published in *Who's Going to Read*

This Anyway?*, Holt, Rinehart and Winston, 1980. Reprinted by permission of the author. **7** "A History of Western Philosophy" by Bertrand Russell, Simon and Schuster, Inc., New York, © 1945. **8** From *A Study in Scarlet*, by A. Conan Doyle, from *The Complete Sherlock Holmes*, by Sir Arthur Conan Doyle, Doubleday and Company, Inc., New York, © 1953. **9** Based on *The Teaching of English Usage* by Robert C. Pooley. Copyright © 1974 by the National Council of Teachers of English, Urbana, Illinois. Reprinted by permission of the National Council of Teachers of English.

Chapter 8 **1** From "Heat Saves," by Harris Mitchell, *Today* Magazine, November 15, 1980. Reprinted by permission of *Today* Magazine. **2** From "Energy Overkill," by Jan Marmorek and Barry Spinner, *Canada and the World* Magazine, April, 1977. Reprinted by permission of *Canada and the World* Magazine, Maclean-Hunter Ltd. **3** From "Adoptive Parents: have they no rights?", The Vancouver *Sun*, August 5, 1980. Reprinted by permission of the author. **4** Reprinted by permission of Greenpeace. **5** From *A Guide to the Peaceable Kingdom*, ed. William Kilbourn, Macmillan of Canada. A Division of Gage Publishing Ltd., 1970. **6** From *The Husband of Xanthippe and Other Short Plays* by Conrad Seiler, Walter Baker Company, Boston. © 1929. **7** From "Hair Does Nothing For People" by Ted Schrader, printed in *The Treasury of Great Canadian Humour*, ed. Alan Walker. Reprinted by permission of the Estate of E.U. (Ted) Schrader. **8** Letter and reply from Ann Landers' column, New Orleans *Times-Picayune*, August 13, 1978. © Field Newspaper Syndicate, reprinted by permission of Ann Landers. **9** From "Cop-Out Realism," by Norman Cousins, *Saturday Review*, September 2, 1978. **10** "Catch-22 Incident," by Joseph Heller, © 1955, 1961 by Joseph Heller. Reprinted by permission of Simon and Schuster, a Division of Gulf and Western Corporation, New York. **11** From *What's Wrong with High School English?*, by Priscilla Galloway, OISE Press, Toronto, 1980.

Chapter 9 **1** Courtesy of Mrs E.B. Farnham, Director of Admissions, University of Saskatchewan. **2** Courtesy of the Vancouver Office of Canada Manpower. **3** Excerpt from an article by Karl Meyer, *Saturday Review*, October 14, 1978, p. 56. © *Saturday Review*, 1978. All rights reserved. **4** From *The Scientific Approach*, by J.T. Davies, Academic Press, Inc., New York, 1965. **5** From *Letters from Pompeii*, by Wilhelmina Feemster Jashemski, © copyright 1963 by Ginn and Company (Xerox Corporation). Used with permission. **6** "Letter to a Brother," Malcolm Lowry published in *Selected Letters of Malcolm Lowry*, by Margerie Bonner Lowry. Copyright © 1965 by Margerie Bonner Lowry. Reprinted by permission of Literistic, Ltd.

Chapter 10 **1** Much of the information in the following sections of this chapter has been adapted from the *Burnaby South Senior Secondary School Research Handbook for Students*, Fred Lepkin and Steve Bailey, 1979. **2** *Indochina: The Colonial War that Failed*, by Kalwant Gill, Burnaby South Senior Secondary School, 1980.

Chapter 11 **1** From Margaret Laurence, *Critical Views on Canadian Writers*, ed. William H. New, McGraw-Hill Ryerson, Ltd., 1977. **2** Excerpt from "Teaching from Eaton's Catalogues" in *Ten Lost Years*, by Barry Broadfoot. Copyright © 1973 by Barry Broadfoot. Reprinted by permission of Doubleday and Company, Inc. **3** "As it Happened," by Sam Roddan, published in *The B.C. Teacher*, January-February, 1979. Reprinted by permission of the author. **4** From *The Women's Room*, by Marilyn French, © 1977 by Harcourt Brace

Jovanovich (Jove), New York. **5** From "A Sin of the Mother Visited upon the Child," by Brenda Rabkin published in *Who's Going to Read This Anyway?*, eds. Matthews and Webb, Holt, Rinehart and Winston. Originally published in *Maclean's*, September 18, 1978. Reprinted by permission of the author. **6** From "When Mount Vesuvius Erupted…," by M.W. Newman, Chicago *Sun-Times*, August, 1978. **7** From *The Great Railway Bazaar*, by Paul Theroux, Ballantine Books, New York, © 1975. **8** From *Remembering Betsy of the Evil Eye*," by Gene Plowden, *Parade*, September 20, 1978. **9** From *Hetty Dorval*, by Ethel Wilson. Reprinted by permission of Gage Publishing Limited. **10** From "The Pompidolium," by Horace Sutton, *Saturday Review*, September 2, 1978, p. 44. © 1978 *Saturday Review*. All rights reserved. **11** From "Repent Harlequin!" Said the Ticktockman*, by Harlan Ellison, © 1965, Galaxy Publishing Corp. Copyright assigned 1969 to Harlan Ellison. All rights reserved. **12** From *Lamp at Noon and Other Stories*, by Sinclair Ross, reprinted by permission of The Canadian Publishers, McClelland and Stewart Limited, Toronto. **13** From *Crime and Punishment*, by Fyodor Dostoyevsky. **14** From *The Mountain and the Valley*, by Ernest Buckler, reprinted by permission of The Canadian Publishers, McClelland and Stewart Limited, Toronto. **15** From *How to Survive in Your Native Land*, by James Herndon, Simon and Schuster, Inc., New York. Copyright © 1971 by James Herndon. **16** From *Breaking Smith's Quarter Horse*, by Paul St. Pierre, McGraw-Hill Ryerson Limited, Toronto, 1966. **17** From *Dandelion Wine*, by Ray Bradbury, copyright © 1953 by Ray Bradbury. Reprinted by permission of Harold Matson Co., Inc.

Chapter 12 **1** From *Survey: A Short History of Canadian Literature*, by Elizabeth Waterston, Methuen Publications, 1973. **2** From *As For Me and My House*, by Sinclair Ross, reprinted by permission of The Canadian Publishers, McClelland and Stewart Limited, Toronto. **3** From *The Invention of the World*, ed., Jack Hodgins, Macmillan Canada Ltd., 1977. Reprinted by permission of the author. **4** From "We Played for Lombardi," by Jerry Kramer, *Life*, Vol. 69, No. 11, September 11, 1970. Reprinted by permission of the author. **5** From "In His Magnificent Heart He Knew He was in Trouble," by Christie Blatchford, The Vancouver *Sun*, September 3, 1980. Reprinted with permission—The Toronto *Star*. **6** From *As For Me and My House*, by Sinclair Ross, reprinted by permission of The Canadian Publishers, McClelland and Stewart Limited, Toronto. **7** From *Coming Into the Country*, by John McPhee, Farrar, Straus and Giroux, New York, © 1976, 1977 by John McPhee. **8** From *Jane Eyre*, by Charlotte Bronte © 1943 by Random House, Inc., New York. **9** "Lightfoot at 40," by Peter Goddard from *Who's Going to Read This Anyway?* eds. Matthews and Webb, Holt, Rinehart and Winston, 1980. Reprinted by permission of the author. **10** From *A Jest of God*, by Margaret Laurence, reprinted by permission of The Canadian Publishers, McClelland and Stewart Limited, Toronto. **11** Excerpt from *Cress Delahanty*, by Jessamyn West, © 1951 by the Curtis Publishing Company. Reprinted from *Cress Delahanty* by Jessamyn West by permission of Harcourt Brace Jovanovich, Inc. **12** From "On Stephen Leacock," by Robertson Davies published in *Our Living Heritage*, ed. Robert L. McDougall, University of Toronto Press, 1957. Reprinted by permission of the author. **13** From "The House on the Esplanade," by Anne Hébert, published in *Canadian Short Stories*, R. Weaver ed., Oxford University Press. By permission of the author.

Chapter 13 **1** From *The Educated Imagination*, by Northrop Frye. © Northrop Frye 1963. Used by permission of the author and the Canadian Broadcasting Corporation. **2** From *Selected Poems and Parodies*, by Louis Untermeyer. Copyright © 1916 by Harcourt Brace Jovanovich, Inc., New York. Copyright © 1944 by Louis Untermeyer. Reprinted by permission of Harcourt Brace Jovanovich, Inc. **3** From *The Well-Wrought Urn*, by Cleanth Brooks. Published by Harcourt Brace Jovanovich, Inc., New York, 1947. **4** From *Sea and Sardinia*, by D.H. Lawrence, © 1921 by Thomas Seltzer, Inc. Copyright 1949 by Frida Lawrence. All rights reserved. Reprinted by permission of the Viking Press, Inc. **5** Student Compositions A to G from *Zodiac*, student poetry published by the Canadian Council of Teachers of English, Project Pandora, 1974-75. All rights reserved. **6** From Frank Budgen, "James Joyce: Two Decades of Criticism" in *The Art of James Joyce/Method and Design in* Ulysses *and* Finnegan's Wake, by A. Walton Litz. Oxford University Press, London, © 1964. **7** From *Serve Me a Slice of Moon*, by Marcie Hans. Reprinted by permission of Harcourt Brace Jovanovich, Inc. **8** From *Laughing Time*, by William Jay Smith, © 1955, Little Brown and Company, Boston, and *The Atlantic Monthly*. **9** From *The Art of James Joyce/Method and Design in* Ulysses *and* Finnegan's Wake, by Walton A. Litz. Oxford University Press, London, © 1964. **10** From *A Portrait of the Artist as a Young Man*, by James Joyce. © 1972 by Viking Penguin, Inc. Reprinted by permission of the publisher. **11** From *The Sound and the Fury*, by William Faulkner. Copyright © 1929 and renewed 1957 by William Faulkner. Copyright © 1946 by Random House Inc., New York. Reprinted by permission of Random House, Inc. **12** From *73 Poems*, by e.e. cummings. © 1963 by Marion Morehouse Cummings. Reprinted from *Complete Poems 1913-1962*, by e.e. cummings by permission of Harcourt Brace Jovanovich, Inc. **13** From *An Introduction to Haiku*, by Harold G. Henderson. © 1958 by Harold G. Henderson. Reprinted by permission of Doubleday and Company, Inc. **14** From *The Book of Humourous Verse*, compiled by Carolyn Wills, © 1920 by Doubleday and Company, Inc., Garden City, N.Y. Reprinted by permission of Maurice O'Connell, Jr. **15** From "Method in Certain Cases" by Jewel Martin in *Creative Youth*, edited by Hughes Mearns, © 1925 by Doubleday and Company, Inc.

Chapter 14 **1** From "Outlooks/Editorial: The Paradoxes of Lyof Tolstoy," *Saturday Review*, October 28, 1978, p. 54. © 1978 *Saturday Review*. All rights reserved. **2** Based on *Elements of Writing About a Literary Work: A Study of Responses to Literature*, by Alan C. Purves and Victoria Reppere, NCTE. Research Report #9, National Council of Teachers of English, 1968. **3** From "A Review of Fairytales and After: From Snow White to E.B. White, by Roger Sale, "by Clara Claiborne Park, *Saturday Review*, December 12, 1978, p. 53 © 1978, *Saturday Review*. All rights reserved. **4** From "Of Rats, Bones, Shadows and Time," by Ray Bradbury, a critique of *The Night Country* by Loren Eiseley, in *The Sunday Record*, Hackensack, N.J., January 23, 1972. © 1972 by Times Mirror Company. Reprinted by permission of Harold Matson Company Inc. **5** From "*A Review of Up Against It: Children and the Law in Canada*, by Jeffery Wilson," by Joan Malcolmsen, *Quill and Quire*, August, 1980. **6** From "A Review of *Madwomen:*

Poems, by Fraser Sutherland," by Barry Dempster, *Quill and Quire*, May, 1980. **7** From "A Review of Alex Driving South," by Keith Maillard," by Paul Hornbeck, *Quill and Quire*, May, 1980. **8** From *Portraits and Protests*, by Sarah N. Cleghorn. All rights reserved. Reprinted by permission of Holt, Rinehart and Winston, Inc. **9** From *The Complete Poems of Paul Laurence Dunbar*. Reprinted by permission of Dodd, Mead and Company, Inc. **10** "Warren Pryor," by Alden Nowlan, published in *Theme and Image*, ed. Carol Gillander, Copp Clark Pitman, 1976. By permission of the author. **11** "Ex-Basketball Player," from *The Carpentered Hen and Other Tame Creatures*. by John Updike. Originally appeared in *The New Yorker*. Reprinted by permission of Harper and Row, Publishers, Inc. **12** From *Selected Poems*, Third Edition, revised and enlarged, by John Crowe Ransom. Copyright © 1927 by Alfred A. Knopf, Inc. and renewed 1955 by John Crowe Ransom. Reprinted by permission of Alfred A. Knopf, Inc. **13** "We Real Cool The Pool Players. Seven at The Golden Shovel." from *The World of Gwendolyn Brooks*, by Gwendolyn Brooks. © 1959 by Gwendolyn Brooks. Reprinted by permission of Harper and Row, Publishers, Inc. **14** "30 Below," by George Bowering, published in *Canadian Writing Today*, ed. Mordecai Richler, Penguin Books, 1970. Reprinted by permission of the author. **15** "Mushrooms," from *The Colossus and Other Poems*, by Sylvia Plath. © 1960 by Sylvia Plath. Published by Faber and Faber, London, © 1971 by Ted Hughes. Reprinted by permission of Alfred A. Knopf, Inc. **16** "Portrait by a Neighbour," from *Collected Poems* by Edna St. Vincent Millay. Harper and Row, Publishers, Inc., New York. Copyright © 1922, 1950 by Edna St. Vincent Millay. **17** Reprinted by permission of Faber and Faber Ltd., from the *Collected Poems*, by W.H. Auden. **18** From *Collected Poems*, by Siegfried Sassoon, © 1918 by E.P. Dutton and Company, 1946, by Siegfried Sassoon. Reprinted by permission of The Viking Press, Inc. and Mr. G.T. Sassoon. **19** From *Selected Poems*, by Al Purdy, reprinted by permission of The Canadian Publishers, McClelland and Stewart Limited, Toronto. **20** "Southbound on the Freeway," from *New and Selected Things Taking Place*, by May Swenson. Copyright © 1963 by May Swenson. First appeared in *The New Yorker*. Reprinted by permission of Little, Brown and Co., in association with The Atlantic Monthly Press.

Style Sheet **1** From *Everything but Money*, by Sam Levinson, Simon and Schuster, 1966.

Index